CISTERCIAN STUDIES SERIES: NUMBER FORTY-FOUR

THE
NAME
OF
JESUS

by Irénée Hausherr

Translated *by* CHARLES CUMMINGS ocso

c. 168 conversatio, etc.

CISTERCIAN PUBLICATIONS INC.
Kalamazoo, Michigan 49008
1978

Prayer: (Not,) "Jesus" all by itself = 321

©Cistercian Publications, In., 1978
W.M.U. Station
Kalamazoo, Michigan 49008

Library of Congress Cataloging in Publication Data:

Hausherr, Irénée, 1891—
    The name of Jesus.

    (Cistercian studies series; no. 44)
    Translation of *Noms du Christ et voies d'oraison.*
    Bibliography: p. 348
    Includes index.
        1. Jesus Christ—Name. 2. Prayer. 3. Jesus prayer.
I. Title. II. Series.
BT590.N2H3813   232.9'01   77-10559
ISBN 0-87907-844-8

Second Printing 1983

*Typeset by The Contemplative Sisters of the Precious Blood
Cloister Printery, New Riegel, Ohio*

Printed in the United States of America

TABLE OF CONTENTS

AUTHOR'S PREFACE

L ONG AGO the sixteenth-century Spanish theologian, Luis de Léon, published a brilliant treatise on the names of Christ, *Los Nombres de Cristo*. The present book aims neither at literary brilliance nor theological disputation but at something more lowly, an investigation of religious practice in Eastern Christian spirituality. What were the names these Christians used when they prayed to the Lord and what was the reason behind their choice? The book is divided accordingly. Part One considers the names of Jesus used by the faithful and Part Two discusses the methods of continual prayer taught and practised by Eastern ascetics.

All prayer can be regarded theologically as a form of calling upon the name of Jesus, since prayer is a means of salvation and 'there is no other name under heaven given to men by which we are to be saved' (Ac 4:12). Eastern Christians have developed a form of prayer which is centered on the literal, vocal invocation of the name of Jesus. How did this form of prayer evolve? How did it gradually develop until for some it ceased to be merely one form of prayer among others and became the only perfect way of prayer to the exclusion of all others?

We are dealing here with matters that have a considerable importance in the history of Christianity. Treating the subject

i

with total thoroughness would require a survey of the whole body of christian literature. I have settled for something less: an investigation of those documents which seem to be either intrinsically more important or else more favorable to the assertions of other people. The following pages are the result of this investigation.

Inevitably there is a danger that this attempt will prove either tedious because of all the details it includes or disappointing because of those it omits. To those who notice only the lacunae I wish to say that gathering the names of the Lord scattered in so many different writings has given me such great joy that I pursued the enterprise until my vision deteriorated almost completely. May I suggest that you, with your good eyes, continue the inventory and add as many new references as you can.

To those who see here only protracted and unnecessary repetition I will say this: if this search for the names of the Lord Jesus does not speak to your heart you are perfectly free to prefer something that has a more immediate and obvious appeal. Only remember how many professors and students are capable of inexhaustible patience and painstaking labor over far less captivating subjects. Since I am a Christian nothing concerning Christ can leave me indifferent, least of all his names, because these are identical in a certain sense with his very person.

Another criticism which could be made is that my division between the names and the invocation of the name is not perfect and is not kept perfectly. Certain details or even paragraphs in the second part could have been put in Part One, and vice versa. All these critical observations, and others too, I accept without objection. May those who are better qualified try, in treating the same subject, to merit them less. One thing which I hope will be evident to everyone is that I feel a deep and sincere sympathy for every human effort to pursue peace and union with God through pure and continual prayer. And if I have given anyone grounds to suspect otherwise, then I must say: 'Lord Jesus Christ, son of God, have mercy on me.' Amen!

AUTHOR'S INTRODUCTION

IN 1925 Reinhold von Walter published a German translation of *The Way of a Pilgrim*. This was how the West became acquainted with the Jesus Prayer—'Lord Jesus Christ, son of God, have mercy on me (a sinner)'.[1] A synopsis of the book was published the following year in *Orientalia Christiana*. It read as follows:

The original Russian title of this book was The True Account of a Pilgrim to his Confessor. *From its contents it could have been titled* The Search For Continual Prayer. *A Russian peasant who was literate but handicapped with a crippled left arm was seized with an ardent desire for continual prayer. Failing to learn the secret of it from sermons he finally met the director he needed, a staretz. The staretz taught him to say the Jesus Prayer 3000 times a day to begin with, then 6000 times, then 12,000, then as often as he wished. In the end it was no longer the pilgrim saying a prayer but the prayer saying itself in the pilgrim's mind and heart whatever his occupation and even while he slept. The effects were marvellous:*

> *In my soul I felt the bliss of loving God, interior peace, ecstasy, purity of thoughts, and a blessed*

teach others than ten thousand words in a strange tongue'
(1 Cor 14:19). *However, these few pages are themselves only
important in the preliminary stages of contemplation. At the
culminating point the formula is condensed into a single cry
which springs from the depth of the heart—'Jesus! My
Jesus!'—until this too disappears into the silence of ecstasy.* [5]

This extensive quotation should give some idea of the
literary genre. Professor Crainic drew criticism from a monk
of the Eastern Church who wrote: 'The article is marred to
some extent by the author's naïveté; he attributes the
discovery of the Jesus Prayer to the Blessed Virgin Mary,
which might be true in a mystical sense but certainly does not
fall within historical perspectives.' [6] Professor Crainic was
relying in his opinion on the authority of Gregory Palamas. [7]
In the second of two homilies on the Presentation of Mary,
published in 1861, Gregory says:

*The Virgin Mary opened a path toward greater and more
perfect things. She discovered and practised and transmitted
to posterity an activity superior to contemplation and a
contemplation more sublime than anything previously known,
as truth is more excellent than fantasy....* [8]
   *Renouncing all blameworthy behavior, she preferred a life
invisible to everyone, free of human entanglements,
attachments and profane influences, in an inaccessible secret
sanctuary where she could rise even above concern for her
own body and give her intellect to reflection, attention and
uninterrupted divine prayer. Thus she attained total self-
possession and arrived at a state above the swirling clouds of
concepts and images. Thereby she pioneered a new and
privileged path to heaven, which might be called the path of
intelligible silence.* [9]

Nowhere does Gregory Palamas explicitly attribute the
discovery of the Jesus Prayer to the Blessed Virgin, but that
conclusion could be drawn from passages like that above,

of enthusiasm he stirred up.

Here I would like to quote a few paragraphs from one of these recent works. A former Romanian government official, now a professor at the University of Bucharest, Nichifor Crainic, wrote a book about the Jesus Prayer which is cited here from a German translation:

Among the theoretical and experimental forms of Orthodox mysticism there is one which is predominant and normative for all the others, the Jesus Prayer, also known as 'prayer of the spirit', 'prayer of the heart', 'isychast [sic] prayer'. There is nothing like it in the prayers of the Western Church. The Jesus Prayer has a history that reaches far back into antiquity and extends to the most famous Russian startsy. It has put its stamp indelibly on Orthodox contemplative prayer by its doctrinal substance, its method, and especially its widespread use.

Because it has been transmitted from master to disciple from generation to generation and guarded jealously according to the strict rules of sacred custom, the Jesus Prayer has preserved its original form and power. In 1782 when the Philokalia *was first published in Greek at Venice every single copy was carried off to the East. This possessiveness, which is perfectly in accord with their traditional discipline, shows how much they consider it private property. The Jesus Prayer is inseparable from the spiritual life of the Orthodox Church. It forms the nucleus of monastic life. 'It can substitute for the divine office and all other prayers for it has universal value.'*[4]

We can ask what gives the prayer this universal value and what explains its historical longevity? What else but the name of Jesus which is the incandescent core of this prayer? The longer form can be abbreviated to 'Lord Jesus Christ, son of God, have mercy,' or simply 'Lord Jesus Christ, have mercy'. This last form consists of five words, and the hesychast authors often apply to this prayer a text from St Paul: 'I would rather speak five words with my intellect in order to awareness of God. In my body a warm sensation in the heart, lightness, freshness, quick pulse and overall well-being. Life became a joy. I was immune to illness and sadness. There were revelations, intellectual insights, interpretations of the scriptures. I felt close to the spirit of nature, free from worldly tumult; I tasted the sweetness of the interior life and sensed the nearness of God and of his love for us.

Thus our pilgrim floated rather than walked over the vast stretches of Russia and Siberia, experiencing everywhere with new astonishment the marvellous effects of continual prayer not only on himself but on other pious souls, and on a child who had to be threatened with a stick before he would say the prayer, and even on wild beasts and the forces of nature. Continual prayer restored the state of original innocence, with all its happiness and dominion over nature. [2]

And these beautiful promises did not go unfulfilled. The world was ripe for such a message. For many, World War I had produced a disillusionment more cruel than all the physical miseries. They had been led by pre-1914 prosperity to believe in an approaching earthly paradise where no one would suffer want. The cataclysm which exploded their euphoria awakened a hunger for spiritual nourishment. In every European country with a free press books and reviews of spirituality knew a sudden popularity which lasted for years. Appearing at this time, *The Way of a Pilgrim* enjoyed a success it never knew in its original language. Even the Communist revolution helped promote it because the Russian refugees were a living advertisement for it, if only because they excited curiosity and sympathy for 'the other Russia'. [3]

The list of books about the Jesus Prayer grows longer by the year. The bibliography at the end of this book is incomplete despite its length, but it is enough to show what a welcome the Russian pilgrim received and what a whirlwind because the Jesus Prayer is precisely the highest form of contemplation. This is the presupposition with which Professor Crainic read Palamas. [10]

The same presupposition could be pointed out in many other books and articles. Usually no distinction is made between the prayer formula and the method which has been its setting since the twelfth or fourteenth century. We have no intention of speaking of this hesychastic method but only of the prayer itself.

The study will follow chronological order as far as possible, both in Part One, *The Names of Jesus*, and in Part Two, *Invocation of the Name*.

1. R. von Walter, *Ein Russisches Pilgerleben* (Berlin: Petropolis, 1925). 'Jesus Prayer' transliterates literally the Russian *molitva Iisousova*, the German *Jesusgebet*, and the Greek *Iesou euche* or *he euche tou Iesou*. The French *prière de Jésus* is not perfectly equivalent because the genitive must be the object not the subject; it is a prayer addressed to Jesus not a prayer made by him. In French *prière à Jésus* would be more exact. John Climacus refers to the Our Father by the term *Iesou he proseuche*.

2. *Orientalia Christiana* 6 (1926) pp. 174-175.

3. *Das andere Russland*, title of a German translation of a book by P. Kologrivof, *Essai sur la sainteté en Russie* (Bruges, 1953).

4. Crainic here quotes from Sergius Boulgakov, *Orthodoxie* (Sibiu-Hermannstadt, 1933), page not given.

5. N. Crainic, *Das Jesusgebet*, trans. W. Biemel, in *Zeitschrift für Kirchengeschichte* 60 (1941), pp. 341-353.

6. A Monk of the Eastern Church, 'La Prière de Jésus', *Irénikon* (Chevetogne, 3rd edition, 1959) p. 7, n. 1.

7. Crainic, *Jesusgebet*, p. 348.

8. G. Palamas, published by Sophocles K. *Ex Oeconomon* (Athens, 1861), p. 169, No. 31.

9. Ibid., p. 176, No. 38.

10. According to strict logic, if the Jesus Prayer is the exclusive property of the Byzantine East and if it is to be identified with mental prayer, then it would follow that the Roman Church knows nothing of mental prayer. So it should not be too surprising to read the following in *Hagioritiki Vivliothiki*, 24th year, No. 279-280 (Volos, 1959), p. 367: 'The official Catholic Church considers mental prayer (*ten noeran proseuchen*) and hesychasm a type of heresy.'

PART ONE

THE NAMES OF JESUS

CHAPTER ONE

SCRIPTURAL AND PATRISTIC NAMES

PLURALITY OF NAMES

"A NAME," wrote Origen, 'is a term which summarizes and expresses the specific quality of the thing named.'[1] Origen then goes on to give his philosophy of the name. Instead of plunging into modern philosophical theories we would do well to begin by reading what Origen has to say about the subject:

The apostle Paul has specific qualities which make his soul the way it is and make his mind able to understand this or that and make his body have particular characteristics. The name 'Paul' designates these specific and incommunicable qualities which make up Paul and distinguish him from every other being in the universe. Sometimes a man's personal character changes and when this happens his name changes too, as Scripture shows. When Abram changed he was named Abraham. When Simon changed he was named Peter. When Saul, the persecutor of Jesus, changed he was named Paul. Since God never changes and remains always the same, we have for him only one name to use forever, the name 'He who is', which is found in Exodus and elsewhere. We all make guesses about God, trying to say something about him.

3

Not everyone knows what he is like, and only a few, or fewer than few, can see his holiness in all things. It is with good reason then that we are taught that the name of God is holy, for this helps us to see his holiness in creating, in exercising providence, in judging, in choosing and abandoning, in accepting and rejecting, in rewarding and punishing each according to his merits. It is in these things and others like them that the specific quality of God is brought to light. And in my opinion it is this quality which scripture calls the name of God.[2]

The best summary of Origen's long dissertation, and of others still longer by other authors,[3] has been given by D. Mollat in a commentary on Jn 3:18: 'Believe in the name of the Son of God'. Mollat notes that 'name' is 'a Semitism for the person'.[4]

The Lord Jesus, son of Mary, has many names. An anonymous, seventh century author has left us a work proposing to be a list of all the scriptural names of the Saviour.[5] He finds a total of one hundred and eighty-seven, which he introduces with the remark that 'some say the Saviour's proper name is *Wisdom*, others that it is *Verbum*; and they say that all other names are not proper names but metaphorical (*tropikos*).' Here are the first few on the list:

> (1) Wisdom, (2) *Verbum*, (3) Son of God, (4) Word of God, (5) Light of the world, (6) True Light, (7) Resurrection, (8) Way, (9) Truth, (10) Life, (11) Gate, (12) Shepherd, (13) Messiah, (14) Christ, (15) Jesus, (16) Lord, (17) Master (*didaskalos*).

Was it by an oversight that the name 'Jesus' occurs only in fifteenth place? It seems not, because the author deliberately put 'Wisdom' first and '*Verbum*' second. In a subsequent list of 'all the names of the Theotokos,'[6] he begins with 'Mary' and concludes with number fifty-four, 'Theotokos properly and truly'.

The compiler of this dogmatic florilegium, which Diekamp calls the most extensive and valuable of all we possess,[7] furnishes no argument for modern authors who claim that the Jesus Prayer can consist of the word 'Jesus' alone inasmuch as this is the heart and essence of the prayer as well as the nucleus of Orthodox Christianity and of its spiritual life. Was the anonymous compiler unfamiliar with 'the philosophy of the name'? If so, Diekamp's hypothesis about the author crumbles. He attributes this florilegium to Anastasius the Sinaite, but the Sinaites would have been more likely to preserve a philosophy of the name than anyone else since Sinai is in a Semitic country and the Jesus Prayer had very great importance in Sinaitic spirituality.[8]

In any case our problem is this: if there is a philosophy of the name, which name is being used since the Saviour has many names? The answer is important not only for the history or pre-history of the Jesus Prayer, but in general for the history of devotion to the name of Jesus.

NAMES OF JESUS IN THE GOSPELS

There was only one way for the Jewish contemporaries of Jesus who were not his followers to distinguish him from others, like Jesus Barabbas, who had the same name. They had to designate the town he came from. Pilate had the inscription 'Jesus of Nazareth' placed on the cross. We never read in the gospels that anyone addresses the Master by his proper name nor as 'Lord Jesus'. The vocative does occur in Mark and Luke but only from the demons speaking through the lips of someone possessed, and then only with the addition of the native town, 'Jesus of Nazareth' (Mk 1:24; Lk 4:34). The Gerasene demoniac uses the title 'Jesus, son of God most high' (Mk 5:7; Lk 8:28). Apart from possessed persons only the blind man, Bartimaeus, calls Jesus by his proper name, adding 'Son of David' (Mk 10:47; Lk 18:38). This is the text which the proponents of the Jesus Prayer usually stress most. The Marcan account puts 'Son of David' before 'Jesus'. After being reprimanded by the crowd Bartimaeus goes on shouting, but only the words, 'Son of David'. In another incident, found only in Luke, the ten lepers call from a distance, 'Jesus, Master, have pity on us' (Lk 17:13). According to some versions the good thief says, 'Jesus, remember me' (Lk 23:52), but a significant variant has 'remember me' without the name of Jesus, while another variant puts 'Jesus' in the dative, 'He said to Jesus'. The Canaanite woman cries, 'Have mercy on me, Lord, son of David' (Mt 15:22).

From this brief survey it appears that the only ones who addressed Jesus directly by name were the demons or people outside the circle of close disciples, and the name was usually accompanied by a special title. One day Jesus would say to his close disciples, 'I call you no longer servants but friends' (Jn 15:15). Nevertheless they did not dare call him by his 'first name'; perhaps the idea never occurred to them. And the Lord seems to approve, for he says, 'You call me Master and Lord, and rightly so, because this is what I am' (Jn 13:13). 'Master' and 'Lord' are not synonymous, and they can be understood either in the nominative sense as the names the disciples used when speaking *about* Jesus or in the vocative sense as the names they used in speaking *to* Jesus (see Jn 20:28). The evangelist probably had both meanings in mind, and this would correspond to the general usage we find in the gospels. Twice the gospels record a phrase spoken by Mary to her son, but she does not call him 'Jesus'. When the boy is found in the temple among the doctors she says, 'My child' (*teknon:* Lk 2:48). At the marriage in Cana she simply says 'They have no more wine' (Jn 2:3), without any name.

Whenever the apostles or the early disciples spoke about Jesus in a narrative context after the ascension, they called him by his earthly, historical name, 'Jesus'. This would be the common practice of any historian when he has no reason to refer to his subject by any but the simplest name. But there are times when it is enough to call Paris 'Paris', and other times when it is better to call it "the capital of France".

And there is a nuance of difference in meaning for the discerning reader. To take an example from the gospels: in one place Luke writes, 'Mary remembered all these things and pondered them in her heart' (Lk 2:19). Then a few verses later he writes, 'His mother kept all these things in her heart' (Lk 2:51). The second phrase delicately suggests the reason behind the fact: Mary treasured these memories because she was his mother.

In some cases when the evangelist places the title 'Lord' on the lips of one of the disciples he may be doing so out of strict fidelity to historical fact. For instance, St John in his gospel habitually writes 'Jesus' when he narrates past events, But when he records one of his own statements, such as the remark made to Peter by the disciple whom Jesus loved, he writes, 'It is the Lord' (Jn 20:7-12). Mary Magdalen uses the same title, 'Lord', after the resurrection (Jn 20:2, 18), and so do the disciples (Jn 20:25). Luke's gospel follows the same practice. When Cleopas and his companion returned to Jerusalem from Emmaus the disciples greeted them with the news 'that the Lord is risen indeed' (Lk 24:34). It should be remembered that the conjunction *hoti* is equivalent to our quotation marks and is used to introduce direct discourse.

Then there are occasions when the evangelist is reporting not the words but the thoughts of the disciples about Jesus, and this mental discourse can be picked up by a reader who pays close attention to nuances of phrasing. A Latin translation would express this by indirect discourse in the subjunctive. In Luke's gospel a clue to these passages is provided by the twofold repetition of the title *Kyrios* first when a disciple addresses Jesus and secondly when the evangelist uses it to introduce Jesus' reply (see Lk 12:41-42; 17:5). Or the evangelist's introduction may come first: 'Zacchaeus stood up and said to the Lord, "Behold, Lord..."' (Lk 19:8). In the scene of Peter's denial Luke is the only one to mention the glance Jesus gave Peter after the third denial (Lk 22:61). The ultimate source for this precious detail must have been Peter himself; it is his voice that we hear behind these words: 'The Lord turned to look at Peter and Peter remembered the Lord's prediction.' Mark and Matthew mention simply the historical fact: 'Peter remembered what Jesus had said to him....'" The title *Kyrios* may occasionally be a later insertion by a copyist, as in Lk 13:15, where a variant reading has 'Jesus'; or in Lk 22:31, where the best manuscripts omit the words 'The Lord said....' Finally, there are a few verses where it would be natural to expect the word 'Jesus' if the evangelist were writing purely as an historian, but instead, because of the author's faith, we find 'the Lord'. For instance: 'Afterwards *the Lord* selected seventy-two other men' (Lk 10:1). It could be said that Jesus was making this selection precisely as *the Lord*. The same would be true for Lk 11:39 (chastising the Pharisees) and to some extent also for Lk 18:6 (explaining a parable).

From all this we can draw the conclusion that the evangelists nearly always use the name 'Jesus' in their ordinary narrative style. When they substitute 'the Lord' it is because they have a special reason for doing so, a reason which can usually be reduced to the faith of a disciple or the author's own faith. Of all the terms used to designate the Saviour, the name 'Jesus' is the simplest, the shortest, and the farthest from connotations of grandeur and honor. When such connotations need to be conveyed, the titles *Kyrios* or *Didaskalos* are used in addition to or in place of the name 'Jesus'.

THE REMAINDER OF THE NEW TESTAMENT

It would be uncritical to expect *a priori* that the usage we have found in the gospels would prevail also in the other parts of the New Testament. With the exception of Acts, we are dealing no longer with historical narrative but with the exhortations and instructions of believers to believers, no longer with historians but with Christ's apostles in the actual exercise of their ministry.

Even in Acts there are several speeches where it is not Luke the historian speaking but other people, believers and non-believers alike. The vivid character of Acts enables us to catch a real-life glimpse of how these people spoke of Jesus. It is rewarding to discern some of the nuances recorded so faithfully by Luke. The following should be especially noted:
1. The Jews who oppose the christian 'heresy' and the pagans who don't know very much about it speak, with or without affectation, of 'Jesus', 'Jesus of Nazareth', or 'a certain Jesus' (Ac 4:2, 13; 5:40; 6:14; 25:19; etc.).
2. When the apostles speak to adversaries or to strangers they adopt their own vocabulary. Peter in his Pentecost sermon and his defense before the Sanhedrin spoke of 'this Jesus whom you have put to death' (Ac 2:22; 5:30; also 13:33; 7:18; etc.). To this category may be added the account of Philip explaining 'the good news about Jesus' to the Ethiopian eunuch (Ac 8:35), or Peter telling Cornelius about 'Jesus of Nazareth whom God has annointed with the Holy Spirit' (Ac 10:38), or the newly converted Paul 'preaching in the synagogues about Jesus and saying he is the Son of God' (Ac 9:20).
3. Believers do not use simply the name 'Jesus'. Luke himself uses it only when he speaks as an historian, and in the first few pages of Acts (see also Ac 18:25). When speaking to one another the faithful almost always show their convictions by completing the name of Jesus with a title expressing faith and respect. The most common title, here as in the epistles, is 'Christ'. This is a proclamation especially to the Jews of the Christians' belief that 'Jesus is the Messiah, the Christ' (Ac 18:3, 28). Adding the title 'Christ' to the name Jesus is an act of faith in the resurrection, according to the line of reasoning expressed in Peter's Pentecost sermon: the resurrection of the Messiah had been predicted by David in the Psalms, and the one who was finally raised from the dead was 'this very Jesus, and we are all witnesses of this' (Ac 2:30-31).

What is to be said about the title *Kyrios*? During the

earthly life of Jesus of Nazareth this word, even when it was used by the disciples, was simply the common form of polite and respectful address, like the Italian *Signore* or the Spanish *Señor*. It was used, for example, by the Greeks who approached Philip of Bethsaida with their request: 'Sir, we wish to meet Jesus' (Jn 12:20-21). After the first miraculous catch of fish Simon Peter 'fell to his knees before Jesus and said, "Depart from me, Sir, for I am a sinful man" ' (Lk 5:8). This is not yet the confession of faith at Caesarea Philippi, but there is already, in the title coming near the end of his statement and in the action which accompanies it, the suggestion of the presence of more than human dignity and sanctity, and the intimation of a respect that will evolve into adoration. When after the ascension the title *Kyrios* occurs in the words or writings of the apostles and early Christians it has the incisive, almost awesome, meaning given it by Peter in his speech to the Jews of all nations who were assembled in Jerusalem: 'Let all Israel know for certain that God has made this Jesus, whom you crucified, both Lord and Messiah' (Ac 2:36).

The incomparable hymn recorded in the Epistle to the Philippians expresses sentiments perfectly familiar to the faithful of the time. St Paul used it to recommend peace, humility and charity in the christian community, after the example of Christ:

He always had the nature of God but did not cling jealously to his equality with God. Instead he emptied himself, taking the nature of a slave; he became like man and appeared in human likeness. Then he humbled himself and became obedient unto death, death on a cross. Therefore God has lifted him to the highest heavens and has given him the name that is above every other name, that at the name of Jesus all beings—in heaven, on earth, and under the earth—should bend their knees and every tongue proclaim that Jesus Christ is LORD to the glory of God the Father (Phil 2:6-11).

The early Christians knew what they were saying when they attributed the name *Kyrios* to Jesus their master. The Greek version of the Scriptures which was familiar to them used it to translate the Hebrew *Adonai* and *Yahweh*. In other words, 'What is said of the *Kyrios* (Yahweh) in the Old Testament is said of the *Kyrios Iesous Christos* in the New Testament.'[9]   St Paul's designation for Christians is 'those who call on the name of our Lord Jesus Christ' (1 Cor 1:2). As Bousset points out, calling on the name of the Lord is a distinctive characteristic of Christians.[10]   It was equivalent to a proper name at a time when the word *Christianos* was still rare.[11]   Calling on the name of the Lord understood as Jesus Christ is an unmistakable sign of faith in him as Messiah and son of God. In this early period to call on the name of the Lord was to have and to profess the christian faith; this was not at all true of pronouncing the name of Jesus even in a prayer addressed to the one who bore that name historically. The name 'Jesus' by itself had no special significance in a time and milieu when it could have been anybody's name. In fact, 'up to the beginning of the second century A.D. the name *Jeshua* or *Iesous* was very common among the Jews.'[12] An indication of its frequency can be gathered from two verses at the end of the Epistle to the Colossians: 'Aristarchus...sends you greetings, and so does Mark.... Jesus, surnamed Justus, also sends greetings.... Greetings from Epaphras, your countryman and a servant of Christ Jesus' (Col 4:10-12). The simple expression 'Jesus Christ' is also an act of faith; specifically, faith that Jesus of Nazareth is Messiah.

For all the reasons we have indicated—the fact that *Kyrios* was the divine name, *Christos* the messianic name, and *Jesus* a farily ordinary name in the Judeo-Christian milieu—it can be said that the first Christians 'used the name Christ more often than the name Jesus'.[13]   The fact is quite certain: Christians, at the beginning and long afterwards, said 'Jesus Christ' or 'the Christ' or 'the Lord Jesus' or 'our Lord Jesus Christ' much more often than they used simply

'Jesus', because they wanted to express their faith in him and their love for him, and they wanted to call on the name of the Lord. They knew from the Master himself that it was not enough to say 'Lord, Lord', in order to be a true disciple, and they knew by instinct and experience that saying simply 'Jesus' was not enough to constitute an act of faith.

THE APOSTOLIC FATHERS

The same conclusions apply also to the period of the apostolic fathers. In the *Didache*[14] we find this picture: three times the name 'Jesus' alone, always in the context of the eucharistic formula (IX:2, 3; X:2); three times 'Jesus' qualified as *tou paidos sou*; and once *dia tou paidos sou* without 'Jesus' (X:3). The Latin translation of *Didache* IX:5 reads *baptizati sint in nomine Jesu*, while the Greek text has *eis onoma Kyriou*—and this is a phenomenon that occurs more than once. *Christos* occurs alone only once, and 'Jesus Christ' also once (IX:4). *Kyrios* occurs eighteen times, twice with the addition of 'our' ('our Lord'—XV:4; XVI:1), once in the vocative (X:5), twice in the phrase 'in the name of the Lord' (IX:5; XII:1).

The *Letter of Barnabas*[15] gives an entirely different numerical picture. There we find 'Jesus Christ' once (2:6) and 'Jesus' fifteen times. *Kyrios* occurs once in the sense of master-of-a-slave (19:7), three times with reference to the owner of swine (10:3), and everywhere else it is used without differentiation either in the Old Testament meaning to refer to Yahweh or else to designate Jesus, the son of God. Two comments may be made: (1) The frequent use of 'Jesus' does not necessarily imply a special devotion to this name, because nearly all the passages are concerned with demonstrating that Jesus is the Messiah promised by the Old Testament (4:8; 6:9; 7:7, 10, 11; etc.). This is basically the same usage we encountered in Acts: 'Philip told him the good news about Jesus' (Ac 8:35). (2) Chapter 12:8 is concerned with the typological similarity of names between Joshua (Jesus), son of Nun, and Jesus, the son of God. This does not indicate a devotion to the name as such.

More important are Clement's *Epistles to the Corinthians* and the letters of St Ignatius. The former are representative of the official usage of the Roman Church, while the latter are filled with the refreshing spontaneity of love. In his first letter St Clement never writes simply 'Jesus'.[16] Instead we find 'Jesus Christ', 'our Lord Jesus Christ', 'the Christ', 'the Lord Jesus', 'your beloved son Jesus Christ' (addressed to God the Father—LIX:3), or 'our high priest and defender, Jesus Christ'. In the second letter attributed to Clement we find the historical style: 'Jesus answered Peter' (5:5). The author says that 'Jesus' is still a sign of contradiction: there are some who now deny him but they will one day discover to their surprise that this Jesus is ruler of the whole world (17:5-6); others call him 'our Jesus', and these will share in 'the mercy of Jesus' (16:2). Everywhere else, because the author is speaking to the faithful without any reference to nonbelievers, he uses a term in conformity with their common faith—such as 'Jesus Christ' (1:1-2, etc.), or 'the Christ' (2:7; 5:5; 6:7; etc.), or 'the Lord' (6:1 and frequently), or 'the Christ, the Lord who has saved us' (9:5). In one place (4:2) he alludes to Mt 7:21, 'Not everyone who says to me, "Lord, Lord", will be saved, but only he who practises justice,' and then he corroborates the thought by a very forceful quotation from an aprocryphal gospel: 'If you do not keep my commandments, then even though you were gathered together in my bosom I would reject you and say, "Depart from me, I do not know you nor where you are from, you sinners"'.

Except for St Paul and St John there is no one who puts us in touch with the reality of life in the early church so concretely as does St Ignatius of Antioch.[17] No one wrote as this man wrote because no other author loved as this man loved. How was St Ignatius accustomed to speak about the Master whom he longed to imitate by giving the supreme proof of love, his own life? How did he reveal his feelings and

express his great tenderness? His letters are totally
spontaneous. In those pages there is nothing of the
conventional or the stock phrase, nothing of the affected or
the forced. It is 'a living water murmuring within' (*Rom* 7:2).
We know what is murmured: the sovereign word put in our
hearts by the Spirit of the Father and the Son, 'Come to the
Father'. What we wish to discover is how, in this same
paternal and filial spirit, Ignatius speaks or is made to speak
of Jesus.

First of all there is his philosophy of the name. For
Ignatius, the name is the person himself. He writes: 'Among
others here with me is Crocus—a name which is dear to me'
(*Rom* 10:1). By 'the name which is dear' he did not mean the
two syllables of 'Crocus' but the man himself in flesh and
blood who bore this name. Similarly, when he writes to the
community of Ephesus and speaks of its 'dearly beloved
name', he does not mean simply the fact of living at Ephesus.
He is referring to the reputation which they had acquired
'through a natural temperament enhanced by faith and love
of Christ Jesus our saviour' (*Eph* 1:1). [18] 'Alce' is another
name that Ignatius calls dear (*Smyrn* 13:2), and he would say
the same for that person whatever her name. He speaks of
the names of all these people because the greeting he sends
them is not something collective or anonymous but individual
(*kata onoma*—*Smyrn* 13:3; or *ex onomatos*—*Ad Polyc* 8:2).

The honor due to a name increases with the dignity of the
person, as St Ignatius well knew. His own highest dignity
came from the chains he bore for Christ, which made him
worthy of the royal name of 'prisoner of Christ' (*Magn* 1:2).
In Greek-speaking countries there are people who try
to inspire respect by their sonorous and imposing names. But
St Ignatius preferred not even to write down the names of
unbelievers (*Smyrn* 5:3). What did he care about the names
of men? So many are merely names inscribed on tombstones
(*Phil* 6:1). For him there was only one name which was
important, a name which one has only to pronounce in the
presence of Christians for them to fill their thoughts with it

and boast of it, the name which is above every name, the person who is above every human being that can be named because he is a divine person.

When Ignatius names this person, what name does he use? He does not stop naming him; the name recurs incessantly. F.X. Funk supplies a word index to the Letters, but under *Iesous Christos* he gives only a dozen references to the Letter to the Ephesians and then contents himself with writing, '*etc. in omni fere capitulo*'.[19]   He could have written, '*in omni fere sententia.*'

Only once does Ignatius use the name 'Jesus' without any addition: 'I take refuge in the gospel as in the flesh of Jesus' (Phil 5:1).[20]   What reason can be found to explain this exception? The 'lengthy and involved discussions occasioned by this passage'[21] have not touched this question, so it is not sufficient simply to refer the reader to these discussions. We can compare the passage in question with two other passages in which the word 'Christ' is used by itself. Writing to the Smyrnaeans, Ignatius says they have been 'confirmed in love through the blood of Christ' (*Smyrn* 1:1). And later in the same letter: 'The principalities both visible and invisible must believe in the blood of Christ or else they will not escape damnation (*Smyrn* 6:1). Once he writes 'the flesh of Jesus', and twice 'the blood of Christ'. I believe that these three expressions have an identical meaning and are to be understood as instances of the historical style. The Letter to the Smyrnaeans is strongly anti-Docetic. The man whose name historically was 'Jesus', or by antonomasia 'Christ', was really born of a virgin and was 'really nailed to the cross by Pilate and Herod, and it is to the fruit of his cross, to his holy and blessed passion, that we owe our life' (*Smyrn* 1:1-2). The flesh received from his mother and the blood shed on the cross prove the historical and human reality of the Saviour, and the name of this historical person was simply 'Jesus' or 'the Christ' for Christians of the second century. A. Lelong, summing up the 'lengthy and involved discussions' on this passage, writes: 'For Ignatius the gospel is Jesus himself in flesh and blood because it is the record of his mortal life.'[22] It would be even closer to the thought of Ignatius to say that for him the gospel is Jesus himself because it is as real as Jesus in the reality of his flesh.

Except for these three instances the illustrious bishop-martyr, the disciple of St John who was an enamored of his Master as John was, never used the name of Jesus without addition and only rarely the name of Christ. The Latin translation of the letters is misleading here because it does not always correspond to the Greek text. For example, the salutation of one letter is translated 'according to the mind of Christ', while the Greek has 'according to the mind of Jesus Christ' (*Phil* salutation; see also Phil 8:2; 11:1; *Rom* salutation). There are three other passages which can be explained easily. 'They who profess to belong to Christ' (Eph 14:2) is a clarification of what the name 'Christian' means. *Magn* 13:2 has: 'be submissive to the bishop and to one another as Jesus Christ was to the Father...and the apostles were to Christ.' Similarly, *Rom* 4:1 has: 'I am God's wheat and I am to be ground by the teeth of wild beasts to become the pure bread of Christ.' In these two cases God and Christ are names for the same person, 'Jesus Christ our God' (*Rom* salutation).

Except for these few instances Ignatius habitually used titles like 'our Lord Jesus Christ', 'the Lord Jesus Christ', 'the Christ Jesus', 'Jesus Christ', 'our God Jesus Christ' (Rom 3:3), 'Christ Jesus our Saviour' (Eph 1:1), and 'the Lord' (*Phil* salutation). Once he wrote 'my Lord' for a reason that is immediately evident from the context: 'What good does it do me if a man praises my person but blasphemes my Lord by denying that he has assumed flesh?' (*Smyrn* 5:2). By his faith and love and concern Ignatius identified himself with his Lord and God, Jesus Christ, and by him and for his sake with the church of Christ. All that remained was for him to imitate the Lord to the point of death: 'Let me become an imitator of my suffering God' (Rom 6:2). Then he would possess him definitively: 'Pray for me that I may attain' (Rom 8:3). Attain to what? Ignatius did not always write in the object, which is obviously God or 'my God' (Eph 12:2), or Christ Jesus' (Rom 5:3). 'If I manage to obtain possession of

God, then alone will I truly be someone, then alone will I truly exist, and it will be purely by his mercy' (cf. Rom 9:2). With such sentiments it is not surprising that the name Ignatius gave his Master most frequently and affectionately was that of 'God'.

Such is Ignatius' philosophy of the name. It did not show itself in the repetition of 'Jesus, Jesus', but in his tireless application to the historical Jesus of all the titles which his faith made known to him, which his hope ardently desired, and which his charity loved above all things. His was not a torpid devotion toward a product of infatuated imagination. He did not linger rapturously over the sweetness of the syllables of Jesus' name in a sentimental fantasy of sublimated eroticism. Ignatius was a man who detested Docetism (see the Letter to the Smyrnians), who disdained show (Rom 2:2), who did not relish with an indirect self-love a feeling of tender affection for the Lord, and who had not the slightest, even subconscious, ambition of winning the world's admiration by the heroism of his love. He wanted only to disappear (Rom 4:2), to die (Rom 7:2), to be sacrificed for his God (Rom 2:2). Nothing, not even his own life, but Christ alone was of value to him. To describe the psychology of this total believer and lover is to attempt an endless task. No saint has ever surpassed this one in his boundless passion for Jesus Christ and for his name. It cannot be by accident that Ignatius is the first one to use the term *Christianismos* (*Magn* 10:1), which he follows up with the incisive comment: 'Whoever calls himself by a name other than this does not belong to God.'

This is how the most illustrious of the apostolic fathers expressed his devotion 'to the name'. It cannot be expected *a priori* that the other Fathers would be anything like him in this respect. *The Shepherd of Hermas* may be mentioned briefly. [23] Hermas knew that 'the name of the Son of God is magnificent, infinite, upholding the entire world' (*Similitud* ix, 14, 5). The 'name' is identifiable with Christianity itself to such an extent that Hermas, like Ignatius and others, used this word by itself to stand for the total christian synthesis (*Visio* iii, 1, 9). [24]   The first place in this synthesis was reserved for 'the royal and glorious name' (*Visio* iii, 3, 5), 'the name of the Son of God' (*Similitud* ix 12, 4), on the well-beloved Son, (Ibid. 5). By such phrases the roman layman-author exalted this name even more than did the Bishop of Antioch, yet he never once wrote either 'Jesus' or 'Christ'.

It seems correct to say that the greater the devotion to the divine name, the less the name of Jesus is used. The omission is not because of forgetfulness but because the idea never occurs. We presume that the actual name should have been used because we no longer understand this 'Christology of the name', this 'theology of the name as designation of the divine person of Christ'. [25]   But our ignorance is pardonable; already in the seventh century a corrector of the *Codex Sinaiticus* felt he had to substitute 'the expression *the name of the Lord* for the typically Jewish Christian expression *the name*, which was no longer understood'. [26]   For us the name is 'Jesus', which is one of the names of the well-beloved Son; for Hermas and others like him the very person of the Son was *the name*, the only name which perfectly expressed the Father.

ST IRENAEUS

St Irenaeus deserves special attention because he was obliged to reflect on the subject of names much more than was his old master, St Polycarp, or others of that generation for whom the instinct of faith was guidace enough. In St Irenaeus's time, Gnosticism was propagating a divided Christ:

One Christ was produced by the Only-begotten for the re-establishment of the pleroma, *another was the Saviour sent for the glorification of the Father, still another the Jesus of the economy who, they say, suffered and died while the*

Saviour returned to the pleroma *bearing Christ.* [27]

Instead of citing the entire refutation which follows, we can content ourselves for our purposes with quoting the first phrase, for it already contains the name which knits together the unity of the one Christ: 'I judge it necessary to review here the complete doctrine of the apostles regarding *our Lord Jesus Christ.*' As St Ignatius did against Docetism, so Irenaeus, fighting a Gnosticism which 'dissolves Christ' (1 Jn 4:3—Vulgate), combined in a single title the divine and human names of the Saviour and never stopped repeating them as a perpetual profession of faith. As for the simple name 'Jesus', gnostic speculation would have made it somewhat ambiguous to use. 'The heretics say that *Jesus* is a symbolic name consisting of six letters whose meaning is known by all who are among the called' (*Adv Haer* I, 14, 4). The context goes on to elaborate the abstruse numerical significance of various names, especially the name of Jesus. Irenaeus had no choice but to give a thoroughly convincing refutation of these pedantic theories because they were taken very seriously by those who invented and propagated them. Irenaeus tried to collapse the foundation of their theories by pointing out that the name 'Jesus' is not originally a Greek name with six letters but a Hebrew name with 'two and a half' letters (*Adv Haer* II, 24, 2). The Gnostics had constructed their own 'philosophy of the name' and Irenaeus had to upset it in order to preserve both orthodoxy and common sense. His method was to go to the very essence of Christology, the union of two natures in one person. In the distant future, defenders of the Jesus Prayer would likewise maintain that this prayer contains an act of faith in both the humanity and the divinity of the incarnate Word. And they are right to say so. By reason of their christian instinct, they are without knowing it the heirs of Ignatius and Irenaeus. The Gnostics 'do away with the Spirit and separate Christ from Jesus' whereas actually 'all the conditions of the human lot have been fulfilled by our Lord Jesus Christ who is always one and the same' (*Adv Haer* III, 17, 4). As is evident, it was impossible for the faithful in such a climate of Gnosticism to speak about or speak to Jesus using simply that name alone.

ORIGEN

Origen was well aware that Christ had many names. He enumerated some of them and commented on the principal ones in the second chapter of the first book of his treatise *Peri Archon*.[28]   Since Christ has two natures, the divine nature of the Son of God and the human nature assumed for our salvation, 'therefore we must first study who the son of God is who is called by many different titles according to the judgments and opinions of those who name him' (*Peri Archon* I, 2, 1). He lists titles such as: Wisdom, *Verbum*, Truth, Life, Son, Image, Breath, Mirror, Splendor, etc. At the end of the chapter Origen remarks: 'It would be a lengthy task, matter for another book and another time, to collect together all the titles of the Son of God, such as Light, Gate, Justice, Sanctification, Redemption and countless others, and to show why each one of them is given to him' (*Peri Archon* I, 2, 3).

This list of names belongs properly to the divine nature of the Son of God. Though Origen does not make a list of his human names, the principal one, which is 'Jesus', does occur in the same chapter (see I, 2, 10). It is mentioned not as part of a list but in relation to Phil 2:10-11 in order to show that Jesus shares the Father's omnipotence since 'at his name every knee will bend in heaven, on earth and under the earth and every tongue will confess that Jesus is Lord to the glory of the Father'. For Origen, as for St Ignatius before him and St Gregory Nazianzen after him, Jesus was the historical name of a person who was a sign of contradiction, ridiculed by philosophers like Celsus, adored by those who accepted him as Messiah and son of God. This principle was evident to Celsus himself and he formulated it by saying that Christians are 'those who follow Jesus, believing that he is the Messiah, the Christ.'[29]   When Christians are among themselves they do not use the name 'Jesus' alone, but 'Jesus Christ' or 'the Lord Jesus' or 'the Christ' or 'our Lord Jesus Christ'. Non-Christians can do nothing but call him by his human name. And Christians themselves follow this practice when dealing with unbelievers or when repeating narratives from the gospel. This was Origen's practice in the *Contra Celsum*. Celsus continually wrote the name 'Jesus' without any title, perhaps deliberately refusing to give him any title. At any rate he could not use a designation which would imply a faith he did not really have. As Origen traced his adversary's line of argument he also adopted his style of speech.

This Jesus whose enemies speak so disdainfully of him, says Origen, has in fact accomplished marvellous works beyond anything ever attributed to the Greek gods and heros, 'except perhaps in the myths which they try to make us believe without proof, though they themselves refuse to yield to historical evidence on our side' (*Contra Celsum* I, 67). Origen goes on to assert that 'the work of Jesus is known over the whole inhabited world wherever are found the churches of God gathered in the name of Jesus, composed of men converted from innumerable sins'. Thus it was to a large extent in response to the challenge of unbelievers that Origen was led to condense in the name of Jesus everything that his faith taught him about the Lord, the Christ, the Son of God. A name that was for an historian neutral and for a keen adversary an expression of disdain became for Origen the epitome of all the glories of Christ.

When not concerned with polemics, however, Origen reverted to the universal practice of giving to his Master all the titles his heart might suggest. Thus in the homilies of the great Alexandrian we encounter another style. There he is not addressing and adapting himself to the learned but to the faithful. There he uses a different means of confessing his faith and expressing his love. He proclaims that he belongs to Christ as Thomas the Apostle did when he cried, '*My* Lord and *my* God' (Jn 20:28). In Origen's homilies phrases such as '*my* Saviour' (*In Ezech* 5:3) and especially '*my* Lord Jesus' (*In Is* 1:2) are very frequent. F. Bertrand has called attention to some of these phrases,[30] and for further study he refers to H. de Lubac.[31]

In all the places cited by F. Bertrand the text reads 'my Lord Jesus' instead of 'my Jesus'. This is true also for almost all of de Lubac's list. Some of the exceptions (e.g., *In Jos* 1:5) can be explained by the context in which 'my Jesus' is contrasted to 'Jesus son of Nun'. The exception in *In Jer* 21:7 may be due to an alteration made by a copyist or translator. There remain only two or three authentic instances of the use of *mou ho Iesous* (*In Jer* 18:5; 21:7; *In Lucam* 18:3). It is scarcely possible on such a slim basis to invoke Origen as a witness for devotion to the name of Jesus used without additional titles. Like his predecessors he took advantage of almost every opportunity to complete the human name of the Master with qualifiers that expressed faith in his divinity. What is new with Origen is the frequent occurence of the possessive adjective first person singular, '*my* Lord Jesus Christ'.

What interests us more than the plain fact of this unusual expression are the reasons that led Origen to adopt it. Were they conscious reasons of faith or unconscious motives of the heart? In the first place this great Christian evidently enjoyed being able to proclaim with the heavens, the earth and the underworld that his Jesus, his Christ, was his Lord, and to confess aloud that he was a disciple of this Lord Jesus. Like Ignatius of Antioch he took pride in the name and even without the stimulus of polemic enjoyed displaying his feeling in these assemblies of believers who shared his sentiments. Secondly, there was the character of his audience. Expressions of piety are likely to take a more openly affective form in the presence of ordinary Christian people than among the sophisticated, though it might be difficult to document this. Still another factor might be a subconscious remembrance of other people named 'Jesus' whom Origen does not wish to confuse or even compare with *his*

Jesus, *his* own Lord Jesus. Finally, as a result of this exclusive admiration and adoration, Origen was obviously a man of deep, virile, discreet, respectful and grateful tenderness of heart, like St Paul and St Peter and St John and the martyrs whom he dreamed of following to the limits of love.

It would be a very spiritually rewarding task to search beneath the words and between the lines to detect the subtle hints of this *agape*, this *philia*, even this *eros* for Christ—to use an expression from Origen's commentary on the Canticle. [32] To succeed one would have to have a delicacy of soul equal to that of the saints and courage sufficient to confront the smiles, if not the displeasure, of professional scholars. F. Bertrand has attempted this, skillfully and creditably and without claiming to have said the last word on the subject. What I like best is his concluding remark: 'The presence of bloody persecutions had given a seriousness and depth to Origen's love for Christ which subsequent ages could well envy.' [33] To speak of tenderness for Christ and especially for *Jesus* is always to risk being misunderstood. If there is anything completely foreign to the mentality of Origen and of the martyrs, it is the pretense of a devotion to Jesus in which a divine love stronger than death has faded and dissolved into a surrogate human love affair. The object of Origen's and the martyrs' tenderness was Jesus, but they knew and were convinced and affirmed that this Jesus, their Jesus, was the Lord, the Son of God, and God in the glory of the Father.

Their tenderness showed itself, without being ostentatious, in their readiness to proclaim his greatness and in their concern for avoiding any word or deed or attitude which could compromise this greatness, even in appearance. One example from Origen will illustrate the delicacy of this adoration, which is more sensitive than a mother's love and more respectful than a son's affection. The example has to do with the name of Jesus:

'*At that time there was a notorious prisoner named Jesus*

Barabbas. Pilate therefore said to the crowd of Jews, "Which one do you want me to release, Jesus Barabbas or Jesus who is called the Christ?" He knew very well that they were prosecuting him because of jealousy' (Mt 27:16-18).

There are many manuscripts which do not mention the fact that Barabbas was also named Jesus, and perhaps they are right to omit it, so that the name of Jesus is not associated with a criminal. For if we look through all the books of Holy Scripture we never come across a sinner whose name is Jesus. Other names are given to both saints and sinners, the name 'Judas' which is given to praiseworthy men like the Apostle, Judas the Zealot, Judas Maccabeus, and to the patriarch Judah, but also to men like Judas the traitor. Similarly we find in Genesis the same names being given to the sons of Lot and to the sons of Cain, like Enoch, Lamech, and Methuselah. It would be unfitting if the same were true of the name 'Jesus'. I suspect that heretics may have made an addition to the text in order to shore up their own theories by pointing to a similarity of names between Jesus and Barabbas. However I suspect that there is also symbolism and mystery here: Barabbas had a reputation for revolution, for war, for the assassination of mens' souls, while Jesus as the Son of God existed for the sake of peace and, as Verbum *and* Wisdom, *for the sake of all that is good.* [34]

What would Origen have said if he could have foreseen the custom in our day whereby anarchists or even good Christians are sometimes named 'Jesus'? He would be quite severe in his criticism of the parents who gave such a name and of the priest who accepted it at baptism. His devotion to the name of Jesus made him sensitive to the least suggestion of disrespect towards this name and caused him to love people in proportion to the respect and love they showed for this person. Thus he wrote that St Peter is not called blessed for having said simply 'You are the Christ', but for having added the words 'the son of the living God'. Mark and Luke record only the words 'You are the Christ', without the addition we find in Matthew, and they likewise omit the blessing and the promise, 'You are Peter....'[35]

We have observed Origen's habit of writing '*my* Jesus'. There were many Greek and Byzantine writers who imitated this pious Origenism by adding to the different names of Christ the possessive adjective 'my'. It is questionable whether they did so with as much spontaneity as Origen did. Too often it gives the impression of being a deliberate imitation, a stylistic flourish. We could only guess or conjecture about the reasons and motives behind Origen's own use of the possessive, because he himself never explains these reasons. In fact he seems to be unaware of them. Other authors have been quite conscious of their reasons and have recorded them for us. One of the first to do so was Gregory Nazianzen. Gregory, surnamed 'the Theologian', found a theological reason:

If the devil tempts you to ambition by showing you in an instant and in a single glance all the kingdoms of the earth, and if he claims that they all belong to him, then do not believe him for he owns nothing at all. You are fortified with the seal of baptism and you can say to him, 'I too am the image of God and I have not been thrown down from the glory of heaven as you have; I have put on Christ; I have taken possession of Christ by baptism. It is you who should adore me!' [36]

Christ belongs to us and we to him. It is impossible to imagine a closer relationship than this one which goes almost to the point of identification. Gregory describes it in another sermon:

Yesterday I was crucified with Christ, today I am glorified with him. Yesterday I was a corpse with him, today I am brought back to life with him. Yesterday I was buried with Christ, today I rise with him.... We have become like Christ since Christ has made himself like us; we have become Gods through him since he became man for us. [37]

It is this fine theological sensitivity for our union with Christ in all his mysteries that led Gregory Nazianzen to express himself as Origen did: 'My Christ, my Jesus.' For example:

Once again, my Jesus, once again a mystery.... [38]

The very first reason for this holy celebration of light is the baptism of my Christ who is the true light who enlightens every man coming into the world, with a light that purifies him....[39]

The theological reason given by Gregory Nazianzen is probably the primary explanation for the use of the possessive 'my' by Origen. But it can be supplemented by the thought of Metropolitan Theophylactus of Bulgaria commenting on 2 Cor 12:21: 'When St Paul writes "my God", he manifests his burning love for God.'[40] What was true of St Paul was true also of Origen spontaneously writing 'my Christ', 'my Lord Jesus'. This deserves to be emphasized. The love we are referring to is not only the love which is shown in obedience to the Lord's commands, though this is the most important and ultimately the only important kind of love. Rather what is meant is the resonance of obedient love felt in the flesh and bones of a person, like the love which the Lord showed for his disciples not only by giving his life for them but also by his human sympathy for their miseries and his delight in their joys. Although St Paul claimed that he no longer knew anyone according to the flesh, not even Christ (2 Cor 5:16), he could not suppress his deep feelings, particularly his love for Christ. St John Chrysostom was able to detect these pulsations of Paul's heart, and we can detect them still today. In the case of Origen too we feel at every instant that we are in contact with a soul enamored of Christ. To give a few more examples from his writings:

Ezekiel refers to himself through his prophecy as 'the son of man'. And who is son of man as much as my Lord Jesus Christ?[41]

When Scripture says, 'Go to the bee' (Prov 6:8), I think the meaning is this: in the hive one bee is supreme, the queen. And just as the bees have their ruler, so my Lord Jesus Christ is a prince and it is to him that the Holy Spirit directs me so that I may eat his honey, for it is good, and so that the honeycomb may fill my throat with sweetness.[42]

What is wisdom's name? Jesus. What does 'may your name be invoked upon us' mean? I am wisdom, I wish to be called by your name so that I, wisdom, might be named Jesus, and so that counsel, fortitude, knowledge, piety and fear of the Lord might be named Jesus, and then your name will become all in all.[43]

As a final example here is a prayer found in Origen's fifth homily on Isaiah:

O Jesus, come, for my feet are dirty. Make yourself a slave for me. Pour water into your basin and come wash my feet. I know that what I say is presumptuous, but I am afraid of the warning which came from your lips when you said, 'If I do not wash your feet you will have no part with me'. Wash my feet then, that I may have a part with you. But why do I say only my feet? Peter was able to say, 'Wash only my feet', because he was clean all over and only his feet needed washing. In my case, however, although I have been washed once, I still need the baptism of which the Lord said, 'I have another baptism which I must be baptized with'.

A. Hamman has commented on this prayer that 'it is all the more remarkable in that Origen's habitual concern was to refer all worship and prayer to the Father, as being the source of the Godhead.'[44] We have one remark to make about this: What is also surprising, at least for a moment, is the vocative 'Jesus' used all alone, the only instance of such a form of address. But it must be remembered that we have this prayer only in St Jerome's Latin translation, and the Byzantine editors may, moreover, have permitted the original terms to be lost. Consequently if someone assures us that with Origen 'prayer was generally addressed to Jesus'[45] this cannot mean the use of the vocative, *Jesu*, by itself. In this matter more than anywhere the principle *testis unus testis nullus* is valid.

Editors in the West have also preserved for us Origen's *Homilies on Jesus Son of Nun*, with their touching preface. 'God has given the name which is above every name to our Lord and Saviour Jesus Christ. The name which is above every name is "Jesus". And because this name is above all others every knee shall bend at the name of Jesus....'.[46] And Origen goes on to give him all the titles his faith and devotion can suggest.

To summarize: (1) Origen, a theologian enchanted with Christ, loved to name him with divine titles as an expression both of Christ's greatness and of man's faith and love; (2) Origen used the historical name 'Jesus' as the evangelists did, when he was writing in a simple narrative style or engaged in polemic with adversaries who did not know or did not admit any other name; (3) When he was at ease and relaxed, with an audience of Christians, Origen allowed himself to be drawn into a more intimate style of conversation characterized by the addition of the possessive 'my': 'my Christ', 'my Lord', 'my Lord Jesus', and even, though infrequently, simply 'my Jesus'. In this expression there is a tenderness that is the more touching for being unself-conscious. Devotion to the point of total submission, and love ready for the sacrifice of life caused the full refinement of human sentiment to burst forth. Origen never lingered to indulge in these sentiments and he might have blushed to discover them in himself, even more so if another had discovered them. In one commentary he wrote:

The evangelist could not fail to remark also that 'He was called Jesus, the name given him by the angel' (Lk 2:21). It was not fitting for this name to be pronounced and glorified first of all my men, but it was right that this be done by creatures of a higher order of being, for this is a name that is adorable and worthy of respect beyond every name.[47]

Compare St Jerome's translation, which is slightly longer but perhaps thereby more faithful to the nuance:

Vocabulum Jesu gloriosum omni adoratu cultuque dignissimum, nomen quod est super omne nomen, non decuit primum ab hominibus appellari neque ab eis afferri in mundum, sed ab excellentiori quadam majorique natura....

SAINT BASIL

St Basil was forced to reflect on the meaning of names and forms of address (*prosegoria*) in order to refute Eunomius. His theory on the subject can be summarized easily:

1. Proper names, whether of creatures or of God, do not in any way signify or describe the essences of things but only the characteristic properties of individuals (*Adv Eunom* II,4).[48]

2. There is a distinction between relative names and absolute names. Absolute names designate objects in themselves, such as man, horse, cow. Relative names include relationships to other things, such as son, servant, friend (Ibid., II, 9).

3. Absolute names 'even though they appear to signify a fundamental reality do not really designate the essence but only the properties surrounding it' (Ibid.; proof given in II, 4).

4. The nature of a thing does not follow its name, rather the

name comes from the thing itself. Though the fourth book of
the tract against Eunomius may have been written by
Didymus, it is true to the thought of Basil when it says that
things are greater than their names and that existential
realities are more effectual than spoken words (PG 29:685A;
cf. 580B).

5.   It is not impossible that one and the same essence have
several names, nor that, among creatures, one and the same
name belong to different essences (PG 29:685A).

6.   In speaking of the incarnate Word one must keep in mind
the distinction between theology and economy, and must not
attribute to the nature of the Word what Scripture says of the
historical Christ as such (PG 29:577A).

Granted these principles, says St Basil, *it is not surprising
that: When our Lord Jesus Christ spoke of himself for the
purpose of teaching men about the philanthropy of God and
the grace coming from the incarnation (the economy),... he
called himself by several names which flow from qualities
that are proper to him: Gate, Day, Bread, Vine, Shepherd,
Light. All these names designate the same subject and in
using them the Lord always meant himself but under
different aspects* (tais epinoiais).[49] *according to the different
effects which he brings about. When he calls himself the
Light of the world he lets the inaccessible glory of his divinity
be glimpsed by that name, along with the splendor of
knowledge with which he enlightens those whose soul's eye is
pure. He calls himself the Vine because he nourishes with the
fecundity of good works all those who are rooted in him by
faith. He calls himself Bread as being the most suitable
nourishment of the rational being, since bread sustains the
strength of the soul and maintains its proper disposition by
providing it with everything it needs, thus preventing the soul
from becoming sick as would happen if it gave way to
irrationality. It would be possible to go through each name
like this and show the different aspect of the one same
subject it described* (Adv Eunom I,7; PG 29:524C).

Later on pseudo-Denys will say that God is both nameless and multinamed.[50] For Basil the multiplicity of titles does not make our Lord Jesus Christ 'someone with many names (*ou polyonymos tis on*), because these names do not all have the same meaning' (Ibid., I:7; PG 29:525A). From this remark we can conclude that Basil thinks there is one name which denotes not a particular aspect but the substance or subject itself (*to hypokeimenon*).

What would this name be? Undoubtedly it is the name that Basil wrote at the beginning of this tract against Eunomius: 'When *our Lord Jesus Christ* spoke of himself....' This expanded, explicit title is very common in the writings of St Basil, especially when some subject of great solemnity is under discussion. Occasionally he embellished it even more: 'The only-begotten son of God, our Lord Jesus Christ' (*Reg Fus Trac* X; PG 31:944C). Basil was annoyed by injury or disrespect towards 'the name of our Lord Jesus Christ' (Ibid., XXVI; PG 31:1009A). This is another reason why he always named him with titles which were in themselves signs of faith, such as 'Christ', or signs of reverence, such as 'Lord', but never 'Jesus' alone except in scriptural citations. This usage is quite deliberate on Basil's part although he may not have been consciously aware of it each time:

All the names which we give to the Word made flesh belong to the economy, not to theology. Of these, the names 'Lord' and 'Christ' are the best expressions of the sovereign dominion which the Father has given him. This is evident from Peter's address on the first Pentecost: 'Let the whole house of Israel know for certain that God has made both Lord and Christ this Jesus whom you crucified' (Ac 2:36).[51]

Once more a great spiritual master bears witness to the tradition that prefers the formula 'Lord Jesus Christ'.

ST GREGORY NAZIANZEN

St Gregory Nazianzen, who is traditionally known as 'the Theologian' and who also possessed an affective temperament as passionate as St Bernard's, has left us an *ex professo* treatment of the names of Christ (*per omnes Christi appellationes*) in one of the nine homilies translated by Rufinus. His list of about thirty titles is obviously dependent on Origen: God, Son, Image, Word, Wisdom, Truth, Light, Life, Power, Breath, Emanation, Splendor, Creator, King, Head, Law, Way, Gate, Foundation, Rock, Pearl, Peace, Justice, Holiness, Man, Servant, Shepherd, Lamp, Priest, Sacrifice, Firstborn before creation, Firstborn of the dead, the Resurrection. These are both names and realities (*onomata kai pragmata*). A priest, before daring to exercise his sacred functions, should be familiar with all of them by experience and contemplation.[52] The name 'Jesus' does not occur in the list, although he could easily have written *Jesu Christi appellationes* at the head of it instead of simply *Christi appellationes*. Gregory's use of the name 'Jesus' alone is restricted to passages quoting from the gospels. The name he usually uses is 'Christ'.

On one occasion Gregory spoke of 'the majesty of Jesus'.[53] Here his choice of the earthly name of the Saviour could be ascribed to his feeling for good oratory, since he wished to make a strong contrast between the lowly appearance of Jesus of Nazareth and the high honors he possesses in the eyes of faith. A similar stylistic device can be noticed a little earlier in this oration:

Christ is baptized, let us descend with him so that we may also ascend with him. Jesus is baptized. Is that all? Should we not also consider who he is and by whom he is being baptized and when? He, the all-pure, is being baptized by John, and it happens when he is about to begin performing miracles (In Sacra Lumine 14; PG 36:350CD).

Something of the same nuance can be detected in an expression which Gregory borrowed from Origen, *Iesous ho emos*. It occurs at the beginning of the same oration: 'Again, my Jesus, and again a mystery' (*In Sacra Lumine* 1; PG 36: 336A)

Gregory the Theologian left us his deepest thought on the subject of names in one paragraph of his thirty-seventh oration, his only surviving exegetical work. The text being discussed was Mt 19:1-12, the question about divorce. Gregory took the opportunity to say something to those 'who were made eunuchs from their mother's womb' (Mt 19:12). 'Be not proud, you who are eunuchs by nature....For a virtue which comes by nature is not meritorious; only that virtue is praiseworthy which is the result of free choice.'[54]   After making this point Gregory continued:

There is something else that I demand from true eunuchs. Do not commit fornication against the Deity. You have been made one with Christ, do not dishonor Christ. You have received the Spirit of perfection, do not try to make the Spirit be like you. St Paul says, 'If I were still trying to win the favor of men I would not be the servant of Christ' (Gal 1:10). If I worshipped a creature I would not be called a Christian. Why is the name of Christian so honorable? Is it not because Christ is God? I hope it is not because, being human, I love him only humanly as one would love a friend. And yet I love and honor St Peter without calling myself a Petrine, and St Paul as well, without having ever been called a Pauline. I do not permit myself to be named after any man because I am born of God. So then if you call yourself a Christian because you acknowledge Christ as God, you are to be congratulated! May you persevere in this name and in the reality which it signifies. But if on the contrary it is out of mere human affection that you call yourself by his name, you will benefit from it no more than from any other title given you by reason of your profession or something like that. Consider people who are fans of horse racing. They are named after the colors

*and the teams which they favor. You've heard these
names, the Greens, the Blues, and so on. If it is like this that
you call yourself a Christian, then your title is a very sorry
thing, however much you may boast of it. If however you are
a Christian because you believe that Christ is God, then show
by your deeds that this is your conviction.*[55]

The best summary of this argument is provided by
Gregory himself in his fourth theological discourse:

*Surely nothing can bring greater honor to the humble state of
man than to be united to God, to become God by this union,
to be visited from on high by the rising sun (Lk 2:78), so that
the holy one who is born should be called the Son of the Most
High (Lk 1:32, 35) and should receive the name that is above
every name (Phil 2:9). What can this name be but the name
of God? Let us add this: every knee should bow before him
who emptied himself for our sake and who united the divine
image to the form of a slave, and the whole house of Israel
should know that God has made him both Lord and Christ (Ac
2:36).*[56]

According to Gregory the Theologian, a philosophy of the
name applies to the human name of Jesus only because it
first applies to the divine name. The Jesus Prayer is well
phrased, 'Lord Jesus Christ, son of God....'

ST JOHN CHRYSOSTOM

We may begin with a principle enunciated by John
Chrysostom on the subject of names and their relative
importance:

*'Behold the virgin will conceive and will bear a son, and they
will name him Emmanuel' (Is 7:14). Why is it then that the
name which he received was not Emmanuel but Jesus Christ?*

Notice that the prophecy does not say, You *will name him, but 'they will name him', meaning the people, and even the course of events. What is prophesied is his ultimate name. Scripture often does this, substituting a future happening for a proper name. So the phrase 'they will name him Emmanuel' means simply that in him they will see God with men. God may have been with men before, but never in so evident a manner.*

Now if the Jews should deny this interpretation we can ask them to tell us when the prophecy was fulfilled that said Isaiah's son should be named 'Quick spoils, speedy plunder' (Is 8:3). *They will not be able to answer.... Or we can ask them about that other prophecy, that the city 'will be called City of Justice, faithful City of Zion'* (Is 1:26). *We never read that the city acquired the name 'Justice', since it has been continuously called 'Jerusalem'. ...for when something occurs that identifies someone more clearly than his ordinary name, scripture says that this event is his name.*[57]

Therefore a person's given name (*prosegoria*) does not necessarily determine from the outset everything that the person wil accomplish in life. This is why some of the famous people of history are given additional names or titles. And in the case of the most famous the new epithet completely replaces the original name. St Thomas' usual name for Aristotle is 'The Philosopher'. And not many know that 'Plato' is a sobriquet for one who had been named Aristocles by his grandfather. And there are other men whom we know now by the names of the functions or achievements or crimes that they were associated with in adult life, rather than by the names they were given in infancy. The Lord himself changed Simon's name to Cephas/Peter, and Saul became known as Paul. Consequently a philosophy of the name will not consist in an effort to show how a name given at baptism or circumcision might contain or prophesy everything that the bearer of that name may become in later life. One man may do his name dishonor, while another may do it so much honor as to render it inadequate. Evagrius Ponticus captures this phenomenon in an epigram: 'In the course of time...worlds change and names do not remain the same.'[58]   In other words the requirements of a genuine philosophy of the name will be met not by simply repeating the original name but by adding to it or replacing it with another name which will better express the fame or infamy of the subject. As fame increases, or appears to increase, new titles may be added, as was the case with the Roman emperors. Not infrequently the original name disappeared altogether.

The works of St John Chrysostom include four homilies entitled *De Mutatione Nominum*.[59]   The title as well as the amplitude of the work might lead us to expect a fully developed, systematic philosophy of the name. In fact, however, the great orator gets carried away by his own eloquence to the extent that his digressions receive more attention than the original subject of the discourse. The introductory parts in particular were prolonged until the audience began to complain, though they were accustomed to 'homilies' of this kind.

In the first of the four homilies Chrysostom managed, at the final paragraph, to come to a statement of the problem. Why was Saul afterwards called Paul and Simon called Peter? Why were James and John called Sons of Thunder? And in the Old Testament why the change from Abram to Abraham, from Jacob to Israel, from Sarai to Sarah, and so on? 'All these changes of names provide us with ample matter for investigation' (PG 51:124).

The next day, after an introduction taking up a quarter of the length, Chrysostom began to explore his subject. The question, he said, is not idle speculation because it deals with names given by God to his saints. In appearance it may be a simple matter but if one digs deeper he will find a treasure, as everywhere in the rich earth of sacred Scripture. We find changes of names in both testaments. Sometimes the pagans have more than one name, such as Porcius Festus, Pontius Pilate, Sergius Paulus, but we are more concerned with the times when names are changed by God himself. Some explain St Paul's case by saying that the name Saul (*Saulos*) suited him as long as he disturbed (*saleuein*) the church, but when he ceased (*pauesthai*) this madness he was known as Paul. Chrysostom admitted that this explanation is a little hard to swallow:

If I put it before you it is only to teach you not to let yourselves be put off by specious etymologies. It is obvious that Saul's parents, who gave him his name, were not prophets and could not foresee the future. Besides, if he had been named Saul because he shook and disturbed the Church, he should have stopped using this name as soon as he was converted (Hom II).

But he is still called Saul after his conversion as is clear from Acts (Ac 9:17; 11:25; 13:1). The Holy Spirit himself calls him Saul: 'Set apart for me Saul and Barnabas for the work which I have in store for them' (Ac 13:2). Thus the matter is not so simple.

Names have a considerable importance even in business affairs, and all the more so in spiritual matters. Consequently, says Chrysostom, two questions must be asked. First of all, why did God give a special name to certain holy men but not to others? In the New Testament, Peter and the sons of Zebedee received new names from the Lord but the other apostles were left with the names their parents had given them. In the Old Testament, there were changes with Abraham and Jacob, but not with Joseph, Samuel, David, Elijah, Elisha or any other prophet. And secondly, why did God give some people their names before they were born, for example Isaac and John the Baptist, and then give new names to others only in adult life, for example Peter, James, John, Abraham and Jacob? Chrysostom chose to treat the second question first. He went back to the first man who received his name from God, Adam. Adam was named after his mother, the earth, to remind him of his humble origin.

Isaac means laughter and joy. And, like Isaac, we too are sons according to God's promise. In the realm of grace 'nature is totally inoperative, for it is the power of God which accomplishes everything'.

The third homily opened with Chrysostom's self-defense—going on for five columns, half the total length—against those who had complained to him about the length of his introductions. Finally he took up the question of why Saul's name was changed to Paul. It was because the Holy Spirit had taken possession of him, just as we often see masters renaming slaves they have just acquired, for example Hananiah, Mishael and Azariah were renamed Shadrach, Meshach, and Abednego (Dn 1:7). Why didn't the change occur immediately after Paul's conversion? Because this might have caused some people to question whether the apostle was truly the persecutor.

The fourth homily still bears the title *De Mutatione Nominum*, but again it treats the subject only incidentally. Chrysostom wrote:

Paul is a simple name but it conceals a wealth of thoughts, as you have been hearing. For if you recall, I have been discoursing for three whole days about nothing but this name, and about the reasons why his name was changed from Saul to Paul and why this did not happen immediately after his conversion.

Without a word about the meaning of the name 'Paul' he continued:

God puts in the names of his saints a reminder and instruction about virtue, like something engraved on a bronze tablet. He gave Peter his name with an allusion to his rocklike strength. He put in Peter's very name a proclamation of his steadfast faith so that the very sound of his name might continually encourage him in his constancy. Similarly he called John and James 'sons of thunder' with an allusion to the resounding echo of their preaching.

And St Paul? Chrysostom sidestepped the question adroitly:

I will not go into that, lest I tire you by repeating the same things, but I wish to make this point: the names of the saints are in themselves feared by sinners and venerated by the friends of God.

Writing to Philemon, Paul based his defense of Onesimus on several considerations, one of which was his own name 'Paul'. Similarly when writing to the Galatians he said, 'It is I, Paul, who tell you this: if you submit to circumcision, Christ will be of no use to you at all' (Gal 5:2). Noticing these details Chrysostom commented:

You have already said, 'I'. Why do you add your name? Isn't the use of the word 'I' enough to identify the writer? Paul's reason must have been to teach us how the bare mention of his name was able to touch his readers; he added it to the 'I' to remind them to remember their master. And this is exactly what we ourselves experience. When we recall the saints we are aroused from our state of laziness or we overcome a temptation to rebel, letting respect guide us back on the right path. With regard to St Paul in particular, I know that whenever I hear his name I think of a man who has experienced many temptations, beatings, imprisonments, a man who spent a day and a night on the open sea, who was snatched up to the third heaven and heard the ineffable dialogue of paradise, a man who was God's chosen instrument, the friend of Christ, who was willing to be anathema from Christ for the sake of his brothers. Like a golden chain the series of wonderful associations follows the mention of his name if my attention is held on it. And the profit from such a train of thought is by no means inconsiderable. [60]

To sum up: as Chrysostom understood it the philosophy of
the name is not primarily a matter of etymology, though this
has its value in certain cases. For some people their name
suggests a particular destiny which they must accomplish and
when they have done so they can say their *consummatum est*.
For others, their name has no special signification and it is
for them to make it significant by a life full of noble works.
Thus the philosophy of the name has a double perspective,
the one prophetic—as for Abraham or Peter, and the other
retrospective—as for St Paul and the majority of men. Among
Greek-speaking people there were many who were given high
sounding names at birth, such as *Onomakritos* (Famous
name) or *Kleitomachos* (Celebrated-fighter), and who failed
ridiculously to live up to their names. In contrast, many
Romans bore very humble names and made them illustrious,
for example *M. Porcius* (Hog) *Cato, Flaccus* (Flap-eared),
Hortensius (Garden).

APHRAATES

Following the principles laid down by R. Graffin for his
Syriac Patrology,[61] Dom Parisot has published along with his
edition of Aphraates an index in which '*signantur cuncta
vocabula, sub omnibus eorum formis quae in...*Demonstra-
tionibus *reperiuntur*'. Unfortunately the name 'Jesus'
includes also Joshua and Jesus the high priest, son of
Josedec. Under 'Jesus' in the Latin *Index Analyticus* Dom
Parisot refers the reader to 'Christus'. A rapid examination of
the material nevertheless permits several conclusions to be
drawn. First of all it is clear from a comparison of the entries
under 'Jesus' and those under 'Christ' that the two names
are rarely found together, but this is because more than fifty
times the reference is to the Jesus of the Old Testament, that
is, Joshua. Since the names are identical, Aphraates drew a
parallel between the two persons, especially in *Demonstration*
XI but elsewhere as well. When he did this he was obliged,

for the sake of clarity, to designate one Jesus by a title which would distinguish him adequately from the other. He often used 'Jesus our saviour' (*Demonstr* XI:12; Parisot p. 502, 504), or again, 'our Saviour, the chosen one, the Lord Jesus, prince of shepherds, light in darkness'. There is a long list of these titles in *Demonstration* XIV:39 (Parisot pp. 681-684). Further examples: 'Jesus, great saviour and son of God' (*Demonstr* XXIII; Parisot p. 29); 'Jesus our vivifier' (*Demonstr* XXIII:47; Parisot p. 93); 'our vivifier, our Lord Jesus Christ' (*Demonstr* VI:18; Parisot p. 308); 'our Lord Jesus Christ' (*Demonstr* I:2; Parisot p. 8 and elsewhere frequently); 'the Lord Jesus' (*Demonstr* I:10; Parisot p. 24); 'Jesus our Lord' (*Demonstr* XVII:2; Parisot p. 788); 'firstborn, well-beloved Son' (*Demonstr* XXIII:12) Parisot p. 36). Finally there are numerous instances of 'Jesus' all alone.[62]

To conclude: it appears that Aphraates, without knowing Origen or perhaps any Greek author, adopted their form of expression when naming the redeemer. He was accustomed to use simply 'Jesus' in quotations, in controversies with unbelievers, or in purely historical passages. Everywhere else he added a title expressing the faith, respect and adoration of a faithful heart. If there was tenderness in this Persian scholar it shows up precisely in the delight he took in lining up and repeating these titles:

Jesus our saviour is a light in the darkness, a lamp on the lampstand which enlightens all the world and purifies the sins of men, the pearl of great price which we have sold all our possessions to buy, the treasure hidden in a field that we have found and acquired in joy, the source of life from which we have slaked our thirst. He is a table heavy laden with abundance and we who are famished have eaten there with delight. He is the wine that cheers the hearts of men, and all who suffer can drink of him and their pains vanish. He is the festal garment and the cloak that conquerors wear. He is the true vine, his father the vinedresser, and we the branches implanted in him. He is the tower....[63]

ST EPHREM

Ephrem the Syrian spoke frequently of names, especially in polemics against heretics. He had a theory on the value of names in general, and he followed certain linguistic patterns whenever he named the Lord Jesus Christ.

Ephrem was concerned not only with proper names but with all words classified as nouns and used either substantively or adjectively, though he was principally interested in the names of God and of his Christ. Some names, Ephrem observed, are hollow, empty of meaning, deceptive—what the Greeks called *pseudonymon*, in phrases such as *pseudonymos gnosis*. Ephrem emphasized repeatedly 'it was not an empty name that God gave to Moses when he called him a god in relation to Aaron' (*Adv Haer* 4:1; Ex 4:11). 'Fate is refuted by the very men who preach it; they succeed one another and thus demonstrate that fate is a powerless name' (*Adv Haer* 4:10). The heresiarchs have done what none of the twelve apostles dared to do: they have given their own names to the Christians who follow them. 'The weeds have given their name to the wheat' (*Adv Haer* 23:1).

'Our names,' said Ephrem, 'are based on our works' (*Adv Haer* 24:11). Those who deny the existence of God deserve the name of Satan from their conduct, because they are led astray by Satan; Ephrem played on the supposed etymology of 'Satan' as derived from a verb meaning 'to deceive, lead astray' (*Adv Haer* 26:4). True names, contrary to false ones, correspond perfectly to a person's works (*Adv Haer* 47:4). This is preeminently the case with God: 'There is only one God and his names parallel his deeds' (*Adv Haer* 50:1). Heretics have given him names that are inappropriate to the all-holy (*Adv Haer* 51:54). Ephrem developed his thought on God's names in the fifty-third hymn of the *Adversus Haereses*:

The divine being is unique and therefore the name of the supreme being far surpasses the names of inferior beings; for if the names were the same the natures would have to be equal (Adv Haer 53:7).

As it is wrong to think that the natures are equal, so it is wrong to interchange the names (53:8).

God revealed his name to Moses. He called himself Ehyeh, a name which expresses his essence. And never, never does he give this *name to another, though he gives many other of his names to different men. Thus he teaches us that he alone and no other is the supreme being with a unique name that he reserves to himself (53:12).*

Although all God's names are glorious and majestic and praiseworthy, it was this name, which God reserved to honor his essence, that aroused the envy of the evil one who led others to deny it (53:13).

You will have to admit without question that angels have one nature since they have one name, and that the soul has one nature since it has one name. The genus is described and explained by the name of its category (54:5).

God has permitted his servants to be called gods and lords, and he has called his children of grace by the name of the Son and has called the family of spiritual men by the name of the Holy Spirit. Their natures are different but their names are the same. This should lead men to praise God's grace and to adore his sovereignty (54:6).

Let them ask therefore who has named creatures with the name of 'being'? If it is the supreme Being himself who did so, then all is grace; but if it is not entirely his doing, then all is rebellion. Who, though, is greater than he is, to be able to take away his own name and give it to creatures? (54:7).

Here we have a fabrication by the heretics, a word without a corresponding reality, a name without an object. Here is a name which has existence applied to a forgery which has no existence. This is to create names of beings rather than the beings themselves (54:8).

In these reflections Ephrem distinguished four different categories of names: false names, borrowed names, analogical names given by divine grace, and true names that correspond to the reality and to its operations. So far there is nothing specifically semitic about his philosophy of the name. It is simply common sense. Origen had the equivalent distinctions. [64]

We begin to discern a possible semitic nuance when Ephrem concerns himself not about names that are properly divine but about names given to beings born on earth, including in particular the incarnate Word. What is his name or what are his names according to Ephrem? He distinguishes two categories:

1. The names of Father, Son and Holy Spirit are equal and concordant in the baptismal invocation (*De Fide* 77:20). Concordant names, concordant movements, and as they are equal in the baptismal invocation so also are they equal in the community of the Trinity (Ibid., 21:22).

2. 'But the Word came down and assumed a human body and with it the frail names of the sons of the human race' (Ibid.).

Thus the incarnate Word has divine names and human names. His divine name in the holy Trinity is 'Son' or 'Begotten'. Ephrem commented:

There is one name which is self-explanatory for us.... As a creature is creature by name and in reality, it should be true a fortiori *that the Son is Son both by name and in reality. If his name were to be untrue, then the names of all things would be untrue in every respect. (De Fide 62:4, 7).*

One of St Ephrem's central notions, directed against the indiscreetly curious, is the inscrutability of God and therefore also the inscrutability of the divine names. 'His name is inaccessible' (*De Fide* 63:7). This fact caused Ephrem to appreciate all the more deeply the condescension of divine love which stooped down to our level 'by taking names that are more suited and appropriate to creatures, thus lowering himself in order to elevate his servants by giving them names proper to himself' (Ibid.).

What moved St Ephrem most, and what he celebrated with tireless poetic verve, was the name of the incarnate Word. It contained everything for him, the whole mystery of the love of almighty God seeking out his own creature to share with it his name and everything which that connotes and implies. He wrote:

The king of heaven has called his slaves kings. And because he is also God he has also called them gods. Because he is a judge his slaves will exercise judgment as well. When they walk on foot he too feels fatigue and whey they have mounts he provides himself with one also, so as to resemble us in all things (De Fide 63:8).

Among all the names of the Word made flesh we are particularly concerned with those names of ours which he has taken to himself and those names of his which he shares with us. But we must not confuse the two:

When he calls us kings, a name proper to himself, we must realize that he retains the reality while we have only a reflection of it. And similarly when he calls himself by the name of his slaves, the nature of a slave remains ours while he accpets only the denomination. Such is the true name and such the borrowed name with regard to ourselves and with regard to him (De Fide 63:10).

To those who can appreciate it, we say that God confers his own names on his slaves because of his mercy, not to make us wonder but to make us joyful. Let speculation now come to an end, my brothers, and let us give ourselves to prayer.... (De Fide 63:11).

The most illustrious name given to us by the son of God made man is that of Christians, sharers in Christ. There could be no greater honor. This is why Ephrem so insistently reproached Marcion, Mani and Bardaisan for having given their own names to their followers. This is a terrible degradation. Ephrem addressed these sectarians in strong terms:

Come then, sheep stolen by heretics, renounce the brandmark and the name of the thieves; come, let yourselves be branded with the glorious name of God and be called Christians, so that you may be a truly Christian flock by name and by brandmark (Adv Haer 56:6).

'Christ' and 'Christians' seem to be the all-important names for Ephrem, but the following strophe may modify this conclusion slightly:

No one should be baptized in the name of any man or named after any man. If however he is named after someone he should also be baptized in the name of that man. Either have yourselves baptized in the name of a man and be called by his name or be baptized in the name of Jesus and call yourselves by the name of Jesus (Adv Haer 56:7).

From this it seems that Ephrem used 'Christ' and 'Jesus' interchangeably. 'The flock is named according to the name of the redeemer; it is Christ who has gathered together the Christian sheep' (*Adv Haer* 56:1). 'The prophets spoke in the name of the Lord and the apostles in the name of Jesus' (Ibid. 56:3). 'The churches of the heretics do not have...the true blood of Christ; they have only an appearance which resembles it, since they do not acknowledge the body of Jesus' (Ibid., 47:1).

There is however a shade of difference in Ephrem's use of these two names. 'Christ' occurs more frequently, as with all Christian writers. 'Jesus' is possibly a more tender form of address since it is the Saviour's human name as the son of Mary and son of God. The fact that others bore the same name presented no problem for St Ephrem. He wrote: 'Joshua, whose name means saviour, directed battles; the

Lord of this name directs the stars' (or 'the cherubim' according to a variant—*Adv Haer* 4:18). There may be many with the name 'Jesus' but only one is the Lord. St Ephrem never forgot this when he pronounced that name. The Jesus who was the subject of his homilies and poems and whom he loved and adored is, by unity of person, one of the blessed Trinity.

> *Marcion...was unable to produce any other names than these three: Jesus who is spoken of in the law, the Holy Spirit who is the treasure of the prophets, and God who is proclaimed by every creature: the three witnesses of our victory (Adv Haer 49:1, with an allusion to 1 Jn 5:8).*
>
> *Jesus is used to being insulted by fools. The names of Father and Son are true; it would be an insult to the Son if his name were false and likewise to the Father if his name were untrue. The Jesus who bore the derision of strangers must also bear harsh insults from those who adore him. It certainly is gravely insulting to the Three if someone is baptized in three other names. (De Fide 22:6-7).*

It is possible to distinguish three different elements in St Ephrem's devotion to the name of Jesus:

1. First, the absolute transcendence of God, the incommunicability of his personal name, the inscrutability of the divine persons, and on our part the adoration which should be our response.

2. The magnificent condescension of the Logos, son of the Father, who lowered himself to the point of sharing our nature and the names that go with it and of sharing with us those names of his which can be shared.

3. These two feelings or currents of feeling, adoration and gratitude, merge in an all-embracing love which centers on the person of Christ the redeemer and encompasses everything that pertains to him: all the titles he has received and accepted, the people he has loved and who have loved him, the things he has used, the places where he lived or

travelled, the doctrines he taught, the very words he spoke. St Ephrem measures, evaluates, judges, respects, loves, hates or condemns everything by its reference to Christ.

Love for Christ made this Syrian doctor a lyric poet of great feeling and strength. Desiring to know no joy outside of Christ, his joy in Christ was exultant. That is why this dreadfully austere-looking man (to judge by his literary portraits and the icons they have inspired) had the word 'happy' on his lips more often than any other word in his vocabulary. Happy, he said, are they who rejoice over Christ; happy they who have renounced every deceitful delight in order to attain true beatitude; happy every man who has approached Christ; happy even the mute earth and the other elements Christ has touched or used.

It is easy to understand why St Ephrem, more than any other ancient writer, became a promoter of various devotions: to the blessed and immaculate virgin Mary, to St John the Baptist, to John the Evangelist. It was all due to his love of Christ; with the very love he had for Christ he loved all those who loved Him, each according to his degree of intimacy with Christ, just as he reserved his hatred for everyone who hated his Christ. The saying *facit indignatio versum* is certainly true of St Ephrem at times, but it is usually love which makes him eloquent and lyrical. He was a man of passionate temperament and Christ was the unique object of his passion. Perhaps this religious temperament was common among Syriac Christians, even those who spoke Greek. Perhaps it is there that we should look for the source of all the currents of tender piety which characteristically mark oriental Christ- ianity, even though we are often told that the Greeks, including the Byzantines, were intellectuals. It might be well to speak rather of 'an oriental substratum of Byzantine spirituality'.

Apart from all such speculation it must be said that St Ephrem had a devotion to the name of Jesus unequalled by any other Greek author before or contemporary with him, including Origen. Consider the following passage:

Jesus—*O glorious name, O mysterious bridge which makes it possible to cross from death to life. I came to you and there I stopped. I am entranced by the very first letter of your name. Be a bridge for my speech that it may cross over into your truth. Out of your love make your very self a bridge for your servant and on you I will cross over to your Father. I will cross over and I will say to him, 'Blessed is he who moderates his severity for his Son's sake' (De Fide* 5:14-16).

This strophe is more intelligible in the light of three strophes in the previous hymn (*De Fide* 5:14-16):

The Son is close to his Father by glory as well as by name. And as he is close in these two respects he is no less close in a third, that as the Father is inscrutable so also is the Son. [65] *Whoever attempts to scrutinize the firstborn will scrutinize the Father also. Investigation of the only-begotten is the bridge; he who crosses by this bridge crosses over to the inscrutable Father. Observe how it is that whoever wishes to examine the fruit finds his attention directed to the root, which is the unbegotten Father. The Son is a treasure that includes both judgment and riches: the indiscreetly curious will find judgment and the merchant of fine pearls will find riches* (Mt 13:45). *Your judgment is full of bitterness but in Your love lies beatitude.*

The hymn goes on to develop this thought very cleverly. What we have read is enough to explain how the name of Jesus can be at the same time a bridge and a sign that prohibits crossing. It says 'No' to indiscreet inquiry but it helps love cross over to the Father and to blessedness.

Such, according to St Ephrem, is the theological basis for devotion to the name of Jesus. In the person of the son of God made man there are two realities which formed the two poles of all Ephrem's thought: the God whom he adored and who is totally inscrutable, and the God whom he loved because he could believe and see that he is humanly accessible. With St Ephrem theology did not extinguish affectivity. Far from freezing into the cold clarity of abstraction, the spontaneity of his love found in theology an increased vitality and warmth. In simpler terms, Ephrem had such great love for the person of Jesus that his supreme joy consisted in adoring him, praising his glory, and repeating over and over both his divine names, because they manifest the grandeur of his majesty, and his human names, because they make the power of his love shine forth. The more a person knows that God is great, the more he will love and adore him if he believes that God has first loved him.

Here lies the explanation of the paradoxical fact that while Ephrem found the name of Jesus the most moving he used other names of the Lord more frequently. For example, in the surviving sections of his commentary on Genesis [66] we usually find 'our Lord' (2:18; 42:6; 43:3; 6, 10) or 'son' or 'Son of God' (2:24; 42:5; 43:2; 3; 44:3). Elsewhere he used a paraphrase suggested by the context, as 'he who hung on the tree and tasted death for the world' (20:3) or 'if someone from the tribe of Dan judges his people how much more likely it is that one from the tribe of Judah, of royal descent, will judge all the peoples of the world' (43:6). The examples can be multiplied:

> Just as it was on Joseph rather than on Reuben his firstborn that Jacob leaned, so in the place of Adam, firstborn and rebel, the world had a son in her old age, towards the end of time, and on him as on a column the totality of the world leaned and balanced itself (In Gen 43:10).

> It was not David who made his royal line illustrious, but Jesus, the son of David, who is the Lord of royalty (In Gen 42:10; cf. 1:25).

> All the saviours of the Old Testament were symbols of that great salvation which was to come to all men through Jesus (In Gen 42:9).

Only twice did Ephrem use 'Christ' ('In Gen 26:2; 44:3).

In his commentary on Exodus there is only 'our Lord' (12:3 twice). The way that St Ephrem's love for the name and the person of the Saviour manifested itself was through the numerous titles of honor which he was continually giving him. We can gain a general idea of the number and variety of these titles by consulting the *Index Rerum* in volume III of Lamy's edition[67] under the word 'Christus', though the authenticity of several of the works indexed may be doubted. For a perfectly accurate picture it would be necessary to revise and shorten Lamy's list, but the majority of titles would surely remain, while the rest would always have some value as a witness to the Syriac spirituality inspired by St Ephrem.

The list of Christ's names is as follows: Second Adam, Admirable One, Lamb, Tree of Life, Supreme Good, Glowing Ember, Leaven, Emmanuel, Fire, Judge, Light and Sun, Mediator, Rock, Dawn, Bread of Life, *Pharmacum Vitae*, Salt, Saviour, Servant, King, Spouse, Only-Begotten, New Life, Word of the Father, God of Gods, Splendor of the Father, Son of God, and so on. For two of these titles, 'Saviour' and 'Son of God', the author of the index gives only a couple of references and then *passim*, because a total enumeration would be too difficult to make and verify. Two other titles, the most frequently used, have been omitted altogether— 'Christ' and 'our Lord'.

The Jesus Prayer is perfectly in line with this tradition in its use of titles: 'Lord Jesus Christ, Son of God....'

In spite of Ephrem's devotion to the name of Jesus, or perhaps because of it, he cannot be invoked as a patron of the practice of frequent repetition of the two syllables of the name 'Jesus' as a form of invocation. The work in which he used the Lord's historical name most often was his *Refutation of Mani, Marcion and Bardaisan.*[68] Curiously, in this work the Syriac form of Jesus' name is ordinarily replaced by the form *Isou* or *Iesou*, transcribed from the Greek *Iesou[s]*. The Greek form occurs sixty-nine times, the Syriac form only a dozen times (*Index* p. CLXVIII). Evidently Ephrem used the

Greek form because he was transcribing Marcionite texts
(*Index* p. CXVIII). Origen, for a similar reason, nowhere used
the simple name 'Jesus' so much as in his work *Contra
Celsum*. This is the historical and polemical style. The
expression 'our Lord' occurs thirty-three times in Ephrem's
Refutation (*Index* p. CLXIX).

PSEUDO-DENYS

Pseudo-Denys the Aereopagite also deserves special
attention. We might expect that an author who wrote
explicitly about the divine names would have discoursed on
the names of Christ as well, but this is not the case. Did he
fail to see any problem with Christ's names? The valuable
Indices pseudo-dionysiani compiled by P.A. van den Doele[69]
make it easy to assemble the statistics: *Christos* twenty-two
times, *Iesous* fifty-five times. These figures, in writings which
have nothing of the gospel-narrative style about them, strike
a dissonant chord in the patristic symphony. In fact, it seems
out of style for any era. But this is completely deliberate, as
is everything in pseudo-Denys, who was an author who left
nothing to chance and spontaneity. What purpose could he
have had in mind to deviate so much from universal custom?
Only twice did he write 'Jesus Christ': in *De Eccl Hierarch*
III:13,[70] and in *De Div Nominibus* XII:2.[71] Here too we
would like to know why. This author never wrote without his
reasons. Most likely it was because he wanted to write on this
point as on everything else, differently from his contemporaries. The *Logia*, that is the gospels, use 'Jesus' most of
the time. The pseudo-Areopagite believed he would appear
closer to the gospels if he imitated them. He failed to make
any distinction between historical style and theological
material, and this blunder led him to become the first
christian writer to speak of 'Jesus' where his predecessors
would have preferred to write 'our Lord Jesus Christ' or
another of the divine names enumerated by Origen or St

Gregory Nazianzen. Pseudo-Denys did, it is true, add adjectives in the superlative which are expressions of his faith, such as 'most thearchical' or 'superessential', and he did use a limited number of substantives like 'giver of life' (*zoodotes*). But these are not names drawn from Scripture like 'Christ' or 'Lord'.

In this way pseudo-Denys has made a greater contribution to the development of devotion to the name of Jesus than many others who were more religious and more christian than he. More precisely, it was the authority he arrogated to himself by claiming to be St Paul's disciple that contributed to making the name 'Jesus' prevail over the other names of the Lord. The effect was to impose on private devotion, in contrast to the liturgy which pseudo-Denys was not early enough to influence, a sentimental and name-centered character which the author himself had certainly not intended. This effect was made all the more inevitable when, in treating of holy chrism, he included a whole contemplation (*theoria*) on 'the superessential fragrance of the most-thearchical Jesus'.[72] The memory of this contemplation, laced with the continual repetition of the name, could not fail to start certain readers down the path toward a *Jesu dulcis memoria*, even if, and especially if, they had little sympathy for the Platonic constructions of the pseudo-Aereopagite.[73]

There is a further consideration. It is now generally admitted that pseudo-Denys wrote in a Syrian country even if in his immediate circle the Syriac language had been replaced by Greek. Syrians have always used the name of Jesus with greater familiarity. Numerous Syriac Christians bear the name 'Jesus' linked with some other name that specifies it or else combined with a verb expressing a special relationship to Jesus Christ, such as 'servant of Jesus' (*Abdiso*, very common). This is evidence of a degree of sentiment and of feeling among Syriac speaking Christians, especially in Persian times, for the name of Jesus, which was not known or not copied by the Greeks. The Greek language is supple enough to form an unlimited number of compound words, but

the Greeks have never done this with the name of Jesus.
Origen, we know, would never have permitted this name to
be given to an infant who might grow up to dishonor it in the
future. Origen's influence was enormous in Greek countries
but it penetrated hardly at all into Syrian lands.

ISAAC OF NINEVEH

Our final witness is 'the greatest mystic of the Eastern
Church', St Isaac the Syrian. He was a seventh century monk
and bishop, and a Nestorian. His works were partially
translated into Greek by the Sabaïte monks, Abramios and
Patricios, in the ninth century. [74]

This great mystic spoke from experience and also from
familiarity with monastic tradition, especially the heros of the
Apophthegmata Patrum. On rare occasions he mentioned a
theologian such as Athanasius (twice) or Basil (four times).
He quoted Athanasius's *Life of Anthony* and his 'biography of
the mirror of solitaries' which would again be the *Life of
Anthony* since Anthony was the ideal prototype of the
hermit. [75] From St Basil Isaac quoted only some observations
on psychology. His great authority in the speculative realm
was Theodore of Mopsuestia and he was particularly
interested in Theodore's doctrine on the different kinds of
revelations (Bedjan pp. 153, 160, 319). Isaac's authority in the
realm of practice and life was Evagrius Ponticus. These and
other characteristics which could be listed do not mark Isaac
out as a theologican or exegete of note. And if we look at the
frequency of his use of the names of the Lord it forms a
startling contrast to someone like St Paul or Ignatius of
Antioch or even Origen. In a very lengthy work of five
hundred eighty-one pages the Lord Jesus is named only one
hundred fifty times. Often this was in scriptural quotations.
The most frequent name was 'Christ' (seventy-five times),
then 'our Lord' (forty-four times, though it is not always easy
to tell whether he means God or Jesus Christ), 'our Lord

Jesus Christ' (three times), 'our Saviour' (five times), 'Jesus Christ' (seven times), and 'Jesus' alone eighteen times.

In one place (Bedjan, p. 34) the Wensinck translation has 'Thirst after Jesus'. However, neither the Syriac text nor the general context will support that translation. The three Syriac words mean literally, 'Thirst, or suffer thirst, for Jesus' sake'. The Greek uses the correct preposition: *dia Christon dipseson* (chap. 44, p. 273). The paragraph as a whole explains the meaning:

It is proper that the best things do not fall effortlessly into our hands or else God's gifts would not be esteemed, for they could be acquired without difficulty. Everything easy to find is also easy to lose (this phrase is omitted from Wensinck's translation). *Anything obtained at high cost is carefully protected. Endure thirst for Jesus' sake, that he might inebriate you with his love. Close your eyes on the precious things of this world that you may deserve to have God's peace reign in your heart.*

Isaac goes on to list a number of good works and their rewards. Many other instances of his style could be examined. [76]

NOTES

1.   Origen, *De Oratione*, chap. 24; PG 11:494B.

2.   Ibid.

3.   See, for instance, Hans Bietenhard, *Onoma*, in *Theological Dictionary of the New Testament* (Grand Rapids: Eerdmans, 1967) pp. 242-281.

4.   *L'Evangile de saint Jean*, trans. D. Mollat (Paris, 1953) 81, note.

5.   Found in F. Diekamp, *Doctrina Patrum de Incarnatione Verbi* (Munster, 1907) 286-290.

6.   Ibid., 291-292.

7.   Ibid., iii.

8.   Un moine de l'Eglise d'Orient, *La Prière de Jésus*, in the collection *Irénikon* (Chevtogne, 3rd ed., 1959), chap. II.

9.   K.L. Schmidt, *Epikaleo*, TDNT 3:500.

10. W. Bousset, *Kyrios Christos* (Göttingen, 1913) 100; English translation (Nashville: Abingdon, 1970) 130.

11. K.L. Schmidt, ibid.

12. W. Foerster, *Iesous*, TDNT 3:285.

13. Rt. Rev. J. Holzner, *Paul of Tarsus*, trans. F.C. Eckhoff (St Louis: Herder Book Co., 1944) 91.

14. See the edition of F.X. Funk, *Patres Apostolici* (Tübingen, 1901) 1-37.

15. Ibid., 38-97.

16. Ibid., 98-184.

17. Ibid., 212-296.

18. A footnote by Funk (213) suggests that there is here 'an allusion to the meaning of the word *Ephesios* which is synonymous with *pothetos*, meaning "dear" or "beloved". But this would be to reduce the philosophy of the

name to a dubious etymology. *Crocus*, another beloved name, means saffron or crocus; it was a not a beloved name because Ignatius did not like this flower or this color or this metaphor!

19. Funk, 668-676.

20. The Latin translation has: *tamquam ad corporaliter praesentem Christum.*

21. A. Lelong, *Les Pères Apostoliques* (Paris, 1910) 72, note.

22. Ibid.

23. F.X. Funk ed., *Die apostolischen Väter* (Tübingen, 1906); M. Whittaker, *Die griechischen christlichen Schriftsteller der ersten drei Janrhunderte*, 48 (Berlin, 1956).

24. Funk, *Die apostolischen Väter*, 431.14.

25. Jean Daniélou, *The Theology of Jewish Christianity*, trans. and ed. John A. Baker (Chicago: Regnery, 1964) 157.

26. Ibid., 39.

27. Irenaeus, *Adversus Haereses*, III, 16, 1; ed. F. Sagnard, Sources Chrétiennes, No. 34 (Paris: Cerf, 1952).

28. PG 11:130-145.

29. Origen, *Contra Celsum*, III, 5; ed. P. Koetschau, *Die griechischen christlichen Schriftsteller der ersten drei Jahrhunderts*, 2 (Berlin, 1899) 206:21; PG 11:785 BC.

30. F. Bertrand, *Mystique de Jésus chez Origène* (Paris, 1951) 147.

31. H. de Lubac and L. Doutreleau, *Origene: Homélies sur la Genèse*, Sources Chrétiennes, No. 7 (Paris: Cerf, 1944) 27-28. De Lubac asserts that Origen frequently says 'my Jesus', and he lists numerous references. Since these passages are worth reading and savoring at leisure they are listed here:

   a. *In Ex* 6:1 *Dominus meus Jesus Christus*

   b. Ibid., 3:2 *Dominum meum Jesus Christum*

   c. *In Jos* 1:5 *Jesus ergo meus* (in contrast to Jesus son of Nun, Joshua)

d. Ibid., 14:1 *Domini mei Jesu Christi*

e. Ibid., 15:7 *Noster autem Dominus Jesus* (again in contrast to Joshua)

f. Ibid., 24:3 *Meo Domino Jesus* (likewise in contrast to Joshua)

g. *In Is* 1:4 *Dominus Jesus Christus*

h. Ibid., 1:5 *Dominum meum Jesum Christum...Domini mei Jesu Christi*

i. Ibid., 2:1 *Dominus meus Jesus Christus*

j. Ibid., 2:2 *Dominus meus Jesus Christus*

k. Ibid., 3:2 and 6:3 *Dominum meum Jesum Christum*

l. *In Jer* 18:5 'The place where my Jesus was crucified...The axe is laid to the root of the trees, said my Jesus.'

m. Ibid., 21:7 *Sed meus Jesus contra fecit* (an alternate reading in Greek has *ho de Iesous*)

n. *In Ez* 3:3 *Domini tui Jesu*

o. Ibid., 6:6 *Domino meo Jesu Christo....Dominus meus Jesus*

p. Ibid., 9:3 *Dominus meus Jesus Christus*

q. *In Lucam* 12:1 *Natus est Dominus meus Jesus*

r. Ibid., 18:1, 3 *Natus est Dominus meus Jesus...in multorum comitatu Jesus meus non potest inveniri*

s. Ibid., 22:4 *Veniet ergo Dominus meus Jesus*

To this list can be added the following:

t. *In Is* 1:2 *Qui sunt ista duo Seraphim? Dominus Jesus et Spiritus Sanctus....Domini mei Jesu nuntiatur adventus....Dum velim glorificare Dominum meum Jesum Christum*

u. Ibid., 4:4 *Quis est iste unus de Seraphim? Dominus meus Jesus Christus.*

32. Origen, *In Cant*, Prologue; PG 13:70.

33. Bertrand, *Mystique*, 153.

34. Origen, *In Mt Com* 121; PG 13:1772C-1773A.

35. Origen, ibid., 15; PG 13:1017C.

36. Gregory Nazianzen, *In Sanctum Baptismum, Or* 40, no. 10; PG 36:372A.

37. Gregory Nazianzen, *In Sanctum Pascha, Or* 1, no. 4 and 5; PG 35:397BC.

38. Gregory Nazianzen, *In Sancta Lumina, Or* 39, no. 1; PG 36:336A.

39. Ibid.

40. Theophylactus of Bulgaria. *In Epis II ad Cor;* PG 124:941C.

41. Origen, *In Ezech, Hom* 1:4; W.A. Baehrens, ed., *Die griechischen christlichen Schriftsteller der ersten drei Jahrhunderte*, 33 (Berlin, 1925), 327.

42. Origen, *In Is, Hom* 2:2; Baehrens, 252.

43. Ibid., *Hom* 3:3; Baehrens, 257.

44. A. Hamman, ed., *Early Christian Prayers*, trans. Walter Mitchell (Chicago: Regnery, 1961) 43, note 1.

45. Ibid., 40.

46. *Hom* 1:1; PG 12:825A.

47. Origen, *In Lucam, Hom* 14; M. Rauer, ed., *Die griechischen christlichen Schriftsteller der ersten drei Jahrhunderte*, 35 (Berlin, 1930) 85.

48. PG 29:577C.

49. On this concept see A. Orbe, *La Epinioa: Algunos preliminares históricos de la distinctión kat' epinoian* (Rome, 1955).

50. Dionisius, *De Divinis Nominibus*; PG 3:596A, 865C.

51. Basil, *Adv Eunom* II:3; PG 29:577AB.

52. Gregory Nazianzen, *Apologetica* 98; PG 35:500BC.

53. Gregory Nazianzen, *In Sancta Lumina* 16; PG 36:353B.

54. Gregory Nazianzen, *Oratio* 37:16; PG 36:301A.

55. Ibid., 17-18; PG 36:304A.

56. Gregory Nazianzen, *Quat Or Theo*, 3; PG 36:106.

57. John Chrysostom, *In Matt, Hom* 5:2; PG 57:56.

58. Evagrius, *Cent* II:17.

59. PG 51:113-156.

60. PG 51:159.

61. R. Graffin, *Patrologia Syriaca* (Paris, 1894-1897) I:1-2; Dom Parisot, ed., *Aphraate.*

62. Page references are to Dom Parisot's edition of the *Demonstrations:*

   a. Sometimes the name 'Jesus' occurs alone when Aphraates is quoting scripture. For instance: *Demonstr* II:5, p. 57; XII:10, p. 529; XX:11, p. 909; XX:18, p. 928: 12 and 20; XXII:5, p. 1017.

   b. Sometimes the context is a discussion with the Jews on prophecies and figures of the Old Testament. For instance: *Demonstr* XVII:1, p. 785; XVII:3, p. 789; XVII:8, p. 800 and 801; XX:12, p. 913; XXI:1, p. 932; XXI: 9, pp. 954, 956, 957; XXI:10, pp. 960, 961, 964, 965, 968, 969, 972, 973, 977, 980, 981.

   c. Sometimes 'Jesus' occurs in a simple historical style. For instance: *Demonstr* XVII:8, p. 804; XVII:11, p. 813; XXII:5, p. 1036; XXIII, Vol. II, pp. 4, 33, 64, 92.

63. *Demonstr* XIV:38; Parisot p. 682.

64. See for instance Origen, *In Cant*, Prologue; PG 13:70BC.

65. This verse is omitted in the translation by Beck, *Corpus Scriptorum Christianorum Orientalium* (Louvain, 1955) 154-155, pp. 21 and 16.

66. R.M. Tonneau, ed., *Corpus Scriptorum Christianorum Orientalium* 152-153 (Louvain, 1955).

67. Th. J. Lamy, ed., *Hymni et Sermones* (Malines, 1889) 995.

68. C.W. Mitchell, ed., *S.E. Prose Refutation of Mani, Marcion and Bardaisan,* 2 vols. (London, 1912-1921).

69. P.A. van den Doele, *Indices pseudo-dionysiani* (Louvain, 1941).

70. PG 3:444C.

71. PG 3:980B.

72. *Eccles Hierarch* IV, IV; PG 3:477.

73. See E. Boissard in *Saint Bernard Théologien* (Rome, 1955) 114-135.

74. Syriac edition by P. Bedjan (Paris-Leipzig, 1909). Greek edition by Nicephorus Theotokis (Leipzig, 1770). There is an English translation by A.J. Wensinck, *Mystic Treatises by Isaac of Nineveh* (Amsterdam, 1923).

75. See Bedjan's edition, pp. 185, 560.

76. Some examples: 'If, my sons, you add to your nightly meditations the labor of the day and the fervor of a heart that loves unceasingly, you will soon rest your head on Jesus' breast' (Bedjan 136; Greek ed. chap. 29, p. 182). 'Jesus' is used here without further clarification because the phrase was a standard expression in mystical writings since Origen. Isaac picked it up from his master par excellence, Evagrius (*Ad Monachos* 118-120; cf. Origen, *Com in Johannem* 19:4 and 32:20).

'Jesus the mediator' (Bedjan 198-199; cf. Heb 12:24).

'The mind cannot be glorified with Jesus if the body has not suffered with Jesus' (Bedjan 222; Greek ed., chap. 16, p. 82). This is a contemplative gloss on Rom 8:17 which Isaac had quoted just above. The Greek translator left the first 'Jesus' but replaced the second by 'Christ'. In the immediate context 'Christ' occurs twice in the Syriac.

'If we have a spiritual zeal for the will of Jesus, all the ennui produced by negligence will disappear' (Bedjan 536; Greek ed., chap. 19, p. 109).

The ascetic should consider 'how the mercy of Jesus has drawn him away from the world' (Bedjan 551; omitted by the Greek ed.). What reason was there to write 'Jesus' rather than 'Christ' or 'our Lord'? Whatever the reason there is no evidence here of a special devotion to this name.

'In the Old Testament fasting was the mediator but we have received it by the grace of our Lord Jesus' (Bedjan 241; Greek ed., chap. 85, p. 494). The Greek translator had difficulty with this passage, as he admits in a footnote. For us it is of interest that he replaced 'our Lord Jesus' simply with 'Christ'.

CHAPTER TWO

THE NAMES OF JESUS USED BY THE CHRISTIAN PEOPLE

W E MIGHT take it for granted that there will be a large degree of uniformity in the manner in which the Christian faithful speak about Christ or call on the name of Christ. Still it is profitable and also enjoyable to verify this hypothesis at least to some degree.

As we have already noted, in the gospels the only ones who use the name 'Jesus' in the vocative are demons speaking through possessed persons and people who are outside the circle of close disciples. In the rest of the New Testament the phrase 'Lord Jesus' occurs twice: on the lips of the dying Stephen (Ac 7:59, followed in the next verse simply by 'Lord') and at the end of the Apocalypse, 'Come, Lord Jesus!' (Rev 22:20). The apocalyptic occurence comes straight from the life and liturgy of the Church after the Lord's ascension. The appearance of *Maran atha* ('Our Lord comes') or rather *Marana tha* ('Our Lord, come!') in 1 Cor 16:24 proves that this exclamation was used in the parousia-oriented primitive community.[1] The two different formulas used by St Stephen, 'Lord Jesus' and simply 'Lord', cannot be cited in favor of a philosophy of the name, unless it is a philosophy that gives more importance to 'Lord' than to 'Jesus'. We may presume that the first Christians continued the apostles' custom of saying '[the] Lord Jesus' or more

63

often '[the] Lord' when speaking about Jesus among themselves or to him in their prayers.

Moreover it was customary at least for official ecclesial prayers to address them to God the Father through Jesus Christ rather than to Jesus Christ himself. This is well known and need not be elaborated. Well known also are the reasons behind this practice. Origen explained them in his treatise *On Prayer*.[2] The theologians have not accepted his explanation without criticism however:

Origen emphasized the idea that christian prayer must be addressed only to the Father.... It is certain that from the beginning of Christianity liturgical prayer was directed to the Father through the Son, but it is no less certain that at every age Christians have prayed to Christ. Origen did so himself fairly often in his homilies.[3]

But the theologians may have forgotten a distinction made by Origen, on the basis of 1 Tm 2:1, between prayer (*proseuke*), supplication (*deesis*), intercession (*enteuxis*) and thanksgiving. It is not out of place to address supplication, intercession and thanksgiving even to the saints. Origen drew a conclusion from this:

How much more proper it is to give thanks to Christ who has filled us with so many gifts according to the Father's will. It is proper also to make intercessory prayer to him as Stephen did when he prayed, 'Lord, do not hold them guilty for this act'. And also we may imitate the supplication of the father of the lunatic boy who prayed, 'I beseech you, Lord, have pity on my son', or on myself or on anyone.[4]

Consequently Origen did not contradict himself when he made supplication to Jesus, nor is his doctrine on prayer proven false by the martyrs who imitated St Stephen's intercessory prayer. The chief difficulty is to know whether these petitions may be called *proseuke* in the strict sense. But this semantic question lies outside our present concern.

ACTS OF THE MARTYRS

A certain amount of reliable information about petitionary prayers addressed to Christ has come down to us despite the degree of silence which naturally surrounds something so personal, so individual and usually so completely interior. Some of the early Christians were forced to give public evidence about their feelings and habits of prayer because of legal action brought against them. We will look first therefore at the acts of the martyrs.

In many of the accounts we can find cries that come straight from the heart, like the cry of the protomartyr, Stephen. They may have been influenced by explicit or implicit recollection of the martyrdom described in Acts, but mere similarity of circumstances would have been enough to cause similar invocations to spring to these Christians' minds. There is no need to dwell on the fact that the situation was the same; for the faithful being accused the matter was one of life or death as it was for Stephen. What may need more explanation is the similarity between Stephen and the later martyrs as regards their interior dispositions of faith and love for Christ. Everything served to impress on the martyrs the thought of their Master; it would be superfluous to offer proof for this. They knew that the hour had come for them to give the supreme testimony of their love by following the Lamb even to immolation. It was not a time for syrupy sentimentality; never did they know better that it was not enough to cry 'Lord, Lord' in a burst of emotional fervor. Nothing is more serious than death. In a way that nothing else can, death marks with a certain attitude of gravity the lives of those who think about it. In the face of death no one tells lies or plays games or spouts slogans. So the Church has need of martyrs, as St Irenaeus had already pointed out,[5] to preserve or recover or test against their example the genuineness of her protestations of love for the Lord.[6]

For our inquiry what is even more noteworthy than the strength of the martyrs' love is their intimacy with Christ at the hour at which they were about to die for his sake. Their Lord was closer to them than ever. Stephen saw 'the heavens open wide and the Son of Man standing at the right hand of God' (Ac 7:56). The *Martyrdom of Polycarp* says: 'At the moment of torment the heroic martyrs made it plain to us that they were no longer in their bodies, or rather that the Lord stood near them and conversed with them.'[7]   St Blandina 'did not feel her sufferings because of her strong hope, her expectation of the rewards promised to faith, and her intimate union with Christ'.[8]   This familiarity brought with it the right to a freedom of speech, *parrhesia*, which would not have been permitted in ordinary circumstances of life. In cases when they survived their tortures by a miraculous escape from death, these Christians were considered by the community to occupy a privileged position in relation to Christ and his Church. In what words did the christian martyrs speak to their Master at the moment of their supreme heroism and their supreme love for him?

The name 'Jesus' rarely occurs alone in any of the Acts of the Martyrs, whether in indirect or in direct quotation. When it does occur it does not seem to be for reasons of close familiarity but simply because 'Jesus' and 'Christ' are synonyms. For instance, we read in *The Martyrs of Lyons*: 'Then there appeared the boundless mercy of Jesus',[9] but a little later we read: '...the boundless mercy of Christ'.[10] Many additional examples are given in the notes.[11]

The evidence permits us to conclude that, with rare exceptions, the dying martyrs did not pray to him for whom they were dying under the name of Jesus alone. In the exceptional cases when they do, it is possible to discover special reasons for it.

INSCRIPTIONS

The coming of an era of peace for the Church did not weaken the love of Christians for their Lord. The Church was in the process of coming to regard virginity and asceticism as a kind of martyrdom; this eventually resulted in the canonization of confessors. There were good grounds for paying special attention to these 'athletes' as they were called, who following the example of St Anthony were trying to make up for lost chances of martyrdom by undergoing a 'martyrdom of conscience'. But it would be unwise for us to overlook the simple faithful if there is trustworthy documentary evidence of their piety. And in fact such evidence is not lacking.

One of the most interesting sources for information about ancient christian customs is Eusebius's *Ecclesiastical History*. Fortunately it is possible to consult a very useful index of its proper names compiled by E. Schwartz.[12] The entry under *Iesous* is only one page long; *Christos* has more than four pages.

According to Schwartz's other findings, in the *Legend of Abgar* only the name 'Jesus' occurs, and not 'Christ'. Similarly, in the citations of Hegesippus 'Jesus' is found predominantly, while 'Christ' occurs only in the sense of 'the Messiah'. In the fragments of *The Acts of Pilate* and of other gnostic texts 'Jesus' is usual. That is to say, this usage is found only in non-christian authors or authors writing for non-Christians. Everywhere the name 'Jesus' is found in a purely Christian context it occurs within a title such as 'our Lord Jesus Christ', 'your beloved and blessed servant Jesus Christ', 'the Christ Jesus'.

L. Jalabert and R. Mouterde have published all the early Syrian Latin and Greek inscriptions.[13] 'These inscriptions date from the first century before Christ to the seventh century of our era.' In the first two volumes the name 'Jesus' occurs around fourteen times including doubtful cases, while

'Christ' is found more than eighty times. Here is one example (no. 214): a bronze reliquary plaque in the shape of a cross. In the center is Christ, arms outstretched, clothed in a sleeveless tunic; beneath, in a border, the inscription *is chs* (that is, *Iesous Christos*). Under the right arm of Christ is our Lady and the inscription *ide o us sou* (that is, *ide ho huios sou*, 'behold your son'). Under his left arm is St John with the inscription *ide he meter sou* ('behold your mother'). The name of Jesus is not used alone. It never is except perhaps in Number 689, where a tiny iota is followed by *eis theos monos*. The editors comment, 'Perhaps this should be interpreted *I[esous]*.' That is highly doubtful. The ordinary formula, which was in use at least since the beginning of the fifth century in the morning prayer, was 'One unique God and his Christ'. [14]

Most of the time the name 'Christ' is used without 'Jesus'. *Kyrios* is also very frequent, especially in the vocative. [15] There are some doubtful instances. *Kyrie* doesn't always necessarily mean Jesus Christ. In most cases though there is no doubt about it even without any further qualifiers. For example: 'O Lord and blessed Mary, come to the aid of the priest, Mara' (no. 489). When *Kyrie* refers to God the Father or to God in the Old Testament sense, it is usually accompanied by some expression such as 'Lord of hosts' (no. 525). Or again, 'the Lord and his Christ'. [16]

It should be noted that the word *theos*, God, can mean Jesus Christ when there is an additional qualifier such as *no theos techtheis ek parthenou Marias*, 'God born of the Virgin Mary' (no. 1862). In particular, *Christe ho theos*, 'O Christ God' is frequently used. We will say nothing about the cryptogram *Ch M L* except that the *Ch* almost certainly stands always or most of the time for *Christos*. Whatever this formula is—an exorcism or even a charm—the name of Jesus is absent from it. [17]

Much more important, and less mysterious, is the cryptogram *I ch th u s* (*Iesous Christos theou huios soter*). There is no doubt at all about its meaning. And what is equally evident is that four of its five words are found in the Jesus Prayer, and the fifth, 'Saviour', is virtually equivalent to the conclusion of this prayer, '...have mercy on me, a sinner'.[18]

From the evidence available we can reach a firm conclusion that for the Greek-speaking Christians of Syria the name most rarely used to invoke Jesus Christ was the name 'Jesus' by itself. Was the case any different in other parts of the world? This is what has to be investigated next.

The Christian Inscriptions of Asia Minor published by H. Gregoire [19] are not limited to the first seven centuries as is the work of Jalabert and Mouterde. In the material that comes from the period before the seventh century we never find the name 'Jesus' by itself. *Christos* is the most common name. In prayers it is either *Kyrie* (see nos. 130, 138) or 'Jesus Christ' (see no. 209). Number 107 from Ephesus, an edict of Justinian in favor of the church of St John, begins: 'In the name of our sovereign (*despotou*) Jesus Christ.' A pastoral letter of Hypatios I, Archbishop of Ephesus, contains the phrase, 'Jesus Christ our God' (no. 108, line 4). Number 116, from the sixth century, says, 'O Christ God, save every soul that comes here'. Number 212 reads, 'O Christ, help (us). Our Christ [is] God. O Christ, help us'. Number 214, from the fifth century, has, 'I cry to you, O Lord. If I am silent you know that it is because of sin. I write this inscription and I cry to you, O Lord, have mercy on me.' Number 219: 'In the name of our master, Jesus Christ our God' (edict of Justinian). Number 239: 'For the glory and honor of God and of our Saviour Jesus Christ.' We can glean only a little useful material from these inscriptions, unlike those from Syria. These consist chiefly of texts from some civil or ecclesiastical magistrate, and only a few represent the common people.

The fourth volume of *Corpus Inscriptionum Graecarum* published by the Academy of Berlin in 1877 contains all the extant Christian inscriptions. [20] The material runs three hundred eighteen pages, a little under a thousand inscriptions (Numbers 8606-9595) from many different countries, Syria, Asia Minor, Greece, Italy, even France and Germany. They include, from each of these countries, official texts engraved on marble, *ex votos*, dedications, seals, pieces of jewelry, vessels for sacred and non-sacred use, and charms. The public documents are not of major interest and are well-known anyway from other sources. Justinian's edicts, for example Number 8636, Trebizond, 545 AD, call Christ 'Sovereign' (*Despota*) and 'God'. When the emperor assumed the title 'despot' he could not do much more.

The jewelry, crosses, and gems worn by Christians almost never have the name Jesus without 'Christ'. Crosses with the inscription 'Jesus Christ: This is your son; this is your mother' are frequent, as are those with the monograms *Ichthus* (Jesus Christ, son of God, Savior) and *I Ch Nika* (Jesus Christ, Victor). Very frequent too are 'God' and 'Lord' with the invocations *sosais* ('save') and especially *boethei* ('help'). Number 9089 is a precious stone with the name 'Jesus' inscribed twice, if the conjectured reading is correct. The only unquestionable example is Number 9090 which has a *Iesou* in the vocative.

On tombs the most common name is 'God', then 'Lord' or 'Lord Jesus Christ', or simply 'Christ'. 'Jesus' alone never occurs in Egypt, Nubia or Africa. The usual invocations are 'Remember!' and 'Grant rest (*anapauson*) in the bosom of Abraham, Isaac and Jacob'. Occasionally the name of the addressee, 'God' or 'Lord', is omitted. Several times God is called 'God of spirits'.

Of the sixteen Syrian tomb inscriptions, (Numbers 9138-9154) only one has the name of Christ: 'Glory to the eternal Christ who forgives sins' (no. 9144). The rest are very brief, usually just 'Here lies....' Two are slightly longer: Number 9153 which has the beginning of Ps 23, 'The Lord is my shepherd', and Number 9154 which has the stock formula, 'One unique God and Christ', along with the name of the deceased.

There are one hundred twenty-three tomb inscriptions from Asia Minor, (Numbers 9155-9287). The most common name is *Theos*, especially in the expression 'servant of God' referring to the deceased. Sometimes the formula is varied, 'servant of Christ'. Also occuring are: 'Jesus Christ, Victor' (no. 9261), 'the God of the tribes of Israel' (no. 9270) and 'God, the Pantocreator'. 'Jesus' never occurs.

From Greech and Illyria we have two hundred fifty-three of these inscriptions, (Numbers 9288-9540). The deceased represent all ranks of men from a series of archbishops of Athens to simple craftsmen. Numerous inscriptions have 'Lord, help', 'Lord, remember', 'Spare, O Lord' (*phise, pheisai*), 'Jesus Christ help the one who engraved this and his family'. There are many inscriptions to the *Theotokos* or *Theodochos*. Once there is 'Jesus, Saviour' (no. 9299). The episcopal tombs never have an invocation, though those of lower-ranking clergy sometimes do. There are epitaphs in verse, usually bad verse, that reflect nothing of the piety of the people (see, for example, Numbers 9291, 9421, 9535, 9536, 9539 and especially Number 9540 where a twelfth-century rhymester delivers a whole little homily without including a single prayer or sacred name).

The epitaphs from Italy and Rome are the briefest of all: a 'here lies' and a name, or even just a name, or 'in peace'. Number 9543 from Naples: 'May you see Christ'. In eighty successive inscriptions from Rome (nos. 9551-9630), there is no mention of Christ or of God. Then come the simple words 'in God' (no. 9631). Then, 'You live in God' (no. 9639), 'May God remember him' (no. 9644), and 'Live in the Lord and pray for us' (no. 9673). The tombs of bishops have simply their name. Further examples: 'The God seated at the Father's right hand' (no. 9686); *Ichthus* (no. 9697, third century); 'In Christ' (no. 9696); 'Christ [be] with you' (no. 9697); 'May Jesus the Lord remember you, my child' (no. 9617); 'Servant of Christ' (no. 9801); 'He lives in God' (nos. 9804, 9811); 'You live in God the Lord Christ' (no. 9816); 'May you live in the Lord' (no. 9821); 'In God' (no. 9822).

That is all. 'Jesus' occurs only once and then is followed by 'the Lord' in the inscription for an infant.

The evidence shows that in all these hundreds and even

thousands of inscriptions coming from every Greek-speaking
country there is not the slightest hint of a particular devotion
to the name of Jesus as such.

The conclusion is the same for G. Schlumberger's
collection of Byzantine seals.[21]   The name of Jesus is never
found alone here. Christ is called either *Christos* or *Iesous
Christos* or, usually, *Kyrios*. It is exceptional to find
'Saviour', 'Word of God', 'Word', 'Thrice-holy Lord', or
'Lord God'. There are a few special titles whose reason is
obvious, like *Philanthrope* on the seal of a monastery of this
name in Byzantium, or 'The All-seeing' (*Pantepoptes*) on the
seal of a convent of the same name. The observations made
by Schlumberger in 1884 are still valid even after the
publication of material that was unknown in his day.[22]

NAMES OF THE LORD JESUS IN THE NEW TESTAMENT APOCRYPHA

The custom of invoking the Lord under the name of
'Jesus' alone could have come from the deuterocanonical
writings. They do contain a number of prayers addressed to
him. Usually these are too lengthy to be important to our
inquiry as examples of christian prayers, but the vocative
which introduces them does deserve to be noticed. In the
Gospel to the Hebrews the man with the withered hand is
reported to have said: 'I was a brick layer and I made my
living by the work of my hands; I beg you, Jesus, to restore
my hand that I may not have to endure the shame of begging
for my bread'.[23]

St John the Evangelist, the Lord's beloved disciple, does
not speak so freely: 'the blessed *Theotokos* told me to pray
and to burn incense. I began to pray in these words, "Lord
Jesus Christ, who have worked such wonders...." '[24]

In the *Acts of Xantippus and Polyxena*, the prayer of
Probus as he went down into the baptismal waters begins,
'Jesus Christ, son of God and God eternal, may all my sins
be absorbed by this water...'[25]   Later Polyxena said, 'Lord

Jesus Christ, co-possessor of the light and of the knowledge of mysteries. ...'[26]

St Bartholomew had a flamboyant style of prayer which the modern ear does not find very inspiring: 'O eternal torch, Jesus Christ, demiurge of the everlasting light....'[27] Another of his prayers is in simpler language: 'Lord Jesus Christ, make this devil go back to hell because he is insolently attacking me.'[28]   In the next paragraph the apostle 'prostrates at the feet of our Lord Jesus Christ and prays with tears, "Abba, Father, who are the single glorious Word of the Father...." ' Then later on he prays: 'Lord, Father, king of eternal life, king of heaven, king of....,' followed by a long string of titles. Then, 'Bartholomew said to the Lord Jesus: "...my Father has had me call upon Jesus that I might forgive the sins of the penitent."'[29]   And finally Bartholomew and all the apostles 'glorified the Lord Jesus saying, "Glory be to you, father of the heavens, eternal king, torch of unextinguishable light...." '[30]

In the *Narrative of Joseph of Arimathea* the good thief, Demas, is reported to have said, 'I know, Jesus Christ, that you are the son of God; O Christ I see you adored by myriad angels.'[31]

But the one who prayed to Jesus most often was Mary, his mother. It is worth the effort to investigate how the apocryphal literature described her prayers. When she was about to die she prayed, 'My Lord Jesus Christ, who out of your supreme bounty have deigned to be born of me....'[32] When all the apostles had gathered around her, she said to them, 'Cast incense because Christ is coming with a host of angels.' Then 'the Mother of the Lord' prayed again in these words: 'O Lord, king of heavens, son of the living God, accept every man who calls on your name, that your birth may be glorified.' She prayed again saying: 'Lord Jesus Christ, who are all-powerful in heaven and on earth, here is the favor I ask of your holy name, that every time and every place where my name is mentioned may be glorified, along with those who glorify you through my name; accept from these people all their offerings and all their supplication and all their prayer.' She spoke much of 'the name' but never once did she say 'Jesus'. She seems to have been able to say only, 'My king and my Lord'. Even when the Lord called her by her own name, 'Mary', she answered, 'Here I am, Lord.' The narrative continues:

The mother of the Lord said to him, 'Lay your right hand on me and bless me, Lord.' And the Lord stretched out his undefiled right hand and blessed her. Grasping his hand, she kissed it and said, 'I adore this right hand which created heaven and earth and I call upon your name infinitely worthy of praise, O Christ God, king of the ages, only-begotten of the Father.'

When speaking to John, the Theotokos adopted a more familiar approach. With maternal feeling she called him *technon Ioanne*, 'John, my child'.[33] In the same narrative, she addressed her son by a title of majesty, *despota*. She said, 'Hear, my Sovereign and Lord, the prayer of your mother Mary who implores you' (Jugie, 380:21). She also used simply *Kyrie* or 'King of glory' (Jugie, 396:18; 397:20). Something different happens when she relates to John the scene at calvary, when she had said to Jesus on the cross, 'You are departing, my son (*huie mou*), and to whom are you going to leave me?' (Jugie, 383:28).

The philosophy of the name is illustrated by a tiny detail in the *Gospel of Pseudo-Matthew*.[34] Jesus tells Joseph to go and raise a dead man by saying the words, 'May Christ heal you'. Joseph goes, but what he says to the corpse is, 'May Jesus heal you'. And the dead man rises from his bed. Changes of names like this from one occurence to the next or from one language to another are not infrequent; it proves simply that the authors and translators considered such changes insignificant.

Finally it may be appropriate to add the Muslims to our list of witnesses. In spite of their well-known veneration for

Christ they never give him anything but his human name, 'Jesus, son of Mary'. In rare instances they will call him 'the Messiah'. But they always add a little phrase which they add to every other human name, either 'May he be saved' or 'May God save him and bless him',[35] whereas Christians would have to add the phrase, 'May he be glorified'.

The apocryphal acts of the apostles which recount their lives and martyrdoms contain, surprisingly, a rather frequent use of *Iesous* all alone. We can begin with the *Acts of the Apostle Thomas*.[36]   Many of these instances can be accounted for by the fact that they are the words or thoughts of non-Christians. For instance: 'to believe Jesus' (65:19), 'to announce Jesus' (17:12), 'a certain Jesus' (18:11). But there remain many cases, especially of direct address, which deserve closer consideration.

The Apostle went in person and said with great joy and gladness: 'I thank you, Jesus, *for you have made me worthy not only of believing in you but also of suffering many things for your sake. I thank you,* O Lord, *because for you I have been treated as an alchemist and a magician.'* (65:13).

When the wild donkey suddenly became calm, the Apostle said, 'What is to be thought of your magnificence, O Jesus? *What shall I say of it? For I cannot,* O Christ, *express such things'* (54:2).

Speaking with the Lord, *the Apostle said, 'Now is the time,* Jesus, *to move quickly, for now the children of darkness are going down into the darkness itself'* (79:34).

Glory to you, Christ Jesus... (79:28).

May your victorious power now come, O Jesus (82:1).

Thomas did use the name 'Jesus' systematically, but he had no scruples about using this simple vocative among all the other names and titles he gave to the Lord. The *Acts of Thomas*, it should be remembered, were written in Syriac, and we have already observed the freedom with which the Syrians used this name. Fortunately the Syriac text has been published.[37]

In a litany-like passage the name of Jesus is repeated thirteen successive times with a list of the glorious attributes of the incarnate Word, as in our litanies of the Name of Jesus. The Greek translator began, out of habit, to write 'Jesus Christ' in this passage (except in one codex); then he abbreviated it to 'Jesus' five times and finally ended with 'Jesus Christ' again. Elsewhere too the translator reduced the number of occurrences of 'Jesus' alone, either by adding 'Christ' or by leaving out any vocative. In one place the Syriac text has:

O Jesus, who are unknown in this country, Jesus, who have never been proclaimed in this city, Jesus, who have never been heard of by these people, Jesus, who sent your apostle to every town and village so that through him you might be glorified and might become known by all who are worthy of it, O Jesus, who have taken a body and become man and were seen by everyone in order that we might not be separated from your love, O our Lord, who have given yourself for us....

Of the five occurrences of 'Jesus' in this passage the Greek translator left only two as they were. He suppressed one altogether and added 'Christ' to the remaining two. In doing this the Greek version betrays itself as a translation from Syriac because it leaves the pronouns in the third person, according to Syriac syntax, instead of making them agree with the second-person subject.[38]

In the *Acts of Andrew* we almost always find 'Lord Jesus' or 'Jesus Christ' or 'our God and saviour Jesus Christ'.[39] An exception is Number 34 (p. 27:24): *onoma andros tinos legomenou Iesou.* This is a quotation of the pagans of Patras. Number 35 (p. 29:10): 'Calling on the saving name of the Lord Jesus', St Andrew cured the sick.

In the *Martyrdom of Andrew* we find the following: 'Andrew and Peter came to Jesus'.[40]   This is in the gospel-narrative style. In the prayer of St Andrew on the cross there is 'O Jesus, son of God' and *Iesou Christe* (no. 35; p. 63:17, 23). *Christos* often occurs alone.

The *Acts of Andrew and Matthias*[41] have Jesus speaking to Andrew in the guise of the pilot of a boat. He says, 'If you are truly a disciple of the one called Jesus (*matheta tou legomenou Iesou*)....' As soon as Andrew recognized the pilot's true identity he began to call him 'Lord' and 'my Lord Jesus Christ' (see 87:6; 88:1). Likewise when he spoke about him (see 114:11-13).

The *Martyrdom of St Peter* by Bishop Linus almost always uses 'our Lord Jesus Christ' or 'the Lord Jesus Christ'.[42] Exceptions are: 'Jesus Christ, true God' (17:24); 'O Lord Jesus Christ, word of life' (18:9); 'Jesus Christ my Lord and my teacher' (18:21).

In the *Martyrdom of St Paul*[43] a young man who was the page and cupbearer of Caesar fell from a window ledge during a sermon of St Paul and was killed. The prayer of the Apostle brought him back to life. Then the following conversation took place between Nero and the page:

Nero asked him, 'Patrocles, are you alive?' 'Yes, Caesar, I am alive.' Nero said, 'Who has brought you back to life?' Then Patrocles answered, from a heart that was full of joy and burning with the flame of faith, 'The Lord Jesus Christ, king of all the ages' (27:17).

Barnabas, Justus and others used a similar title: 'The invincible king, our Lord Jesus Christ' (28:13). Likewise Paul himself: 'My God and eternal king, the Lord Jesus Christ' (31:19). A moment after St Paul was decapitated, 'the name of the Lord Jesus Christ was heard distinctly in the Hebrew language' (40:18). We are left to guess what the Hebrew words might have been.

In the *Acts of Peter and Simon* we find almost always 'our Lord Jesus Christ' or some variation of this.[44] The same is true for the *Martyrdom of SS Peter and Paul*.[45] The name of

the Lord is rare in the *Acts of Paul and Thecla*. [46] It occurs in
a prayer by Thecla: 'O my God, son of the most high, you who
are in heaven' (256:10). Throwing herself into the water
Thecla cried, 'In the name of Jesus Christ, I am being
baptized for the last day' (260:7). Finally in one codex there
is an additional story in which Thecla says, 'I am a little old
lady, a servant of my Lord Jesus Christ' (271).

In all these documents the name of 'Jesus' alone can be
found only about fifteen times. These instances deserve to be
examined more closely: [47]

a) 28:15   Nero hears some Christians 'call Jesus an
unconquerable king'. The phrase represents Nero's
thought; the Christians themselves had said, 'We fight for
an unconquerable king, Jesus Christ our Lord.'

b) 47:4   'Jesus, the living God'

c) 66:25   Peter saw a blind old woman leaning on her
daughter's arm. He said to her, 'Come here, Mother.
Today Jesus gives you his right arm.... He says to you
through me, "Open your eyes, see, and walk by yourself."'
This affectionate and familiar tone of speech towards
women is not uncommon (see *Acts of Thomas*, Bonnet, ed.,
70:4).

d) 68:11   Peter has been speaking of Christ, of his glory,
his mercy, his transcendence, and he continues:

*This is the Jesus whom you possess, my brothers. He is the
gate, light, way, bread, water, life, resurrection, consolation,
precious pearl, treasure, seed, delight, mustard seed, vine,
ploughshare, grace, faith, word. He is all these things and
there is no one greater than he. To him be glory forever.
Amen.*

e) 71:24   'Jesus of Nazareth' They are the words of Simon
Magus, denying the divinity of this 'workman's son, a
worker himself'.

f) 84:26   '...strengthened by the power of Jesus' The
phrase refers to four women converted by Peter. The old
Latin translation had 'strengthened by the Lord', and one

Greek variant has 'by Christ the judge'.

g) 98:10   'Jesus undefiled (*aniante Iesou*). From his cross
Peter said a prayer to Christ under the title of king, or as
the Latin has it, 'good king Jesus Christ'. Peter had
already spoken of Christ as the 'Word of God' and then he
wished to emphasize that Christ meant everything to him:

*You are to me a father, a mother, a brother, a friend, a
servant, a steward. You are everything and everything is
contained in you. We ask of you what you have already
promised to give us, O Jesus undefiled. We praise you, we
thank you, and we proclaim...that you are God.*

In such a context it does not seem that this 'Jesus undefiled' can be counted as an example of devotion to the
name of Jesus as such. The Latin, furthermore, translated
it, 'Lord Jesus'.

h) 111:3   'Jesus, unconquerable king'
i) 205:6   'I am Jesus whom you are persecuting' (spoken
to St Paul).
j) 233:3   'Peter asked, "Lord, where are you going?"
Jesus said to him, "I am on my way to be crucified
again."' This is the historical narrative style. The same is
true for several instances in the story of Abgar, King of
Edessa (see 274:3; 279:3; 282:5; 7, 10, 14, 18).

THE NAMES OF THE LORD IN LITURGICAL TEXTS

This section, though important, can be short because the
picture is quite clear.

The Byzantine liturgy is marked by its highly serious
theological and anthropological tone. The transcendence of
God calls forth the response of adoration; mankind's fall is a
call for mercy. This sense of solemnity and compunction does
not exclude liveliness but it gives to joy a dimension that the
well-meant but disrespectful frivolity of superficial piety could

never attain. The majesty of God and human honesty prevented from the outset any indiscreet familiarity with the Lord Jesus, son of God, and in this the liturgy only followed the example of all the great early saints, the apostles, the beloved disciple and the mother of God herself.

If anyone ought to have preserved 'the original freedom of centering on the name' of Jesus alone, it was the woman who stood at the source of 'the oldest historical record' of conversation with him, Mary the Theotokos. [48] But Eastern liturgy and iconography are unanimous in picturing the Virgin in an attitude and with expressions of the highest respect towards the God who, in her, became man. It is not that Mary remained servant and adorer in spite of her dignity as mother, but that she became servant and adorer in the highest degree precisely because of her incomparable dignity. It is always a source of surprise for a Westerner when he sees for the first time the *deësis* of Mary and John the Baptist standing in prayer before the enthroned Christ. But this is one of the classic representations of the glorious virgin mother in her role as mediatrix.

The eucharistic liturgy never portrays Mary as speaking, but other liturgical forms do. For instance, in a hymn by Romanos the Melodist, Mary is made to say, 'My child' (*technon*) as in Lk 2:48; but the refrains which set the tone for the hymns always place on the lips of the Theotokos phrases like 'my son and my God' [49] or 'new-born infant, God from all eternity' (repeated also by the Magi). [50]   At Bethlehem Mary calls the infant she suckles 'sovereign King' (*hypsele basileu*), 'my saviour and leader, my son, my creator, my redeemer' (Strophes 3 and 24). We never find simply 'Jesus'.

We will consider the Byzantine canonical office and menology in closer detail. The Horologion contains the parts of the office that never change: [51]

The midnight office (*Mesonycticon*): *Lord Jesus Christ, our God, have mercy on us* (1). *Let us kneel before Christ the king, our God* (4). *Adored and glorified always and at all times in heaven and on earth, Christ our God...* (with a list of titles—17). *The Lord, the only son, Jesus Christ* (18). *The day of your only son our Lord and God and Saviour Jesus Christ* (19). *O Christ* (21). *The Christ our God* (22). *With awe let us glorify Christ the giver of life* (35).

Lauds (*Orthros*): *Christ God* (38, 48). *The Virgin Mother hymns her son and God* (followed by the Magnificat—65). *Christ our God* (72). *Lord, only son, Jesus Christ* (72).

Prime: *'Begin with compunction'* (76). *You* [Mary] *hold in your holy arms the Son, God of the universe* (79).

Terce: *Lord our God, who have given your peace to men* (Prayer of St Basil—93).

Sext: *Christ God* (97, 98). *Christ our God* (98). *Of your only Son our Lord Jesus Christ* (Prayer of St Basil—102).

Typica: *The only son and word of God* (105). *O Christ God...Sovereign Lord Jesus Christ* (Despota Kyrie—105). *Remember, O Lord,...remember, O Sovereign...remember, O holy One* (106).

And so on. These are the titles that the liturgy tirelessly repeats. [52]

Next we will consider the menology. In the Venice edition of 1763 we notice first of all an engraving, more Venetian than Byzantine, with the inscription 'Jesus teaching in the temple'. In the Athens edition of 1952 this has disappeared and in its place is a sort of *deësis* with the inscription 'the Christ teaching in the temple' (the two figures standing on either side of the throne are Mary and Joseph).

Apart from this detail the titles of the Lord are quite ordinary. One exception, which can be related to what we have seen in an earlier chapter, occurs in the troparion of women martyr saints:

Your little lamb, O Jesus, crys aloud to you. It is you for whom I long, O my spouse. It is to find you that I entered the combat and that I was crucified and buried with you in baptism.... (Saints Euphemy, Thecla, Caritone, Anastasia,

Ecatherina and Julian).

This is an example of the *parrhesia* of the martyrs, as well as of feminine affectivity. Only this troparion of women martyrs speaks in such terms.

One other exception that deserves further comment is found in a certain 'Office of the most sweet Jesus'. What we have here is something quite unique, 'a litany beseeching our Lord Jesus Christ'. It is deliberately oriented to contrition, almost with a vengeance and to the point of weariness. Systematically and relentlessly it repeats its invocation, 'O sweet Jesus' (*Iesous glykytate*).

PENTHOS AND AFFECTIVITY

There are two paths which could lead to a deep and tender love of the Lord Jesus, his divine goodness since he is God (*dulcedo Dei*) and his human amiability since no man has ever spoken or ever loved as this man. These paths ultimately merge because the Lord is a single divine person, but because he has two natures these two paths can be distinguished, can run side by side along parallel lines or can even split off and go in different directions. Something has already been said about this in the context of the philosophy of the name, particularly with respect to Origen and St Ephrem, but this is the place to treat the subject more thoroughly.

The Old Testament speaks so often of the divine goodness that a book has been written about the theme.[53] The Psalter particularly—and this was the book most familiar to the faithful—contains invitations to 'taste and see how good the Lord is' (Ps 34:8; 100:5). This phrase turns up frequently and spontaneously in the writings of the mystics. Jesus is the Lord. In him the goodness and kindness of God have become visible and tangible (Tt 3:5; 1 Jn 1:1). Jesus, in his divine person and his theandric nature, in his life and words, in his passion and resurrection, is himself the supreme manifestation of the love with which God loves us. It would be impossible ever to imagine anything more likely to arouse a loving response. 'When you have realized this, with what love will you not love him who has so loved you the first!'[54]

The fact that christians love Christ is not surprising. 'If someone does not love the Lord, let him be anathema,' says St Paul (1 Cor 16:22). But what kind of love should they have? It is often said that Eastern spirituality is characterized by a vivid awareness of the divine transcendence and that it contemplates the divinity of the Word incarnate more than his humanity. Their liturgy praises, thanks, adores and implores in terms befitting a poor and sinful creature. And they have an 'Office of the most sweet Jesus' which 'antedates the *Jubilus* attributed to St Bernard'.[55]   St Bernard's *Jubilus*, however, is not the Roman liturgy. Nor does the Byzantine liturgy begin in the style of the following:

Most sweet Jesus, joy of my soul!
My Jesus, giver of peace to my soul, master most merciful!
O Jesus, save me!

One hypothesis is that this 'Office of the most sweet Jesus' comes from the ninth century, and this is very far from the period of the origins of the Byzantine liturgy.

What is beyond doubt is that this Office is thoroughly monastic and thoroughly oriented to contrition:

O Jesus, my Saviour, have mercy on me;
Keep me from every punishment....
O most sweet Jesus, glory of monks...
O Jesus, save me,
Snatch me, O Jesus Saviour, from the dragon's claws....
Draw me away from the abyss of hell...
O Jesus, open for me the gates of repentance.
Give ear, O Jesus, O my Jesus friend of mankind, to your
   servant's cry of sorrow.

Prostrate at your feet, in tears,....
O Virgin who gave birth to my Jesus, pray that I may be
saved from hell.

In what follows, the poet goes to the very limit of self-condemnation, saying that he is worse than 'the sinful woman, the prodigal, Manasses, the publican, the thief and the Ninivites,' and that 'no one on earth, O my Jesus, has ever sinned as I have sinned....'[56]

Father Salaville has some penetrating comments to offer along with his translation of this Office. He says that basically the poet was saying the same thing over and over, and that it would be extremely difficult to find a logical development of thought running through all the strophes that would be comparable to the development Dom Wilmart has discovered in the Latin *Jubilus*. The point of comparison that Father Salaville wishes to make between the two works is 'their similarity as regards the tone of affectivity and tender familiarity'.[57]

This conclusion needs a slight modification because in the *Jubilus rythmicus de nomine Jesu* there is no mention of sin, whereas the Byzantine Office is full of talk about forgiving sin and escaping punishment. This introduces a significant difference between the two, which affects even the similarity of their accent on tenderness. On the one hand we have, in Dom Wilmart's words, 'a progressive search, like the one in the Canticle, a pursuit which ends in heaven'.[58]   On the other hand there is an interminable *Miserere* expressing the hope that 'all who turn to you may be delivered from temptations, dangers and eternal fire' (from the concluding *Theotokion*, 258).

From this perspective, the purely literary similiarities are less impressive. To repeat: the Byzantine liturgy did not begin with anything that resembles either the compunction or the forced affectivity of the 'Office of the most sweet Jesus'.

Is there anything dating from before the ninth century that might compare with this Office? As far as the tone of repentance is concerned there is an overabundance of similar material. What of 'the accent of tenderness towards Jesus'? Father Salaville writes: 'It is safe to say that the accents of tenderness towards Jesus had already been heard in the East.' Even, we may add, to a greater degree because more discreetly. For instance, there is an alphabetical hymn probably dating from before the sixth century which says in one verse, 'O my Christ, save your people and bless this house'.[59] There are also some lines from Romanos the Melodist. These particular pieces are not later than the sixth century. In the fifth century Diadochus of Photice had already spoken repeatedly of the 'sweetness' (*glykytes*) of God, and this 'God' is the Lord Jesus.[60] Worth quoting is the second half of his Chapter sixty-one; everything is delicacy and respect:

It is grace itself that murmurs and repeats with the soul, 'Lord Jesus' as a mother would teach her little child the word 'father' by repeating it with him until she has given him a habit, which not even sleep can obliterate, of distinctly calling his father instead of babbling incoherently. Thus the Apostle says, 'In the same way the Spirit comes to the aid of our weakness, for we do not know how to pray as we should, but the Spirit himself intercedes for us with ineffable groanings' (Rom 8:26). Since we are babies when it comes to the art of perfect prayer, we absolutely have to have the help of the Spirit, so that all our concepts and thoughts may be penetrated and sweetened by the effect of his wondrous sweetness, and so that we may thus be led with all eagerness to the remembrance and love of God our Father.

Just previously, in the same spirit of fervent love, Diadochus had written of 'the glorious and much longed-for name' (*polypotheton*) of the 'Lord Jesus' (chap. fifty-nine). This style or at least the atmosphere surrounding it would have been enough to bring the phrase *Iesou glykytate* to the lips of a pious monastic reader, though Diadochus himself deliberately avoided using anything but 'Lord Jesus'.

The breeze of warm, human piety was blowing from other quarters too. There is not only the general tendency 'towards a progressive humanization' in iconography and in religion as a whole, which we note in passing,[61] but also, rather surprisingly, there is the phenomenon of unconcealed tenderness among the famous hermits and ascetics especially towards the end of their lives and after long practice of those austerities recounted in the *Vitae Patrum*. We can see here the symptoms not of neurotic babbling but of a freedom of speech, *parrhesia*, that is the fruit of a long period of purification. Perfection, after all, consists in becoming like little children again. The innocence of a child can and perhaps should accompany a perfectly mature judgment (see 1 Cor 14:20).

A good example of affectivity among the ascetics is furnished by St Antony the Hermit. There are two versions to compare, the Greek text of St Athanasius and the Latin translation by Evagrius of Antioch:

Athanasius	Evagrius of Antioch
The Lord *had not thus far forgotten Anthony's fierce struggle.*	Jesus *did not forget the struggles of his servant.*
He was at hand to give him help....	*He came and protected him..*
Feeling this help and breathing easier again, since his pain had ceased, he asked the vision that appeared to him: 'Where were you? Why did you not come immediately and prevent my suffering?' And a voice said to him: 'Antony, I was here, but I waited to see how you would fight....'	*As soon as Antony recognized the Lord's presence he drew a long, deep breath and said to the light which had appeared to him: 'Where were you, good Jesus, where were you....?'*

In his preface the translator, Evagrius, had already
advised his readers in a succinct phrase that he meant to give
the sense not the words: 'I have translated in such a way as
to lose nothing of the meaning though perhaps something of
the words.'[62]   Subsequent generations are always curious
about things which never troubled their forefathers. We
would love to know what idea or habit or inadvertence
influenced Evagrius to replace 'the Lord' by 'Jesus' and to
add 'good Jesus' in a place where no name was expressly
given. A reader of the book *Spiritual Terminology in the Latin
Translations of the Vita Antonii* by L. Th. A. Lorié, SJ, might
expect the author to have treated this question, but
apparently the names of the Lord can be of less interest to a
Jesuit than terms like *acediosus* or *amentia* which appear
among the 350 entries in two indices.[63]   Since Evagrius was
a Latin author, perhaps the reason why he replaced the
solemn 'Lord' by the familiar 'Jesus' might lie in his Latin
style.[64]   However, an earlier Latin version followed the
original Greek literally.[65]   And in fact this Evagrius was born
and raised in Syrian Antioch. Would it be incorrect to suspect
a Syrian influence?

Not long after Evagrius, St John Chrysostom lived at
Antioch; like Evagrius he was the son of a roman official. We
have already studied Chrysostom's philosophy of the name.
Even if he had thought of it, he could never have permitted
himself to speak about the Lord or even address him without
giving him a title. But in reading John Chrysostom one has
the impression that he was tempted to do so at times. We are
even told by one author that 'John shows us Christ personally
imploring our love.'[66]   To quote the passage in question:

*Who can be more generous than I? I am father, I am brother,
I am spouse, as well as food, clothing, home, root,
foundation, everything you could wish for. You need nothing
else. I will even become your servant for I came to serve, not
to be served. I am also friend, member, head, brother, sister,
mother. I am everything to you. You have only to be my*

friend. I became poor for your sake, a beggar for your sake; I was cricified for you, buried for you. In heaven I implore the Father for you. You have become everything for me—brother, coheir, friend, member. What more can you desire?[67]

Reading such pleas might bring to mind the picture of a lonely child pleading, 'Won't *you* at least love me?' But John Chrysostom would never make Jesus Christ beg for love in such a pitiable, untheological way. The Christ whom he pictured was speaking as the redeemer preoccupied with saving men and not as some misunderstood soul tormented by its own sentimental loneliness. The love which Christ asks of us begins with serious renunciation:

Why do you beat the air and run in vain? Every occupation has a purpose, obviously. Tell me then, what is the purpose of all the activity of the world? Answer, I challenge you! It is vanity of vanity; all is vanity. [68]

Without a doubt this strong, virile love can become a tender, affectionate love, and in fact it did. But it was still far from being anything like an 'Office of the most sweet Jesus'.

One point should be clarified before we go further. There were several factors that prevented the early monks and ascetics from openly showing their affection toward God; their sense of modesty and their sense of humility prevented it especially. The only expression of devotion that was not completely hidden by this twofold scrupulosity was mourning and weeping for past sins. When it was a question of compunction (*penthos*), they felt free. There is small risk involved in the admission of being a sinner; there is the possibility of incurring scorn but that is a gain. 'We shall never know very much about the ardent love for God that burned in the hearts of our great monastic forefathers except by reasoning about it as did Theodoret.'[69]

The situation can be illustrated by a story which is told about John Colobos. [70] Some have seen in it only a titillating anecdote, but actually it is a gem of literary craftsmanship which catches and holds the reader's interest right up to the surprise ending. According to the story Paesia, a rich orphan lady who had been a benefactress of the monks, turned to a life of sin. When the monks heard of it they were deeply grieved. They dispatched Abba John Colobos to save her, saying: 'Take the trouble to go to her home and try to straighten her out, using all the wisdom that God has given you.' The man of God did so. He had great difficulty getting past the gatekeeper and then past the servants. But finally the lady consented to see him because, as she told her maid, 'these monks are beachcombers along the Red Sea and sometimes they find precious stones.' She dressed and waited for him sitting on her bed. John came in and sat down beside her. 'Then he looked her in the eye and asked her, "What do you have against Jesus that you have come to this?" When she heard this a shiver shook her whole body. Abba John lowered his head and began to weep bitterly.' The outcome was the lady's conversion.

At the risk of seeming an idiot, I will say that in my opinion Abba John's remark is sublime. To explain why would only be to invite ridicule, but as far as our subject is concerned this remark speaks more eloquently than the most subtle dissertation and the most solemn documents. In order for that very revealing question to escape from the ascetic's heart, it took something as urgent as the salvation of a soul.

Before the sixth century, slightly earlier than Diadochus, St Nilus of Ancyra wrote the following note to a distressed monk. It says a great deal despite its brevity. Nilus was not one to beat around the bush when he felt he had to set someone straight. He wrote: 'This unbearable sadness and deep discouragement is a temptation which you can overcome by copious tears, by strong hope, and by a burning love (*pothos*) for our sweet saviour, Christ (*ton glykyaton sotera Christon*).' We should note that this sweetness can be present without mention of the name 'Jesus'.

The most effective means of inspiring affective feelings for

Christ has always been, in every country and in every
christian era, the remembrance of his passion. Even if
documentary evidence were lacking we could take this for
granted. But we happen to have a fourth-century witness who
tells us this explicitly in regard to Jerusalem. The author is
Egeria, the well-educated, truthful and curious pilgrim from
Southern Europe, who is also known as Sylvia, Silvania,
Aetheria, and Echeria since she neglected to mention her own
name in her travel memoirs. Her words may be surprising
but evidently she felt they were well chosen because she
repeated them in three different places. [71]   In the Basilica of
the Resurrection the bishop read the gospel: 'As soon as he
began to read there arose from the assembly a moaning and
groaning capable of moving the hardest heart to tears,
because the Lord suffered so much for our sake.' When the
gospel passage describing the arrest of the Lord was read
in the garden of Gethsemane, 'there was such a moaning and
groaning from all the people that their moaning could
probably be heard in the city itself in spite of the distance.'
On Calvary for three hours the messianic prophecies were
read:

*At each prophecy and every prayer there was so much
emotion and groaning from all the people, it is hard to
believe. On that day, during those three hours, there was not
one who did not weep more than can be imagined, because
the Lord endured all these sufferings for our sake.*

To understand, it would be necessary actually to have
been at Jerusalem. The reason is not that Palestinians were
more emotional than anyone else. There were people from all
points of the compass in that crowd, and perhaps those who
came the furthest were the most likely to be filled with
emotion since their journey was over and they had reached
the place they had longed for. Gerontius, the author of a biography of St Melany, followed the Roman rite but he stood
out among all of them for the gift of tears when he celebrated

the synaxis on the mountain of olives. [72]

Why is it that the Holy Land has so attracted Christians of all times? Faith ought to be able to transcend the desire to see the holy places; blessed are they who have not seen and have believed. But the need for feeling also has its legitimate reason for being, and the prospect of giving free rein to one's devotion without the impediment of human respect can be quite compelling. As substitutes for going to the Holy Land the stations of the cross were invented and different centers of pilgrimage gradually developed, like so many focal points radiating fervor of spirit and warmth of feeling. Places like these have always played an important part in the history of piety in every country. It is not astonishing to discover signs of a more emotional form of religion appearing near these centers of pilgrimage.

The people of Syria are next-door neighbors to the Holy Land. They feel at home there and experience no language barrier. [73] It was easy for them, on the very ground where Christ lived, to have an imaginary picture of his humanity, and it was natural that they should take an interest in the events of Christ's life which happened in those very places. At Bethlehem the most cerebral of pilgrims cannot help imagining the infant with Mary and Joseph, just as a visitor at St Anne's in Jerusalem cannot help thinking of the *bambina*. The whole atmosphere has a gradual but definite effect on the spirit and on the feelings.

Furthermore, Syria was a country where poetry and religious music flourished long before melodies were known among the Byzantines. Liturgical music—like the liturgy itself—came to Byzantium from the Semitic orient. From Bardesane, Ephrem, James of Sarough and Narsaï of Nisibis we have a multitude of *memra*, *tesbohta* and even rhymed homilies. One could easily become bored by all these if he approached them with a 'time is money' mentality. After the reader has made his way through interminable verbiage and finally reached a turning point he is liable to find the author saying that he intends to repeat what he has just said so that no one will misunderstand. [74] The reader has to overcome his annoyance, make an effort to get into the mentality of the early Easterners, and realize once and for all that the time given to such repetitions is time well spent because it will bear fruit precisely through the repetition. Then gradually a new dimension begins to open up: a world that is more human, more interior, more tranquil, an oasis of quiet freshness where one would like to settle down and stay and never have to go back to the madness of a modern city.

Syrian Christians have a third characteristic. They distrust intellectual speculation about God and his mysteries much more than Greeks do. Their most vigorous thinkers will inevitably repeat with personal conviction a refrain learned from St Ephrem: 'A man who believes that there is a God will not be curious to know when and how he became God.' Indiscreet curiosity about God may indicate:

that the soul has not experienced God. One who has truly experienced God should have the spirit of a child and should feel towards God and His providence just as a child feels towards his father and mother; he is a child and he listens as a child listens to his lessons and accepts it on faith.

These are the words of a formidable polemicist, Philoxenus of Mabburgh. [75]

Philoxenus spoke in the same intimate, familial terms about God's love for us, for instance in his seventh homily. As for our love of Christ such expressions as 'the sweetness of the love of Christ', 'the feeling of the burning fire of Jesus', 'the princely dignity of the beauty of Christ' repeated like a leitmotif in his twelfth homily all show that this thinker did not have an arid, sterile heart.

The same features can be observed in more debonaire authors like James of Sarough. He constantly refused to scrutinize God, and stressed faith and love instead:

Woe to him who examines you too closely, O Son of God....

*Speak within me because I do not attempt to scrutinize you.
Jesus, light of the sun, rise in your love above my thoughts...
You are most loving toward him who adores and believes in
you but most terrifying toward one who attempts to examine
you too closely.* [76]

Faith works the astounding miracle of permitting a sinner
to attain familiarity with God. Two of James's homilies are
particularly illustrative of his style, one about the thief on
Jesus' right and the other about the cherubim and the
thief. [77]   They are little dramas calculated like medieval
mystery plays, to arouse the devotion of the people. But
though they are short they are too long to be quoted in their
entirety here, and to abridge them would take away their
exotic charm. Besides, none of this was ever translated into
Greek and so it could not have had a direct influence in
bringing about that climate of affective piety which was
favorable to the birth of the Jesus Prayer. The Jesus Prayer
originated in Greek-speaking lands and so we are primarily
concerned about writings that circulated in the Greek
language. At the same time we must remember that currents
of thought and of feeling can exist independent of all literary
transmission.

Among authors who were translated into Greek, John of
Dalyatha and the Greek Ephrem deserve special notice.
Among St Ephrem's works we have, first of all, a piece 'On
the Life of Abraham and his Niece, Maria'. [78] This is almost
a paraphrase or expanded version of the anecdote about John
Colobos and the orphan lady, Paesia. Here terse prose has
been replaced by verbosity, however, and sublimity by
buffoonery. At the moment of crisis, Maria, like Paesia, is
struck speechless; finally she manages to say, 'I cannot look
at you for shame; how can I call on the spotless name of *my
Christ* when I am filthy from the mire of impurity?' Should
we consider 'my Christ' a form of affectionate address?
Copyists have not preserved it: the *Acta Sanctorum* has 'my
God' [79] and the metaphrastic *Life* has simply 'God'. [80]   In the

sequel the author seems to lose interest in his two heroes and
writes in the first person, 'My Lord is near....' Then he
concludes with a prayer of contrition for his sinfulness, during
which he carries his foolishness to the point of explaining to
the good Lord in parentheses the meaning of the words he
uses.

The vast majority of these writings were intended to foster
compunction and were meant primarily for monks. They are
concerned much more with the practice of asceticism than
with affectivity. Occasionally, though, a glimmer of feeling
breaks through: 'My son, cast off the yoke of the enemy with
all his pride and submit your neck to the yoke of our sweet
Master, our Lord and Saviour, Jesus Christ'.[81]   This is
Ephrem's customary title for the Lord. In rare instances it is
'our Lord and Saviour, Jesus' (see *Paraenesis* 31, p. 121E),
and this may be due to a copyist's error. The ordinary name
is 'Christ'. *Kyrios* alone is frequent. 'Jesus' alone, never. A
typical example of the tone of this genre is the following:
'Love mourning (*penthos*) because this is what Christ
commands; it was he who said, "Blessed are they who weep
now for they shall be comforted" ' (*Paraenesis* 41, p. 153F).
Prayers also occur; they are generally long and always
oriented to contrition (see, for example, *Paraenesis* 42, p.
160C).

At times the mood of mourning is carried to extremes.
The author of a sermon on the second coming of the Lord
gave a lengthy description of the despair of the damned.
Then he made these tortured souls say:

*'God's judgment is just. We shall never see the throng of
saints, never gaze upon the true light. We are completely
orphaned. What shall we say? Farewell, all you saints;
farewell, apostles, prophets and martyrs; farewell, choir of
patriarchs; farewell phalanx of monks; farewell, precious and
life giving cross; farewell, kingdom of heaven; farewell,
Jerusalem on high, mother of the firstborn, paradise of
delights; farewell also, Lady Theotokos, Mother of God,*

friend of mankind; farewell, father and mother, sons and daughters—we will never see any of you again.' Then they depart, each to the place he has prepared for himself.

After delivering this exhortation, which runs five folio columns, the author remarked, 'There, I have now done what you asked me to do, I have fulfilled your desires' (202A). And then he goes on for another seven pages.

If there is any warmth of affectivity in all this, we can also see from what fire it comes. Sermons on the last judgment are found again and again. The listeners must have been insatiable. While today people say they don't care to hear any more sermons on hell, these early Christians asked question after question. 'Tell us about the interrogation at the last judgment' (215F). 'And after that, O servant of God, what will they hear and suffer?' (216D). The preacher declines because the matter is too dreadful to discuss, but the 'friends of Christ' beseech him: 'Speak, for the love of the Lord and for our benefit.' Later they ask, 'Is there only one kind of punishment or a variety of kinds?' (218D). 'We beg you, O servant of God, to hide nothing from us in this matter and tell us how the wretched go to their punishment' (219D).

Shall we stop? The same sort of thing turns up again on pages 377-393, but the sample given may already be too much for our sensibilities. They go on at it interminably. As is obvious, this whole spirituality revolves around compunction. 'We have to do much praying and weeping,' they say (219D).

In another of St Ephrem's works, the sinful woman sitting at the Lord's feet in the home of Simon the Pharisee is made to say a lengthy prayer which comes from her heart and contains many tender words and much emotion, but it is all directed toward gaining forgiveness of sins, as we might expect:

I do not look upon you as does this Pharisee, Simon, who has invited you to dine with him today. I look upon you as God, the great demiurge of all things. I am a ewe lamb who has strayed from your flock; make me come back, O Saviour, into your fold, for you alone are the good shepherd....O my master (despota), *I am your dove, carried off by a dreadful hawk.* [82]

All the names of Christ are there, with the sole exception of 'Jesus'.

Here is a prayer in a similar vein, which forms the conclusion of a long sermon by Ephrem on patience:

O Christ, light of truth, scion of the blessed Father, stamp and radiance of his substance (Heb 1:3), *seated at the right hand of his majesty, incomprehensible Son, inscrutable Christ, unfathomable God, glory and joy of those who love you, my life, O Christ, I beseech you to save me in your kingdom, sinner though I am, and do not repay me according to my deeds but save me by your grace and pardon me by your mercy because you are blessed and glorious forever and ever, Amen.* (II,333).

Calling on the divine name comes naturally. We are told that it should be habitual. 'Pray to God always and everywhere, saying, "Save me, O God, by your name" (Ps 54:1), and he will immediately send his help and renew the courage of your heart.'[83] This is the 'all holy name' that delivered Daniel, Jonah and the three children in the fiery furnace.

The love of Christ is often the subject of St Ephrem's sermons. Those who have given proof of their love are called martyrs or athletes of Christ or soldiers of Christ. The one who inspired in Ephrem the most enthusiastic response was the mother of the last of the forty martyrs of Sebaste, who 'lifted her son in her arms and ran to bind him to the sheaves' of his companions (II, 250). After that she delivered a three page discourse explaining her action (251-254).

In the *Testament of Ephrem* we read the following (II,

359):

O Jesus, be yourself my judge and do not delegate my judgment to another; for he who is judged by God will have mercy done to him at his judgment. I have heard it said to wise men and I have been taught by the lips of learned men that whoever has seen the face of the King, even if he has sinned, will never die. Hosea greatly frightens me because of what he says about 'Ephrem'.

The Greek version of this passage alters the tone somewhat:

O Lord Jesus Christ, do not pass judgment on your servant and do not give to another the responsibility of judging me. Let me appear before your glorious tribunal, for he whom God judges will receive mercy. I believe, because I have heard it from wise and learned apostles, that whoever sees the King, even if he has sinned, will never die. But woe to me, my brothers, what is this that is pressing me hard? Weep and lament for I am being crushed....

In the *Life of St Anthony* we saw how the Latin translator, Evagrius of Antioch, added the name 'Jesus' and the vocative 'good Jesus' not found in the Greek; here the Greek translator replaced the tender 'Jesus' of the Syriac with the more formal 'Lord Jesus Christ'. Would it be right to conclude from this that the Byzantines were more cautious than the Syrians or Latins about overfamiliarity in their relationship with God. Perhaps so; at any rate it is a possible conclusion.

A rapid glance at the remaining Greek writings attributed to St Ephrem justifies the following observations:

1. What predominates is definitely *penthos*, a feeling of compunction, mourning and grief.
2. Any affectivity springs from that source.
3. The Jesus Prayer occurs nowhere;

4. but this prayer does summarize in a few words the thrust of this whole spirituality.

A simple glance at the table of contents is enough to show how *penthos* is all-pervasive. It is a list of sermons on the last judgement, self-accusations, grief over the passions, and prayers of contrition. Even when the title might suggest otherwise, the content is the same. The 'prayers to the Theotokos' weep and lament over sin as much as do the most terrifying meditations on death.

Especially relevant to our study in all this are the prayers which often conclude and sometimes interrupt these austere considerations. A list of these, far from complete, can be seen in the footnotes.[84] A rapid survey of this material, and even a closer examination, reveals the total predominance of the spirit of *penthos*, compunction, sorrow for sin.

But one feeling begets another. Compunction turns easily into affectivity because it is itself a form of affection. Yet, the love which is born of compunction always bears the mark of its origin; when it expresses itself in tears it is not clear whether they are tears of pure affection for the Lord or tears of self-pity. Even when the invocation 'O sweet Jesus' comes back again and again, it always has the undertone of a *Miserere* rather than an *Alleluia*. A good example is the work entitled 'Canon of Contrition to our Lord Jesus Christ'. Transplanted among the prayers of the Greek Ephrem it stands out in the collection only by a systematic repetition of the invocation to the 'most sweet Jesus Christ'.

It is also relevant and instructive to study the literature of heretical sects like the Nestorians, the Monophysites and the Messalians. The Monophysites would seem, *a priori*, to be less rationalistic than the Nestorians and therefore more inclined to an affective form of piety. The Messalians, for their part, believed that spiritual feelings should be avidly esteemed as the sign of a great spiritual gift or of the presence of the Holy Spirit. It would be out of the question to analyze all this literature. A few exploratory soundings will have to suffice, but this will be enough to illustrate the significant trends.

From the century of Chalcedon we have the Monophysite *Life of Peter the Iberian*. Like orthodox hagiography, the original Syriac version habitually used 'Lord Jesus', 'Christ', 'Lord Jesus Christ', 'Christ our Saviour', 'our Saviour Jesus Christ'. Two exceptions are worth pausing over. Peter, lying on his sickbed, saw the devil appear at the foot of his bed and begin to mock him in these words:

See now what has come to you from the one whom you love! See to what condition you have been reduced by him whom you have followed and for whom you have sacrificed everything. Now then, curse him and be free of your complaint!

But Peter merely sighed at him with indignation, like a man who has experienced this sort of effrontery many times. He answered:

'You are talking about my Jesus, *you unclean, impudent swine, you vicious blasphemer of God. You are asking me to imitate your own perversity. May the power of Christ annihilate you!'*

As soon as he heard the name of Christ, the Evil One vanished like smoke and was seen no longer. Then Peter began to weep and to call upon the Lord with bitter tears and sighs. Immediately the Lord appeared to him as it is written, 'While you are still speaking he will say, "I am here!"' (Is 58:9). *He said to Peter, 'What is wrong? Why this disturbance, man of little courage? Do you not know that it is I who have power over life and death?'*[85]

Notice first of all that the expression of 'my Jesus' springs from Peter's indignation against the devil's mockery. However, it was not when he heard the name 'Jesus' that the devil vanished, but only at the name of Christ. Note further that the story deals with the world of visions and sensory communications with invisible realities. Finally, there is the text from Isaiah which we met once before in the apophtheg-mata, with the same reproach from the Lord; it comes back again in Peter's biography, on page ninety-two.

The second example is also instructive. The incident took place when Peter was the guest of an official on a country estate near Tripoli in Syria. Peter was reading. Suddenly he broke into tears of joy and said:

Who would not be overcome with wonder at the goodness and power of the holy martyr Leontius [martyred at Tripoli under Vespasian]! This very night I saw him speaking with someone and saying to him, 'My fellow exile, pray for this young man that he may get well.' And the man replied, 'I will ask you to do it yourself, O martyr of the Lord. You can effect his recovery, for you have freedom of speech (parrhesia) *with* Jesus. *As for me, I am but a sinner.'*[86]

From this it appears that to say simply 'Jesus' is the privilege of a *parrhesia* or a special intimacy reserved to the martyrs and their equals. This is a traditional viewpoint.

A third passage gives the same impression, though not as clearly. Two youths, named Nabarnugios and Mithradates, travelled to Jerusalem. When they finally caught sight of the city: 'They wept and praised and sang and rejoiced as if they had already met the *Jesus* whom they loved and whom they would live with in heaven hereafter.'[87]

A famous friend of Peter the Iberian was Abba Isaiah.[88] A man of great depth and sensitivity, a Monophysite but not a militant, Abba Isaiah commanded respect among all the Eastern ascetics by writings that had universal appeal. The austerity that shows through his writings is second to none, but it comes wrapped in such a delicate sensitivity that every chapter, as well as the author himself, becomes amiable rather than frightening. Isaiah prescribed the traditional, strict, monastic asceticism with all its detailed practices, but through all these pages the reader senses that the whole reason for it is the Abba's great love of Christ and his charity for his spiritual disciples. He has grasped, more deeply than many, the idea that true freedom lies in shaping our nature according to the nature of Jesus, in following the footsteps of Jesus, and in undergoing the cross of Jesus in order to enter into the repose of the Son of God (for all this, see the article cited in Note 88).

This gave Abba Isaiah a very authentic style of expression when he spoke of the Lord Jesus. Ordinarily he used the common name 'our Lord Jesus Christ'. But we also find: 'our ruler, the beloved Jesus',[89] 'our beloved Jesus, ruler', 'our beloved Jesus', 'our beloved Lord Jesus', (nos. 3, 6). Often he wrote 'the Lord Jesus'. The transcendent titles of the divine Christ and the expressions of human affection provoked by his condescendence both flowed so naturally from Isaiah's lips that they must have sprung straight from the heart. His love led him to adore and he rejoiced in adoring him whom he loved:

The goodness of the great and holy King Jesus has awakened repentance (metanoia) *which has given the soul great joy. Metanoia has opened it up, and Christ the great King has entered in....(Logos 25, no. 11)*

Another time Abba Isaiah said: 'If a man does not struggle till his dying day to make his body like that borne by the beloved Jesus in his earthly life, he will never be able to meet him with joy ' (*Logos* 26, no. 2).

The principles of asceticism and mortification are seen and expressed in relation to Christ, in a way that makes them highly attractive: 'If a man keeps an attentive spirit and wishes to be a pupil at the feet of the Lord Jesus, he will willingly cut off his own self-will so as not to be separated from his beloved Lord' (*Logos* 26, no. 2).

Penthos is not neglected. It is recommended more than once, not counting a litany that repeats 'Woe....' a hundred times (*Threnody*, 198-207). It seems to be held within bounds and to have a certain character of peace and joy: 'Do not be afraid! Take heart! God knows that a man is weak and he will strengthen him.'[90]

The ascetical life consists in following the sacred steps of Jesus to the end.

Blessed is the man who is crucified and who dies and is buried and rises again in newness of life, following the sacred steps of Jesus who became man for our sake. His intention was that we should become like him by humility, poverty, bearing injury and dishonor. Thus, free from all concern about the body and without fear of sudden attack by criminals, we shall be at peace with everyone. The man who rids himself of his vices and seeks this peace is a true Christian, a son of God and brother of Jesus.[91]

Abba Isaiah had recovered, or had never lost, the spirituality of the martyrs. He accented it with a personal intimacy which tempered its tragic aspect without decreasing its seriousness. Here it would be well to read his meditation 'on what was done for our benefit to our beloved Lord God, Jesus, who is our model in all things'.[92] The title, 'On those who have been in combat and have fought to the end', recalls the vocabulary of the era of persecutions. The whole work draws a parallel between the exigencies of the ascetic life in pursuit of perfection and 'what our beloved Lord God, Jesus, has done and suffered'.[93] If we remember that these pages of Abba Isaiah were read and pondered in every christian country, east and west, at least since 1754,[94] we will have good grounds to suspect his influence when we see similar expressions and emphases in later authors.

The next sample is the most remarkable one I know. It is John of Dalyatha, surnamed John Saba.[95] He was a Nestorian of the eighth century. The patriarchs of his sect condemned him, but this did not prevent him from acquiring the renown and the title of a spiritual sheik as far away as Ethiopia.[96] Like Abba Isaiah or Abba Macarius or the

Imitation of Christ, he owed this success to the fervor of his love for Christ. For example, in a chapter on renunciation of the world we find what must be called one of the most beautiful contrition prayers imaginable. 'It is like a more developed *Anima Christi*, radiant with humility and tenderness.'[97]

O Lord Jesus Christ our God, as you wept over Lazarus and shed tears of sadness and compassion for him, accept these bitter tears of mine. By your passion heal my passions, by your wounds comfort my wounds, by your blood purify my blood, and spread over my body the life-giving perfume of your body. The gall which your enemies offered you brings sweetness to my soul and makes it lose the bitterness which the enemy poured upon it. May your body stretched on the wood of the cross make my mind fly toward you when the demon tries to drag it down below. May your head which had to rest on the cross lift up my head when I am insulted by enemies. May your sacred hands nailed to the cross by unbelievers draw me up toward you from the abyss of perdition, as you yourself have promised (Jn 12:32). May your face which was so often struck by the slaps and spittle of cruel men make my face shine again after it has been disfigured by sin. May your spirit which you gave back to your Father on the cross lead me to you by your grace. I am without a heart that mourns and looks for you; I lack the spirit of penance and compunction that brings children back to their heritage. I cannot weep, O Lord. My mind is clouded with earthly concerns and cannot direct its attention in sorrow. My heart has grown cold from a multitude of temptations and can no longer warm itself with tears of love for you. But may you, O Lord Jesus Christ, treasury of blessings, grant me perfect repentance and a sorrowful heart that I may set myself to follow you with all my strength. Without you I can do nothing good. Give me your grace, O generous one! May the Father who from all eternity engendered you from his bosom renew in me the features of your image. I have abandoned you, but

*do not abandon me. I have strayed away from your flock, but
come and look for me and lead me back to your pasture; give
me a place among the sheep of your chosen flock and feed
me, and them, with the delights of your divine mysteries.* [98]

It should be remembered that this 'pious prayer' comes at
the end of a chapter on *'Penthos* and Sorrow with
Discretion'. [99] The psychological matrix most favorable to
affective outpourings is compunction.

It is time to conclude a chapter that has been both too
long and too incomplete. The passages from John Saba which
we have seen came to the attention of the Byzantines
together with the works of Isaac of Niniveh in the ninth
century. This date brings us to the furthest limit of the period
we are studying. The Jesus Prayer had by that time reached
its definitive formulation.

CONCLUSION

The Jesus Prayer did not begin with the name of Jesus. It
had its beginning in *penthos*, in mourning, in sorrow for sin.
It is not correct to say: 'He who would like to return to the
original freedom and concentrate on the name of Jesus alone,
without using the fully developed formula....would be only
taking up again the oldest historical practice of the Jesus
Prayer.' [100] For the developed formula, at least as regards its
substance, we have many pages of documentary evidence; for
the use of the name alone we have very few witnesses;
formally we have nothing at all.

The truth is that the Jesus Prayer is not the result of a
development but of an abbreviation. It condenses the whole
monastic spirituality of *penthos* in one short formula suited to
the needs of 'meditation'. And this formula was invented and
propagated, as Cassian noted, as a means of attaining
continual prayer.

To call on the name of Jesus does not mean saying 'O

Jesus'. At least it did not mean this for Christians of the early centuries. Orthodox Christians loved to confess their faith by saying: 'Jesus Christ', 'Jesus Messiah', 'Son of God', and especially 'Lord'. They did so the more readily as the heretics refused to do so. The Gnostics, according to St Irenaeus, [101] would not call the Saviour 'Lord' though they loved to make all kinds of mystic speculations on the name 'Jesus'. Non-Christians said 'Jesus' as they would say 'Socrates' or 'Pythagoras'. Everything induced the faithful to say something different as a profession of faith and in reaction to those who did not share this faith. They were wary of a love that was verbal, sentimental, superficial. They knew that they had to love *their* Lord Jesus as God with their whole heart and soul and mind and strength. No name, no title was meaningful unless backed up by deeds: 'The most perfect way to say "Lord" is to speak it with your whole life; it is evident therefore that to call on the name of the Lord implies holiness, and indeed great holiness.' [102]

The theological sensitivity of the early Church, the fidelity of Christians to the teachings of the Church, and to some extent also the imperial Byzantine or Roman magnificance created a spontaneous as well as a deliberate preference for the more elaborate titles like 'Lord Jesus Christ, son of God' or 'Jesus Christ, son of God, Saviour'. History and theology are in perfect harmony here, to the greater glory of our ancestors in the faith. The first Christians who said simply 'Jesus' in their devotions, and perhaps out of their devotion, were the Syrians. Among the Syrians those who adopted this usage most freely were the (heterodox) authors of such apocrypha as *The Acts of Thomas*. How this usage spread in subsequent ages to different countries and even to the West is a further question. Part Two will provide a partial answer but the question awaits a more thorough treatment particularly for the period after the fourteenth century.

NOTES

1. See E. von der Goltz, ed., *Das Gebet in der ältesten Christenheit* (Leipzig, 1901) 82.

2. Origen, *De Oratione* 15; PG 11:464D, 468B.

3. G. Bardy, *Origène, de la Prière* (Paris, 1932) 77, n. 2.

4. Origen, *De Oratione* 14; PG 11:164C.

5. Irenaeus, *Adversus Haereses* IV, 9; PG 7:1078A.

6. See the fine article by P.J. Madoz, 'El amor a Jesucristo en la Iglesia de los Mártires,' *Estudios Ecclesiasticos* 12 (1933) 313-344. St Ignatius is inadvertently misquoted on page 332: 'Let us then imitate his patience and even if we do not suffer for his name let us glorify him.' St Ignatius actually wrote: '...if we suffer for his sake let us glorify him', namely, in and by suffering.

7. F.X. Funk, *Patres Apostolici* (Tübingen, 1911) 316:8.

8. 'Letter from the Christians of Lyons and Vienne' in Eusebius, *Hist. Eccl.* V,1; E. Schwartz, ed., *Die griechischen christlichen Schriftsteller der ersten drei Jahrhundert* 9 (Berlin, 1903-1909) II, 424.

9. See R. Knopf, *Ausgewählte Märtyrerakten*, 3, neubearb. Auflage von G. Krüger (Tübingen, 1929) 22, 32ff.

10. Ibid. 24, 23ff.

11. *Sts Perpetua and Felicity:* never 'Jesus' alone; instead we find 'Christ', 'Jesus Christ', 'our Lord Jesus Christ'.
    Pionius: never 'Jesus' alone, but 'the Lord Jesus' (xi, 9), or 'Jesus Christ' with different titles. 'He had been praying in a low voice and when he came to the end of his prayer he looked up. While the flames were rising higher and higher he said the final "Amen" with a face reflecting joy. Then he said, "O *Lord*, receive my soul" ' (xxi, 9; p. 56).
    Acacius: 'Marcianus said, "Who is the son of God?" Acacius replied, "The Word of truth and grace." Marcianus asked if that were his name and Acacius responded, "You did not question me about his name but about his prerogative of sonship." "Explain his name," demanded Marcianus. Acacius said, "He is called Jesus Christ" ' (iv, 59, On the question of authenticity see H. Delehaye, *Analecta Bollandiana* 33 (1914) 346.
    Eugenia: 'The venerable bishop Helenus said, "I thank you, good Jesus" ' (vii; PL 73:610A). Eugenia herself says, 'My Lord Jesus Christ', and then, addressing God the Father, 'Your son, my Lord Jesus Christ' (xiv; PL 73:613D).

Carpus answers: 'Because of the religion and the name of my Lord Jesus Christ I cannot cooperate with you' (Knopf-Krüger, 9:10ff).

Pamphilus, a companion of Carpus: 'Looking up to heaven he said, "I thank you, Lord Jesus, because when I was a vessel of dishonor you made me a vessel of honor according to your good pleasure" ' (Ibid., 9:34ff).

Agathonice, a companion of Carpus and Pamphilus: 'when the torch was put to the faggots the servant of God cried out three times, "Lord Jesus Christ, save me because it is for you that I suffer". And after these words she gave up her spirit' (Ibid., 10:34ff).

Conon, who was from Nazareth and a compatriot and distant relative of Jesus: 'as for me, I obey the great king, the Christ' (iii, 3; Knopf-Krüger, 65:16). He always says 'the Christ' except in vi, 4: 'Lord Jesus Christ, receive my soul' (Ibid., 66:27ff).

Montanus and Lucius (Knopf-Krüger, 74-82): always 'Christ'. In xxiii, 3 (82:20): 'Our Lord Jesus Christ'.

Marian and Jacob (Knopf-Krüger, 86-87): 'The Christ my God' (ii, 4); 'my Lord Jesus Christ, son of the living God' (ii, 6); 'the Christ, my Lord' (ii, 10). Never simply 'Jesus'.

Euplus or Euplius (Knopf-Krüger, 100-101): '...this my Lord Jesus Christ knows also' (i, 2). 'By my Lord Jesus Christ, the son of God' (i, 4). 'While they tortured him Euplus said, "Thanks be to you, O Christ; keep me who suffer this for you" (ii, 3). "Thanks be to you, O Christ; Christ help me; for you I suffer this, O Christ," these phrases he repeated often. When his strength was gone his lips moved without a sound, repeating the prayers' (iii, 3). After telling us this the author comments, 'Euplus was always joyful and he said continaully, "Thanks be to Christ God." '

Crispina (Knopf-Krüger, 109-111): always 'our Lord Jesus Christ' or 'my Lord Jesus Christ'. 'I have never sacrificed nor will I offer sacrifice except to our one, true Lord Jesus Christ, his son, who was born and who suffered' (i, 3). 'The living and true God who is my Lord...my Lord Jesus Christ.... For the name of our Lord Jesus Christ she bared her neck and was decapitated' (i, 6).

Irenaeus of Sirmium (Knopf-Krüger, 103-104): 'my Lord Jesus Christ' (iv, 6). 'I thank you, Lord Jesus Christ' (v. 2). 'Lord Jesus Christ who have willed to suffer for the salvation of the world, may your heavens open and may your angels bring in the soul of your servant, Irenaeus, who bears these sufferings for your name and for your people. I implore you, I beg for your mercy, that you might receive me and strengthen these people in their faith' (v, 4).

Saint Julius, martyred at Dorostor in Moesia (Knopf-Krüger, 105-106): always 'Christ' or 'Lord'. 'Christ himself, the same who is God' (iii, 4). '...he exposed his neck to the sword and said, "Lord Jesus Christ, for your name I am about to die; I pray you, graciously receive my soul with all your holy martyrs" ' (iv, 4).

St Felix of Tibiscus (Knopf-Krüger, 113-116): 'Christ' or 'Jeus Christ' or 'Lord Jesus Christ' or 'our Lord Jesus Christ'. Never 'Jesus' alone.

Claude, Aster, and companions (Knopf-Krüger, 106-109): always 'Christ'.

Testament of the Forty Martyrs of Sebaste (Knopf-Krüger, 116-119). Never 'Jesus'. Often 'Christ'. Once: 'We the forty martyrs of the Lord Jesus Christ' (iii, 4).

St Acacius of Cappadocia (PG 115): 'My Lord Jesus Christ' (220A, 228B). 'The name dear to me and to all my fellowmen, *Christian*' (220D). 'Our Lord Jesus Christ' (221C, 224A). 'Jesus Christ, help me, your wretched servant; Lord do not abandon me' (228A). 'Lord Jesus Christ' (228B). 'My Christ' (228D). The following prayers of St Acacius are also noteworthy:

He began to pray to the Lord in these words: 'Glory to you who deal mercifully with those who love your name. Glory to you who have called me, a sinner, to such a testing. Glory to you, Jesus, who know the weakness of our flesh and who give me strength to endure my torments. You see, O Lord, the multitude of evils that weigh me down so that my soul is on the point of leaving the body. Therefore, O Lord and Master (Deposta Kyrie), *send me a healing angel to heal me of my wounds and the accompanying misery, and make it happen somehow that the judge's verdict may put me out of my pain to be with you in peace, for to you belong power and glory forever. Amen '* (229D).

Ten men took turns striking him and the martyr cried out in his torments, 'O Christ, help your miserable servant.' Whereupon the judge angrily ordered them to strike him in the stomach. In his pain the blessed martyr cried in a loud voice, 'Lord Jesus Christ, help your servant ' (236D).

When the servant of God realized that his mission had been accomplished he cried out under the impulse of the Holy Spirit, 'With innumerable voices I bless you, O Christ, author of life, son of the living God, for showing mercy and patience towards me, a sinner, whom you permitted to have such a destiny as this ' (237D).

Before he died, Acacius asked for another delay in order to pray. Kneeling down he said, 'Glory to you, O God....Blessed be your glorious name, O Lord. Give grace and pardon to those who call upon your name, O Lord....Receive, O Lord Jesus Christ, my soul as well ' (240A).

Only once did Acacius use 'Jesus' all alone: when he referred to the One who had to be like his brothers in all things in order to show them mercy.

Sabas the Goth (Knopf-Kruger, 119-124): 'Our Lord Jesus Christ' (i, 1); 'our God and saviour, Jesus Christ' (i, 1); 'our saviour and Lord, Jesus Christ' (i, 3). Upon being condemned to die, Sabas cried out in the joy of the Holy Spirit: 'Blessed are you, O Lord, and may your name be glorified, *O Jesus*, forever, Amen! Atharides has condemned himself to eternal death and perdition but he has sent me to the life that lasts forever, for such has been your good pleasure towards your servants, O Lord our God' (vii, 3).

12.   In *Griechischen christlichen Schriftsteller* 3 vols. (Leipzig, 1903-1909).

13.   L. Jalabert and R. Mouterde, *Incriptions grecques et latines de la Syrie* (Paris 1929-1955).

14.   See E. Peterson, 'Jüdisches und christiches Morgengebet in Syrien', *Zeitschrift für Theologie und Kirche* 58 (1934) 110.

15.   See the following numbers: 223,1; 281,1; 285,7; 291,3; 295; 322A; 328A; 355B; 363; 364; 369; 378; 380; 392; 400; 412; 414; 415; 421; 431; 441; 457; 458; 489; 525, 2-3; 526; 552; 562; 572; 573, 1; 609; 613; 616; 627; 634; 642; 651; 653; 675; 679; 694; 1234.

16.   No. 382. On the formula 'One God, the helper (*boethon*)' see E. Peterson, *Eis Theos* (Göttingen, 1926). These questions lie outside our subject. Jalabert and Mouterde, *Inscriptions* list in their index of names twenty-six instances of the formula 'One God and his Christ'.

17.   See Peterson, *Eis Theos*, 16; Jalabert and Mouterde, *Inscriptions*, no. 171, p. 152.

18.   F.J. Dölger, *ICHTHOUS*, 5 (Rome-Münster, 1910-1927, 2nd ed. Münster, 1928-1943).

19.   Thus far only Fascicle I has appeared (Paris, 1922).

20.   A. Boeckh, ed., 5 vols.

21.   See G. Schlumberger, *Sigillographie de l'Empire Byzantin* (Paris, 1844), 35.

22.   For instance, V. Laurent, *Documents de Sigillographie: La Collection C. Orghidan* (Paris, 1952).

23.   Compare St Jerome, *Comm in Mt 12:13*; PL 26:78B.

24.   *Logos de saint Jean le Théologien sur la dormition de la sainte Theotokos* in C. Tischendorf, *Apocalypses Apocryphae* (Leipzig, 1866); or in De Santos Otero, *Los evangelios apócrifos* (Madrid, 1956) 622.

25.   *Acta Xantippae et Polyxenae* xii, in *Texts and Studies* Vol. II, n. 3 (1893) 73.

26.   Ibid., xxviii, p. 78.

27.   A. Wilmart and E. Tisserant, eds., 'Evangile de Barthelemy', IV, 9, *Revue Biblique* (1913) 328.

28.   De Santos Otero, *Evangelios*, 603.

29.   See N. Moricca, *Revue Biblique* (1922) 20.

30.   De Santos Otero, *Evangelios*, 607.

31.   Tischendorf, *Evangelia Apocrypha* (1853) 442.

32.   *Logos of St John the Theologian* in De Santos Otero, *Evangelios*, 621.
The subsequent quotes are taken from this work, pp. 621-638.

33.   M. Jugie, *Homélies Mariales Byzantines X* in *Patr. Orient.* XIX,
384:26; 385:24; from the *Dormitio Dominae Nostrae Deiparae* by John of
Thessalonica.

34.   De Santos Otero, *Evangelios*, 255; Tischendorf, *Evangelia*, 102.

35.   See M. Asin Palacios, *Logia et Agrapha Domini Jesu apud moslemicos
scriptores,* in *Patrologia Orientalis* XIII, 335-341.

36.   Ed. Max Bonnet (Leipzig, 1883).

37.   There is an 1871 edition by W. Wright and an 1892 edition by F.C.
Burkitt (Paris).

38.   See Th. Nöldeke, *Kurzgefasste syrische Grammatik* (1898), 275, no.
350B.
39.   See the edition of R. Lipsius and M. Bonnet, *Acta apostolorum
apocrypha* (1903) Vol. II, pp. 1-127.

40.   Ibid., no. 2; p. 47:7.

41.   Ed. M. Bonnet (Leipzig, 1893) pp. 65-116.

42.   Lipsius and Bonnet, *Acta*, I, pp. 1-22.

43.   Ibid., 23ff.

44.   Ibid., pp. 45-103. The variants are: 'Father of your holy son, Jesus
Christ', 'You, Lord Jesus Christ', 'O God, Jesus Christ', 'the Lord Jesus
our God', 'The Christ Jesus', 'to believe in the name of Jesus Christ, son of
God', 'Jesus Christ'.

45.   Ibid., pp. 118-177. Here the variants are: 'We have only one Lord,
Jesus Christ', 'in Christ Jesus our Lord'."Who is your Lord?"'Peter replied,
"Jesus Christ." ' In one place, p. 170:10, the Latin translation has 'my Lord

Jesus Christ' where the Greek has 'our Lord'.

46.   Ibid., pp. 235-272.

47.   Page references are to the Lipsius-Bonnet edition.

48.   See Un moine de l'Eglise d'Orient, 'La Prière de Jésus', *Irénikon* (Chevetogne, 3rd ed., 1959) 69.

49.   'Threnody of the Virgin' in N.V. Tomadakis, ed., *Romain le Mélode* (Athens, 1954) 156-172.

50.   G. Camelli, *Romain le Mélode*, (Florence, 1930) 88-118.

51.   The following page numbers refer to the Venice edition of 1763.

52.   The following should also be noted:
Mary always says, 'My son and my God' (121, 124).
The famous *Phos Hilaron*, ascribed to Sophronia of Jerusalem or to Athenogene the martyr, contains this phrase: 'Jesus Christ,...it is right to sing hymns at all times, O son of God, lifegiver. That is why the whole universe glorifies you' (131).
The Great Compline: 'O God be propitious to us sinners and have mercy on us' (147).
The Prayer of Manasses (152).
The *Te Deum*: 'Lord, only son, Jesus Christ' (154).
An eleventh century prayer of Paul Evergetinos: 'Your only son, our Lord, God, and Saviour Jesus Christ' (160).
'Sovereign, most merciful Lord, Jesus Christ our God' (162).

53.   J. Ziegler, *Dulcedo Dei* (Münster, 1937).

54.   *Letter to Diognetus* x, 3; H.J. Marrou, ed., *Sources Chrétiennes* 33 (Paris, 1951).

55.   This is the title of an article by S. Salaville in *Revue d'ascétique et de mystique*, 25 (1949) 247-259.

56.   For the 'Prayer of Manasses' see the *Grand Apodeipnon* (Venice, 1763) 152-153.

57.   S. Salaville, 'Office du Très Doux Jésus', *Revue d'ascétique et de mystique*, 25:258.

58.   Quoted by S. Salaville, 'Office', 258.

59. S. Gassisi, 'Gleichzeilige Hymnen in der byzantinischen Liturgie', *Byzantinische Zeitschrift* 17 (1909) 347-348.

60. Diadochus of Photice, *One Hundred Gnostic Chapters*, chaps. 15, 44, 63, 90; E. des Places, ed., *Sources Chrétiennes*, 5 bis (Paris, 1955).

61. See S. Salaville, 'Christus in Orientalium Pietate', *Ephemerides Liturgicae*, 52 (1938) 234.

62. PG 26:833-834. The passage quoted is from col. 860:10.

63. L. Th. A. Lorie, 'Spiritual Terminology in the Latin Translations of the *Vita Antonii*', *Latinitas Christianorum Primaeva*, 11 (Noviomagi, 1955).

64. See S. Damasi Papae, *Carmen IV de Nomine Jesu; V De Eodem* (acrostics and telestichs); *VI De Cognomentis Salvatoris*; PL 13:378.

65. See G. Garitte, *Un Temoin important du texte de la Vie de S. Antoine par S. Athanase*, (Brussels-Rome, 1939) 26.

66. A. Moulard, *Saint Jean Chrysostome* (Paris, 1941) 108.

67. Cited by Moulard, ibid.

68. St John Chrysostom, *Im Matth.;* PG 58:700; Moulard, *Chrysostome*, 109.

69. I. Hausherr, *Penthos, La Doctrine de la componction dans l'orient chrétien*, (Rome, 1944) 60. See Theodoret, *De Divina et Sancta Charitate;* PG 92:1497-1521.

70. PG 65:217.

71. *S. Silviae Peregrinatio*, P. Geyer, ed., *Corpus scriptorum ecclesiasticorum latinorum* 39 (1848) no. 24, p. 74; no. 36, p. 87; no. 37, p. 89.

72. R. Raabe, *Petrus der Iberer* (Leipzig, 1895) 31.

73. See *S. Silviae Peregrinatio*, Geyer, ed., no. 47, p. 99.

74. See, for instance, James of Sarough, *Homiliae Selectae*, P. Bedjan, ed., (5 vols., Paris-Leipzig, 1905-1910) IV, 60, verse 3.

75. French translation by E. Lemoine, *Homélies* (Paris, 1956) 52.

76. Bedjan, *Homiliae*, III, 582.

77.   Ibid., II, 428-446 and V, 658-680.

78.   *Sancti Ephrem Syri Opera Omnia* (Rome, 1743) Vol. 2, pp. 2-20.

79.   Pars II, p. 747D.

80.   PG 115:76A.

81.   *Paraenesis* 17, *Sancti Ephrem Opera* (Rome, 1732-1746), Vol. II, p. 93E. Subsequent page references are to the same volume.

82.   *In mulierem peccatricem, Sancti Ephrem Opera*, Vol. II, p. 303.

83.   *In quadraginta martyres, Sancti Ephrem Opera*, II, 346C.

84.   Citing the Rome edition, *Sancti Ephrem Opera:*
In Vol. I:
    19E-22E: Self-accusation, confession.
    28E: Note the following in a contrition sermon: 'Let us cry out in the words of the blind man, "Have mercy on me, son of God the most high." '
    37E: 'Let a psalm be always in your mouth because the name of God drives away demons.' The psalm seems to have the same effect as the Jesus Prayer.
    53F: 'Weep before him day and night.'
    58A: Prayer oriented to contrition.
    63F-66A: The same.
    68AB: A short prayer to be recited with sighs and tears.
    69D-70C: A long prayer for forgiveness to be recited with tearful contrition.
    110F-111C: Prayer of the same sort: 'Lord Jesus Christ, King of Kings.'
    145E-147E: 'Lord, son of God....'
    153EF: 'God most high, only immortal one, give to this sinner....'
    154A-156C: Prayer for contrition, breaking into an apostrophe to a sinner.
    158B-D: 'Save me, O my Master, save me, son of God, sinless Christ.'
    161A-E: Contrition; always *Huie, Christe, Kyrie.*
    171D-F: *Christe,* Son of God, Lord.
    184C-185A: A prayer interrupted by a parenthesis: 'O *Despota,* Christ Saviour, see the fountains of our tears.'
    187B-F: 'I have sinned against heaven....'
    193-197A: 'How the soul should pray, weeping....' Always *Kyrie* and *Despota.*
    197B: A prayer that turns into a sermon.
    199A-201C: Reconciliation of penitents.
    255C: Prayer oriented to contrition.
    256F-258B: The same; *Kyrie Iesou Christe.*
    258A: *Soter tou kosmou.*

298B-299B: Especially 298C: *Despota Iesou Huie tou theou.*

302A-D: Prayer oriented to contrition.

315B: Prayer of a sick man for health of body and soul: 'Lord Jesus Christ....'

In Vol. III:

19-21: Brief treatise on continual prayer which mentions nothing about short prayers.

82C: A four-line prayer to the 'merciful Lord'.

91E-92F: Prayer oriented to contrition; always *Kyrie.*

93E: 'Present yourself always like the sacrificial ox.'

94C: 'O monk, present your heart like the [sacrificial] ox' (cf. Ps 27:14).

97F-98B: The first verse of the *Miserere* paraphrased in prayer.

99F: 'Pray like Hannah, the mother of Samuel.'

100E-101: To 'meditate' Scripture: *mnemoneuein, meletan.*

101D: To repeat the verses 'within your heart'.

101E: A prayer before reading: *Kyrie Iesou Christe.*

126A-127C: A prayer oriented to contrition which begins with the prayer of the publican.

142E-143A: Universal *penthos* at the time of the parousia.

155F: *Melete.*

222S: Advice for praying without distraction.

222F: The blind men: *eleeson emas Huie David.*

223B: The Canaanite woman: *eleeson me Kyrie.*

224B: Not to petition relentlessly (*apotomos*). See St Nilus, *De Oratione,* 34.

225D: Models of prayers to be said for different purposes.

229B-E: Prayer oriented to contrition.

231E: Same as 99F.

234: Same as 102E.

248A-E: A prayer to the crucified Saviour in litany form, with *doxa soe.*

251E: Prayer to the martyrs, full of compunction.

253E: The same again.

256BD: Another prayer of compunction.

311E: 'O Jesus Christ, save those who have perished.' Grief-stricken plea.

354: Martha and Mary: the primacy of prayer.

372: 'Sign all the members of the body with the sign of the cross'. This practice is mentioned more than once.

379E: 'O Sovereign (*Despota*), son of God.'

394D-395: Prayer of the sinful woman. This occurs elsewhere too.

436-438: Same as 262.

439-455: Self-accusation with a list of 'my vices'.

455-458: On prayer. Notice 457F: 'Be propitious (*hilastheti*) to me a sinner.'

482: A prayer: 'O just and praiseworthy God....'

483: A prayer: 'O Sovereign Lord (*Despota Kyrie*), God of heaven and

earth, King of the ages....'
   484: A prayer: 'Lord King, heavenly Paraclete....'
   485: Prayer for a happy death.
   486: A prayer: 'Lord Jesus Christ, son of God....'

The remainder of the volume consists primarily of prayers. Notice especially the following pages: 487, 489B, 489E, 490A, 490C, 492, 497C, 502D, 507E, 512E, 516D, 520; 521; 523DE, 524, 524E, 526C, 528B, 532D, 536B, 539C, 543C, 545D, 548A, 551. Latin translations begin on page 552. Note that the prayers to the Blessed Virgin Mary always address her by her most glorious titles. These prayers are second to none in self-accusations.

85.   R. Raabe, *Petrus der Iberer* (Leipzig, 1895), 35-36 (from the Syriac text).

86.   Ibid., 110.

87.   Ibid., 27.

88.   Abba Isaiah was held in renown by orthodox Nestorians as well as by Monophysites. See 'L'imitation de Jésus-Christ dans la spiritualité byzantine', *Mélanges F. Cavallera* (Toulouse, 1948) 237ff.

89.   *Logos* 21, no. 5; Augoustinos, ed., *Isaie* (Jerusalem, 1911).

90.   *Logos* 16; Augoustinos, p. 90. See also the text published by F. Nau in *Patrologia Orientalis* VIII, 104.

91.   *Logos* 18, no. 3; Augoustinos, 90; PG 40:1155B.

92.   *Logos* 13, no. 3; Augoustinos, 76; see also *Mélanges Cavallera*, 242ff.

93.   Latin translation PG 40:1138B.

94.   A Latin translation was published in 1754 by Pierre François Zinus (Venice, de Vérone). The *Precepts and Counsels to Novices* (Augoustinos, 209-217) had already been included by St Benedict of Aniane in his *Codex Regularum*, PL 103: 427-434. On the popularity of Abba Isaiah see Antoine Guillaumont, *L'Ascéticon copte de l'abbé Isaïe* (Cairo, 1956).

95.   See A. Baumstark, *Gerschichte der syrischen Literatur* (Bonn, 1922) 225ff.

96.   See R. Bidawid, *Les Lettres du Patriarche nestorien Timothée I* (Rome, 1956) 83.

97.   I. Hausherr, 'Dogme et spiritualité orientale', *Revue d'ascétique et de mystique*, 23 (1947) 24.

98.   See Hausherr, *Penthos*, 149ff; and B. Schultz, 'Untersuchungen über das Jesus-Gebet', *Orientalia Christiana Periodica*, 18 (1952) 339-343.

99.   PG 86:858C, 857C.

100.   Un moine de l'Eglish d'Orient, 'La Prière de Jésus,' *Irénikon* (Chevetogne, 3rd ed., 1959) 69.

101.   Irenaeus, *Adv Haer* I, 1, 1; W. Harvey, ed., (Cambridge, 1949) 12:1-2.

102.   Origen, *Sel Ps 4*, 2; PG 12:1136C.

PART TWO

CALLING ON THE NAME OF THE LORD

CHAPTER THREE

WAYS OF CONTINUAL PRAYER

MEANING AND PURPOSE OF THE JESUS PRAYER

C ALLING on the name of Jesus does not mean simply pronouncing the name 'Jesus' in prayer or directing a prayer explicitly to Jesus. There are some who say his name but who do not pray in his name. As St Augustine has said, no one can be praying in the name of the Saviour who prays for something opposed to salvation. Besides, the Lord has several names, as we have seen, and it is not the name 'Jesus' that the faithful usually give him when they speak about him. Should we expect that they will use it more often when they are praying to him?

The meaning of the phrase 'calling on the name of the Lord' or 'calling on the name of our Lord Jesus Christ' as found in St Paul has been studied many times and commented on at length. As a sample it will be enough to quote the judgment of Père Allo: 'It means that one adores Christ as he adores God, and this in spite of the irreproachable monotheism of St Paul and of his readers.'[1]

But there have been people who took this expression in a very literal and more or less magical sense, even very early in the history of the church. We read in Acts:

Some of the Jewish exorcists who travelled about the country tried to invoke the name of the Lord Jesus on

119

> *those who were possessed, saying, 'I adjure you by*
> *Jesus whom Paul preaches....' The evil spirit answered,*
> *'Jesus I know and Paul I know, but who are you?' (Ac*
> *19:13-16)*

These exorcists got no thanks for their efforts, as St Luke
goes on to relate. But the report of these unfortunate
attempts to invoke the name of Jesus had the unexpected
result that 'the name of the Lord Jesus came to be held in
great honor' (Ac 19:17). It did the Jewish exorcists no good to
pronounce the holy name because they did not regard Jesus
as Lord.

The exorcists in question, who learned at their own
expense the consequences of a faulty philosophy of the name,
were the seven sons of the high priest, Sceva (Ac 19:14). It is
not surprising that in later times others, less well educated,
would make the same mistake. Throughout the history of the
Church it has been necessary to correct aberrations in this
matter caused by well-meaning but poorly instructed souls.

At the beginning of his *Longer Rule* St Basil made this
point:

> *But if someone claims that it is written: 'Whoever calls*
> *upon the name of the Lord will be saved' (Jl 2:32; Ac*
> *2:21), and that therefore a Christian need only invoke*
> *the name of God to be saved, let him read what the*
> *Apostle has said: 'How can they call upon him if they*
> *do not believe in him' (Rom 10:14). And besides this*
> *there are the words of the Lord himself: 'Not everyone*
> *who says, "Lord, Lord", will enter the kingdom of*
> *heaven, but only he who does the will of my Father who*
> *is in heaven' (Mt 7:21). Moreover, if someone is doing*
> *the will of the Lord and does not do it exactly in the*
> *way God has ordained or does not do it out of the*
> *proper motive of love for God, then all the effort he*
> *puts into the action is useless, as Jesus Christ himself*
> *has said in his gospel: 'Hypocrites do these things so as*

*to be seen by men; I tell you truthfully, they have
already received their reward' (Mt 6:16). It was in this
divine school that St Paul learned the lesson which he
taught when he said: 'If I give away all my possessions
to feed the poor and give my body to be burned, but
lack charity it profits me nothing' (I Cor 13:3).* [2]

And how much less profit it would be simply to cry
'Jesus, Jesus!' without adding 'Lord' or another title to
express the faith that is on one's lips or in one's heart.
Warnings such as we find in St Basil could be duplicated in
the writings of the Western fathers. St Augustine was even
more forceful than Basil:

*When the scripture says 'In my name', it does not refer
to the letters and syllables of a word but to the meaning
which these normally and truly signify. Consequently
those who believe something about Christ which should
not be believed about the only son of God are not really
praying in his name even if they faithfully pronounce
the letters and syllables of the name* Christus. *Everyone
prays in the name of what he believes when he prays.* [3]

The important thing is not so much the name that is used
but the intention behind the use of it or the goal that is
sought by means of that name. Now the Jesus Prayer has a
number of special characteristics. They may be listed as
follows:

1. It is short.
2. It is meant to be repeated frequently.
3. It is addressed to Jesus Christ.
4. It gives him several different titles.
5. It implores his mercy.
6. It calls the suppliant a sinner.
7. It constitutes a 'secret occupation', as it is called.
8. Above all it is a means for attaining the goal of every

interior life, communion with God in continual prayer.

It is the last of these characteristics that gives meaning to all the others and so it is to the last element that we should first direct our attention—*quod ultimum est in executione, primum est in intentione*. This should give us a perspective from which to see the whole question clearly.

A brief examination of representative sources will show that there is complete unanimity, from Cassian to *The Way of a Pilgrim*, about the fact that the ultimate goal truly is continual prayer or union with God through continual prayer.

In Cassian, Abba Moses makes a distinction between the ultimate goal (*telos*) and the immediate end (*skopos*) which must be reached to attain the goal. The goal is the kingdom of heaven, but the immediate end 'which if pursued without faltering will lead us to our goal' is said to be 'purity of heart, without which it is impossible to reach the ultimate goal.'[4] Pure and continual prayer is at the same time the cause and the effect of purity of heart. Cassian wrote:

> *The monk's goal and the perfection of his soul consist in uninterrupted perseverance in prayer. It is an attempt to attain perfect purity and tranquillity of mind as much as is possible for human weakness. This is why we undertake manual labor and practise compunction of heart in every form with unremitting zeal. There is a mutual and indissoluble bond between these things, for the whole arch of the virtues has but one purpose, the attainment of perfect prayer, and without this keystone which unites the different parts into a self-supporting whole the structure would have neither solidity nor durability. On the one hand the perpetual tranquillity of prayer we are discussing could neither be attained nor brought to perfection without the virtues, but on the other hand the virtues which serve as its foundation could not reach their own perfection without it.[5]*

The kingdom of heaven, purity of heart, pure and continual prayer, beatitude—these are merely different names or aspects of the infinitely rich reality of charity, which is not only a reflection of the love which God is, but is also a real participation in it. This is the christian realization of the perennial human dream of 'becoming like God as much as possible'.[6]

Cassian continued:

> *It is then that we shall see the fulfillment of our Saviour's prayer to the Father for his disciples: 'May the love with which you have loved me be in them and they in us.... May they be one as you, Father, are in me and I in you, may they also be one in us' (Jn 17:21, 26). That perfect love wherewith 'God has first loved us' will come about in our hearts through the fulfillment of this prayer of the Lord, and our faith tells us that his prayers cannot be in vain. These are the signs that will accompany the fulfillment: God will be our whole love and desire, our whole study and labor, our whole thought, our whole life, our speaking and our breathing. The unity which exists between the Father and the Son will be communicated to our soul and emotions. Just as God loves us with a true and pure and unfailing charity, so we will be united to him by the indissoluble unity of constant love. We will be so attached to him that our whole yearning and thinking and speaking will be about him alone.*
>
> *Thus we will gradually come to that goal which we have mentioned and which the Lord desired for us when he prayed, 'May they all be one as we are one, I in them and you in me, may they be made perfectly one.... Father, I wish that where I am they also may be whom you have given me' (Jn 17:24).*
>
> *This should be the hermit's goal and the object of all his efforts: to merit to possess already in this life and in his mortal body a preview of future blessedness and a*

foretaste of the glorious life of heaven. Such, I repeat, is the summit of all perfection, when the soul is so free of carnal attachments that it can rise daily to the lofty realms of the spirit, until its whole life and every stirring of its heart becomes one continual prayer.[7]

The early monks did not flock to the desert to pursue chimeras and to live in misery, nor even simply to immolate themselves for the glory of God, but in order to concentrate all their inner powers on the achievement of a single goal, the love and service of God. They tried to free themselves from the innumerable worries that can eat away all spiritual vitality at its roots, and they tried to have instead one sole concern, that of attaining a state of total interior integration and wholeness which is literally health or salvation (*soteria*), the well-being and joy that comes from living for the greater honor and glory of one's maker.[8]

Many centuries later, in *The Way of a Pilgrim*, the very same ambition was expressed by a 'Russian pilgrim of interior prayer'. Or rather, the Pilgrim demonstrated the realization of these ambitions in his own life brought about by nothing other than his famous prayer leading to a blessed state of continual prayer and union with God. In the Pilgrim's words:

I am by my own deeds a great sinner but by God's grace a Christian....

On the twenty-fourth Sunday after Pentecost I went to the Church for the Liturgy. The reading was from the first epistle of Paul to the Thessalonians and it contained the command, 'Pray without ceasing' (1 Th 5:17). The words stuck in my mind and I began to ponder how it was possible to pray without ceasing since a man is obliged to do very many other things....

I thought to myself, What shall I do? Where can I find someone who will teach me? I decided to visit all the churches that were renowned for their preaching, in the hope of hearing something that would make things clear for me. This is what I did, and I heard many excellent sermons on prayer telling what prayer is and how necessary it is and what are the fruits of prayer. But no one told me how I could pray unceasingly. I did hear one sermon on continual and uninterrupted prayer but nothing was said about the means to reach that state. And so I stopped going to public sermons because I could not find in them what I was looking for. I decided instead to search with God's help for a man of great learning and experience who could teach me privately how to obtain what my heart longed for so desperately.

So I began to travel far and wide, always reading my Bible and inquiring everywhere whether there was a wise and holy spiritual guide in the vicinity.

One day I was told that in the country on a certain estate there lived a man who had for a long time been seeking the salvation of his soul. He had a chapel there and never left the property. All day he prayed and read devout books. Without delay I went there and found the man. 'What do you want from me?' he asked. I replied, 'I have heard that you are a man of sound judgment who fears God. I beg you in God's name to explain to me the hidden meaning of the Apostle's words, "Pray without ceasing." How is it possible to pray continually? I want with all my heart to learn how, but nowhere have I found anyone who can teach me.'

The man gazed at me for a long time before speaking and then he said: 'Continual interior prayer is the spontaneous leaping forth of man's spirit towards God. You have to pray to God to enlighten you about the means by which the spirit may accomplish this activity. Pray hard and fervently; prayer itself will reveal to you how it can be prolonged unceasingly. But this will take much time.'9

Many other men in preceding centuries had asked
themselves the same question the Pilgrim asked. And the
answers given have varied widely. It was from this very
search for continual prayer that the Jesus Prayer was born. In
order to understand and appreciate and situate this prayer we
will have to accompany that search, discover its guiding
principles and observe the results which it has produced.
Then the Pilgrim of nineteenth-century Russia will no longer
look like an eccentric or a dropout who is trying to live in a
dream world in order to compensate for his inability to cope
with reality. He will appear instead as the heir of a tradition
as ancient as Christianity itself, and one which counts among
its numbers some of the finest men who have ever lived.

ACTS OF PRAYER

Orthodox biblical exegesis has never, it seems, interpreted
as mere hyperbole the commandment to pray always. The
exegetes disagree only about the meaning of the two words,
'pray' and 'always'.

Among the early Christians it was the heretical sect of the
Messalians who took the words in their most literal sense
without any attempt to introduce distinctions. 'To pray,' they
reasoned, meant to say prayers, either aloud or mentally.
And 'always' meant never to do anything but pray. Hence
their name, 'the praying ones' (Syriac: *Mesaliane*; Greek:
Euchetai; Latin: *Precatores*). They were predictably unsuc-
cessful in maintaining their literal observance. Almost from
the beginning they stretched the concept of prayer to include
all spiritual occupations such as reading. Nor did they refuse
to eat or sleep, but they did refuse all forms of worldly
occupation, especially manual labor. They believed that the
Lord had condemned manual labor with the words, 'Do not
labor for bread that perishes' (Jn 6:27). Convinced of this
they felt that they, as perfect Christians, had the right to
receive the necessities of life from other Christians, who were

called 'the just' in their *Book of Degrees*,[10] and who were
excluded from perfection because they did not know how to
practise 'the great commandments'. Faced with pretensions
like these, their adversaries could employ a wide range of
tactics. The quickest way to reach them proved to be through
the stomach. The *Apophthegmata* record this incident:

> *A brother came to the monastery of Abba Sylvanus and*
> *when he saw all the brethren at work he said to the*
> *elder, 'Do not labor for the bread that perishes. Mary*
> *has chosen the better part.' At this the elder called a*
> *disciple and said, 'Zachary, give this brother a book and*
> *show him to an empty cell.' The ninth hour, which was*
> *the hour for dinner, came and passed. The guest was*
> *intently watching his door to see if someone would*
> *come and get him for dinner, but no one called him. At*
> *length he rose and went to find the elder. 'Abba,' he*
> *said, 'are the brethren fasting today?' 'No, they have all*
> *eaten,' replied the elder. 'Why wasn't I invited?'*
> *'Because,' answered the elder, 'you are a spiritual*
> *person and have no need of bodily nourishment. But*
> *we, carnal as we are, are obliged to eat and this is why*
> *we work. You, however, have chosen the better part;*
> *you read all day long and have no desire for bodily*
> *nourishment.' At these words the man made a*
> *prostration and said, 'I beg your pardon, Abba.' The*
> *elder pardoned him and concluded his lesson with the*
> *words, 'That is how Mary herself stands in need of*
> *Martha. It was because of Martha that Mary could*
> *receive her praise.'*[11]

Even the illustrious John Colobos [the Dwarf] had to be
taught a lesson like this, and it was his elder brother who did
it for him:

> *John said to his brother one day, 'I desire to be*
> *perfectly free from care* (amerimnos) *like the angels;*

*they never work and are satisfied to serve God
unceasingly.' Accordingly, he took his cloak and went
deep into the desert. One week later he came back to
his brother. When he knocked on the door his brother,
without opening, shouted to him, 'Who's there?' 'It's
your brother John,' was the answer. 'John has become
an angel,' was the reply, 'and he no longer associates
with men.' In vain John repeated, 'It is I.' His brother
would not let him in and made him stand outside in the
cold all night. Finally he opened the door and said to
John, 'You are only a man after all, and you must learn
to work for your living.' Thereupon John prostrated
before him and begged for pardon.* [12]

St Augustine too, in his book *De Opere Monachorum*, was
obliged to deal with quixotic and disedifying conduct of this
sort. [13] These and many other indications suggest that in
practice the Messalians were not easy to convince. And this
was not only because of their love of leisure but even more
because of their determination to achieve the continual prayer
which they believed necessary for salvation and for
perfection. Their adversaries—not always easy to distinguish
from their partisans—implicitly or explicitly admitted the
validity of their cardinal principle and were opposed to them
only on the question of the means and the manner of
applying the means. One of the more ingenious means by
which they attempted to pray continually was to have
someone else come and pray in their place at the times when
they were unable to pray for themselves. Despite its artful
naïvete, the practice attained an astonishing popularity in the
institution of the Acoemiti or 'sleepless ones'. But it had
already been tried and recorded in the *Apophthegmata*. Take
for example the following anecdote about Abba Lucius who
had the habit of reciting ejaculations while he worked:

*Once some Euchites came to visit Abba Lucius in the
Enaton, near Alexandria. When he asked them what*

*type of work they did, they replied, 'We never lift a
finger to do manual labor; instead we pray without
ceasing, in accordance with the Apostle's command.'
The Elder said to them, 'Don't you eat, then?' 'We do,'
they assured him. 'When you are eating, who prays in
your place?' No answer. He asked them another
question: 'When you are sleeping, who keeps up your
prayers?' They could give him no answer. Then he went
on: 'I beg your pardon, but you do not do what you say
you do. Let me show you how I manage to pray always
even when I busy myself at manual labor. I sit down
with my supply of palm fronds soaking beside me and
as I weave them together I say, with God's help, "Have
mercy on me, O God, according to your great goodness,
and wipe out my transgressions according to your
abundant mercy"* (Ps 51:1). *Tell me, is this not a
prayer?' They assured him that it was. Then he said:
'By working and praying like this all day long, I can
complete around sixteen baskets. I give away two of
these to any beggar who comes to my door. I make my
living from the rest. And the man who has received the
gift of two baskets prays for me while I am eating and
sleeping. That is how, by God's grace, I manage to
pray without ceasing.'*[14]

That, in short, is continual prayer attained by teamwork.
This was the principle that inspired the founder of the
Acoemeti, and it is essentially the same principle that under-
lies our [contemporary western] practice of perpetual
adoration or perpetual rosary.[15] But this was not a solution
that satisfied everyone even in the monastic milieu. The
command to pray continually was addressed to particular
individuals not to the Church as a whole or to moral persons
such as a monastery or confraternity. Besides, this solution
was concerned only with vocal prayer, which always entails
inconveniences and almost inevitably distractions.

St Thomas Aquinas had an opinion on this matter (II-II

83:13, *Utrum oratio debeat esse attenta*) which could be very consoling for us moderns who esteem the first two effects of prayer—merit and petition—far above the third—which is 'spiritual nourishment of the soul'. The ancient monks and hesychasts were striving to achieve conscious, actual union with God. And for that, says St Thomas, attention in prayer is strictly necessary. What these Christians were attempting was continual prayer on the third level of attention, which St Thomas explains as follows:

> *The third level is when the attention is directed toward the goal of prayer which is God and the thing being prayed for. This degree of attention is the most necessary, and it is within the reach of all, even the feebleminded. Sometimes this concentration of the mind on God is so intense that all other things are forgotten.*

St Thomas refers the reader to Hugh of St Victor (*Liber de modo orandi*, cap 2). He could also have quoted many Eastern authors, especially, and perhaps exclusively, Eastern monastic authors.

Apart from the monks and those, like St Basil and St Gregory Nazianzen, who wrote for a monastic audience, the verses of the New Testament on continual prayer have generally been given the interpretation which Origen gave them in his treatise on prayer. This was the earliest treatment of the subject in the East. According to Origen prayer is not interrupted by taking time out to perform good works or to obey God's commandments. He wrote:

> *The man who prays continually is the man who combines prayer with necessary works and works with prayer. This is the only way it seems possible to fulfill the precept of unceasing prayer. We have to envision the whole life of a pious Christian as one long prayer, and the exercise we commonly refer to as prayer is merely a part of this whole.* [16]

This teaching of the greatest of the Greek exegetes became also that of the greatest Latin exegete, St Augustine,[17] and of the earliest Syriac exegete, Aphraates.[18]

Their position must be clearly understood because it too is subject to misinterpretation. They saw the lives of Christians as made up of two distinct temporal sequences: moments of explicit prayer when time is devoted to nothing but prayer, and moments of implicit prayer when time is spent in doing good works which are themselves a form of prayer. What would be the proper proportion between the two elements? Origen said it is necessary to pray explicitly three times a day. In the course of time the practice of praying at fixed intervals evolved into the seven canonical hours of the divine office. Before the number came to be fixed at seven there were many variations. And even afterwards most of the saints believed that it was necessary to pray more often than seven times a day. Then there is also the question about the length of time that should be devoted to each of these privileged moments of prayer. And, most important, the question about the psychological influence that formal prayer must have on the hours of work in order for these to be justly considered periods of true, implicit prayer.

When St Basil, or someone using that name, said to his monks, 'Let your whole life be a time of prayer',[19] he was undoubtedly alluding to Origen's exegesis, but he was far from thinking that it would be enough for the monks to pray explicitly three times or even seven times a day and the rest of the time to give themselves to their various tasks without any thought of prayer. The psalmody and the kneeling have to be interrupted but the act of prayer does not. On these grounds the *Sermo de renunciatione saeculi* could be attributed to St Basil because it recommends offering 'secret prayers which God will see in secret and will reward on the great Day of the Lord'.[20]

Often the best interpretations of the Scriptures and the Fathers is that given by the lives of other Fathers. The *Vitae Patrum* deliberately excluded all Messalianism but did not reject a number of anecdotes which seem to lean very far in the direction of this heresy. For example, this is said of Abba Apollo of Scete: 'He never did manual labor but instead spent all his time saying over and over, "I have sinned as men will, but do Thou pardon me as God pardons." '[21] This Abba was trying to make up for forty years of his life spent without any prayer at all.

Even without such a motive monks were expected to pray more often than the canonical times. An example comes from a certain Palestinian monastery:

> *The Abba of this cenobium wrote to Epiphanius, Bishop of Cyprus, saying: 'Thanks to your prayers we have been faithful to our canonical hours. We never omit the office of terce, sext, none or vespers.' But the Bishop wrote back and reproached the monks in these terms: 'Evidently you are neglecting the remaining hours of the day which you spend without prayer. The true monk should have prayer and psalmody in his heart at all times without interruption.'[22]*

The *Verba Seniorum* gives a slightly different translation: 'The true monk should have prayer or at least psalmody in his heart at all times without interruption.' Book Twelve of the *Verba*, where this occurs, could be quoted at length in the same vein. It begins, quite properly, with the sayings of the St Arsenius, the perfect model of hesychasts:

> *It is told of Abba Arsenius that on Saturday evening, beginning with first vespers of Sunday, he stood with his back to the sun, lifted his hands to heaven, and prayed until the rising sun shone in his face on Sunday morning. Then he would sit down.[23]*

That does not imply, of course, that all the other nights he would go to bed for a good eight hours. It was the opinion of Arsenius that one hour of sleep should be enough for a monk who was serious about the spiritual struggle (see no. 13). His own practice, as Abba Daniel related, was to keep vigil throughout the night, and only when morning had come would he 'yield to nature and say "Now come, Sleep, you unprofitable servant," and then he would fall asleep for a short time, sitting down, and before long he would be up again' (no. 14). All day long he worked unceasingly at his weaving, praying all the while as was evident from the tears he continually shed (no. 41).

The example of this great champion of *hesychia* had more influence on monks than any amount of lengthy explanation. It is unfortunate that we have no record of what Arsenius' prayers were; he scrupulously guarded the secret of his rule of life (*politeia*). He must have had his own method, his own special formula, judging from what we know about many of his associates. It would have been, in the first place, a prayer oriented to contrition, since Arsenius was the unexcelled paragon of *penthos*. Those who came after him and wrote about prayer, such as the famous Abba Isaiah, could claim his authority for saying, 'Force yourself to say countless prayers.'[24] Or Hyperechios: 'The measure of prayer for a monk is to pray without measure.'[25] Or the anonymous author who recorded this aphorism: 'If a monk prays only at the times when he is standing at formal prayer, he does not pray at all.'[26] In briefer form: 'To pray only at the appointed hours of prayer is not to pray at all.'[27]

All these authors, following the Origenist tradition, admitted the validity of implicit prayer. They seem though to have been distrustful of it, granting it only grudgingly as a poor substitute which it were better to use as little as possible. And where is the limit of what is possible? We have the following example of an ascetic named Paul who lived at Pherme and who seems to have come very close to the limit:

> *His rule of life* (politeia) *consisted in never doing any sort of work and never accepting gifts except what was*

necessary to live on. His occupation and his penance was to pray without interruption. He said a daily quota of three hundred prayers. In order to keep track of the number, he began by collecting three hundred pebbles to carry with him; at the end of each prayer he threw one pebble away. One day this man met St Macarius the Citizen. 'I am troubled, Abba,' he said to him. Macarius insisted that he explain the reason. Paul replied: 'In a certain village lives a virgin who has practised the ascetic life for thirty years. I have been told that she eats only on Saturday and Sunday, fasting for five days at a time, week after week all year long, and furthermore she says seven hundred prayers a day. When I heard that, I lost all my self-esteem, for three hundred prayers a day is all I can manage to say.' [28]

At that Macarius gave him a good lesson to think about. His own rule, we know, was to say only a hundred prayers a day. Compare these practices to the thousands of 'adorations' which St Simon Stylites made on top of his pillar. Theodoret described this:

At times he would remain standing motionless and at other times he would bow down low again and again to offer God his adoration. The spectators would often count these adorations. Once a companion of mine counted 2144, then he got mixed up and stopped counting. [29]

'And each time he bowed over he touched his forehead to his toes,' says our eyewitness, Theodoret.

Writing much later, John Moschus recounted a story which proves that these feats were still actually being imitated and not merely admired. The story concerns a Roman monk maned Christopher of the monastery of St Theodosius in Palestine. What he did many others have also done in their own way and according to their own strength. A certain Theodoulos was about to ask Christopher a question for the benefit of his soul. Knowing what was coming, Christopher prayed at length and then said to Theodoulos:

> *My son, when I renounced the world I was filled with the most intense ardor for the monastic life. By day I would busy myself as the rule prescribed and by night I would withdraw to the grotto which holds the tomb of St Theodosius and the other fathers in order to pray there. As I descended to the grotto I made a hundred genuflections to God on each of the eighteen steps. [These exist still today.] And when I had gone down all the steps I stayed there until the bell rang; then I went up to attend the office. For ten years I lived like this, in fasting, in strict continence and in manual labor. Then one night I went down into the grotto as usual, making my genuflections on each step. When I reached the floor of the grotto I was rapt into ecstasy and saw the whole floor of the grotto covered with candles. Some of these were burning, others were not. Then I saw two men clothed in white cloaks busying themselves with the candles. I asked them, 'Why are you arranging those candles? Why don't you go away and let me pray here?' They answered me, 'These are the candles of the fathers.' I asked again, 'Why are some burning and others not?' They replied, 'Those who wanted to do so have lit their candles.' Then I said to them, 'Tell me please, is my candle lit?' 'If you pray,' they said, 'we will light it.' I answered almost indignantly, 'Pray! What else have I been doing all this time?' Saying these words I came to myself again, and when I looked around there was no one there.* [30]

These few examples are enough to show that there was a strong and evident tendency in the monastic world, quite apart from Messalianism, to spend the greatest possible amount of time in explicit prayer, using words or gestures. This meant that the monks had to learn how to manage their time very carefully and prudently. An illustration of this can be found in the life of St Melanie the Younger:

> *Wounded thus with divine love...she would have liked to lock herself up in a cell away from everyone in order to give herself to uninterrupted prayer and fasting. This was impossible because of the many who found profit in her inspired teaching and constantly came asking for it. So she set aside certain hours, known to everyone, when she would make herself available for the benefit of the visitors, and the rest of the day she consecrated entirely to spiritual activities and dialogue with God in prayer.* [31]

The rule, then, for prayer is this: not to set a certain minimum time for prayer in order to devote all the remaining time to work, but to decide on the maximum amount of time which will be spent on necessary business and then turn immediately afterwards to prayer.

THE STATE OF PRAYER

In spite of the multiplicity of their vocal prayers, none of these great men of prayer, or even the most deluded Euchite, could pretend that he really prayed uninterruptedly. Between the hours of their office there were always intervals without prayer. Even St Simon Stylites devoted a minimum amount of time to sleep and the other necessities of nature. Even St Arsenius conceded an hour a day to sleep. Besides, there is the fact noted in a famous dictum of St Antony, that the bow which is bent too far will break, and to avoid this it is necessary to unbend a little and relax the tension from time to time. All of this interrupts prayer or causes distractions.

Surprising as it may seem, distractions occur almost

inevitably in the recitation of psalms, interrupting one's attention to God. Because of this, some have held or pre-supposed as self-evident that psalmody of its very nature hinders deep prayerful concentration because it demands constant mental attention to the words. Referring to this phenomenon, St Maximus the Confessor described a novice asking the question: 'How can the mind pray uninterruptedly when we are obliged to distract it with many thoughts and considerations when we sing psalms or read or meet people or work?' Maximus tried to prove that none of these occupations makes prayer impossible; in the process he put psalmody on the same level as the other apparent obstacles to prayer:

> *Sacred Scripture never commands us to do what is impossible. The Apostle himself recited psalms, read Scripture, and served others, yet he prayed without ceasing. Continual prayer means keeping the soul attentive to God with great reverence and love, constantly hoping in him. It means entrusting ourselves to him in everything that happens, whether in things we do or in events that occur.* [32]

Maximus did not deny for a moment the inherent dangers and difficulties in the recitation of lengthy prayers and in intellectual or manual labor. He knew the occasions of distraction both by personal experience and from the teaching of his masters. He must have read, for example, this sentence of Evagrius Ponticus which was known to all the Eastern monks and which had been given a prominent place in the *Apophthegmata:* 'A great thing indeed—to pray without distraction; a greater thing still—to sing psalms without distraction.' [33] The saying does not of course imply the superiority of psalmody over contemplation. As the same author wrote elsewhere, 'Psalm-singing is an image of wisdom which is many-sided (*polypoikilos sophia*—Eph 3:10), prayer is the prelude to immaterial and uniform knowledge.' [34]

Multiplicity is an obstacle to the contemplation of God
which is what Evagrius meant by 'prayer'. This was stated
more explicitly by Evagrius in a treatise on prayer that
circulated among the Byzantine monks under the name of St
Nilus.[35] The matter is further clarified by one of the most
famous spiritual writers, John Cassian:

> *A certain verse from the psalms may come to mind and
> then slip away almost imperceptibly as our attention is
> drawn, without our knowing it, to another text of
> Scripture. We begin to meditate on this second text but
> have not yet penetrated the depths of it before a new
> text rises in the memory and expels the previous one.
> Before long still another text comes to mind and claims
> the attention in its turn. In this manner the soul turns
> from one psalm to another, skips from the gospel to St
> Paul, and from there jumps to the prophets and thence
> to some edifying story. Our wandering and inconstant
> attention is tossed about here and there over the entire
> Bible, unable to choose or reject as it pleases, unable to
> penetrate and study and exhaust the contents of any
> one passage. It momentarily touches and tastes the
> spiritual meaning without reaping and possessing its
> full benefit. It is always in motion, always circling aim-
> lessly. Even during the synaxis it finds itself going off
> in all directions, as if it were under the influence of
> some intoxicant. Thus we never perform our office as
> we should.*[36]

Cassian's whole teaching can be summed up in a term
which he used in the following chapter and which he learned
from Evagrius: prayer is a 'state', *orationis status*. It will be
worth our effort to try to understand this term more
profoundly. The word *katastasis* has a long history and only
the principal stages will be indicated here. The antiseptic,
colorless notion of a 'state' is actually a derived meaning.
Originally it carried a connotation of well-being which is not

conveyed by the Latin *status* or the English 'state'. Leopold's Greek *Lexicon* defines it very well as 'something established in its proper place'.[37] Used in the active sense it would mean putting things in order, and used passively it refers to harmony, permanence, rest, and firmness in a condition conformed to a thing's nature, laws and perfection. Protagoras wrote a treatise, now lost, which he entitled *Peri tes en arche katastaseos*. The experts have various opinions on what it was about but the title is noteworthy because we find spiritual writers frequently speaking of man's 'original state', but with a meaning which no doubt differed greatly from that of the Sophist from Abdera. Aristotle in his *Eudaemian Ethics* (VI, ii, 6-7) distinguished the *kathestotes* from children and animals: 'Between the weak-minded evildoer and the well-balanced wise man exists the same difference as between children or animals and a man who is *kathestos*.' Children or animals are ruled by instinct, while the wise man, who is never deceived by appearances and always guided by reason, will enjoy a firmly established position, an even temperament, and a calm outlook.

A true 'state' cannot be something transitory. It shares the characteristics of habit or disposition (*hexis*).[38] It lasts until it is modified by some extraordinary occurrence such as the transition from life in time to life in eternity.[39] According to the Origenist school of theology, three states can be distinguished: the angelic state, the human state, the diabolic state. They are alterable, but only with difficulty.[40]

The nuance of permanence and peaceful possession is often made explicit by an accompanying adjective such as *eirenike*,[41] or by a closely linked substantive, for instance *katastasis kai praotes*.[42] But the word *katastasis* by itself is sufficient to convey this meaning, as in Ammonas: 'to walk in God's path with *katastasis*.'[43]

A significant passage from Abba Isaiah revolves around the concept of *katastasis*:

Wine first goes through a stage of fermentation. This

> *symbolizes the age of adolescence which is a period of*
> *excitement inevitable until maturity and steadiness*
> (katastathe) *are attained. Wine does not reach maturity*
> *unless the proper amounts of quicklime and yeast are*
> *added, and in the same way it is impossible for youth to*
> *advance in the practice of self-denial unless it receives*
> *the proper leaven from a spiritual father in the form of*
> *guidance along the right path until God's grace gives*
> *him clear vision. People leave wine in a cave until it is*
> *perfectly settled* (katastathe). *Likewise, without aus-*
> *terity,* hesychia, *and all sorts of good works it is not*
> *possible to attain* katastasis.[44]

St Dorotheus used this term very freely but without emphasis on the duration of the state. He used it to mean a degree of the spiritual life or else the emotional and moral disposition of the soul or even the quieting of a passion.[45] For him it referred to a 'state of the soul', in the comprehensive sense that the term is used today. Dorotheus preferred to limit himself deliberately to the psychological and the ascetical or moral level and to avoid the mystical. He spoke very little about prayer, and then gave only elementary advice.

Whether it is considered as a permanent habit or as a temporary disposition, *katastasis* cannot be conceived as a series of acts. Every human act demands the intervention of the will and the cooperation of other faculties, intellect, memory, and sense appetite. A state can exist without the activity of any of the powers, spiritual or physical. It is a contradiction in terms to speak of continual acts of prayer. And frequent repetition of the act ends inevitably in weariness—which are two good reasons why it is futile and even disastrous to expect prayer to be continual in terms of quantity or number. It will have to be something that is quantitively discontinuous or discrete. Attempts to achieve habitual union with God through incessant repetition of prayers will not succeed, though this method can be useful in combination with other practices. By itself it will tend to bring about a state of weariness and strain, if not mental disturbance, instead of the true state of prayer which is completely peaceful and restful even for the body.

Something else is needed, something that is a quality or habit. The soul must acquire a habitual disposition which in some way can rightly be called prayer by its very nature, without reference to special acts of prayer which may occur more or less frequently. This state of implicit prayer, which is like an *actus primus proximus* always ready to become explicit prayer, is known by different names according to the different schools of spirituality, but they are all in agreement about the general method of reaching it. According to the clear and constant teaching of tradition, the method is asceticism—*praxis*. Vocal prayer must find its place in a full program of exercises and virtues which touch every single aspect of life. Only the strict Messalians, and they alone, failed to grasp this fact on the speculative level; on the level of practice there are many people in every age who act as if prayer in large or small amounts were enough in itself, without any other effort or mortification. Except for the strict Messalians, all the Eastern spiritual authors stress with impressive unanimity the necessity of asceticism for all who seriously desire to advance in the ways of the spirit and until they reach the very summit. Once this summit, which is the state of perfection, of imperturbability, of peace, of prayer, and of paradise, has been attained, a question might be raised about the need for further mortification. But this question is not our concern at the moment. What needs to be considered now is the testimony of tradition about the essential features of this state of prayer and the means of acquiring it.

BEFORE EVAGRIUS

In the earliest period there is a great diversity in

terminology because philosophical presuppositions differ from one milieu to another. Before neoplatonic categories succeeded in dominating the language of asceticism the monks expressed their convictions in simpler terms drawn from Scripture or from common speech, utilizing easily understood metaphors. Underlying everything was the truth which all had read in the sixth beatitude: 'Blessed are the pure of heart for they shall see God.'

This verse is never quoted in the writings of the apostolic fathers because they never treated the subject of contemplation or continual prayer; from this it should not be concluded that they knew nothing about these realities, but simply that there was no pressing need to discuss them. The apostolic fathers did not fail to speak of prayer, but they were concerned with intercessory prayer and especially with the common prayer, the one prayer, of the community as such (for instance, St Ignatius to the Magnesians, 7,1). During this period the prayer of individuals had a breathtaking universalism about it, both on the part of the one who prayed and on the part of those he prayed for. An example is St Polycarp. When arrested, Polycarp asked and received permission from the imperial police to pray as long as he wanted to. Then we read that 'he prayed standing up and was so full of the grace of God that he did not stop praying for two solid hours; those who heard him were amazed and many even repented of having come with arms to capture such a pious old man.' During that prayer Polycarp remembered 'all the people whom he had ever met [in his eighty-six years of life], the great and the little, the famous and the unknown, and he also prayed for the whole Catholic Church throughout the world' (*Martyrium Polyc* vii, 2-viii, 1). We could wish that everyone who prays and everyone who has written about prayer down through the centuries might imitate the example of this great disciple of St John and might recommend it for imitation.

The Shepherd of Hermas does not explicitly quote the verse that promises the vision of God to the pure of heart, but he seems to allude to it when he writes the following at the beginning of his commandments: 'If you keep these rules and make them your guide and do it with a pure heart, the Lord will surely reward you as he himself has promised.' [46] At any rate it soon became a commonplace in ascetical writings to insist that the higher state of perfection presupposes observance of all the commandments.

St Irenaeus expressed the same things when he wrote that God 'will grant to all who love him the grace of seeing him as is' according to the predictions of the prophets and the promises of our Lord. It is instructive to read his words in their context:

> *Because of God's great majesty and his stupendous glory, no man may see him and live. But out of his goodness and his love for man, and his almighty power, he permits himself to be seen by those who love him. Not that man can attain this vision of God by his own unaided strength! It is entirely up to God, who lets himself be seen by those whom he chooses, when he chooses, and in the manner he chooses.* [47]

This is the first principle of all christian mysticism and no one can be too careful about keeping it in mind. Without it, one is simply living on the plane of naturalism, however much he may surround himself with christian symbols and observances.

A benedictine scholar, Dom Gerard Békés, has given us a Latin dissertation on Clement of Alexandria's doctrine of continual prayer. [48] Continual prayer is not only the permanent union of the mind with God; it extends to the entire life of the gnostic with all its activities and powers. This is, as Dom Békés calls it, existential prayer, prayer that implies a total transformation of man into God's servant by means of adoration, thanksgiving, obedience and works of charity. The *state* of continual prayer presupposes a soul and an intellect purified by the practice of virtues and by divine gnosis. In this contemplative state the gnostic experiences conformity to the Logos and is enabled to pray everywhere, 'not openly (*antikrys*) or in the sight of men, but when he is walking or conversing or resting or reading or doing the tasks dictated by reason (*logos*)—he is always at prayer.'[49] The word *antikrys* which Clement used in this context could be translated very well as 'explicitly'. Here Clement is recommending a solution to the problem of continual prayer by means of a distinction between explicit and implicit prayer. The state of continual prayer becomes identical with the state of perfection. It should be added that Clement clearly attributed this transformation to the grace of God (see Békés, p. 104).

There is, however, a problem which Dom Békés did not consider. It has to do with Clement's choice of terms. He always used the word *euche* for prayer; only once did he use *proseuche* and then it was with reference to the Lord's Prayer. The verb *proseuchesthai* is rare too, and it always has the connotation of making a request for oneself or interceding for others. Is this choice of words merely accidental? It does not seem to be. And the question is not an insignificant one, because Origen for his part has a serious discussion of it at the beginning of his treatise *On Prayer*. What is the distinction between *euche* and *proseuche*? Does St Basil's dictum, 'The time of prayer (*proseuche*) is the whole of life,' have exactly the same meaning as this sentence from Clement: 'Prayer (*euche*) and communion with God is the whole of life'?[50] The word *euche* is never used in the gospels, nor is the verb form *euchesthai*. In the rest of the New Testament, *euche* is very infrequent (Ac 8:18; 21:23), and it has the meaning of 'vow', except for Js 5:15; 'This *prayer*, made in faith, will heal the sick man.' And even here there is a variant which reads *proseuche*. The verb *euchesthai* is a little more frequent, but almost always in the sense of 'to wish'. Only Js 5:16, 'pray for one another', has the meaning of truly praying, and again there is the variant *proseuchesthai*. The Vulgate translated St Paul's reply to

Agrippa quite correctly by *opto apud Deum* (Ac 26:29), and
this example casts doubt on the usual translation of 2 Cor
13:7, 'We *pray* to God that you will do no wrong.'

Because of all this it is very much to the point to ask
whether Clement of Alexandria meant by 'prayer' (*euche*) the
same thing meant by the gospel before him and by Origen
and the monks after him. Is Clement's lofty, psychological,
gnostic state really the same as the state of prayer envisioned
by the disciples of the simple, unsophisticated fathers of the
desert? If so, we would have to conclude that they were
follwers not so much of Origen but of Clement in this very
important matter. What we are saying is that there may be a
difference between the gnostic state described by Clement,
the philosopher, and the *katastasis tes proseuches* desired by
all the monks and hermits we read about in Cassian and the
Vitae Patrum. I believe this difference exists and that it is as
substantial as the difference Clement himself saw between
gnostics and the simple faithful. If *gnosis* is beyond the reach
of the simple faithful, then so is continual prayer. They can
say prayers which are acts of petition or of praise addressed
to God on certain occasions, this much Clement would grant.
Can they also have a form of continual implicit prayer which
would occupy the more or less lengthy intervals between
times of explicit prayer? Clement was not interested in the
question. He did not concern himself with the ways in which
the humble faithful, who are excluded from *gnosis*, might still
reach the perfection of christian life that is reserved for the
gnostics.

Looked at from another angle, the difference appears even
more plainly. According to Clement the state of prayer is a
communion of the mind with God (*homilia nou pros theon*).
By no means does it fall in the category of making humble
petitions for mercy, although when the gospel enjoins
continual prayer it does so in a context of supplication and
petition. The gnostic state as presented by Clement is 'uninterrupted contemplation' (*adialeiptos theoria—Stromata* vii
35, 4). This is far from being a state of perpetual supplication

or the habitual posture of a beggar before God, and it seems
that such a posture was positively excluded or at least
omitted by the Alexandrian philosopher. The true gnostic
appears to have gone beyond the stage of asking God for
anything at all, since he is prepared to renounce everything,
even his eternal salvation.[51]

The christian solution of the problem of continual prayer
cannot be found purely along the lines of *homilia nou pros
theon*. The christian solution, if it is not to remain on the
level of a completely natural philosophy or to anticipate
prematurely the final blessedness of heaven, must never fail
to take into account another aspect, more evangelical, more
humiliating for man and more pleasing to God, the aspect of
petitio decentium a Deo. What happened in actual fact was
that the ascetics of the desert and their successors, with few
exceptions, avoided the vocabulary of *gnosis, theoria*, and
apatheia. Their prayer life consisted essentially in prayers
that were truly supplications, even in the case of the genuine
mystics among them. The Jesus Prayer is simultaneously the
most ardent and the most humble of supplications.

EVAGRIUS

The philosopher-monk *par excellence* of the fourth century
was Evagrius. More than one classic spiritual writer adopted
his categories and his terminology. The thought of Evagrius
is marked by a great clarity which is due in part to a mathe-
matical cast of mind and in part to a characteristic common of
disciples of great teachers. Consequently Evagrius is a good
place to begin.

Evagrian spirituality is resolutely centered on contemplation in the strict sense of the term. His goal was not a kind
of global perfection in which contemplation is included
somewhere but not necessarily recognized by those who
practise or teach it. Evagrius aimed knowingly and
deliberately at intellectual contemplation and ordered every-

thing else, even the practice of fraternal charity, to this end which is 'the supreme good'. Charity, towards both God and neighbor, is defined within this perspective: 'Charity is the highest state of a reasonable soul, by which it is unable to love anything in the world more than the knowledge of God' (*Cent* I, 86). This definition is somewhat surprising. Love in this sense would be less concerned about God himself than about the psychological function which constitutes human blessedness, namely *gnosis* or *theoria*, the union of the soul with God by knowledge and contemplation.[52]

No one thought to challenge the validity of the definition of charity. St Maximus the Confessor copied the idea without any change of meaning: 'Charity is a good habit whereby the soul esteems the knowledge of God above all else' (*De caritate* I, 1). Others used different terms but they began from the same basic presupposition that the love of God consists in seeking union with God and the happiness which comes from that union. They may not have stressed as much as did Evagrius and Maximus the intellectual character of union with God. For instance, Nicetas Stethatos (*Cent* II, 1) made a distinction between the beginning, the middle, and the end or perfection of charity, and said of the final stage: 'This is a spontaneous desire (*eros*) for the supernatural gifts of God and a deep longing for union with God and for resting in him.'

Thus we see a synthesis or blend of contemplation, perfect charity, and beatitude into a single psychological state which is given different names from different points of view: 'state of peace' (*eirenike katastasis*) or 'primeval state' (*archike katastasis*) because it is a return to the original condition of man. More important for our purposes, this state has also been identified with the state of prayer, so that 'pure prayer' (*proseuche kathara*) is only another name for perfect love. To understand this, it is necessary to refer to the Evagrian definitions of the forms of prayer listed by St Paul in 1 Tm 2:1:

> *Intercession* [enteuxis] *is a petition made by spiritual persons to God for the salvation of others* (Cent *Supplement, no. 33*).
> Euche [*Syriac:* nedra, *'wish'*] *when it comes from a good will is the promise of something good*(Ibid.,*no. 32*).
> Deesis *is conversation of the soul with God and confident supplication for favors such as security in time of war* (Ibid., *no. 31*).

The question arises whether pure prayer is possible at all in terms of the prayer-forms listed here. The answer must be in the negative as far as Evagrius and his disciples are concerned. They applied the adjective 'pure' never to these three prayer-forms, but only to *proseuche* which is prayer in a special sense. This is how Evagrius defined it: 'Prayer (*proseuche*) is a state of the intelligence in which all thoughts of earth have been destroyed' (Ibid., no. 29). Again: 'Prayer is a state of the intelligence which can be brought about only by the light of the holy Trinity' (Ibid., no. 30).[53] If it is a state, then *deesis* and *enteuxis* are automatically excluded because they are acts. At most these acts could occur without detriment to the already existing state of prayer, or so it would seem.

In the Evagrian system 'states' of various kinds assumed great importance and they led Evagrius dangerously, if not fatally, close to heretical Origenism. He loved to classify things in degrees, a trait which he shared with many others (for instance, John 'Climacus' or the Syriac *Liber Graduum*). But for Evagrius the degrees of perfection were ontological, not merely psychological, states. They classified intelligent life according to a hierarchy of being—demons, men, angels—so that one went up or down the ladder of being depending on whether his actions proceeded from *gnosis* or from ignorance (*Cent* II, 79). The angelic condition came first historically and is known as 'the first or primordial state' (*Cent* III, 17, 61). Pure, authentic prayer (*proseuche*) characterized the angelic condition and was identical with it.

It is possible to return to this primordial state: 'The monk becomes *isangelos*, like an angel, through true prayer' (*Chapters on Prayer*, 113). Numberless readers of the *Chapters on Prayer* have, without succumbing to Origenism, given this sentence an interpretation of their own. The word *isangelos* or *angelikos* can take on different nuances, all the way from an Origenist realism which also spoke of *ischristoi* to the innocuous metaphor still used in phrases like 'angelic virtue'. For Evagrius, it is clear, the angelic state was the state of prayer (*proseuche*). A person became an angel in a very real sense if he possessed the vision of an angel; *gnosis* implied an ontological transformation of the intellect in which it ascended to a higher degree of being. Whoever aspires to true prayer aspires by that very fact to the vision of the angels who 'see always the face of the Father who is in heaven' (Mt 18:10). It is not necessary, at this time, to analyze the nature of that vision.[54]

Evagrius mentioned angels very often, and one of the reasons why, perhaps the main reason, was precisely his perspective of coming to be like the angels through the contemplative vision of true prayer. Angelology is the master key for his whole system, as it is also for St Thomas. Angels are pure intellects, full of true *gnosis* (*Cent* II, 7). Intellectuality is their identifying characteristic, corresponding to concupiscence in men and anger in demons (*Cent* I, 68). They have a body of light (*Cent* III, 5). There is nothing in them that could be an obstacle to contemplation. Consequently they live continually on *theoria ton onton* (*Cent* III, 4), and especially on 'the highest spiritual contemplation' which is the contemplation of God (*Cent* II, 61). They know everything that can be known about the Father by a creature (*Cent* IV, 2). Their *gnosis* is named 'heavenly Jerusalem or Sion', symbolizing the vision of God (*Cent* V: 6, 21, 40, 88; *Cent* VI, 49). Unlike men the angels remained in their first state, continuing to enjoy the 'first contemplation', which has the holy Trinity for its object (*Cent* VI, 75). In a word, they are in the state of pure intellectuality (*katastasis noos*).

It is possible for men to join the angels in that state by
acquiring the 'state of prayer' because the two terms
designate the same reality. 'Prayer,' said Evagrius, 'is
activity which is appropriate to the dignity of the spirit; or
better, it is appropriate for its nobler and adequate
operation.'[55] The dignity of the spirit or intellect (and the
intellect *is* man—*Cent* I, 6) comes from the fact that it is the
only creature capable of attaining knowledge of the holy
Trinity. The human intellect is in some way the summit of all
creation since everything was created to be a revelation of
God and the intellect is the very image of God, able to know
him because of the resemblance it bears to him. The rest of
creation manifests only God's omnipotence and wisdom.
'*Gnosis* of the holy Trinity' and 'theology' are two names for
the highest contemplation, and 'true prayer' is another name
for the same thing. 'If you are a theologian you truly pray; if
you truly pray you are a theologian.'[56] What Evagrius called
a theologian is not the professional scholar who speculates
about divine mysteries but the mystic who attains the vision
of God through ascesis and spiritual contemplation of created
beings. Earlier we quoted Evagrius's statement that 'prayer
is a state of the intelligence which can be brought about only
by the light of the holy Trinity'. It is evident then that the
state of prayer is equivalent to the primordial state, the
angelic state, the state of peace, the state of intelligence, the
state of pure intellectuality. When a man's spirit reaches this
stage it sees itself and seeing itself it sees God as in a mirror.
Evagrius formulated this in a very remarkable passage: 'The
intellect must totally put aside the old man and be clothed
with the new man of grace and then it will see itself in the
time of prayer like a brilliant sapphire or like a cloudless sky,
a state which Scripture refers to as "the place of God" (Ex
24:9) which our ancestors saw on Mount Sinai' (PG
40:1244A). Evagrius repeated this idea almost literally in four
or five different works, which is an indication of the
importance he attached to it.[57]

Would it be correct to see in this doctrine the solution to

the problem of continual prayer? If so, it would be necessary that this state of prayer, once acquired, persist continually. That, however, seems to be an impossibility both in itself and according to the mind of Evagrius. The duration of the state of prayer (*katastasis proseuches*) is limited to the time of prayer (*kairos proseuches*). None of the spiritual masters has ever taught that the highest mystical experience lasts for long periods of time. In later ages there are records, if the biographies are trustworthy, of visions that went on for hours or even days and weeks; St Sabas the Younger in the fourteenth century had a vision lasting forty days.[58] But these phenomena have nothing in common with the gospel command to pray without ceasing, and if the ancient spiritual authors had such things in mind they would never have proposed continual prayer as a goal that could be attained by all. Continual prayer is something that has to be for everyone. The Messalians, perhaps, thought that they were in a mystic state which was coextensive with their ordinary life thanks to their special indefectible charism; but Evagrius and his followers were not Messalians.

TWO KINDS OF PURE PRAYER

We have postponed until now an analysis of the concept of 'pure prayer'. It will bring us very close to the ultimate solution of the problem of continual prayer. 'Pure prayer' has a broad range of meaning, from Evagrian philosophical abstractions all the way to the real life of simple, christian ascetics. The term is so frequent in Greek and Syriac spiritual writings that a complete list of occurences would be interminable.[59] It does not occur literally in the New Testament but Scripture does contain a doctrine on purity of heart. The prayer of the Pharisee in the temple was not pure because it was self-conscious and directed by regard from men, as the spiritual writers did not fail to point out (see Evagrius, *Chapters on Prayer*, 102). The Pharisee's self-complacency and disdain for the publican destroyed the purity of his prayer. St Paul recommended prayer with the lifting up of pure (*osious*) hands, without anger, without *dialogismos* (1 Tm 2:8). Elsewhere he spoke of 'those who call on the Lord with a pure heart' (2 Tm 2:22), referring again to moral purity.

The phrase which was destined to have the greatest repercussions was 'without anger or *dialogismos*'. The Lord himself taught that anger hinders the quality and purity of prayer (Mt 5:24). And Evagrius paraphrased this: 'Leave your gift before the altar, go and be reconciled with your brother, and then you shall pray undisturbed. For resentment blinds the reason of the man who prays and casts a cloud over his prayer.'[60] As for the term *dialogismos*, it can mean simply dialogue or discussion or even argument. Since it occurs during prayer it must be understood as an interior dialogue in the form of disturbing or passionate thoughts. St Paul remained firmly on the plane of morality. But this term was a convenient scriptural point from which philosopher-ascetics could take off with their own theories. It is possible to give a more philosophical meaning to *dialogismos* (usually shortened to *logismos*), and the concept of prayer takes on a different nuance according to whether *logismos* is understood in the moral sense or as something more intellectual. The difference is that in the first case passionate thoughts are excluded insofar as they soil the purity of the soul, while in the second case all thoughts and concepts are considered an obstacle to prayer and must be excluded. Besides a purity of the soul there is also a purity of the *nous*, a mental purity. Purity of the soul is compatible with making intercessions and petitions to God. But *proseuche* in the strictest sense demands something more—the exclusion of all concepts, all multiplicity and all reasoning.[61]

This type of prayer definitely deserves to be called a 'state' because it excludes acts, though it is not necessarily prolonged in duration. It is known as 'the state of pure intellectuality' (*katastasis noos*). Spiritual writers characterized it with descriptions such as: without images (*aneidos*), without form (*amorphos* or *amorphotos*), without feeling (*anaisthetos*), immaterial (*aylos*), naked or unencumbered (*gymnos*), free of any trace of created reality (*atypotos*), free of multiplicity (*apoikilos*), undeviating (*aplanes*), and authentic or true (*alethes*).

The treatise on prayer ascribed to St Nilus and other works of Evagrius and his school treat frequently of this state, of its special qualities, and of the means to attain it. But no one treated it more thoroughly than Theodore of Edessa. This little-known writer is the author of a *Century* composed in the Evagrian style.[62] The work is full of praise for pure prayer. Such prayer should be perpetual, as the gospel commands, or at least '*almost* continual and uninterrupted' (*Cent* 60, 16). He described it as 'a safe rampart, a calm harbor, the protection of virtues, the destroyer of passions, the vigor of the soul, cleanser of the mind, rest for the weary, consolation for the sorrowful'. His highest form of praise for it was to list all the metaphors and definitions that he could discover:

> *Prayer is communion with God, contemplation of invisible things, progress in virtue, the substance of things hoped for, the preoccupation of the angels. Cling to this queen of virtues with all your strength, my brothers! Pray night and day, in sorrow and in joy; pray with fear and trembling, pray with a vigilant and wakeful mind, and then your prayer will be pleasing to God.* (*Cent* 60).

We can see from this that Theodore of Edessa did not quite succeed in remaining on the Evagrian level of pure prayer, however much he tried to use the appropriate terminology. Sorrow, for instance, is incompatible with pure prayer, which is the state of pure intellectuality, vision of the holy Trinity, and so forth. As Evagrius wrote, 'Effort and weariness belong to the lower stages but in the contemplation

of the Trinity there is only peace and ineffable tranquility'
(*Cent* I, 65). Evagrius conceived pure prayer as the natural
condition of the intelligence, so that everything which disturbed that state—passions, reasoning, multiplicity of
concepts—was contrary to its nature. If this doctrine were
pushed to its logical conclusion it would mean that the state
of prayer is the normal state of the human or the angelic
intellect and everything that interrupted or interferred with
this state would be unnatural. Obviously it is impossible to
remain in pure prayer 'night and day, in sorrow and in joy'.
The only reasonable thing is to propose this prayer as a goal
to be desired and attained through the use of appropriate
means. Unless a doctor is a miracle-worker he cannot
command his patient to show immediate and continual signs
of good health; what he does is to tell the man to build
himself up and gradually to develop his strength by suitable
exercises.

Many of the early spiritual authors of the East understood
the term 'pure prayer' in a less lofty, more accessible way
that Evagrius did, and Evagrius himself departed occasionally
from the strict definition he had given. That explains how
Theodore of Edessa, for instance, could slip from one
meaning to another without noticing it. Prayer is not only
communion of the intelligence with God or the ascent of the
mind to God or 'a state of the intelligence in which all
terrestrial thoughts are eliminated'.[63] For the majority of
men, including Christians who are very familiar with the
gospel, prayer is simply asking God for something. Even on
this level, however, prayer can be either pure or impure. This
distinction was made in Porphyry's letter to Marcella: 'Prayer
accompanied by evil deeds is not pure and not acceptable to
God; prayer accompanied by good works is indeed pure and
pleasing to God.'[64] This author, we can be sure, would never
have given the name 'prayer' to that state of superior wisdom
which he described so willingly for his correspondent.[65]

St Maximus the Confessor, who knew his Evagrius and
had read many other theologians, distinguished three degrees

of prayer corresponding to the three stages of the spiritual life. For the man engaged in *praktike*, prayer is a request for the virtues; for the man concerned with the *psychikos*, prayer is a request for the 'scientific' knowledge of beings; for the theologian, prayer is ineffable silence.[66] Ordinarily petitionary prayer at the first two stages would be called *deesis* rather than *proseuche*. If all three degrees of prayer were called *proseuche* the terminology would be ambiguous, for only the first two degrees actually imply requests while the third degree asks for nothing at all (presumably because it brings possession of the supreme good and leaves nothing more to be desired). The two lower degrees might be termed 'pure' in their own way, since they ask simply for what is suitable at that particular point along the path of salvation. In fact, anything else would be impossible since no one can pretend to be in a state of prayer if he really isn't. Evagrius described the highest degree as 'an habitual state of imperturbable calm, which snatches to the heights of intelligible reality the spirit that loves wisdom and is truly spiritualized by the most intense love'.[67] This could not be simulated any more than a man in chains could pretend to run or a man with something in his eye could pretend to see clearly.[68] That is why Evagrius taught that the first thing to pray for was to be purified from passion and the second to be liberated from ignorance.[69] He continues: 'In your prayer seek only after justice and the kingdom of God, that is to say, after virtue and true spiritual knowledge. Then all else will be given you besides.'[70] It is especially important to free the prayer from all the vices that could destroy its purity, particularly egotism, lies and profanity.[71]

We can cite several other authors who understood purity of prayer in the moral sense. One of the *Apophthegmata* asks the question directly, 'What is pure prayer?' The elder replied, 'That which is of few words and is abundant in deeds; for if your actions be not more than your petition, your prayers are mere words empty of seed.'[72] The biography of St Syncletice speaks of *kathara proseuche* as a weapon of the

spiritual combat in parallelism with ascetical practices; it is
therefore not the prayer at the summit of the spiritual life.[73]
Similarly, the biography of St Hypatius reports that this saint
begged his children not to be disobedient because when he
lost his temper with them his prayer would no longer be
pure.[74] This recalls the text from St Paul which we quoted
previously (1 Tm 2:8).

Moreover, when the treatise *De Malignis Cogitationibus*—
which is substantially from Evagrius—affirmed that anger
drives out pure prayer, it does not seem to have had in mind
only the highest state of the intellect. Every impurity
contaminates prayer. Origen had already said as much when
he observed that pure prayer is impossible to the degree that
the *katastasis* of the soul is not yet pure.[75] Usually it is in
this negative form that the doctrine is expressed, but those
who understood it in the positive sense and called every
prayer of a pure soul 'pure prayer' were not presenting the
matter in a false light. The Syriac authors who did not yet
know the Evagrian theories based their doctrine quite simply
on the teaching of Scripture. For example, according to
Aphraates prayer is pure under the same conditions that
fasting is pure, that is, when it rises from a pure
conscience.[76] Special attention is called for so as not to
destroy purity by failures in fraternal charity, especially by
bearing a grudge and refusing to forgive. All the ancient
masters of prayer including Evagrius stressed this important
point. If they did not all give the name of pure prayer to
prayer that was *morally* blameless, it was because they
wished to reserve the term, according to their systems of
classification, for an *intellectual* state that was free of disturbance and distraction.

Enough has been said about these two meanings of 'pure
prayer'. Some concluding observations can now be made from
a theological and a psychological point of view, which
correspond also to history. By itself theology probably never
would have reached the point of identifying pure or perfect
prayer with the contemplative vision of the holy Trinity. It

would have followed faithfully the common exegesis of the gospel passages on continual prayer, as given by Origen, Aphraates and Augustine, who represent the three principal traditions of the Church. Theology would have gone on repeating the doctrine that a man prays continually if he prays at fixed times during the day and the rest of the time occupies himself with good works—implicit prayer in the period between moments of explicit prayer. Prayer would cease only if a man 'ceased to be just'.[77] The state of prayer would have been equated with the state of justice or the state of grace, supported at certain moments by deliberate acts of prayer. Theology would have continued thinking, with Aphraates, that 'doing what pleases God, relieving the weary, visiting the sick, helping the poor—this in itself is prayer'.[78] And positive fraternal charity would have been emphasized much more, though without prejudice to prayer in the exclusive sense. Fraternal charity itself, with all its demands for continual renunciation, patience, devotion and detachment, obliges a person to have recourse to prayer in every situation.[79] The gospel teaches nothing else, provided it is read without gratuitous philosophical presuppositions.

From the psychological point of view, pure prayer in the Evagrian sense is not attainable by everyone, or by anyone as an habitual state. This is evident from a glance at all the necessary prerequisites listed by the very ones who propagated the practice. The witness of history could also be invoked, if more documentation were available. We have no statistics on the number of Christians who reached that prayer-contemplation-vision of God in this life, but we know quite well what the most influential spiritual masters of the East have said in this regard. They are unanimous about the extreme rarity of the highest gifts of prayer. In fact it is a common complaint among them. Each one deplored his own times; every age has its Jeremiah. Here, for example, is the lament of the greatest byzantine father, St Maximus the Confessor:

> *O where in this present generation can a soul be found*
> *that is totally free of passionate thoughts and worthy to*
> *enjoy that pure and immaterial prayer which is the mark*
> *of the interior monk? (De Caritate IV, 51)*

'The interior monk' is an Evagrian expression.[80] Here, in a
similar vein, is the greatest of the Syriac fathers, Isaac of
Nineveh:

> *How hard it is to find one man among ten thousand who*
> *has kept the commandments and been judged worthy of*
> *having purity of soul! And it is just as rarely that a*
> *single person can be found who has obtained the gift of*
> *pure prayer, who has entered upon this path and been*
> *judged worthy of this mystery. It is not the multitude*
> *who are judged worthy of pure prayer, but only a*
> *chosen few. As for the mysteries beyond, it would be*
> *hard to find a single person in every generation who has*
> *come that close to the knowledge of the grace of God.*[81]

THE MEMORY OF GOD

Spiritual authorities of the highest repute have indicated
that pure prayer, the state of pure intellectuality and the
vision of the holy Trinity, is extremely rare. If we accept their
judgment, it means that the vast majority of men, even the
majority of monks and hesychasts, must give up all hope of
attaining union with God in this state of prayer. Indeed, the
more realistic of the fathers seem to have renounced such an
ideal for themselves, or at least they never spoke of it. In
place of such lofty ambitions they proposed striving for a
state which may be more lowly in appearance but is perhaps
not inferior in excellence, a state which is generally far more
attainable though it does not lack difficulties of its own. The
traditional name for this state is 'the memory of God'
(*mneme theou*).

Philo of Alexandria seems to have been the first to discuss the concept explicitly, but before him the Stoics had already outlined a theory of memory. Zeno defined the memory as the treasury of fantasies (*thesauros ton phantasion*), where every impression on the soul is stored, whether concepts constructed by reason or images received from the senses. Many similar memories go together to form an 'experience'; repeated mental conclusions retained by the memory constitute knowledge. Memory is the faculty that gives permanence and duration to what would otherwise be transitory. The Stoics did not push their analysis much further than that. Yet, it was enough to indicate, if indications were needed, that the problem of permanent union with God might find a solution in terms of memory. Aristotle, whom Philo knew well, had made important contributions to the psychology of memory and of reminiscence. Philo probably showed the influence of all these philosophers in his panegyric of the ascetic community of Therapeutae in the treatise *De Vita Contemplativa*. Describing their form of life he wrote:

> *Always and incessantly they preserve the* memory of God, *so that even in their dreams they think of nothing but the beauty of divine virtues and powers. Indeed many of them while under the influence of dreams give utterance to the dogmas of holy philosophy in their sleep. They have the custom of praying twice a day, at dawn and at sundown.* [82]

The last sentence is noteworthy because it shows that Philo did not have an explicit idea of continual prayer.

'Always to preserve the memory of God and never to forget it'—this was the ideal of the ascetics who lived by the Mareotic Lake. It is not necessary to go into the history of this group. [83] The point to be noted is that their spirituality was considerably more down-to-earth and free of angelism than was the school of pure prayer. For Evagrius the memory was the great enemy of pure prayer. He wrote:

> *Remember this: the memory has a powerful proclivity*
> *for causing detriment to the spirit at the time of prayer.*
> *The devil so passionately envies the man who prays*
> *that he employs every device to frustrate that purpose.*
> *Thus he does not cease to stir up thoughts of various*
> *affairs by means of the memory.* [84]

In time the Evagrian attitude toward memory developed into something like a phobia, similar to that which in our age has had the imagination for its object. As J. Pegon observes: 'The fool of the house was memory instead of imagination.' Perhaps the fool was 'the imaginative memory'.

Instead of being deprecated, the complex faculty of the human memory should be recognized as a marvellous gift from God. And there must be an effective way of utilizing it as a means to attain God. St Basil, St Gregory Nazianzen and the other masters of the *mneme theou* certainly thought so. They were not the type to write off the products of the six days of creation as so many temptations. Forgetting all the creatures God has made is not the only way of going to him. It would seem that if we could look at creatures precisely as created by God we would continually have the memory of God and never forget him. But the fathers were not unaware that it is psychologically very difficult to maintain a continual vision of the invisible Creator by contemplating his visible creatures. Indeed, the encounter with some of them is far more likely to turn our minds away from God than towards him. The solution is to break away from certain created things and deliberately to attach ourselves to others. St Basil taught exactly this in an important chapter of his *Longer Rule* entitled 'On the necessity of living in seclusion':

> *Consequently, in order that we may not receive through*
> *our eyes and ears the stimuli of sin and thus become*
> *unconsciously accustomed to it, and so that the*

> *impressions and pictures of things seen and heard may*
> *not lodge in the soul to work its ruin and damnation,*
> *and for the sake of perseverance in prayer, we should*
> *first of all seek a secluded dwelling place.*[85]

The following chapter goes on to discuss 'The difficulties and dangers of living as a hermit'. The solitary life, which Basil called literally the 'monastic' life, is hazardous and difficult; man is naturally social and not 'a monastic animal' (Chap. 3; PG 31:917A).

The same line of reasoning was applied to material things: some of them must be carefully avoided, others must be prudently used. St Basil has left us some homilies on the six days of creation. His purpose in these homilies was not to exhort people to close their eyes to the world's beauty but to form men who would be, as he says, 'free of fleshly passions, not entangled in worldly cares, not afraid of labor, dedicated to the search for God, carefully observing (*periskopousa*) everything so as to form an idea of God which is worthy of Him'.[86] Basil may have been recalling here his own youth which was spent on a country estate affording him many opportunities to observe nature carefully and there discover God or the memory of God.[87] His desire was to communicate to those who heard his homilies something of this memory of God.[88] Basil's spirituality was not the spirituality of a philosopher in his tower or his cell, as was that of his former disciple, Evagrius. It was something incarnate, like the soul which lived it; it was a spirituality which knew how to adjust to the cosmos so as to live with God in the midst of the world.

According to St Basil the secret of reaching God does not lie simply, as with Evagrius, in *apothesis*—in renunciation, suppression, forgetting—in order to cleanse the mind. Basil was more specific. What must be suppressed and forgotten, he said, is our bad habits, our strong emotional attachments. Without effective separation (*anachoresis*) from these things we will be unable to carry with us everywhere 'the holy thought of God stamped into our soul like an ineradicable seal by means of a distinct and continual remembrance'. [89] In a word, we must exclude everything that could distract us from 'the precious remembrance of God'. [90] It is perfectly possible to conserve this remembrance in all circumstances even while doing physical labor, the Messalians notwithstanding. Occupations outside the time of formal prayer are perfectly compatible with prayer of the heart or even of the lips; they provide opportunities for such prayer, stimulate it and, so to speak, prime it. When we are busy at our tasks, or in between tasks, we spontaneously begin to pray:

> *We express our gratitude to him who has given strength to our hands as well as cleverness and ingenuity to our minds, and who has made us capable of learning skills and has provided tools to work with and also the materials we need.* [91]

The memory of God is kept alive by gratitude, and gratitude can be continual because God is offering us new graces at evey moment and because his best gifts are beyond the limits of time, lasting forever. The preface of the Liturgy speaks of 'always and everywhere giving thanks', an idea which is taken at face value by the spirituality we are considering. A passage from St Mark the Hermit illustrates this:

> *Here, my son, is the way to gain merit and make progress in the sight of God. You must make a list, in your memory and in your constant meditation, of all the providential benefits which have been allotted to you by God, the lover of men, for the salvation of your soul. You must never forget them. Do not permit negligence and wickedness to cover these memories with the veil of forgetfulness so that you lose all remembrance of the great and numerous graces you have received. If that were to happen you would spend the rest of your life in*

ingratitude, without any merit at all.[92]

After recommending gratitude in glowing terms that show by themselves how important the thought was to him, St Mark enumerated all the fruits of gratitude. He concluded with this remark, which sums up everything: 'The man who always and everywhere keeps such sentiments alive and never forgets his blessings will be a deeply humble person, always prepared to correct himself, zealous for the practice of every virtue, ready for any holy work, and disposed to do the will of God in all things.'[93] Further on he writes:

> *In this way your heart is moved to give God its best efforts to live a life of strict discipline, virtuous behavior, prudent judgment, and well-regulated speech. You will want to give yourself entirely to God prompted by remembrance of the great gifts you have received from such a generous and loving Lord. It will come about almost automatically* [automato tini tropo] *that your heart will be wounded with love and longing brought about by the constant memory of your blessings and even more by the help of heaven's grace.*[94]

To follow the path traced here is to be on the way towards the ceaseless memory of God and by that very fact towards continual prayer as well, since recollection of that kind can certainly be called *homilia nou pros theon*, communion of mind and heart with God. This is a form of spirituality which achieves perpetual prayer through an appeal to one of the most noble sentiments of the human heart. However, it must also be said that the prayer which is derived from and nourished on gratitude is not so much prayer of petition but rather 'confession' of praise, as St Mark the Hermit put it.[95] Furthermore, this spirituality does not seem to have promoted the practice of short, fervent prayers. And finally, it does risk straining the bow a bit too much.

St Basil never taught the practice of short, repeated

prayers. Either he did not know of it or else he knew of it but did not think it had any special importance. Basil tended more toward exegesis and theological analysis than toward psychology. He analyzed prayer into two moments, confession and petition, or thanksgiving and supplication.[96] He drew conclusions simply by grouping the pertinent texts of Scripture together, with no commentary except the heading or title which introduces the group and provides a resume. Rule Fifty-five of his book of *Morals* has two chapters with the following titles:

That we must recognize and be grateful for every blessing, and that when we are suffering for Christ patience is a gift of God.
That we should not let God's blessings go unremarked but should give thanks for them.

This is the prayer of confession or gratitude. Rule Fifty-six goes on to describe the prayer of petition:

That we should never give up the practice of vigils and of prayers. [The scriptural quotations all speak of petitions.]

That we should first give thanks before eating what is necessary to sustain the body.

That we should not give way to verbosity in our prayers nor pray to the Lord for things that are corruptible and ignoble.

Then he quotes from the synoptic gospels without further commentary. St John Chrysostom, in contrast, has a lengthy commentary on these very same texts and he draws from them his teaching on short prayers.

What interested St Basil more than the material continuity of prayer was the state of soul. He entitled the next chapter of his *Morals*: 'How we should pray and in what dispositions.' Perhaps the reason for his emphasis may have been the distortions of the Messalian position. We find allusion to the Messalians when he warns against those who 'refuse to work, alleging prayer and psalmody as their excuse', as if prayer and work were mutually exclusive.[97] Basil quoted Qoheleth, 'There is a time for all things, a time to be born and a time to die...' (Qo 3:1). He agreed with the principle of doing certain things at certain times but he made an exception for prayer. Prayer is suitable at all times and it can accompany all our other occupations under the form of praise and gratitude to God, either out loud or at least in the heart.

St Basil did not suggest using short prayers or any method of counting or measuring in order to attain continual prayer because he believed that *everything* can and should be a means of maintaining *mneme theou*, the memory of God. Obviously this requires a continual effort of attention. Basil thought the subject of 'attention' was important enough to warrant a long homily on the words of Deuteronomy, *'attende tibi ipsi'* (Dt 15:9).[98] From beginning to end he repeated the refrain, 'Attend to thyself'. The final line recapitulates the theme: 'Attend to thyself so thou mayest be attentive to God.'

But we may well ask whether any human nervous system can stand the strain of continual tension, or attention. The venerable old fathers of the desert, and their interpreter, John Cassian, showed themselves good psychologists when they looked for 'a sacred formula which would lead to the perpetual memory of God'.[99]

THE FATHERS OF THE DESERT: **POLITEIA**

The desert fathers had an explicit doctrine on the means of attaining continual prayer. In the first place they insisted, with all the Eastern masters, on the necessity of praxis or ascesis. Evagrius spoke for them all on this point when he said, 'The ascetical life (*praktike*) is the spiritual method for cleansing the affective part of the soul.'[100] Evagrius did not offer the beginner a choice of methods; praxis is the only method, the only way (*odos*), if one wishes to go from vices to virtues and through virtues to union with God. Origen and Gregory of Nazianazen had the same conviction,[101] and Cassian emphasized it for the West:

> *Whoever wishes to arrive at the stage of contemplation* (theoretike) *must first put all his efforts and ambition into the acquisition of practical knowledge. It is possible to have the ascetical life without the contemplative life, but to attain the state of contemplation without ascesis is completely impossible.* [102]

The only scope for personal initiative within the universally necessary practice of the virtues and keeping the commandments lies in the individual's free choice of what is called a *politeia*, in the restricted sense of 'a rule of life' or 'a special resolution'. For example, Abba Dioscorus of Namisias began every year with 'a particular resolution (*politeia*), one year proposing not to go and visit anyone, then another year not to speak, then to eat only fruit, then not to waste vegetables'.[103] Each ascetic was permitted to follow a program of his own, which he could keep all his life or else change if he discovered something better. St Hilarion had a meal with Bishop Epiphanius but refused to eat the fowl which was served because, as he explained, 'From the time I took the habit I have never eaten meat.' To this St Epiphanius replied, 'For my part, since taking the habit I have never let anyone go to sleep while he still held something against me, nor have I ever gone to sleep myself with bitterness towards any man.' Hilarion's response was, 'Your *politeia* is better than mine.'[104]

Politeia can go by other names or be given no special name at all. We read in the *Vitae Patrum* that twelve fathers assembled and told one another about their *katorthoma*. The term was Stoic in origin but became a common term for any accomplishment, especially a successful one; Cicero defined it as something *recte factum* (*De Fin* 3, 7; *De Off* 1, 3). Another equivalent term is *melete*, which will be studied in the following section. There is also 'daily occupation' (*ergasia*), or simply 'work' (*ergon*). But most often the *apophthegmata* which recount one of these special ascetical practices do not give it a technical name at all. They simply report the fact, attributing it to a definite person or to an anonymous source: 'Abba A said...' or 'It is said of Abba B...'.

The word *politeia* has a long and illustrious history. Plato used it for the title of one of his most important dialogues, *The Republic*, which is a lengthy discussion of the ideal state constitution. Using the same title, Aristotle wrote a book, no longer extant, which described one hundred fifty different political constitutions. The form of government (*politeia*) differed from country to country and there was always ample material for a discussion of the relative merits of each.

Transferred to the domain of private life, *politeia* was a good term to designate the personal life-style or habits of a particular individual. It occurs in the New Testament in this sense only once, though even here the meaning is not certain: 'At that time you [Gentiles] were excluded from Israel's way of life (*politeia, conversatio*)' (Eph 2:12). In Clement's Epistle to the Corinthians the term was used twice by itself and twice in a context that gives it the nuance of 'virtuous conduct' which it was ultimately to have. Clement wrote:

> *Previously you were governed by conduct* (politeia) *that was full of reverence and all the virtues.* [105]
> *Live a life* (politeuesthai...politeian) *which you will not have to be ashamed of before God.* [106]

As time went on the term became frequent in christian usage, and in the special sense given it by Greek-speaking Christians it played a role whose importance would be hard to exaggerate.

Greek hagiography consecrated the term by coining the stereotyped phrase *bios kai politeia* used in the title of lives of the saints. *Bios* meant the external details of their lives, the places, dates and events; *politeia* referred to their inner lives of virtue and holiness together with all the means and methods they followed. It was the *politeia*, or in Latin the *conversatio*, that made the saint.

Monasticism was born in a search for the optimum *politeia*. From that source springs the prodigious vitality of the monastic movement and the inexhaustible relevance of the texts which bear witness to it, the *Vitae Patrum*, the *Apophthegmata*, the *Life of St Antony*, the *Life of St Pachomius*, and so on. Nothing captivates a man's attention more than the spectacle of someone like himself whose life is a quest for the one thing which is of supreme concern to all men, salvation. Or in other words, the quest for a way of growing in goodness and happiness, a way of finding complete happiness by finding God. All this is implied and understood in the question which the monks were continually asking one another, 'Give me a word to teach me how I can be saved.'

These special practices or life-styles included everything except salvation itself and the commandments obligatory for all. They referred especially to the evangelical counsels and the means of observing them perfectly. In short, they embraced all the 'instruments of good works' (*ergaleia areton, instrumenta virtutum*), from the most obvious to the most subtle, from a spectacular flight from the world into the desert solitudes to the little ejaculatory prayer unnoticed by anyone.

Some of these *politeiai*, it is true, aroused lively interest, and this is reflected etymologically in the very names given to the ascetics: 'anchorites', 'hermits', 'monks'. But contemporary curiosity did not penetrate much below the surface. What was and always remained essential was the motive which led such men to seek solitude; and this was not the desire for fame and public attention but the desire to be forgotten. And also the desire to forget, and so to establish contact with God. What was true of solitude was true also for silence: men sought to be alone in order to enjoy a more desirable companion, and they practised silence in order to experience an interior colloquy. A love for silence and solitude constitutes the living dynamism of prayer.

Consequently there is nothing more contrary to the search for God than a spirit of vainglory and ostentation. When Symeon the Elder first had the idea of taking up residence on top of a high pillar, the monks of Egypt would have nothing more to do with him because they could not approve this 'strange *politeia*'. [107] They did not change their opinion until the stylite demonstrated by his prompt obedience the authenticity of his calling. [108] Their initial reaction was understandable, considering their love of hiddenness. Elsewhere we read: 'It is said of the monks of Scete that if someone happened to find out about one of their special austerities or caught them practising it, they would consider it a sin, not a virtue, to continue doing it.' [109]

They knew that pride lurked everywhere and that it could spoil everything. [110] This is why they tried to make themselves disappear as much as possible from the sight of men, and even to disappear in their own sight by the practice of self-accusation. [111] In spite of the reporter-instincts of a Palladius or a John Cassian or others who collected their sayings and doings, we are completely uninformed about the greatest of these men and will remain so until the last judgment.

They were wary also of falling into illusions and of mistaking beautiful phrases and terminology about the love of God for that love itself. They were afraid, as Evagrius remarked, of looking like invalids who discoursed about health. [112] Evagrius might have read a similar thought in Aristotle:

Most men will not do virtuous deeds but will content themselves with speculating about them and thus they

> *imagine they are becoming philosophers or men of*
> *virtue. They are like those who listen carefully to every-*
> *thing the doctor says but refuse to follow his*
> *prescriptions. As the latter will never regain physical*
> *health by such a course of therapy, neither will the*
> *former find health of soul by such a course of*
> *philosophy.* [113]

Even apart from Aristotle, the common sense and honesty
of the desert fathers, together with the teaching of the gospel
(Mt 6:3) and the example of the saints would have been
suficient to explain their desire for hiddeness. St Ignatius of
Antioch had a maxim that is as forceful as anything we read
from the monks of Scete: 'Nothing that can be seen is
good.' [114]

The lives of the ascetics were often marked with repeated
retreats from the demonstrations of public esteem which
swept upon them like waves threatening to submerge them.
They were at peace only when they were alone before God.
Antony and Pachomius desired to remain hidden even in
death. When Antony was about to die he moved to the inner
mountain and commanded the two disciples who assisted him
not to tell anyone the location of his tomb. St Athanasius
adds, 'No one, in fact, knows where his body lies except
those two persons.' [115] This prevented the Egyptian populace
from giving honor to the dead man by preserving his final
resting place. It was similar in the case of Pachomius: 'To
this day no one knows the place where he lies.' [116] These
saintly men, in contrast to the vast majority of people, were
obsessed with the desire to be unknown. If they could not
escape publicity entirely, which was quite difficult, they
would at least try to be held in contempt, even feigning
madness sometimes to assure this.

In spite of their love for anonymity it is true that we are
well informed about the spectacular performances of a great
many of them. One reason is that secrets and mysteries
naturally stimulate curiosity, especially when imprudent souls

suspect that something valuable is being hidden. I once saw somewhere a wall five feet thick drilled full of holes because a faint outline of a human figure painted on the stone was enough to around suspicions of buried treasure. We know from the biography of St Antony that candidates for the eremitical life 'imitated the wisdom of the bee' by going from one veteran ascetic to another in order to be trained in the particular virtue in which each one excelled:

> *...the cheerful disposition of this one, the perseverance in prayer of that one; the gentle heartedness of another and the generosity of still another.....the charity showed to all men for the sake of Christ, and the love which filled their hearts. Filled with all these examples they would return to their cells and go over in their minds the virtues they had seen exemplified separately in so many different persons, so as to be able to incorporate all of them into their own lives.* [117]

St Athanasius described all this with reference to his subject, St Antony, but we are justified in putting it in the plural because the many collections of *apophthegmata* prove that the custom was widespread. If in reading these lives and sayings we find greater pleasure than from any novel, we owe a debt of gratitude to the compilers for their curiosity, for without them we would know nothing at all. None of the earliest ascetics left us his 'Confessions'. The only autobiography of any importance is that of Nicephorus Blemmydes, 'the great ill-tempered savant of the Nicaean Empire'.[118] But Nicephorus died around 1272, well after the period we are studying.

What we are concerned with right now is the subject of continual prayer and the means of obtaining it. Of all the secret *politeiai* this was the most carefully hidden, because it was valued above all the others. We are fairly well informed about fasts, vigils, sleeping on the ground, and other austerities practised by many of the elders because these 'corporal virtues' were visible and verifiable. But how can we penetrate into their interior lives in order to learn about the intimate aspects of their communion with God?

THE FATHERS OF THE DESERT: **KRYPTE MELETE**

Other things have to be deliberately hidden and concealed but the deepest reality of a man's prayer is already by its very nature something secret. No one can observe it; at the most we can conjecture about it somewhat. We may suppose for instance that when the desert fathers were alone in their cells they prayed as they had learned to pray in their families or in the communities or parishes where they had been raised. Since they had become accustomed to the liturgical recitation of psalms and prayers commonly used in the churches, they would have been inspired by these in their personal, private prayers outside the time of divine services. While they were busy at manual labor or other indispensable activities they surely would have recalled and repeated certain verses from the liturgy, depending on each one's temperament, his present disposition, and the bent of his piety. Probably they would also have made up new formulas of their own. It is this intimate life of prayer that we would like to discover, observe and analyze.

Everything about a man at prayer is opposed to that sort of observation. There is a study by F. Heiler that stresses this very point.[119] He quotes Deissmann, Kierkegaard, Plotinus and others, though it is scarcely necessary to multiply the testimony of authorities. Everyone experiences how shyness and reticence grow and deepen in direct proportion to the degree of intimacy. And communion with God in prayer takes place or tends to take place at a level too deep for another creature to fathom. One of the supplementary delights of the blessed in heaven will be that they can watch this dialogue unfold. Here below we have to content ourselves, though even this is sometimes sublime, with catching a glimpse of that universe of souls as it is shown in a few dazzling flashes of revelation.

We are well enough informed about the liturgical life of the early fathers but not about their private prayer. And it is the latter which we would like to investigate. A beginning can be made by collecting the fragments of data we do possess.

There is one thing which is very well attested, the fact that the ascetics did carry on a secret interior occupation (*ergasia*). They revealed this much when they advised everyone not to talk about it. The fact of carrying on a mental dialogue is not itself surprising since no one who is capable of reason is without his interior life. However busy a man may be in external affairs there are certain moments when he must reflect, must enter within himself. The difference among men in this matter lies in the object of their musings and the duration of their reflections. The early fathers were well aware of all this. Evergetinos has written:

> *One of the fathers said, 'Man of necessity [physical not merely moral necessity] has within himself some sort of mental activity* (he entos ergasia). *Now if his mind devotes itself to an activity concerned with God* (eis ergasian theou)....' [120]

The rest of the sentence does not pertain to our present subject. Two phrases deserve analysis here. The first, *he entos ergasia*, refers to a universal phenomenon. The second, *eis ergasian theou*, describes the special variation which this activity assumes in a man of God. A saying attributed to Arsenius contains the first phrase with a minor difference: 'Strive with all your might that your interior activity (*he endon ergasia*) be according to God.' [121]

This shows that interior activity is not automatically 'according to God'. A struggle, an *agon*, is needed first, and it requires all one's effort. What is involved is a spiritual combat (*aoratos polemos*) with the hostile powers that seek to divert our attention from God. In different terms it is the struggle to replace forgetfulness (*lethe*) with remembrance (*mneme*) of God. The title of the chapter from Evergetinos quoted above says this very thing: 'Distraction and forgetfulness are death for the faithful disciple, but continual remembrance of God brings him life and frees him from every evil.' The enemies of this interior mental life are designated as *logismoi*, that is 'reasonings' or 'thoughts' which do not have God or the things of God for their object. The preceeding chapter of Evergetinos (Chapter VI) taught how to deal with *logismoi*. The doctrine of the fathers on this subject runs to twenty-five columns, which illustrates what an important and difficult subject it is. Finally Chapter VIII treats of continual prayer, which is the goal and outcome of the invisible combat against *logismoi* and of mental activity concerned with God. We have already discussed the problem of *logismoi*. As for continual prayer, it cannot be obtained or understood except by means of the inner activity concerned with God, and consequently this is what we must examine first.

Interior activity has another name which if properly understood is both richer and more exact in meaning. It is called 'secret meditation' (*krypte melete*). We will study the general meaning of *melete* and then the special object given to it by christian ascetics.

Meletan was usually translated by *meditari* in Latin, and the two words seem to be perfectly equivalent. Our verb 'to meditate' carries a more restricted connotation which is not exactly equivalent to *meletan/meditari*. According to the *Thesaurus Linguae Latinae*,[122] there are three principal meanings of *meditari*:

1. It refers to the thinking process and means *to reflect, to consider*.
2. It refers to the process of deliberation and means *to weigh alternatives, to take counsel*.
3. It refers to a kind of preparation and means, in general, *to prepare*; in particular it means *exercendo*

preparare, to do preliminary exercises, to learn an art or science by practising.

The third sense would usually correspond best to the Greek *meletan*, as it was used by the monks and by certain philosophers before them.

At this point a seminal book by Paul Rabbow must be mentioned. [123] In it the author demonstrates that there existed in the Greek schools of philosophy, in addition to abstract academic studies, a course of methodical training in the ways of living according to the principles of these schools. Among the exercises which Rabbow describes there is one especially, called 'soliloquy,' which foreshadows the *meletan* of the fathers. 'Soliloquy' is defined as a method of training oneself by the spoken word or by writing. It includes elements of 'meditation' in the more restricted sense of the term, but primarily it consists in saying over and over to oneself, either quietly or more loudly, certain sentences which the student wishes to engrave on his memory. In the process the thoughts sink not only into his memory but into the depths of his psyche as well, with the result that they cause reactions and reflexes in him which are in conformity with the principles of wisdom taught by the masters. They had discovered the pedagogical, or rather the 'psychogogical', power of repeated verbalization. For example, Thrasea, the roman Stoic, repeated incessantly the words, 'Nero may kill me but he cannot harm me.' This is based on a saying of Socrates. [124]

In our day there is a tendency to dismiss repetition as the most unimaginative of rhetorical devices; so much so that most writers have an evident phobia of repetition, considering it evidence of an impoverished vocabulary. We have left the exploitation of this psychological law to the science of propaganda and to the art of advertising. And the advertisers know that one single billboard is worth little or nothing; as a result in certain countries the words 'Coca-Cola', 'Rasurel', 'Motta', or 'Cinzano' stand out everywhere you look.

The monks of old were not afraid to 'meditate' intensely. This was their *krypte melete*. Several studies have shown the meaning of *meditari* as used in sacred Scripture and in early monastic literature.[125] Two kinds of verbal meditation or repetition can be distinguished, depending on the verbal formula used or the purpose in view. We are chiefly concerned with the frequent repetition of short prayers. But is was also common to select a verse from Scripture which was suitable for inculcating a salutary thought or affection. In certain cases it is difficult to say which type of *melete* is being recommended, as for instance in the following saying:

> *An old man said, 'Chastity is the offspring of tranquillity, taciturnity [probably in St Benedict's sense of the term], and secret meditation.'*[126]

Usually it is clear that this is a question of 'ruminating' or 'chewing over' a passage of Scripture. For example:

> *An old man said, 'The shepherd gives his sheep good forage to eat, but they also consume many of the weeds they come upon. If they swallow burning nettles they will seek out grass to ruminate on* (anamerychatai) *until the bitterness of the nettles disappears. In the same way* meditation *on the Scriptures is a good remedy for men against the attack of demons.'* [127]

Paul Rabbow has written that men of antiquity had the habit 'of talking to themselves out loud, softly or not so softly, to a degree that seems very peculiar to us'. The early monks belonged to the same tradition; they were taught to 'meditate' under all circumstances. The Rule of St Pachomius frequently recommended it: *de scripturis aliquid meditari* (see *Penthos*, 76). In order to be capable of doing this, Pachomius expected his novices to learn at least the New Testament and the psalter by heart.[128] The monk's obligation to memorize certain sacred books or spiritual writings was always stressed.

One of the reasons why the genre of *apophthegmata* held such a place of honor in monastic literature was that it furnished so much material for secret rumination in the form of ready-to-eat mouthfuls of different sizes, never too large, and suited to every taste.

Like men of antiquity the monks did their meditating out loud, usually in a low murmur or mutter. In those days people also read aloud. St Augustine recorded his surprise at seeing St Ambrose read without moving his lips. [129] Ambrose had learned to read silently so as not to be overheard by visitors, for his home was open to anyone. The monks did not have to be careful about that; their solitude permitted them to indulge freely in their soliloquies. Sometimes, though, they were overheard:

> *Abba Ammoes said, 'Once Abba Bitimios and I went to visit Abba Achilles and we could hear him* meditate *this phrase, "Fear not, Jacob, to go down to Egypt"* (Gen 46:3). *He spent a long time* meditating *this verse. When we knocked he opened the door for us.'* [130]

Several observations might be made. First, the hermit must have been speaking rather loudly in his cell because his visitors could hear through the closed door and make out the words. However, the main point of the anecdote was not this 'meditation' but what is described in the sequel, the Abba's great zeal for manual labor. Meditating in a loud voice even for a long time was nothing extraordinary. Sometimes these meditations lasted for years:

> *Pambo could not read, so he went looking for someone who would teach him a psalm. He listened to the first verse of Psalm 38* [Hebr 39]: *'I have said, I will watch my ways that I sin not with my tongue', and then he refused to hear any more. 'This one verse is enough', he said, 'if I can succeed in learning how to practise it.' Six months went by and Pambo did not come back to*

> *his teacher. So the teacher reproached him and Pambo*
> *replied, 'It is because I have not yet learned to practise*
> *the first verse of the psalm.' Thus he lived for many*
> *years. Finally one of his acquaintances asked him if he*
> *was making any progress with his verse. The Abba*
> *replied, 'In nineteen long years I have barely succeeded*
> *in learning how to put it into practice.'* [131]

One thing which stories of this kind illustrate—and this is the only point we wish to make—is that the fathers encouraged their monks not to let themselves be overcome by monotony or boredom but to persevere indefinitely meditating one single thought. Here we see already the meaning of a term which will be studied later: 'a prayer of one word' (*monologistos*).

In place of a scriptural text it was also permitted to whisper or sing a more spontaneous formula:

> *Abba Arsenius was in the habit of whispering* (ypadein)
> *to himself the words, 'Arsenius, why have you come*
> *here?' In other words, 'For what purpose have you left*
> *the world?' He also had the practice of singing to*
> *himself this refrain: 'I have often had regrets for*
> *speaking, but never for keeping silence.'* [132]

Another synonym for *meletan* is *apostethizein*, a word unknown in the classical era. The lexicon sees it as a conflation of *apo stethous legein*, and gives the meaning as 'to say or repeat by heart'. [133] It can also mean 'to learn by heart'. The two meanings go together because it is by repeating something that a person learns it by heart. The monks learned certain texts by heart in order to be able to say them without the help of a book while at work or coming and going from one place to another. Abba Marcellinus recited a passage from Scripture by heart as he walked to the church every Sunday, but he murmured (*meletan*) it without moving his lips so as not to be heard by anyone. [134] But the achievement of Abba Ammonius who memorized six hundred thousand lines from both testaments, from Origen, from Didymus and others is not an example of *meletan*. Memorizing was for Ammonius what studying Hebrew was for St Jerome, a weapon in the struggle against the flesh.[135] Palladius, who reported this, says that many other of his heros knew the whole Bible by heart.[136] This should not be surprising since Palladius was an admirer of Evagrius. Evagrius's book, the *Antirrheticos*, was written to provide ascetics with a text from sacred Scripture appropriate for warding off each particular variety of diabolic suggestion. It is noteworthy both for its psychological subtlety and for a great lack of sound psychology. Anyone who attempted to follow this catalogue and drive away one of the 487 *logismoi* by reciting the appropriate formula would soon go out of his mind or give up the effort entirely. Then he might declare, as did St Barsanuphius, that this method is useful only for the perfect. We shall return later to this point.

Another possible synonym, according to H. Bacht, is *philologein* as used by St Athanasius.[137] This may be correct but it is a usage peculiar to Athanasius and need not be stressed. Besides, it is possible that the verb does not mean 'to recite by heart' but 'to read'. For instance, Athanasius wrote, 'The virgin was taken away to be whipped while she was reading (*philologousa*) and with the psalter still in her hands.'[138] Elsewhere he used *meletan* with the meaning 'to recite': '[The heretics] pretend to recite and to read (*meletan kai legein*) the words of sacred Scripture so as to deceive the simple.'[139] Whatever may be his terminology, Athanasius is not a key witness in the present study.

The word *melete* can also have the connotation of reading, but with the probable nuance of 'meditative reading'. Abba Isaiah (†488), made this recommendation to a novice: 'Sit in your cell and apply yourself diligently to three things—manual labor, *melete*, and prayer.'[140] The recommendation found its way into St Antony's *Rules*: 'When you sit in your cell take care to busy yourself with these three things—

manual labor, *reading the psalms,* and prayers.'[141]

What we have seen thus far can be summarized under three conclusions:

1. In general the monk should see to it that his practice of virtue remains hidden. This is 'secret activity' (*krypte ergasia*) in the broad sense.
2. Further, the monk should have an inner life which of its very nature precludes observation. This will consist in a struggle against harmful thoughts and an effort to retain the memory of God (*mneme theou*). One of the very best means of doing this is meditation (*melete*), in the sense of ruminating or tirelessly repeating formulas drawn from Scripture or the fathers.
3. The most efficacious form of this meditation consists in the use of short and frequent prayers.

With that we come to the heart of our investigation.

NOTES

1.   E.-B. Allo, *Première epître aux Corinthiens* (Paris, 1934), p. xxx. N.B. After these pages had been written, J. Dupont *osb* published an article on 'Nom de Jésus' in the *Supplement au Dictionnaire de la Bible* (Tome VI, pp. 514-541). This erudite study does not render our own work superfluous but actually supports it by providing a more solid biblical foundation.

2   St Basil, *Regula fusius tractata,* Preface no. 3; PG 31:893D.

3.   St Augustine, *In Johannem Tr*, 102, no. 1; PL 35:1896.

4.   J. Cassian, *Collationes* I, iii and iv; PL 49:483.

5.   Ibid., *Coll* IX, ii; PL 49:771.

6.   Plato, *Theaetetus*, 176.

7.   J. Cassian, *Coll* X, vii; PL 49:827-28.

8.   See I. Hausherr, 'L'hésychasme, Etude de spiritualité', *Or Christ Per* XXII (1956) 256ff.

9.   'Récits d'un pélerin russe', *Irénikon* IV (1928) p. 5.

10.   This was a Syriac book written around the year 400. There is an edition by M. Kmosko in *Patrologia Syriaca*, Vol. III (1920).

11.   *Apophthegmata Patrum*, Alphabetical Series, 'Silvanus' no. 5; PG 65:409B-D; CS 59:187.

12.   Ibid., 'John Colobos', no. 2; CS 59:73.

13.   St Augustine, *De Opere Monachorum*, PL 40:547-82. See also G. Folliet, 'Des Moines euchites à Carthage en 400-401', *Studia Patristica* II (Berlin, 1957), 386-99.

14.   *Apophthegmata Patrum*, Alphabetical Series, 'Lucius' no. 1; CS 59:102.

15.   On the Acoemeti see the article 'Acémètes' in the *Dictionnaire de la Spiritualité*. Besides this successive collaboration mention should also be made of simultaneous collaboration as envisioned, for instance, by St Julian Saba (see Theodoret, *Hist Relig* II; PG 82:1309BC). This is aimed at making a more lengthy prayer possible by sharing the burden.

16.   Origen, *De Oratione*, no. 12; PG 11:452.

17.   St Augustine, *De Haeresibus*, LVII: PL 42:40.

18.   Aphraates, *Demonstr* IV, 14-17.

19.   St Basil, *Sermo Asceticus* I, no. 4; PG 31:877A.

20.   *Sermo de renunciatione saeculi*, no. 2; PG 31:645A.

21.   *Apophthegmata Patrum*, Alphabetical Series, 'Apollo' no. 2; CS 59:31.

22.   Ibid., 'Epiphanius' no. 3; CS 59:48-9.

23.   *Verba Seniorum*, Bk. XII, no. 1; PL 73:941D. This corresponds to *Apophthegmata Patrum*, Alphabetical Series, 'Arsenius' no. 30; CS 59:12.

24.   Abba Isaiah, *Logos* 4; Augoustinos, ed., p. 14 (Jerusalem, 1911).

25.   Hyperechios, *Sententiae*, 95; PG 79:1482D.

26.   See P. Evergetinos, *Synagogé* IV (Constantinople, 1861) p. 45, col. 2.

27.   At the beginning of his seventh volume on *La métaphysique des saints* (Paris, 1929) H. Bremond quoted the saying, 'God is ill-pleased with prayers that come to an end.' See Hamon, *Traités de piété* II, 19.

28.   Palladius, *Lausiac History*, chap. 20. The ancient Latin translation adds: 'I whom God created a man with the superior strength of a man.' (PL 73:122C).

29.   Theodoret, *Philotheus;* PL 74:106D.

30.   John Moschus, *Pré Spirituel*, Sources Chrétiennes XII; (Paris: Cerf) 150.

31.   Cardinal Rampolla del Tindaro, ed., *Vie de sainte Mélanie la Jeune* (Rome, 1905), no. 32.

32.   Maximus the Confessor, *Liber Asceticus*, no. 25; PG 90:929D; 932A.

33.   Evagrius, *Prakticos*, I, 41; J.E. Bamberger, trans., *Evagrius Ponticus: Praktikos, Chapters on Prayer*, Cistercian Studies 4 (Spencer, Mass., 1970) no. 69, p. 35.

34.   Evagrius, *De Oratione*, 85; Bamberger, trans., pg. 69

35. Nilus, *De Oratione*, chaps. 55-57; PG 79:1185C; 1177D; 1180A; Bamberger, trans., 63-64.

36. J. Cassian, *Coll* X, xiii: PL 49:840B.

37. E.F. Léopold, *Lexicon graeco-latinum manuale* (Leipzig, 1917).

38. Clement of Alexandria, *Stromata* II, 133; O Stählin, ed., Vol. II, p. 186:19 (Leipzig, 1905-1936).

39. Clement, *Eclogae Propheticae* 56:3; Stählin, III, 153:6. See also Cosmas Indicopluestes V; PG 88:300A, and VI, PG 88:323B.

40. Origen (or perhaps Evagrius), *In Prov* XVII, PG 17:197B. Evagrius, *Cent* III, 17; 29-40.

41. Nilus, *Oratio ascetica*, no. 21; PG 79:748A; also no. 41, col. 769D; no. 72, col. 805B.

42. Ammonas, ed. by F. Nau, *Patrologia Orientalis* XI (de Graffin) p. 466:13.

43. Ibid., p. 405:12. This phrase has also been preserved in the *Apophthegmata*, Alphabetical Series, 'Ammonas' no. 6; CS 59:23.

44. Abba Isaiah, *Logos* 12; Augoustinos, ed. (Jerusalem, 1911) p. 71. When the word *katastasis* is transcribed into Syriac it loses the neutral meaning of 'state' and usually signifies 'good order' or 'to put in order' or even 'to ordain, to consecrate'.

45. See Dorotheus, *Doctrina* 17, no. 2; PG 88:1801C.

46. Hermas, *The Shepherd*, Visio V, 7; ed. by F.X. Funk, *Die apostolischen Väter* (Tübingen, 1906) p. 468.

47. Irenaeus, *Adversus Haer* IV, 20; PG 7:1035A.

48. Gerardus Békés *osb*, *De continua oratione Clementis Alexandrini Doctrina, Studia Anselmiana*, 14 (Rome, 1942).

49. Clement, *Stromata*, VII, 49:6-7; Stälin, ed. (Leipzig, 1905-1936) p. 37.

50. St Basil: see note 19 above. Clement, *Stromata* VII, 73:1.

51. See Clement, *Stromata* IV, 22:136; PG 8:1345-1348.

52.   It is certain that the fathers, including Clement of Alexandria, were not preoccupied with the problem of a 'pure love' which abstracts even from the salvation of one's soul. This is true in spite of the passage just quoted, note 51, from Clement which was used in a later day to support a quietist spirituality (see Fénelon, *Le gnostique de saint Clément d'Alexandrie* [Paris: P.P. Dudon, 1930]). It was Clement and not Origen who supplied Evagrius with his definition of charity. The only similar text from Origen which could be brought forth by P.M. Viller (*Revue d'ascétique et de mystique*, XI, p. 240, note 118) was found in the *Selecta in Psalmos*, and Hans Urs von Balthasar has demonstrated that this work is Evagrian ('Die Hiera des Evagrius,' *Zeitschrift für katholishe Theologie* 63 [1939] 86-106; 181-206). Clement wrote: 'The man who is pure of heart is a friend of God, not because of keeping the commandments but because of his very knowledge [of God]' (*Stromata*, VII; PG 9:424B). Pure love as seen by Clement and Evagrius was not a love which no longer cares about blessedness but a love which cares for nothing else, renouncing everything else and ready to renounce even eternal salvation if it were possible that this salvation might be incompatible with knowing God, or in other words if this salvation lay elsewhere than in God. But since they were absolutely sure that human happiness can be obtained only by cognitive union with God, Clement and Evagrius and all the rest believed that they were loving God out of completely pure love by consciously desiring this beatifying knowledge and directing their whole lives towards attaining it.

53.   See *Orientalia Christiana* 22, no. 69, p. 117; and 24, no. 73, p. 39.

54.   See my commentary on chap. 114 (PL 114) of the *De Oratione* in *Revue d'ascétique et de mystique*, 15 (1933) 145ff.

55.   Evagrius, *Chapters on Prayer*, 84; Bamberger, p. 69.

56.   Ibid., 60; Bamberger, p. 65.

57.   See W. Bousset, ed., *Apophthegmata* (Tübingen, 1923) p. 286.

58.   See Philotheus Kokkinos, *Life of St Sabas the Younger*, ed. by A Papadopoulos Kerameus, *Analecta Hierosol Stachyol*, Vol V, p. 274.

59.   See the list given by M. Viller in *Revue d'ascétique et de mystique*, 11 (1930) p. 251.

60.   Evagrius, *Chapters on Prayer*, 21; Bamberger, p. 58.

61.   See Evagrius, *Chapters*, 55-57, and the commentary in *Revue d'ascétique et de mystique*, 15, p. 86ff.

62. Included in the *Philokalia* of Nicodemus the Hagirite (Venice, 1782) 265-281.

63. See the list of definitions given by F. Diekamp in *Doctrina Patrum de Incarnatione Verbi* (Münster, 1907) 264.

64. Porphyry: see *Recherches de science religieuse*, 23 (1933) p. 112.

65. See Nauck, *Jamblichi de Vita Pythagorica liber* (St Petersburg) 284ff.

66. In *De caritate* II, 6, Maximus distinguished two stages of pure prayer, one for actives, the other for contemplatives. This suggests a reaction to Evagrius rather than an influence from him. See the remark of J. Pegon, Sources Chrétiennes, Vol. 9 pg. 95.

67. Evagrius, *Chapters*, 52; Bamberger, p. 63.

68. Ibid., 71; 64.

69. Ibid., 37.

70. Ibid., 38; Bamberger, p. 61.

71. Ibid., 40; 127.

72. E.A. Wallis-Budge, *The Paradise of the Fathers* II (London, 1907) no. 695.

73. *Vita Syncleticae* xxix; PG 28:1504D; see also no. xix.

74. *Vita Hypatii* (Leipzig, 1895), p. 64.

75. Origen, *In Prov* XIX; PG 17:208C.

76. Aphraates, *Demonstr* IV, 1; Dom Parisot, ed., *Patrologia Syriaca*, p. 138.

77. Origen, *In I Reg*, Hom I; Baehrens, ed., p. 15.

78. Aphraates, *Demonstr* 14; Parisot, ed., p. 170.

79. Ibid., *Demonstr* 16 (Parisot, ed., 174); 6 (Parisot, 239; 255); 8 (Parisot, 271); 20 (Parisot, 311).

80. See *Revue d'ascétique et de mystique*, XV (1934) 76-77.

81. Isaac of Nineveh, Bedjan, ed., (Paris-Leipzig, 1909) p. 167.

82. Philo, *De Vita Contemplativa*, 475; *Loeb Classical Library* edition, no. 26-27.

83. The essential facts are given in the article devoted to them in *Dictionnaire de Spiritualité*, Vol. II: col. 1856-1862.

84. Evagrius, *Chapters*, 44, 46, see also 45, 61, 68; Bamberger, p. 62.

85. St Basil, *Regula fusius tractata*, Question 6; PG 31:925B.

86. *In Hexam, Hom* I,1; PG 29:3A.

87. See P Humbertclaude, *La doctrine ascétique de saint Basile de Césarée* (Paris, 1932), p. 119ff.

88. See *In Hexam*, Hom IX, 6; PG 29:208B.

89. *Regula fusius tractata*, Question 5, ii; PG 31:921AB.

90. Ibid., Question 6, ii; PG 31:928B.

91. Ibid., Question 37, ii; PG 31:1012C.

92. Mark the Hermit, *Ad Nicolaum Praecepta*, no. 2; PG 65:1029CD.

93. Ibid., PG 65:1032C.

94. Ibid., PG 65:1037B.

95. Ibid., no. 2; PG 65:1029D.

96. See St Basil, *Homilia de gratiarum action*, PG 31:217B. See also *Moralia, Regula* lv; PG 31:781C; 788B.

97. St Basil, *Regula fusius tractata*, Question 37; PG 31:1011B.

98. PG 31:197C; 218B.

99. J. Cassian, *Coll* X, x; PL 49:832B.

100. Evagrius, *Praktikos*, chap. 78; Bamberger, p. 36. See also J. Cassian, *Coll* XIV, i.

101. See the article 'Contemplation' in *Dictionnaire de Spiritualité*, Vol. II:

col. 1802.

102. J. Cassian, *Coll* XIV, ii; PL 49:955A.

103. *Apophthegmata Patrum*, Alphabetical Series, 'Dioscorus' no. 1; CS 59:46.

104. Ibid., 'Epiphanius' no. 4; CS 59:49.

105. Clement, *Prima Epis ad Cor*, II, 2; ed., by Funk, *Patres Apostolici*, p. 102.

106. Ibid., LIV, 8; Funk, p. 168.

107. Theodorus Lector, *Eccles Hist* II, 41; PG 86:205A.

108. Evagrius, *Eccles Hist* I, 13; ed., by J. Bidez and L. Parmentier (London, 1898) 21ff.

109. Paul Evergetinos, *Synagogé*, III, 26 (Constantinople, 1861) p. 72.

110. See Evagrius, *Praktikos*, 13, 30, *passim*; *Letter* 51; W. Frankenberg, ed., p. 598.

111. See Hausherr, *Penthos*, 55-62.

112. Evagrius, *Gnost;* Frankenberg, ed., p. 598.

113. Aristotle, *Nichomachean Ethics* II, chap. iv.

114. Ignatius of Antioch, *Ad Rom* III, 3; Funk, ed., p. 256; see also Origen, *De Oratione,* chap. xx; PG 11:480A.

115. St Athanasius, *Vita Antonii*, 91; PG 26:969.

116. L. Th. Lefort, *Les view coptes de saint Pachome et de ses premièrs successeurs* (Louvain, 1943) p. 51.

117. St Anthanasius, *Vita Antonii*, 3ff; PG 26:844.

118. S. Runciman, *Byzantine Civilisation* (London: Edw. Arnold, 1933) p. 247.

119. F. Heiler, *Das Gebet* (5th ed., Munich, 1923), 26ff.

120. Paul Evergetinos, *Synagogé* IV, 7; p. 43, col. 1.

121. *Apophthegmata Patrum*, Alphabetical Series, 'Arsenius' no. 9; PG 65:89BC; CS 59:9. See also 'Eulogius the Priest' and 'Silvanus' no. 4; CS 59:51-2, 187.

122. Leipzig, 1939; col. 574-581; article signed Buchwald.

123. Paul Rabbow, *Seelenführung: Methodik der Exerzitien in der Antike* (Munich, 1954).

124. Plato, *The Apology of Socrates*, 30c.

125. See Emmanuel von Severus, 'Meditari in Sprachgebrauch der hl Schrift', *Geist und Leben* 26 (1953) pp. 365-375, and H. Bacht, 'Meditari in den ältesten Mönchsquellen', Ibid. 28 (1955) pp. 360-373.

126. *Vitae Patrum* V, 25; PL 73:880A.

127. Evergetinos, *Synagogé*, IV, 15; p. 63.

128. See A. Boon, *Pachomiana Latina;* S Pach Paaecepta, no. 140 (Louvain, 1932).

129. St Augustine, *Confessions,* VI, iii; PL 32:720.

130. *Apophthegmata Patrum*, Alphabetical Series, 'Achilles' no. 5; PG 65:125A; CS 59:25.

131. Socrates, *Hist Eccles* IV, 23; ed. by Hussey (Oxford, 1853), Vol. II, p. 521.

132. Evergetinos, *Synagogé* IV, 5; p. 21, col. 2. This is equivalent to *Apophthegmata Patrum*, Alphabetical Series, 'Arsenius' no. 40; PG 65:105.

133. H. Estienne in *Thes Gr Linguae*, sub verbo *apostethizein*.

134. Evergetinos, *Synagogé*, IV, 29; p. 110.

135. See Palladius, *Lausiac History*, XI, 4.

136. For instance, Mark the Ascetic, Heron, Serapion the Sindonite, and the inhabitants of Tabennesis.

137. H. Bacht, in *Geist und Leben* 28 (1955) p. 368.

138. St Athanasius, *Epistola Encyclica*, no. 4; PG 25:232A.

139. Ibid., *Epistola ad Episc Aegypt et Libyae*, no. 4; PG 25:545C.

140. Ed. Augoustinos (Jerusalem, 1911), p. 65.

141. Anthony, *Regulae*; PG 40:1071B.

CHAPTER FOUR

SHORT PRAYERS

EXISTENCE AND OBSCURE NATURE

ALL THINGS impel the Christian to prayer: meta-physics and life, logic and experience, faith and history, hope, fear, and especially love, which is both a longing for God and a resting in him. Everything impels him, everything above the level of sinful passions, though even these can call forth prayer as a reaction or as the only means of regaining integrity. All these factors are at work, along with our Lord's injunction and St Paul's exhortation, to make the Christian want to pray always and in all circumstances. Cassian shows, in the lives of the desert fathers whom he quotes, how the impulse to pray can take on all the force of an elemental urge reinforced by deliberate and frequently renewed intention. These champions of asceticism wanted to be happy, as all men do, and it was their conviction that happiness could be found only in anticipating eternal blessedness by living in God through pure and continual prayer. Cassian wrote:

> *This ought to be the goal of the solitary, this should be the aim of all his efforts: to merit to have in this life a preview of future blessedness, and to have in his mortal body a foretaste of the life and glory of heaven. This, in my*

> *opinion, is the summit of perfection, that the mind be so*
> *purified from material concerns that it rise each day*
> *toward the most sublime spiritual realities until the whole*
> *life and the whole longing of the heart become one*
> *continuous prayer.* [1]

The Jesus Prayer had its origin in this matrix, in a milieu impregnated with these ideas. It utilized the law and psychology of *krypte ergasia* and *krypte melete* in order to actuate the experience of continual prayer, which is the foretaste of heaven.

In what follows we are going to penetrate deeper and deeper into the private experiences of holy men. We have to expect to encounter a greater proportion of silence than of discourse, and more questions than answers. It will be best to proceed systematically, according to chronological order.

The care people ordinarily take to preserve a certain secrecy is based on solid reasons dictated by prudence. Anything that is valued, important or precious runs the risk of being disturbed and destroyed if it becomes known to indiscreet persons. When it concerns the spiritual life, which is essentially something hidden, every gaze from the outside except that of a spiritual director will seem indiscreet. The spiritual director cannot publish what he is told in confidence because such things are revealed, before God, only for purposes of help and guidance. So it is evident *a priori* that information about our subject will be scanty.

But without fear of mistake we can be perfectly certain of one thing, that the ascetics did have a hidden spiritual activity which was their principal concern and in a sense the aim of all their works and sacrifices. This inner life is of the essence of christian perfection and even of virtue in general. What is visible and external, the outward act, is not the true virtue but only the instrument of virtue. The consequences of this obvious principle are far reaching. An anecdote from the *Lives of the Fathers* illustrates this quite well:

> *One morning as Abba Macarius was returning to his cell*
> *with an armful of palm fronds he met the devil armed*
> *with a reaper's scythe. This he tried to swing at Macarius*
> *but could not do so. He cried out, 'Something terribly*
> *strong is holding me back, Macarius. I intended to cut you*
> *down but I cannot do it. And yet, everything that you do I*
> *do even more: you fast at certain times but I never eat;*
> *you keep vigil often, but I have never slept. Only in one*
> *single thing do you surpass me, and I have to admit it.'*
> *Macarius asked what this thing was. 'Your humility,'*
> *replied the devil, 'and that alone has beaten me.'*[2]

But nothing destroys this fundamental virtue so much as publicity.

To conceal an 'interior life' presupposes that one really exists. The masters of Eastern spirituality often tell us how the interior life can be lost, and from that we can deduce something about its structure and content. Not infrequently these lessons take the form either of a saying attributed to a famous desert father or of a story, real of fictitious.

On no point has Cassian so faithfully reported the teaching of the desert fathers as on the goal of the ascetical life. In response to a drawn-out forty-five line question about the *telos*, the ultimate goal, the proper object, of monastic life, he gives an answer in three lines, but these three lines are so important that they form the whole of Chapter Three. 'It is for the kingdom of heaven that we do all this.'[3] Perfectly plain, perfectly simple. The *telos*, or ultimate end, is distinguished from the immediate end, called *scopos*, which is purity of heart. This must be attained by every possible means if the *telos* is ever to be reached.[4] Cassian was insistent: 'Whatever helps lead us toward purity of heart we must practise with all our might, but whatever separates us from it we must shun as a harmful danger.'[5] Purity of heart has another name—love. All other things, including fasting, vigils, separation from the world, meditation on Scripture, renunciation, leaving all possessions, are only instruments of perfection, not perfection itself. As Cassian put it:

> *Whatever is likely to disturb that purity and tranquillity*
> *of mind, even if it seems to be useful or indispensable,*
> *must be avoided as something harmful.* [6]
> *This then should be our main effort and the perpetual*
> *intention of our heart, that we always remain absorbed in*
> *God and the things of God. Whatever has nothing to do*
> *with this, however important it may be, should be given*
> *second place, or even treated as negligible and potentially*
> *dangerous.* [7]

This doctrine, developed and repeated tirelessly by
Cassian, can be condensed in a single word. It is
'contemplation'. Or in a word with a less complex history,
'prayer'. The great problem of the monk or of the Christian
who is striving to attain perfect charity is the problem of
continual prayer. Cassian devoted two conferences to this
subject, the ninth and tenth. All this teaching must be taken
into account if we are to understand the Jesus Prayer, and it
is particularly necessary to see how all this is related to the
monk's secret occupation (*krypte ergasia*).

SHORT PRAYERS IN THE FOUR GOSPELS

Our study will begin with the gospels and then go on to
the rest of the New Testament and into the patristic era until
the point when the Jesus Prayer has crowded out all other
short prayers.

We notice in the gospels that many people ask favors of
the miracle-worker from Nazareth. Neither Matthew nor Mark
nor John records any prayers containing the vocative, 'Jesus'.
Mk 1:24 and 5:7 are not prayers but the cries of demons
coming through the mouths of the possessed: 'Jesus, son of
the most high God, I implore you, do not torture me' (Mk
5:7). We may be sure that this verse was not the model that

inspired the Jesus Prayer, though there is a similarity in the initial words.

Luke has parallels to Mark's passages, plus several that are original with him. In the prayer of the ten lepers who cry out from afar, 'Jesus, master (*epistata* or *rabbi*), have mercy on us', (Lk 17:13) we see the second half of the Jesus Prayer. Here it is a request for immediate physical help. Then there is the blind man of Jericho. In Luke's gospel he crys, 'Jesus, son of David, have mercy on me' (Lk 18:38). Mark names him Bartimaeus and says that he cried, 'Son of David, Jesus, have mercy on me' (Mk 10:47). In Matthew there are two blind men and they cry together, 'Lord, have mercy on us, son of David' (Mt 20:31). The elements are the same in all three accounts; again, the favor requested is physical aid. Finally Luke has the words of the good thief, 'Jesus, remember me....' And a variant reading has: 'Turning towards the Lord he said to him, "Remember me...." ' We will meet prayer formulas inspired by these words of the good thief, but this is not the Jesus Prayer.

Petitions addressed to Christ under the title 'Lord', either in the vocative or in the nominative with a vocative meaning, are much more frequent. And it seems that the Master may even have grown weary of being called 'Lord' by men who did not act as if they believed it: 'None of those who call "Lord, Lord" will enter God's kingdom' (Mt 7:21).

There is a certain type of implicit and discreet petition, sometimes merely in the form of a suggestion, which is a speciality of sensitive souls. The Master never refused these prayers, even if he did respond a little sharply at first as he felt himself being overcome by a great act of faith. It was in this way, St John tells us, that Mary prayed to Jesus at Cana and the sisters of Lazarus prayed at their brother's tomb. Matthew's gospel records a number of such prayers. The leper says simply, 'Lord, if you wish, you can make me clean' (Mt 8:2). The roman centurian, with greater faith than the Israelites, says, 'Lord, my servant is lying paralyzed and in great pain' (Mt 8:6). A disciple asked, 'Lord, may I first go

and bury my father?' (Mt 8:21), but this petition Jesus cannot
grant because that would be to compromise the great
commandment to love God above all else. In the incident of
Peter walking on the water there are two ejaculation-like
prayers: 'Lord, if it is really you, tell me to come to you over
the water....Lord, save me!' (Mt 14:28, 30). The Canaanite
woman repeated her petition three times. First, 'Have mercy
on me, Lord, son of David' (Mt 15:22). Then, 'Lord, help me'
(Mt 15:25). And finally, in terms that would justify the
definition of prayer as 'compelling God' (*coactio Dei*): 'Yes,
Lord, but the little dogs eat the scraps which fall from their
master's table' (Mt 15:27). A father prayed for his son, 'Lord,
have mercy on my son' (Mt 17:15). The blind men of Jericho
say twice, 'Lord, son of David, have mercy on us', and finally
make an explicit request: 'Lord, open our eyes!' (Mt 20:29,
31, 33). And their wish was fulfilled. Finally, the foolish
virgins beg, 'Lord, Lord, open up for us', but the door
remains closed because they are too late.

Mark used *Kyrios* sparingly. When it occurs it is usually
in an Old Testament quotation. It is used in the vocative once
by the Syrophoenician woman (Mk 7:28), and perhaps again
by the father of a possessed boy (Mk 9:24, Vulgate). The
father had asked the disciples but they were unable to cure
the boy. The man addressed Jesus as 'Teacher' in Verse 17
and then asked him, 'If you can do anything, please help us,
out of the kindness of your heart (*splangnistheis*)' (Mk 9:22).
Jesus replied, 'If I can? Everything is possible for one who
has faith.'

Besides the parallels with the other synoptics, Luke's
gospel contains several other prayers addressed to Jesus as
Kyrios. After the first miraculous catch of fish, Peter said,
'Depart from me, O Lord, for I am a sinful man' (Lk 5:8). The
Centurion said, 'Lord, do not trouble yourself; I am unworthy
to have you enter my house' (Lk 7:6). James and John asked,
'Lord, do you want us to command fire to descend from
heaven and consume them?' It was a juvenile suggestion and
the Master was forced to reprimand two of his favorite

disciples (Lk 9:54). An anonymous person declared, 'I will follow you, Lord, but first let me go and take leave of my family' (Lk 9:61). The request was denied, for no one who puts his hand to the plough and then looks back is fit for the kingdom of God. The seventy-two disciples returned jubilant with their first apostolic success and said, 'Lord, even the demons were subject to us in your name' (Lk 10:17). At the end of his response to them Jesus addressed his heavenly Father using the same title, 'Lord' (Lk 10:21). In Chapter Eleven an anonymous disciple who had observed Jesus at prayer asked, 'Lord, teach us to pray'. This request must have pleased him more than any other, and he answered with the words of the most sublime prayer of all. Another anonymous disciple asked him, perhaps out of idle curiosity, 'Lord, will only a few be saved?' (Lk 13:23). The question was inappropriate, like Peter's question about John in the episode on the lakeshore after the resurrection (Jn 21:21). Jesus replied, politely, that everyone should mind his own business. Another curious questioner asked, ' "Where, Lord, will all of this happen?" And he answered, "Where the body lies, there will the vultures gather" ' (Lk 17:37).

Special attention should be given to the short prayer which Jesus himself composed in one of the parables as a model to be imitated. It is the prayer of the tax collector, 'O God have mercy on me a sinner (*hilastheti moi to hamartolo*)' (Lk 18:13). The evangelist used the imperfect tense here—'he would beat his breast and say'—implying that the prayer was repeated more than once, perhaps a number of times. In this prayer we can see the second half of the Jesus Prayer, in content as well as in terminology, for *hilastheti* is synonymous with *eleison*. It is not surprising that the prayer of the tax collector was highly recommended in the teaching and practice of the desert fathers.

To sum up, the Jesus Prayer is present in the four gospels in fragmentary form. The tone and feeling of the prayer is best expressed in the parable of the pharisee and the tax collector. The title 'Lord' is the title most frequently used by those who speak to Jesus. No prayer is addressed to him under the name 'Jesus Christ'; it took a number of years before these two words were combined into a single name. The title 'Son of God' does not occur but 'Son of David' is used by Bartimaeus and by the Canaanite woman. The transition between these two titles under the promptings of faith is explained by Origen in one of his commentaries:

> *'Have mercy on me, son of David!' Go through the gospels and observe who are the ones who call him 'son of David,' like the Canaanite woman and the blind men of Jericho, and who call him 'son of God'. Of those who use the second title some add the word 'truly' like the disciples who adored him in the boat saying, 'Truly you are the son of God'. Others omit the word 'truly', for instance the possessed persons who said, 'What is there between you and us, son of God?' I believe you will find a comparison of this sort very instructive. It will enable you to distinguish between those who approached him as a branch of the stock of David according to the flesh and those who saw him as the one who has been 'established son of God in power according to the Spirit of holiness'* (Rom 1:4). *And in the latter category there are those who add the word 'truly' and those who do not.*[8]

Despite the fact that all the elements of the Jesus Prayer were on hand in the gospels, and Origen's principle was there to inspire someone to bring all the elements together, and in the process to change 'son of David' to 'son of God' as a sign of the christian faith, nevertheless we have no documentary evidence from the first centuries to show that such a synthesis actually took place.

SHORT PRAYERS IN THE REST OF THE NEW TESTAMENT

Outside the gospels we find a great many examples of

invocations addressed to 'the Lord'. In the book of Acts the vocative *Kyrie* often introduces questions—for instance Saul's two questions in the vision on the road to Damascus (Ac 22:8; 9:5; 26:15; see also 1:6; 10:4)—or else some reflection made by a disciple—Ananias (Ac 9:13), Peter (Ac 10:14; 11:8). It also occurs four times in prayers: two of the prayers are addressed to God the Father as is clear from the context (Ac 1:24; 4:29); one is Stephen's prayer addressed explicitly to the 'Lord Jesus' (Ac 7:59); this is followed immediately by Stephen's second prayer, 'Lord, do not hold this sin against them', which could be directed either to the Lord Jesus or to God the Father.

In all the epistles the vocative *Kyrie* occurs only in Rom 10:16 and 11:3, both times in quotations from the Old Testament. In the book of Revelation there are eight occurrences. Six times the reference is to God the Father (Rev 4:11; 11:17; 15:3-4; 16:5-7). Once it is the author speaking to one of the twenty-four elders (Rev 7:14). The final occurrence is in the famous acclamation that expresses longing for the glorious return of the *Kyrios*, 'Amen! Come, Lord Jesus!' (Rev 22:20). This is similar to the *Maranatha* of 1 Cor 16:22.

Thus, of all the prayers which must have been directed to the Lord Jesus after his ascension the New Testament recorded only two, the prayer of the martyr Stephen, 'Lord Jesus, receive my spirit', and the final 'Come, Lord Jesus!' which closes the book of Revelation. Unlike the Jesus Prayer, these are not prayers oriented toward contrition, begging for mercy and pardon; they are the expression of a deep longing for the Lord's presence. Expectation of the parousia must have frequently put the prayer 'Come, Lord Jesus' on the lips of the early Christians, and it is not entirely absent from liturgical prayers even today. Is *Maranatha* the Aramaic equivalent of the prayer 'Come, Lord Jesus'? Or should these Aramaic syllables be separated to read 'the Lord is coming', which would no longer be a prayer but an act of faith? Whatever its original meaning, the expression completely eluded the grasp of the Greek and Latin-speaking Christians. It was even mistaken for a formula of imprecation because of its similarity with the *anathama sit* of 1 Cor 16:22. It furnishes no evidence for the origins of the Jesus Prayer.

SHORT PRAYERS IN THE APOSTOLIC FATHERS

The writings of the apostolic fathers do not teach us very much more. The prayer they are concerned with is public liturgical prayer, far removed from the realm of the hidden and secret. Still, it is worth noting the general tone of these liturgical prayers so that later we can discuss the question of continuity or transformation. The formula used most frequently is an acclamation of praise to the Lord: 'To him be the glory and the power throughout all ages!' Eastern Christians conclude all prayers, even the Our Father, with one form or another of this doxology. This is an expression of their belief that a Christian's primary duty is to praise and thank God, knowing that for him, as for Mary, the Lord has done marvellous things. The graces asked for in personal prayers differ according to the circumstances, but some requests are quite frequent, especially those formulated in general terms. The call for help dominates all others, as we saw in the Acts of the Martyrs.

Collections of sigillography provide documentation about medals, seals, amulets and the like.[9] A summary is provided by G. Schlumberger:

The figures which are featured on the seals are predominantly sacred figures. Ninety percent of the time they portray the Virgin, Christ or one of the saints. The following list gives, in order of frequency, the principal images that I have observed on official documents: the Virgin Mary with or without the Christ child, a saint, the cross, Christ, the archangel Michael, the Virgin or Christ with a saint [or two saints]; several saints, often two warrior saints; a religious scene including one or two persons (the crucifixion, the annunciation, Daniel in the lions' den); an angel; the lamb symbolizing Christ; the reigning emperor or empress; forms of animals; a picture of the holder of the document (rare).[10]

The numerical ratio between the images of the Virgin and the images of Christ will not necessarily be the same in all collections. Besides, the inscriptions are not always addressed to the figure pictured. Sometimes the figure of the Virgin may be accompanied by a prayer to Christ. We are more interested in the inscriptions than in the pictures or the arrangement of the different elements.

Despite the variety of images the invocations are monotonously the same. They ask for help (*boethei*), usually from Christ or the Theotokos, occasionally from a saint.[11] Or they ask for protection (*skepe, skepois*), most often from a saint, occasionally from the Virgin, rarely from Christ.[12] Help is something more than protection. The latter is a request for safety from enemies, the former has the connotation of a prayer for eternal salvation. It should not be surprising that these appeals for help and salvation turn up also in the pagan mystery cults.[13] E. Peterson has discovered that among Christians the cry for help is more characteristic of Syrian than of Egyptian epigraphy.[14]

The high frequency of these prayers for help is something remarkable. I have counted one hundred sixty-four prayers to Christ and one hundred eighteen to the Theotokos, including doubtful cases, in the Orghidan collection alone. However great may have been the influence of fashion or custom both on the engravers and on their clients in these manifestations of piety, the fashion itself is evidence of a general trend in society, either as its cause or as its effect. The fact that there is an almost equal number of appeals to Christ and to his mother, and a relatively high number to the saints, suggests that the favor being asked for was more important than the donor or patron for whom it was being asked. In fact that seems to be the case always and everywhere, except for a few advocates of the ideal of pure love who tend not to ask for any graces at all. The request for help does not imply any particular form of spirituality at all; in contrast, the Jesus Prayer points unmistakably to monastic origins. A good illustration of the difference would be the *Sub tuum praesidium*, which has been called 'the oldest Greek marian antiphon'.[15] It does not ask for mercy to sinners, but for help, protection, and removal of dangers. It is not the prayer of the tax collector but of the child of God who feels danger approaching. It is inspired by a piety that is concerned more about the future than about the past. In the same connection reference might be made to the psalm verse, 'O God, come to my assistance' (Ps 70:1), which Cassian recommended as a method for continual prayer (*formula spiritualis theoriae-Coll.* X, 10). It belongs to the same tradition of praying for help that we find in the inscriptions on byzantine seals of all kinds. Imperial officials, palace guards, government clerks, stewards, notaries, protonotaries (with the possible exception of the patriarchs of Constantinople), hegumens and even monks all have *boetheson* stamped on their seals, and never *eleison*. It is a detail which should be kept in mind as an indication of the prevailing mentality.

With regard to the names of Christ in these invocations, we nearly always find simply *Kyrie*. Occasionally it will be 'Lord God' (*Kyrios ho theos*) or 'Christ our God' or simply 'Christ' or 'Master of all' (*pantanax*).[16] Sometimes it is 'Jesus Christ' or 'Emmanuel', but without any prayer.[17] Correlative to *Kyrie*, whether explicitly present or not, is the term 'servant' (*doulos*) which is what the owner of the seal ordinarily calls himself. To judge from this evidence, it appears that byzantine piety has once again demonstrated its preference for profound reverence instead of tender sentiment.

To this can be added the testimony of tombstone inscriptions and other monuments. Here too it is *boethei* that predominates, with occasional alternatives like *sosais* or *phylatte.* Tombstones often have the name of the deceased together with a phrase like 'Remember, O Lord' or 'May he live in Christ or in God' or 'Give rest to his soul'. The plea for mercy, *eleison*, seems never to occur, though a synonym can be seen in the word 'spare' (*phise, pheisai*). The names of the Lord most frequently used are *Kyrios, Christos, Iesous Christos* (usually abbreviated). 'Jesus' by itself is very infrequent. [18]

SHORT PRAYERS IN MONASTICISM

The Jesus Prayer, since it is ordered specifically to contrition, must have originated in a special subculture rather than in the common christian society. So we now focus our investigation on the world of monasticism. In this field the first author to have left us a systematic approach to the attainment of continual prayer by means of a *formula spiritualis theoriae* is John Cassian, who in his youth visited most of the monastic centers of Egypt and Palestine.

The core of Cassian's teaching is contained in Chapter Ten of his tenth conference, one of the longest and perhaps the most eloquent chapters in the book. A résumé can be made with the aid of the commentator in the Migne edition, Dom Alard Gazet. [19] Gazet tells us that the first effect of the psalm verse 'O God, come to my assistance; O Lord make haste to help me' is to awaken every devout sentiment in our hearts; that is why Cassian called it a sacred formula (*formula pietatis*). Secondly it helps to overcome and banish all temptations. Thirdly it is effective against every such spiritual infirmity as evil inclinations, evil feelings, vices especially of the flesh, illicit desires, bursts of anger, various dangers and occasions of sin. Fourthly it is powerful against dreams and illusions inspired by the devil. And finally it is a means of retaining the continual memory of God and maintaining unceasing, assiduous prayer, without strain or difficulty.

Cassian himself treated the subject with much more

vitality than these scholarly enumerations might suggest. It would be worth the effort to read Chapter Ten at this point in order to see the great enthusiasm with which he sings the praises of this marvellous and all-powerful formula. No panegyrist ever made greater claims for the Jesus Prayer than Cassian did for his psalm verse in this 'most subtle and intricate dissertation'.[20] The *Deus in adiutorium* leads, as will be said later of the Jesus Prayer, to the perfection of contemplation and to a degree of purity which Cassian described as follows:

> *It relies on no image of the imagination, nor on any speech or words, but it springs up like a spark from a burning coal in an ineffable surge of the heart and an inexhaustible alacrity of spirit. The mind is carried beyond all material things that can be seen or felt and pours out its prayer with inutterable sighs and groanings.*[21]
> *This is the kind of prayer that St Antony the Great would call perfect. Antony made this inspired and heavenly remark: 'The prayer is not perfect in which the monk is conscious of himself or of the fact that he is praying.'*[22]

Abba Isaac assured Cassian and his companion that this doctrine or art was a deep secret: 'It has been handed down to me by a few of the oldest fathers still left, and I speak of it only to those rare souls who have a true thirst for prayer.'[23]

In other words, the formula is a piece of esoteric wisdom ordered to the perpetual remembrance of God. But a closer look at Cassian's doctrine raises several questions. For instance, the two conferences on prayer can be dated with complete accuracy; the ninth was just before and the tenth just after the Feast of the Epiphany in 399.[24] At this early date who would be 'the oldest fathers' of the first generation monks? Where did they live? Why did they select this particular psalm verse instead of something like the Jesus Prayer? I personally cannot give an apodictic answer to these questions, but perhaps the bits of information I have gleaned here and there may put someone with greater perspicacity on the track towards a final solution.

The practice of saying ejaculations goes back to very early times.[25] In the soul of one who believes in God such prayers spring out as spontaneously as the commonplace exclamations that rise from any human heart. The believer knows that God is listening everywhere. His devout exclamations do not echo in an empty universe that is deaf to every cry. Spontaneous usage naturally comes before systematic practice based on theory or thematic experience. But once a thing is experienced as useful, theory and improved technique are quick to follow. If this seems to be true as a general principle, something of the sort should also take place with respect to the *politiai* and the *meletai*.

Every effort to systematize is preceeded by a period of liberty, even anarchy, the era of the virgin forest. Now prayer is the most total and profound manifestation of life because it involves the whole man and puts him in communication with his Creator and with all other creatures. That is why prayer is hard to confine within fixed forms and formulas. The person who prays tends spontaneously to use the expression that is most in accord with his own temperament and tends to vary the expression according to changing moods, without ever exhausting the richness of his inner life.

This accounts for the amazing variety of prayer formulas that can be seen in the accounts of those few ascetics who have left some record of their prayer life. They all knew that what counts most is the interior disposition, not the material formula. As one of the *Apophthegmata* puts it:

> *The Canaanite woman cried out and was heard, but the woman with an issue of blood said nothing and was called 'blessed'. The Pharisee prayed in a loud voice and was condemned. The tax collector did not open his mouth and he was heard.*[26]

The supreme law is *simplicity*. The Rule of St Benedict, in perfect conformity with monastic tradition, says, *simpliciter intret et oret* (Chap. 52). Prayers should also be marked by their brevity: *omnino brevietur oratio*, says St Benedict in a phrase which perplexes the commentators but which is again a faithful echo of tradition.

Using these criteria in our inquiry we can safely bracket nearly all the long prayers since length usually means absence of spontaneity. It is however possible to have a long series of short phrases one after the other and all very spontaneous. Also in highly emotional situations it can happen that there is a moment of surprised silence followed by a flood of words. Orientals are more exuberant and voluble than most Westerners, and their improvisations can sometimes take the form of lengthy prayers spoken aloud but obviously coming from the depths of the heart. We have many examples of this, from the song of Zachary and the song of Mary in the New Testament to the impromptu poems of a nineteenth-century Carmelite of Bethlehem.[27] But ordinarily these outbursts of feeling do not take the form of prayers and, if they do, it happens only rarely and to exceptional individuals; consequently they are not too important to the question of continual prayer and we need not consider them.

In order to classify some prayers as short and others as long, we need some objective standard. Judging from the example given by Cassian a short prayer may be defined provisionally as a formula that can easily be repeated several hundred times a day by people who are preoccupied with other tasks. We will give special attention to those which could be said in the time it takes to make a prostration or walk a few steps. Monastic literature provides many examples that fit this definition, as the following survey will show.

The alphabetical collection of *Apophthegmata* begins with St Antony the Great. One day in the desert Antony was overcome by *acedia* and by troublesome thoughts. He said again and again (imperfect tense): 'O Lord, I desire to be saved but my thoughts are fighting against me. What shall I do in this affliction? How can I be saved?'[28] As Antony spoke to God in the desert the great problem that was weighing on his mind was salvation. The eternal question which the monks in the apophthegmata are always asking their elders turns up first as an ejaculatory prayer to God: 'How can I be saved?' Perhaps it never ceases to be a prayer even when it is directed to the spiritual father. It can certainly qualify as a short prayer—three syllables in Greek (*pos sotho*). In the *Life of Antony* we see him as a master in the art of opposing just the right scripture text to the wiles of the devil. For instance, he would use a psalm verse: 'If an army encamp against me, my heart will not fear" (Ps 27:3). When the battle was over he had another ejaculatory prayer which should be carefully noted: 'Where were you, *O good Jesus*, where were you? Why did you not come at the very beginning and cure my wounds?'[29] When St Barsanuphius recommended that *antirrhesis* (fighting the devil with verses from Scripture) be left to the perfect, he must have been thinking especially of Antony, who wielded this weapon with amazing dexterity.[30] Some of Antony's words of advice were: 'pray continually', 'sing psalms', 'repeat by heart', 'remember the precepts of Scripture'. 'Above all he counseled them to meditate (*meletan*) continually the Apostle's command, "Never let the sun set on your anger" (Eph 4:26), and to meditate in the same way all the other commandments.'[31] Continual prayer, constant meditation, short prayers, the name of Jesus-everything is there except the Jesus Prayer itself.

After the great Antony comes the great Arsenius. The first of his sayings records one of his short prayers, the one which made him move from the royal palace to the desert: 'Lord, lead me in such a way that I may be saved.' It is the *pos sotho* again. The second saying informs us that after Arsenius became a hermit he said this prayer again 'using the same words'.[32] Another formula of his is this: 'O God, do not forsake me; I have done nothing of value in your sight but in your goodness give me the grace of beginning now.'[33] Arsenius is the great champion of compunction (*penthos*).

Macarius, surnamed 'the Great', also practised short
prayers, so short in fact that he could say twenty-four of them
as he walked down a passageway which was about sixty paces
long—which would be at a rate of one every three steps.[34]
He explained his theory of prayer as follows:

> *There is no need to go on and on* (battalogein—as in Mt
> 6:7). *All you have to do is stretch out your hands and say:*
> *'Lord, have mercy on me* (eleison) *as you wish and as you*
> *know how.' If a strong temptation comes, say, 'Lord,*
> *help!'* (boethei). *He himself knows what is best and he*
> *will have pity.*[35]

These words—*eleison, boethei*—should be kept in mind. They
belong to two different trends of spirituality. Macarius
probably made a synthesis of them, to judge from a variant in
the *Verba Seniorum*: 'May it be done, O God, as you wish
and as it pleases you.'[36] This could be described as a prayer
of abandonment to God; yet it is also a positive request and
not a refusal to ask for anything.

Mention might also be made of the prayer attributed to
Macarius in an ancient codex from Vienna.[37] It begins with
the words of the tax collector, 'O God, be merciful to me a
sinner', and goes on in terms that we have already heard
from Arsenius: 'I have done nothing of value in your sight.'
This is followed by praise of the holy Trinity. The author
pauses briefly to mention a lack of full control over his actions
and then goes on to win his plea for grace by accusing
himself of having committed every conceivable crime, a tactic
also attributed to St Agathon.[38] Finally the prayer concludes
with the usual request for help (*boetheson*) and calls on the
intercession of our immaculate Lady, the Theotokos, and all
the saints. From internal evidence this prayer must be dated
later than the period of Macarius. Each of the separate
fragments of the prayer could be spontaneous but when they
are strung together they form something like a piece of
literature. Still there are a few noteworthy phrases. One of

these, 'Be merciful to me a sinner', was to become a formula so stereotyped that it could be abbreviated to the definite article *to*.[39] Notice also the use of *hilastheti* and *boetheson*, but not *eleison*.

Cassian chose Psalm 70:1 as a short prayer formula. A commentary on the psalms preserved among the works of Origen suggests that a verse from Psalm 38 was also in use: 'Do not forsake me, O Lord; be not far from me, O God' (Ps 38:21). The commentary says: 'This makes an excellent beginning for prayer because it contains the holy Trinity itself.'[40] How it refers to the Trinity I will leave to others to explain; but the remarkable thing is that the author of this commentary was very probably Cassian's master, Evagrius Ponticus.[41] Was Evagrius repeating a first generation monastic tradition here or was he the first to point out the possibilities of this verse as a short prayer? Both alternatives are possible but the second seems more likely because the intention of Evagrius was to go through the psalter and pick out verses that would be appropriate for all the vicissitudes of the spiritual life. He frequently writes, 'This verse can be used for....'[42] In the chapter on sadness in the *Antirrheticos* Evagrius drew attention to this same psalm verse: 'The soul that desires to find spiritual consolation [literally, *logoi*] in prayer during periods of sadness should employ the verse, "Do not forsake me...."'[43]

Evagrius is known for certain to have utilized the method of short prayers himself. Palladius tells us that he said a hundred of them a day.[44] For a busy man that is a great many. Besides writing his own treatises, Evagrius earned his living by copying manuscripts. He himself recommended the use of brief prayers. In his *Chapters on Prayer* he counseled the monk to 'make use of short and intense prayer' at the time of temptation, which was often enough for those who pursued the ideal of pure prayer.[45] But it is in the *Antirrheticos* that Evagrius most explicitly taught the use of ejaculatory prayers drawn from Scripture. It is not at all surprising that from all this complex machinery only a few detached components survive, such as the *Deus in adiutorium.*

Next in the *Apophthegmata* there is Ammonas who may have been an acquaintance of Evagrius. When asked whether it was best to wander over the desert or to go abroad where you are unknown or to become a recluse, Ammonas answered: 'You will profit from none of these things. Stay in your cell instead. Eat a little every day and have the words of the publican continually in your heart. Then you can be saved.'[46]

We read of an old monk who was relentlessly plagued by demons. He finally cried out, 'Jesus, help me (*boethei moe*),' and his persecutors fled. The old man began to weep. Then he heard a voice from on high asking him, 'Why are you crying? You have only yourself to blame. You saw how I made my presence felt as soon as you turned to me.' Then the monk understood and he began to apply himself diligently to the 'activity concerning God' (*ergasia kata theon*).[47] The story was designed to promote invocation of the name of Jesus in an age when the practice was being neglected or forgotten.

In another anecdote some of the brethren paid a visit to one of the elders and began by praying with him. When their visit was over they suggested saying another prayer. The old man said, 'But haven't we prayed already?' 'Yes, when we came in', they answered, 'but then we had a conversation.' 'I beg your pardon, my brothers,' the old man said, 'but while I sat talking with you I said one hundred and three prayers.'[48] After relating a few more stories like this, Evergetinos slips in the comment that it is erroneous to believe that all prayer must be made with the voice or the body. But if one has not yet attained the stage of spiritual prayer he should at least employ the more visible kind, as another story teaches. A questioner tried to get to the bottom of the problem and received this noteworthy reply: ' "What prayer should I say?" he asked. The elder answered, "Say the Our Father." '[49]
49

Abba Isaiah gave this advice: 'Force yourself to say numerous prayers, for prayer is the light of your soul.' [50] The nature of these prayers is clearly indicated:

> *Examine yourself every day to see if you have sinned. If you pray about these sins, God will forgive them.... Force yourself to say many prayers with tears. Perhaps God will have mercy on you* (eleisei) *and strip you of the old man, the sinner.* [51]

Isaiah was recommending prayers oriented toward contrition. Prayers of petition were given the same orientation:

> *When you pray to God in time of temptation do not say, 'Take this or that away from me', but pray like this: 'O Jesus Christ, sovereign* (despota), *help me and do not let me sin against you....'* [52]

He goes on for ten more lines with similar supplications: 'Have mercy on me', 'Save me', and so on. Abba Isaiah's principle concern was deliverance from past sins (*eleison*) and from possible sins in the future (*boetheson, soson*). He came back to the prayer of petition in his precepts to novices:

> *In the struggle against temptation, prostrate yourself before God again and again saying, 'Be willing to help me* (boethos), *O Lord, because I am weak and cannot keep up this battle.'* [53]

We have already seen how Abba Lucius of Alexandria was accustomed to pray. His formula, as he explained it to the Euchites who visited him, was the first verse of Psalm 51, the *Miserere*. He would say it over and over as he sat weaving his palm fronds. [54]

Abba Sisoes asked for God's help to control his tongue. He prayed, 'Lord Jesus, protect me against my tongue.' He used a common word for shelter or protection (*skepason*) but gave it a moral or spiritual connotation. We are told that Sisoes had been saying this prayer for thirty years and yet he still fell into sin with his tongue once a day.[55]

In the treatise *On the Eight Vices*, attributed to St Nilus, we read: 'Every time the urge for fornication comes upon you when you are alone, get up, throw yourself down before God, and cry, "Son of God, help me."'[56] For Nilus the invocation of the name of Jesus could take place without audible words. Writing about the struggle against demons he particularly recommended 'the invocation of the name of Jesus Christ our God and saviour, the lover of men', though he added that this prayer will not be enough all alone, 'without the other combats'.[57] Elsewhere he commented on the prayer of the blind men of Jericho: 'Have mercy on us, Lord, son of David, for you are God and man in a unity of person; have mercy on us (*eleison*) for it is you to whom we call for help (*boethon*).'[58] Always these two terms! In another letter, to Bishop Philochriste, he wrote that just as the demons never grow tired of tempting us, so we should avoid weariness, *acedia* and idleness by continually calling the sacred name of Christ to our assistance (*eis boetheian*).[59] He went on to explain in detail the theory of this invocation of the name:

> *The weapons to use against the demons are: remembrance of our saviour, fervent invocation of the sacred name day and night, frequent signs of the cross on the forehead, the breast, the heart, and other places, and also the meditation* (melete) *of inspired texts.*[60]

It appears from all this that Nilus understood 'invocation of the venerable name of Jesus' more in the theological than in the phonic sense.

The monk Apollo had been a shepherd, an uneducated man. At the age of forty he was led by sinful curiosity to commit a crime. To make reparation for this, he went to Scete:

'If I live another forty years,' he said to the fathers, 'I will spend them in praying constantly that God will forgive my sin.' He did no manual labor but spent all his time in prayer, using these words: 'I have sinned as men will, but do Thou pardon me as God pardons.' This prayer became his melete *day and night. A brother living with him heard him say one day, 'Lord, let me rest a little, for I have been pleading with you constantly.' And God assured him that all his sins had been pardoned.* [61]

In the *Historia Monachorum* we read of an Apollos, perhaps the same person as in the *Apophthegmata*, whose occupation was 'offering prayers to God for days on end, bending his knees a hundred times by night and a hundred times by day.' [62]

Abba Poemen recommended the practice of *melete* in the form of prayers said aloud, but he also advised the monks not to neglect interior prayer, or secret meditation (*krypte melete*). [63] Without going into details he indicated the general tone of this practice: 'He who wishes to redeem his sins should redeem them by mourning, for this is the traditional way according to Scripture and the fathers...and there is no other way.' [64] The numerous *apophthegmata* attributed to Poemen, one hundred eighty-seven altogether, show how assiduously he 'meditated' Scripture. And 'it was his practice to do everything in secret'. [65]

Here is the rule observed by a soldier-monk of Alexandria named John:

Every morning until the ninth hour he would remain alone in his monastery [i.e. his place of retreat] near the steps of St Peter's, keeping silence and speaking to no one. He stayed in the oratory, wearing a hairshirt and weaving baskets. As he worked he would say, 'O Lord, cleanse me of my hidden faults, that I may not be confounded in my prayer' (cf. Ps 19:12-13). After saying this verse once, he was silent for about an hour, then he said it again. He repeated this verse seven times a day, without adding anything else.[66]

These examples should be sufficient to corroborate Cassian's doctrine. Cassian was true to the tradition of the fathers and not simply projecting his own ideas when he recommended the use of frequent short prayers and extolled their value. Of the many prayers employed by the fathers he chose the *Deus in adiutorium meum intende*, just as others would later choose and publicize the Jesus Prayer.

As we study that process of selection as it took place through the centuries, we will discover still other prayer formulas which were current in hesychasm and the byzantine spirituality influenced by hesychasm. The following section will place the whole process in perspective, showing the point of departure and the terminal point.

FROM FREEDOM TO UNIFORMITY
CHRYSOSTOM TO PSEUDO-CHRYSOSTOM

St John Chrysostom knew and recommended the practice of short, frequent prayers:

> *'Now it happened as Hannah multiplied her prayer before the Lord that Eli the high priest observed her mouth'* (1 Sm 1:12).
> *...why does it say that she 'multiplied her prayer'? It does not seem that her prayer was very lengthy at all. She did not indulge in prolonged discourse or draw out a long entreaty. She said only a few simple words: 'Adonai, Lord God of hosts, if you will look upon the humiliation of your handmaid and remember me and not forget your handmaid, but will give to your handmaid a male child, then I will make of him an oblation in your sight all the days of his life. He will never drink wine or strong drink*

and the razor shall never touch his head' (1 Sm 1:11).

Can that be called a multitude of words? Why then did the sacred author say she 'multiplied her prayers'? The explanation is that she was saying these words over and over again. She spent a long time repeating the same words. This was the way that Christ himself in the gospels commanded us to pray. When he told his disciples not to babble on and on like the pagans in their prayers, he taught us that prayer should be limited. We will be heard not because of a multitude of words but because of the attention of the mind.

Someone may be inclined to object that if Jesus had wanted us to pray in few words he would not have told a parable that teaches us to pray always. He told of the widow who by persistent entreaty and frequent visits succeeded in moving a cruel and inhuman judge who neither feared God nor respected men. And St Paul for his part exhorted us, 'Persevere in prayer' (Rom 12:12), and 'Pray without ceasing' (1 Thes 5:17). There seems to be a contradiction if on the one hand we are to pray assiduously and yet we are to avoid long prayers.

But there is really no contradiction. Far from it! Instead there is perfect agreement. Both Christ and St Paul prescribed prayers that are short and repeated at frequent intervals. The reason is that if you prolong your discourse there will inevitably be moments of inattention which will give the devil an opportunity to get in close and trip you up and draw your mind far from the words you are pronouncing. But if you make use of frequent, successive prayers which break up the time into brief intervals, it will be easy for you to keep alert and thus you will pray with much more presence of mind. [67]

This was the way Hannah the mother of Samuel prayed, says Chrysostom. If we compare length, the 'short' prayer of Hannah was fifty words long, as long as the Lord's Prayer, longer than a Hail Mary. The short prayers of the fathers of

the desert, including the Jesus Prayer and the *Deus in
adiutorium* were hardly more than a dozen words long.

Chrysostom's homily goes on to mention something else
which can be briefly noted and which is also found in other
authors. According to Exodus, Moses prayed without making
a sound and yet God heard him and said, 'Why do you cry to
me?' (Ex 14:15). Men hear only the sound of the voice but
God listens to the cry of the heart. A person can make his
prayer heard without speaking out loud. 'One can be walking
through the agora,' says Chrysostom, 'and be praying
interiorly with great fervor; or one can be with his friends or
be doing anything at all and still call upon God with an
intense, interior cry that cannot be detected by anyone
present.' This is what Hannah did: 'Her voice was not heard'
(1 Sm 1:13). But God heard her, 'so loud was her interior
cry'.

This teaching is in perfect accord with the secret
meditation of the desert fathers. Chrysostom taught his
antiochene audience the monastic custom and built a theory
around it. This is the result, we may suppose, of the four
years that Chrysostom spent as the disciple of 'an old
ascetic'.[68]

In his commentary on the psalms, Chrysostom had further
opportunities to speak of short prayers and their content. For
instance the verse: 'Have pity on me and hear my prayer' (Ps
4:1). The first thing that struck Chrysostom about this verse
is that it does not seem to follow logically after the
preceeding verse which said, 'When I called him, the God of
my justice heard me.' 'My justice' in verse one implies that
the psalmist was already holy, but in the very next verse he
is pleading for mercy. Chrysostom explained it as follows:

> *Even if we have thousands of acts of great virtue to our
> credit, our confidence in being heard must be based on
> God's mercy and his love for men. Even if we stand at the
> very summit of virtue, it is by mercy that we shall be
> saved. Consequently it is necessary to have not only*

holiness but also a contrite heart. If a sinner prays with humility—which is already a part of virtue—he can obtain great blessings. If a just man presents himself arrogantly he will lose all he has gained. This is what the parable of the publican and the Pharisee teaches.

So it is very important to know how we should pray. What is the right way? You can learn it from the publican; and do not be embarrassed to have as a teacher one who had mastered the art so well that only a few simple words were enough for him to obtain perfect results.... He called himself wretched, he beat his breast, he did not presume to raise his eyes to heaven. If you pray as he did your prayer will become lighter than a feather. For if this way of praying could justify a sinner, how much more easily will it lift a just man to the heights![69]

It is possible that St John Chrysostom knew of the formula, 'Lord Jesus Christ, son of God, have mercy on me a sinner.' In any case his teaching vindicates several aspects of the prayer—brevity, the plea for mercy, secret meditation. Only on one point is there a considerable difference between Chrysostom and the promoters of the Jesus Prayer: freedom of choice. This will be clear from a comparison with pseudo-Chrysostom.

Among the works ascribed to Chrysostom there is one called *A Letter to Monks*. Montfaucon, in the introduction to the Migne edition, has some harsh words for its author:

The fame of St John Chrysostom was so great that a phenomenal number of writers who had no chance of making a name for themselves on their own merits tried to win an audience by putting Chrysostom's name to their own works.... The result was a large body of pseudepigraphal works. Nearly all of these are compilations made by authors who stand out only for their bad Greek. Such is the Letter to Monks, *a completely superfluous and silly work, which Pierre Poussines has for some reason placed at the beginning of his* Thesaurus....[70]

Pierre Poussines was a knowledgeable authority on works of spirituality and should not lightly be accused of bad taste. Apart from that, the one thing that can be said for the author of the letter is that he knew Chrysostom's teaching. It is all there: the recommendation of short prayers, the interior prayer which crys out in silence, a virtuous life as the precondition for prayer, and even Chrysostom's example of Hannah and Moses copied from the second sermon on St Hannah. The letter deserves to be quoted:

The Apostle has told us to pray uninterruptedly, without anger or passionate thoughts [dialogismos, *a word which Byzantine ascetical writers habitually interpreted in terms of their theory of the eight evil passions*]. *And this is excellent advice, for every thought which takes the mind away from God is not merely from the devil but is the devil himself, for the whole essence and effort of the devil is to separate and remove our attention from God and entice it toward worldly concerns and pleasures. He works interiorly, in the heart, suggesting good works and resolutions and reasonable, or rather unreasonable, thoughts. We must not pay the slightest attention to these things. The spiritual combat consists in keeping the mind fixed on God, in not entertaining or approving impure thoughts, and in not paying any attention to the phantasms which the detestable, diabolic picture-maker stirs up in our imagination. Sometimes he conjures up colors, shapes, and forms, even human figures, and he is such a master at it that the poor deluded victim imagines himself to be someplace where he is not, like a madman who in his hallucinations sees and speaks to people and plans grand things. The devil can deceive us in all these ways and so it is important to be on guard and keep the intellect on a leash, governing it with a firm hand. Every* logismos *and every temptation of the Evil One must be controlled by the invocation of the name of our Lord Jesus Christ.* [71]

A little further on he tells us that the invocation which should be repeated without ceasing is: 'Lord Jesus Christ, son of God, have mercy on me.' He even wrote it five or six times, like a refrain, in order to impress it on the reader's memory. The author considered the memory the highest power of the soul, the first cause of everything good and everything bad. 'The soul which makes an effort may obtain everything by the power of the memory, good things or bad things.' The seat of this wonderful and all-powerful faculty is the heart. If the name of our Lord Jesus Christ is inscribed on the memory and if the heart is filled with this memory, then that soul experiences true life and salvation. 'Remain therefore in your heart, crying out the name of the Lord Jesus so that the heart may penetrate deeply into the Lord and the Lord into the heart, and the two become one.' Evidently this is the work of a lifetime and it will not be accomplished without trials and sufferings. The author exhorts us to persevere: 'I urge you never to give up this rule of prayer but instead, whether you are eating or drinking or travelling or whatever you are doing, cry out unceasingly, "Lord Jesus Christ, son of God, have mercy on me' ".

The terms are reminiscent of some of Cassian's lines in which he recommended, with equal insistence, a different formula of prayer. What follows in the *Letter to Monks* must have been written with Chrysostom's sermon on St Hannah at hand to be copied from. [72] After referring to the example of Hannah, the author continued: 'The one who prays must therefore avoid long, drawn-out discourses, and instead make frequent prayers at short intervals as Christ commanded through the Apostle; the reason is that if you prolong your discourse....' From there on it is word for word like Chrysostom, quoted above. Then the author goes on to copy Chrysostom's passage on Moses and the silent power of his prayer.

In this way pseudo-Chrysostom compiled a letter in which he made the great doctor say what he could have said about the Jesus Prayer had he wished to do so. The letter is consistent with Chrysostom's authentic teaching on prayer except on two points: (1) for pseudo-Chrysostom the prayer formula is stereotyped and immutable, whereas St John Chrysostom left complete liberty as to choice of formula; (2) the *Letter to Monks* makes a specific point about 'the implantation of the name of Jesus in the depths of the heart'. This has nothing in common with the psycho-physical technique developed by the thirteenth-century monk, Nicephorus.

Between Chrysostom and pseudo-Chrysostom there is all the difference which separates freedom of choice from uniformity. For Chrysostom *monologistos proseuche* meant any short prayer chosen prudently by an individual as matter for secret meditation. But with the *Letter to Monks* the term *monologistos* comes to mean one particular formula to the exclusion of all others. Whether this is a sign of progress or regression is not the point. The point is that once this step has been taken the authentic spirit of the fathers has been lost, even though much of their authentic doctrine may be preserved.

DIADOCHUS OF PHOTICE: SHORT PRAYERS
AND
THE PSYCHOLOGY OF THE MEMORY OF GOD

Diadochus of Photice deserves special attention because it is precisely to him that several scholars have traced the origins of the Jesus Prayer.[73] The accuracy of their thesis will have to be tested. First it is important to grasp the central idea and logical consistency of Diadochus. When this is clearly understood it will not be difficult to see at what point in the tradition Diadochus must be placed.

Diadochus spoke constantly of the memory of God, either

using the actual expression *mneme theou* or making the reader supply it from the context and the general thrust of his argument. But the memory of God, central though it was, remained only a means to a higher goal, love (*agape*). Yet it was an indispensable means, and this is where Diadochus showed himself a profound psychologist. According to his teaching man or man's intellect (*nous*), which is what makes him human, was originally something simple and this state of simplicity must be recovered. Three questions are involved here: (1) In what did the state of simplicity consist? (2) How and to what extent was simplicity lost? (3) How can the wound be healed and pristine integrity be recovered?

Regarding the first problem Diadochus taught that man's nature was simple and undivided prior to Adam's disobedience. This was not the Origenist doctrine that the *nous* preexisted in an incorporeal state equal to that of the angels. Diadochus held that man always had a corporeal body and the spirit did not lose any of its purity or its nobility by being united with matter; the body was the docile instrument of the soul, with harmony reigning among all the faculties. The senses of the body cooperated with what Diadochus called 'the sense' (*aisthesis*) of the *nous*. Speaking of this original simplicity Diadochus wrote: 'The very fact that we can know divine things tells us that originally there was *one* natural sense of the soul which as a consequence of Adam's disobedience was divided into two operations.'[74] The unity of the *nous* implied, as a consequence and a sign, the unity of the sense (*aisthesis*). This key term in the vocabulary of Diadochus must be analysed and seen in its relationship to the memory.

By *aisthesis* Diadochus meant consciousness in the full sense, including both intellectual and volitional acts. In his psychology feeling and understanding are not to be regarded as two separate, essentially different functions. *Aisthesis* is an integral property of the *nous*. It is an intellectual sense, made to know invisible realities and attracted to them by connaturality.[75] But it also has an affective or volitional aspect; because of this Diadochus could speak of the 'sense of the heart' (*aisthesis tes kardias*) by which we love God.[76] Free will must intervene here, however, because we love God 'when we want to' and to the degree that we want to (*symmetros*).[77] Diadochus, using his terminology very carefully, made a distinction between the love which is natural to the soul and is controlled by it and another love which is poured forth by the Holy Spirit and sweeps the soul up into a blazing flame.

Distinguishing the intellectual sense from the five corporal senses Diadochus wrote: 'As I have maintained, and as the Holy Spirit of God teaches us in his love for men, there is but one natural sense of the soul, though there are indeed five bodily senses which correspond to the different needs of our body.'[78] Diadochus seems to have been trying to forestall a certain objection which would see a discrepancy between five senses in the body and only one sense in the soul. He granted that there are five corporal senses, called sense organs (*aistheteria*), but maintained that this was no argument against the existence of only one intellectual sense. The multiplicity of organs of perception is perfectly compatible with the unity of the mind's consciousness, which is the faculty of accurately 'tasting' what the mind discerns, tasting particularly the consolation of the Holy Spirit.[79]

What destroyed the natural unity of consciousness (*aisthesis*)? Diadochus traced the cause to Adam's sin of disobedience which made the intellect partially subject to the different movements of the soul.[80] The soul does not of itself possess simplicity; it merely participates in it to the degree that it submits to the higher principle of the intellect, which is itself informed by the Holy Spirit. Disobedience withdrew the soul from the unifying influence of the *nous* and made it the hotbed of 'psychic' passions.[81]

The memory is closely connected with the *aisthesis* and suffers the same sort of split or duality as a result of Adam's sin. Thus division runs through the whole structure of the personality:

Because the nous *[which was originally simple and undivided] has fallen into a state of cognitive duality it is obliged to experience both good and evil thoughts even when it does not want to. This is especially true of those who have highly sensitive powers of discernment. Every time the mind tries to think of something good it immediately also remembers something evil, because the human memory has also split into a kind of duality in consequence of Adam's disobedience.*[82]

Furthermore, since the *aisthesis* has an affective dimension, the split produced by sin divided the will into two inclinations, one towards good and the other towards evil. Like most of the Greek fathers, Diadochus did not place this tendency to evil in nature itself; rather, it is a disposition or habit which is actualized whenever free will accepts a suggestion made by the demons or by the flesh.[83]

What can be done to heal this schizophrenic condition which affects the whole human being and inclines it towards sin? The foregoing analysis holds a key to the process of reintegration. The simplicity of the *nous* cannot be regained straight off. Therapy will have to follow the steps of the illness in reverse. This means beginning from free choice, going on to memory, then to sense, and finally to intellect. The final goal of the ascetical life, as of the incarnation of the Logos, is to 'strip off the memory of evil and put on the love of God'.[84] This presupposes the good use of freedom. Freedom has to be trained 'to move only toward the good, in order to destroy the memory of evil by repeated good works.'[85]

According to the psychology and ethics proposed by Diadochus, acquiring the habit of good will and virtuous action is not an end in itself but should lead to the reintegration and unification of the memory. Of course it is not enough to think about noble things, however diligently; we must actually do good works and keep the commandments of God:

If therefore we begin to keep the commandments of God
with fervent zeal all our senses (aistheteria) *will be*
illuminated deep within by the power of divine grace
which will fill the heart with an imperturbable, loving
peace and destroy our sinful thoughts, preparing us to
reason no longer according to the flesh but spiritually. [86]

The memory must also be set free and unified by use of
direct methods. Since it was the devil who brought about, or
helped to bring about, the state of division, the devil's
suggestions must now be counterattacked and the soul must
maintain the one thing which contradicts all the devil's
purposes, the continual memory of God. Diadochus knew a
potent means of accomplishing both these objectives. With
this we come to the heart of his spirituality. What Diadochus
had in mind was the Jesus Prayer, or invocation of the name
of Jesus, but he did not use these terms. He never once
wrote simply 'Jesus' without modifiers. His usual terminology
was 'the Lord Jesus'. At times he does refer explicitly to 1
Cor 12:3, 'No one can say Jesus is Lord except in the Holy
Spirit'. But to speak of 'the Lord Jesus' or to say 'Jesus is
Lord' is not primarily an act of love but an act of faith and of
adoration, and it is not primarily and principally an
invocation. Only once did Diadochus speak of calling on the
Lord Jesus: 'If a man begins to make progress by keeping the
commandments and by calling ceaselessly on the Lord Jesus,
then the fire of divine grace will penetrate even to the outer
senses of the heart.' [87] Here the accent is not so much on the
act of invoking as on the adverb 'ceaselessly' and the direct
object 'the Lord Jesus'. What Diadochus always stressed was
the need for remembering; invocation was a means of
maintaining the memory of God. [88]

These steps on the road toward reintegration correspond
to the stages of the downfall. Free will has a direct part to
play only at the first step, keeping the commandments and
thereby striving to maintain the memory of God. Even here,
of course, the Holy Spirit must intervene with his grace, as

Diadochus often recalls. In baptism we receive two tremendous gifts of grace. The first is that the image of God in us is renewed and washed clean. The second has to do with the restoration of the divine likeness. The second gift 'infinitely surpasses the first' and it is here that our response to grace becomes critical. Grace 'awaits our cooperation that the divine likeness may be added to the image'.[89] On the external level cooperation takes the form of good works and the practices of the ascetical life; interiorly it is primarily a matter of continually meditating the words 'Lord Jesus'. Without the effort of asceticism it would be impossible for the mind and heart to keep up their interior meditation: 'When the soul is troubled by anger or clouded with overindulgence or weighed down by anxiety and depression the *nous* cannot immerse itself in the memory of the Lord Jesus however much a man may try to force it.'[90]

The index of perfection is the habitual thought or memory of God and of the Lord Jesus. The health of the whole person depends on the healing and reintegration of the memory. Chapter 85 explains this:

At first, grace conceals its presence within the soul of the baptized person, waiting to see what option he will choose. If the man turns completely to the Lord, grace manifests its presence in the heart with indescribable sweetness. Then it waits again to observe the movement of the soul. If it does not prevent the arrows of the demon from penetrating to the depths of the soul's interior sense, it is in order to incite it to seek God with a more ardent fervor and with humility. If then the man begins to make progress by keeping the commandments and continually calling upon the Lord Jesus, the fire of divine grace reaches out even to the external senses of the heart, burning out the cockle from this human field. As a result the temptations of the demon are driven back and scarcely ever penetrate beyond the sensible part of the soul. Finally when a man has put on all the virtues, especially

*that of perfect poverty, grace illumines his whole being
with a still greater sweetness and by its warmth moves it
to a most fervent love of God.*[91]

That should provide an adequate summary. Our purpose
is not to explore all the riches of Diadochean spirituality but
simply to point out the important place occupied by
cultivation of the memory of God through continual
meditation of the formula 'Lord Jesus'.

Diadochus nowhere used the classical formula of the Jesus
Prayer or even came close to it. Evidently he did not know it.
His spirituality was based on the memory of God (*mneme
theou*) in the tradition of St Basil, St Gregory Nazianzen,
Mark the Hermit, and others. But Diadochus explored much
more systematically the implications of a principle which all
these theologians admitted, the spiritual unity of man.

At this point, if I may be permitted to do so, I would like
to quote a page written twenty years ago in a study of the
theology of compunction:

'Today, men's thoughts, however sincere, do not always
resonate on the level of their feelings. This is a primary
difference between modern man and ancient man. They were
not so dichotomized as we are, in spite of a Platonism which
made them often think of the body as a mere container or a
prison of the soul. It was their conviction that asceticism
could and should integrate the intellectual and the sensible
into a higher, spiritual unity. This was because they had a
lofty conception of the "nature" which a perfect man should
have. The battles which we are used to experiencing, and
which we sometimes welcome as opportunities for merit, they
would have regarded as definite signs of imperfection. They
would continue to reproach themselves and complain about
their lack of holiness as long as they had not arrived at a
state of total peace through the perfect unification of the
passions with the will, the imagination with the intellect, and
the will and intellect with the norm of truth and the will of

God. Evagrius wrote: "The intellect originally had the revelation of the spirit for its master but it turned away from this teacher and became the pupil of the senses; when it has reached perfection in Christ it will once again rejoice in its original master" (*Century* III, 55).

'Here we see the deepest reason for the famous doctrine of *apatheia*; to see it as something purely Stoic is to make a travesty of it. *Apatheia* aims not at the elimination of feeling but at its return to the rule of the spirit; the feelings were meant to be docile instruments of the spirit, but passion turned them into rebellious mischief-makers. We have seen already how spiritual sensitivity is awakened to the degree that the exterior senses are mortified. This is what Symeon the New Theologian called "the life-giving death" (*zoopoios nekrosis—Oratio* 57; PG 120:297). Symeon and his school taught the theory of an original unity in the human soul which was destroyed when sin introduced division.

'Symeon found this theory in the first book given him by his spiritual father, the *Hundred Chapters* of Diadochus of Photice: "The very fact that we can know divine things tells us that originally there was *one*, natural sense of the soul which as a consequence of Adam's disobedience was divided into two operations" (Chap. 25). And in Chapter 29 Diadochus drew out the implications of this theory:

> Because it slipped into disobedience, the one natural sense of the soul has been divided into parts corresponding to the movements of the soul. That is why one part of this sense follows the passions and finds enjoyment in the pleasures of this life. The other part finds enjoyment in the activities of reason and intellect, and so the intellect of a wise man stretches out toward heavenly beauty. If we acquire the habit of despising the pleasures of this world we can even unite the earthly appetite of the soul to its rational inclination, with the assistance of the Holy Spirit. For indeed if his divine light does not efficaciously illumine the depths of our heart we will never be able to

taste the good with an undivided sense, that is, with our whole soul.' [92]

Here is the soil in which the roots or at least the tap root of the Jesus Prayer will be found: an anthropology that believes in the possibility of reintegrating the human psyche after it has been split into two opposing elements by sin. The fathers of the desert, perhaps without knowing it or at least without using such a formidable terminology, were seeking for that psychic healing as well as for their eternal salvation. Their therapy like that of Diadochus was based on ascetical practices and on meditation. This included short prayers which constituted their 'secret occupation' (*krypte ergasia*). The formula for these prayers might be variable and spontaneous, or it might be fixed as with Cassian. In either case, and whether the name of Jesus was used or not, these prayers were essentially the same sort of thing as the Jesus Prayer: a methodical exercise for attaining perpetual prayer. As Diadochus put it:

> *Whoever wishes to purify his heart should set it afire with the continual memory of the Lord Jesus, taking this alone for his meditation* (meleten) *and his ceaseless occupation* (ergon). *For those who wish to purge themselves of their corruption must pray not only once in awhile but must give themselves to prayer continually.* [93]

In several places Diadochus emphasized that the invocation of the Lord Jesus is quite enough by itself—'this alone' (Chaps. 58, 59, 81, 97). Likewise he stresses that this work be 'ceaseless', without interruption, excluding every other occupation. For Diadochus this simple formula, diligently employed, was enough to bring healing to the whole personality, just as the *Deus in adiutorium* recommended by Abba Isaac and Cassian was guaranteed to foster all the virtues.

When Diadochus writes 'this alone', his meaning may be

that the memory of the Lord Jesus is to be maintained by any available means, not simply by repetition of these two words. In two places he put the formula in the vocative and modified it with the definite article: 'the "O Lord Jesus" ' (Chaps. 59, 61). This would seem to indicate that the words were a prayer. But there are many other passages in which the meaning is simply the 'memory of God'. The prayer was intended to make the memory permanent and indelible.

Diadochus must be classed as a witness to an intermediate stage in the evolution towards a fixed formula of prayer to Jesus. Cassian, some sixty years before Diadochus and in another milieu, bore witness to a similar evolution at its final term, the *Deus in adiutorium*. The process seems to move in the same direction everywhere—from variety to uniformity, from spontaneity to rigidity, from freedom to determinism.

PRAYER AND SHORT PRAYERS
ACCORDING TO ISAAC OF NINEVEH

No one has preached the need for continual prayer more than the Ninevite mystic.[94] His main purpose in writing was to lead his disciples and readers to this goal. There is in his teaching one untraditional feature which comes from his reliance on a faulty translation of Evagrius. He taught that there was a state superior to continual prayer, where prayer ceased and the soul entered a kind of ecstatic delirium.[95] This theory serves to make the state of continual prayer even more desirable, since it is a step toward something greater.

The means for attaining continual prayer are perfectly traditional. Isaac faithfully transmitted what he had learned from the fathers concerning asceticism, solitude, silence, and spiritual exercises. But he added to their doctrine a distinctively personal touch based on his own experience and expressed in appealing figures of speech. It is worth examining what he says about training oneself for prayer as well as his teaching on the practice of prayer itself:

*Prayer demands prolonged practice until the intellect
finally calms down. We begin by renunciation in order to
free ourselves from slavery to impulse. Then we must set
about praying with perseverance so that eventually the
mind is trained to control its thoughts and learns by
repeated experience the lessons which it is impossible to
learn in any other way. Every spiritual practice (politeia)
develops out of the practice which preceeds it; the first
practice is always a prerequisite for the one that follows.
Prayer develops out of solitude and solitude is the
prerequisite of prayer.*[96]

The prayer Isaac has in mind is evidently interior prayer.
There are many preparatory exercises for this and they are all
done in solitude; they are efficacious to the degree that they
lead one deeper into recollection and interior quiet. This
comes from Evagrius.[97] The interiority and hiddenness of
such exercises as reading, recitation of praises, prayers of
compunction, prostrations, and psalmody is more important
than the relative value of each. Isaac saw them all as infused
with prayer: 'You must remember, my dear friends, that
every hidden occupation, every application of the mind to
God, and every meditation on spiritual things is penetrated
with prayer and falls under the name of prayer.'[98]
Isaac was influenced by Evagrius but he did have his own
ideas about the life of prayer which he had discovered from
personal experience:

*If you love truth, love also the practice of silence
because this, like the sun, will enlighten you in God. It
will free you from the fantasies of imagination and unite
you to God himself.*

*If you reach the point of finding sweetness in the
exercise of kneeling, then do not be quick to give up the
practice. If only we could do this uninterruptedly all our
life!*

When your thoughts reach a state of recollection, do not

interrupt your prayer. Don't worry that prolonging this prayer of recollection may interfere with your psalmody. Psalmody is not as important as praying with genuflections. If you are able to pray thus, it can take the place of your office of psalms.

When you receive the gift of tears during the office, do not think that this sweetness is an interruption of the office, for the charism of tears is the consummation of prayer....

If your thoughts are in a state of distraction try to read rather than pray. [*The Wensinck translation speaks of 'recitation' instead of 'reading', taking the Syriac* queriana *in the sense of the Arabic* quran]. *You should choose your reading matter in accordance with your rule of life* (politeia). *Not every book is conducive to recollection. Books that deal with speculative theology are not usually helpful for purification of the heart. Changing from one book to another leads to wandering thoughts. Do not think that every book of instruction on the fear of God will lead automatically to purity of conscience and to recollection....*

Love stillness (hesychia) *even more than works of asceticism. Hold reading* [*or recitation*] *in higher esteem than standing, because it is a source of pure prayer. Never, never despise reading* [*or recitation*]. *Watch out for the devil's snares.*

Psalmody should be the basis of your rule of life (politeia). *And remember that psalms recited even with distraction are better than corporal works* [*the Greek has: 'corporal works are more profitable than recitation of psalms'*]. *Compunction of the mind is preferable to weariness of the body. When you feel lazy, try to stir up your zeal....*

The good arrangement of works depends on the enlightenment of the intelligence. Nothing is worth more than this knowledge.[99]

Isaac attached considerable importance to 'the good

arrangement' (*eutaxia*) of the exercises of the ascetical life. He maintained that nothing is more basic. The section quoted above is a literal translation of the Syriac and can serve as an accurate reference for any reader who cares to work out a relative scale of ascetical values according to the Ninevite master.

It must be emphasized that Isaac, the greatest mystic of the Eastern church and the master whose burning desire was to lead all his disciples to the summits of prayer and union with God, nowhere recommended either the Jesus Prayer or any other invariable formula to be repeated or meditated at all times and places. He showed no familiarity with the doctrine of Cassian or the *Philokalia* on this matter.

Isaac has left us many prayers both long and short, however, which are worth examining. His longer prayers, which are of lesser interest to us, occur very often as part of the text itself, similar to the peroration prayer of a sermon, yet spontaneous.[100] Short prayers are frequent too. They come either from the fathers or from Isaac himself. A few of these may be quoted:

> *Let us pray continually to our Lord saying, 'O Christ, supreme truth, make your truth shine in our hearts that we may know how to walk in this life according to your will.'* [Chap. 65; Bedjan, p. 449. Since this is a prayer which is to be said 'continually' it would seem to be like the Jesus Prayer. But in fact Isaac was describing a desirable disposition of soul rather than a prayer formula.]
>
> *O Lord, fill my heart with life eternal.* [Chap. 62; Bedjan, p. 431. This is a marvellous ejaculatory prayer which springs spontaneously from the ideas and sentiments expressed in the context.]
>
> *When you pray to God say simply, 'Lord, make me worthy of truly dying to the affairs of this world'* (Chap. 62; Bedjan, p. 435).
>
> *The prayer of the humble man goes straight to God's ear, 'O Lord my God, illumine my darkness'* (Chap. 6;

Bedjan p. 93).

Do not approach the mysterious words of sacred Scripture without first praying and asking God's help saying: 'O Lord, let me feel the power of these sacred words.' [Chap. 45; Bedjan p. 329. Thus, prayer is the key that opens the Scriptures. The Greek editor in a marginal note—Chap. 81, p. 461—calls this a 'prayer before reading.'] [101]

By way of conclusion, it seems that the Semite, Isaac of Nineveh, cannot be numbered among the advocates of a philosophy of the name or of devotion to the name of Jesus or of assiduous meditation of a single formula as an aid to continual prayer. Nor can he be numbered among the advocates of the Jesus Prayer. Still he will always be counted as one of the greatest mystics of the East and of the whole church. [102]

NOTES

1. Cassian, *Coll* X, 7; PL 49:828B.

2. *Vitae Patrum* IV, 124; also V, libellus XV, no. 26; PL 73:748AB; 959AB.

3. Cassian, *Coll* I, 3; PL 49:485A.

4. Ibid., I, 4.

5. Ibid., I, 5.

6. Ibid., I, 7.

7. Ibid., I, 8.

8. Origen, *In Mt* XI, 17; Klostermann, ed., p. 61.

9. See G. Schlumberger, *Sigillographie de l'empire byzantin* (Paris, 1952); also V. Laurent, *La Collection C Orghidan* (Paris, 1952); and the works listed by Schlumberger pp. 2-3 and by Laurent pp. 9-12.

10. Schlumberger, *Sigillographie*, p. 14.

11. For instance, St Nicholas, in Laurent, *Collection*, no. 426.

12. Ibid., nos. 111, 364.

13. See E. Peterson, *Eis theos* (Göttingen, 1926) p. 3.

14. Ibid., p. 63.

15. This is the title of an article by P.F. Mercenier, *Le Muséon*, 52 (1939) pp. 229-33.

16. See Laurent, *Collection*, nos. 81, 102, 219, 425, 364.

17. Ibid., nos. 4, 5, 68.

18. See ibid., nos. 9076-9816.

19. PL 49:832D.

20. Cassian, *Coll* X, 9; PL 49:830B.

21. Ibid., X, 11; PL 49:839A.

22. *Non est perfecta oratio in qua se monachus vel hoc ipsum quod orat intelligit, Coll* IX, 21; PL 49:807A.

23. Ibid., *Coll* X, 1; PL 49:832B.

24. E. Pichery, *Cassien, Conférences,* Sources Chrétiennes 42, Introduction, p. 16.

25. L. Gillet in *Sobornost,* series 3, no. 12 (Winter, 1952) p. 585, does not like to see the Jesus Prayer called an ejaculation, but the term may be used for convenience' sake.

26. *Apophthegmata Patrum,* Alphabetical Series, 'Epiphanius' no. 6; CS 59:49.

27. See Denis Buzy, *Vie de Soeur Marie de Jésus Crucifié (1846-1878),* (Paris, 1926) p. 128ff.

28. *Apophthegmata Patrum,* Alphabetical Series, 'Antony' no. 1; CS 59:1.

29. Athanasius, *Life of Antony,* chap. 9.

30. Ibid., chaps. 12, 39, 40, etc.

31. Ibid., chap. 31.

32. *Apophthegmata Patrum,* Alphabetical Series, 'Arsenius' nos. 1, 2; CS 59:8.

33. Ibid., no. 3.

34. Palladius, *Lausiac History* XVIII, 10; *Vitae Patrum* VIII; PL 73:1111AB.

35. *Apophthegmata Patrum,* Alphabetical Series, 'Macarius' no. 19; CS 59:111.

36. *Verba Seniorum* III no. 207; PL 73:806B.

37. PG 34:445.

38. *Apophthegmata Patrum,* Alphabetical Series, 'Agathon' no. 5; CS 59:18.

39. See for instance, *Nicétas Stéthatos, Vie de Syméon le Nouveau*

Théologien (Rome, 1928) no. LIX.

40.　*Selecta in Ps* 37:22; PG 12:1368D.

41.　See H.U. von Balthasar, "Die Hiera des Evagrius Pontikus', *Zeitschrift für katholische Theologie*, 63 (1939) pp. 90-106; 181-189. On Evagrius as one of Cassian's masters, see S. Marsili, *osb, Giovanni Cassiano ed Evagrio Pontico* (Rome, 1936).

42.　For example, *In Ps* 126:1; PG 12:1614B: 'This verse should be used against thoughts of pride.' See *Antirrheticos*, Frankenberg, ed., p. 541, no. 30.

43.　Frankenberg, p. 508.

44.　Palladius, *Lausiac History* XXXVIII, 11.

45.　Evagrius, *De Oratione*, 98; Bamberger, trans., p. 71.

46.　*Apophthegmata Patrum*, Alphabetical Series, 'Ammonas' no. 4; CS 59:22.

47.　Evergetinos, *Synagogé* IV, chap. 19, p. 75, col. 2.

48.　Ibid., IV, chap. 6, p. 45, col. 2.

49.　Ibid., p. 46, col. 2.

50.　*Logos* IV, no. 1; Augoustinos, ed., *Isaie* (Jerusalem, 1911), p. 15.

51.　*Logos*, IX, no. 2; Augoustinos, p. 66.

52.　*Logos*, IV, no. 7; Augoustinos, p. 24.

53.　*Logos* IV, no. 67; Augoustinos, p. 217; see also no. 68.

54.　*Apophthegmata Patrum*, Alphabetical Series, 'Lucius' no. 1; CS 59:102; see above, pp. 128-9.

55.　Ibid., 'Sisoes' no. 5; CS 59:179.

56.　*De octo vitiis*; Cotelier, *Eccl Graec Monum* III, p. 197A.

57.　PG 79:260AB.

58.　*Ep* II, 240; PG 79:324.

59. *Ep* III, 273; PG 79:530C.

60. Ibid., 278; PG 79:521BC.

61. *Apophthegmata Patrum*, Alphabetical Series, 'Apollo' no. 2; CS 59:31.

62. E. Preuschen, *Palladius und Rufinus, Texte und Untersuchung* (Giessen, 1897) p. 34.

63. *Apophthegmata Patrum*, Alphabetical Series, 'Poemen' no. 168; CS 59:160.

64. Ibid., no. 119; 155.

65. Ibid., no. 138; 157.

66. John Moschus, *Le Pré Spirituel,* Sources Chretiénnes 12 (Paris, 1946) p. 73.

67. St John Chrysostom, *Sermo II in St Hannah*; PG 54:646.

68. See PG 47:LXXXVII.

69. St John Chrysostom, *Expositio in Ps 4*; PG 55:44.

70. PG 60:751-752.

71. PG 60:751.

72. Compare especially Chrysostom, PG 54:645, with pseudo-Chrysostom, PG 60:753.

73. See K. Popov, *Doctrine of the Blessed Diadochus on the Prayer of Jesus* (in Russian), *Travaux de l'Académie ecclésiastique de Kiev* (1902), Vol. III, p. 651ff.

74. Diadochus of Photice, *Oeuvres spirituelles: Cent Chapitres Gnostiques*, ed. by E. des Places, *sj*, Sources Chrétiennes (Paris, 1955) Vol. 5, chap. 25.

75. Ibid., chaps. 1, 7, 11, 24, 30, 32.

76. Ibid., chap. 14. 16.

77. Ibid., chap. 34.

78. Ibid., chap. 29.

79.   Ibid., chap. 30.

80.   Ibid., chap. 29. Diadochus calls original sin a 'slip' (*olisthon*); through a typographical slip the Sources Chretiénnes translation has *plissement* (wrinkle; for *glissement* (slip).

81.   Ibid., chap. 81.

82.   Ibid., chap. 88.

83.   Ibid., chaps. 3, 43.

84.   Ibid., *Sermon for the Ascension*, VI; Sources Chretiénnes 5, p. 168.

85.   Ibid., *Gnostic Chapters*, chap. 5.

86.   Ibid.

87.   Ibid., chap. 85.

88.   In Chapter 31 Diadochus spoke of having the habit of 'clinging by a fervent remembrance to the name of the Lord Jesus and of using this holy and glorious name as a weapon against diabolic illusions'. The idea is not that the name is a charm or formula of exorcism with guaranteed results. It is a method of avoiding illusions by discerning the spirits, relying on the truth that no one can say 'Lord Jesus' except in the Holy Spirit. The demon may not fall back in panic but he will 'give up fighting by ruse and will attack the soul directly, in person'.

In Chapter 32 Diadochus was concerned with the distinction between authentic consolation and illusory consolation. The first is accompanied by 'a fervent memory of God' and the second by 'a mediocre memory of God'. He concluded: 'If therefore the tempter finds the intellect united attentively to the memory of God, his false consolation will be swept aside....'

Chapter 59 is a good summary of the thought of Diadochus. He very clearly explains that saying 'Lord Jesus' is a means of maintaining the memory of God and of dispelling all distractions. He speaks of 'meditating (*meletosin*) ceaselessly this holy and glorious name in the depths of the heart', making it one's 'whole occupation' and using the 'utmost carefulness'. If this is practised for a long time it will bring about the disappearance of every distracting thought, the unification of the memory, and the reestablishment of the mind and heart in their original simplicity.

89.   Ibid., chap. 89.

90.   Ibid., chap. 61.

91. Ibid., chap. 85.

92. Hausherr, *Penthos*, pp. 186-188.

93. Diadochus, *Gnostic Chapters*, chap. 97.

94. Paul Bedjan, ed., *Mar Isaacus Ninivita, De perfectione religiosa* (Paris-Leipzig, 1909) chap. 35, p. 259; chap. 40, p. 304. This is the Syriac edition (eighty-two chapters).

95. See Hausherr, 'Par delà l'oraison pure', *Revue d'ascétique et de mystique* 13 (1932) pp. 185-188.

96. Isaac, chap. 63; Bedjan, ed., p. 439. In the Greek edition by Nicephorun Theotokis (Leipzig, 1770), this is chap. 35, p. 228.

97. See *Revue d'ascétique et de mystique* 15 (1934), p. 77ff.

98. Bedjan, p. 239; see also p. 439.

99. Isaac, chap. 65; Bedjan, p. 446ff.

100. For example:

   a. Chap. 34; Bedjan p. 233: twelve lines (eighteen in the Wensinck translation)

   b. Chap. 65, p. 453: thirteen lines (not in the Greek).

   c. Chap. 80, p. 456: a 'preparatory prayer' of ten lines (fifteen lines in the Wensinck translation) beginning with the words, 'My Lord and my God' (rendered 'Lord Jesus, my God' in the Greek).

   d. Chap. 40, p. 306: ten lines, beginning, 'O Christ, sole omnipotent one'.

   e. Chap. 30, p. 209: eight lines, beginning 'Our Lord, possessor of every power'.

101. In addition see the following:

   a. Chap. 80; Bedjan p. 584; Greek edition chap. 28, p. 179. This is a *monologistos* prayer borrowed from the *Apophthegmata*: 'I have sinned as men will, but do Thou pardon me as God pardons' (see *Apophthegmata Patrum*, Alphabetical Series, 'Apollo' no. 2; CS 59:31).

   b. Chap. 62, p. 435: 'Jesus Christ, King of the universe, make me worthy of desiring you.' This is a conjectural translation. The Greek translator could make nothing of it and has omitted it.

   c. Chap. 62, p. 436: 'O Lord give me the grace of hating my own life for love of life in you.' Also this reflection: 'Meditation of a mediocre thought only saps the strength of patience.' All the strength of a martyr is needed in the life of prayer.

d. Chap. 36, p. 278; Greek edition chap. 54, p. 319: 'Do not let me fall victim of illusions, O Lord, because even strong and experienced souls can scarcely emerge from such things victorious.' Isaac was referring to diabolical hallucinations and fantasies which are very hard to recognize and overcome. The Greek has repeated the vocative, *Kyrie, Kyrie.*

e. Chap. 74, p. 518; Greek edition chap. 81, p. 461. Earlier (Bedjan, p. 514) Isaac had raised the question, 'What are the signs of true humility?' Now he replies with a lengthy and profound psychological analysis of humility: 'As the soul is hidden and invisible to the bodily eye, so is the humble man unknown among men.' Then he concludes his response magnificently with three small words, five syllables altogether, affirming that the humble man wishes to be in the world 'as someone who is not there'. Such a man would enjoy the deepest interior peace because he would belong totally to the Lord. As for the prayer life of such a man, Isaac says: 'I ask myself and I wonder whether the truly humble man even dares to petition God when he prays or believes that he is worthy of making any requests to God or even knows what he should ask for.' Like the seraphim the humble man would be so penetrated with the feeling of God and so helpless before 'the waves of his mysteries, that he would not have the boldness to say more than this: "As you will, O Lord." ' The Greek version amplifies a little: 'As you will, O Lord, so let it be done to me.' This is practically the reply of the 'handmaid of the Lord', but Isaac never spoke of her.

102. Two final remarks.

First, in the Greek version of *Our Holy Father Isaac of Nineveh, the Syrian*, there is a lengthy prayer of forty lines beginning with the words, 'Lord Jesus Christ our God'. If this were an authentic work it would be necessary to modify the above conclusion on one or another point. We have quoted this work under the name of its real author, John of Dalyatha, called John Saba (see above, pp. 103-104).

Secondly, the Syriac edition of Bedjan contains other prayers of the same sort and probably by the same author in Appendix I, pp. 587-589. It is unlikely that they are authentic works of Isaac. They may have been attributed to him after the condemnation of John of Dalyatha by the Nestorian Catholicos, Timothy, in the Synod of 790.

CHAPTER FIVE

THE PETITION FOR MERCY

A
S WE HAVE SEEN, the prayers of the early Christians were usually requests for help (*boethei*) or for protection (*skepason*). Early christian piety was oriented toward the future. The monks never completely lost this orientation.[1] But they developed something else which was not so evident in earlier times, the feeling of *penthos*, of contrition, of compunction, which led them to multiply *Kyrie eleisons*. They were looking back on the past, but only for the sake of transforming the future.[2]

An evolution took place which must be recognized but not exaggerated. We do find among the apostolic fathers a concern for repentance though without any emphasis on mourning or on tears of compunction. Only once did Clement of Rome speak of *penthos* and that was in praising the Corinthians for their past accomplishments: 'You shrank from any sort of schism or sedition; you wept (*epentheite*) for your neighbors' sins; you looked on the failings of others as if they were your own.'[3] But with the monks there was a definite shift of accent. Origen was undoubtedly a major influence here, but it was also something that corresponded to the new spirit of the times. The evolution did not take place everywhere at the same rate. In this respect the biography of St Antony contrasts with that of Arsenius and his followers,

241

though on the whole they were seeking and attaining the same goal. This nuance, or difference in emphasis, can be seen also between Aphraates and Ephrem though they were only a few years apart. Ephrem did much to establish the image of the monk as 'one who mourns', one who specializes in compunction (in Syriac: *abilā*; in Greek: *penthikos*). Pachomius, in upper Egypt, had already gone further than Ephrem in this direction.

All this raises in the history of religious psychology a problem which ought to be approached without presuppositions or prejudice or preconceived judgments. A movement as widespread as monasticism, with a spirituality that has been lived and preached by some of the greatest saints of the Church, deserves our every effort to see it in terms of the underlying principles of theology and sound christian anthropology which justify it. For the purposes of our present investigation it is enough to recognize the existence of the two currents of tradition described above. Both currents coexisted in monasticism. We can see them crystallized in the two prayer formulas which were most widely used as a means to pure and continual prayer: 'O God, come to my assistance; O Lord, make haste to help me', and 'Lord Jesus Christ, son of God, have mercy on me a sinner'. The first is a *boetheson* formula, the second an *eleison* formula.

In their final verbal form the first prayer is definitely anterior to the second. This was primarily because it could be found word for word in the psalter and did not have to compete with a number of other formulas. When the *Deus in adiutorium* began to be used, the Jesus Prayer existed only in fragmented form and there was no one to put all the pieces together and publicize it far and wide as Cassian was doing. Cassian was the panegyrist of a formula that had been used only by a select few before him; he asserted that it was 'a secret learned from the oldest fathers still left'. Certainly it represents an early tradition, because prayers for help and protection were in general use among the faithful before the invasion, so to speak, of the *Kyrie eleison* style of prayer.

C.M. Kaufmann's manual of ancient Christian epigraphy shows only two instances of *eleison* and these are undated and almost illegible.[4] In A. Hamman's collection of primitive Christian prayers, the *Kyrie* turns up only in the liturgy of St James:

> *After the Alleluia, the deacon says the litany and all reply,*
> Kyrie eleison. *...the people say* Kyrie eleison *three times.*
> *Have mercy on us, O Lord God, father all-powerful....*
> *Have mercy on us, O God our saviour.*[5]

The date of this text is not certain but it is not earlier than the fourth century and perhaps considerably later. The country of its origin was Syria.

Much research has already been done on the *Kyrie eleison* and has been summarized by Dom Cabrol as follows:

> *It is to A. Probst that credit must be given for research-*
> *ing the usage of this early christian acclamation. What is*
> *surprising is that he has not found a single* Kyrie eleison
> *in the apostolic fathers, in the apologists, in Tertullian, in*
> *Cyprian, in Hippolytus, in St Irenaeus, in Clement of*
> *Alexandria, in Origen, in Novatian, even in Book Two of*
> *the* Apostolic Constitutions *Harnach in* Der christliche
> Gemeindegottesdienst, p. 482, *notwithstanding.*
>
> *It must however be noted that it is possible to find*
> *acclamations very similar to the* Kyrie eleison *in some of*
> *the ancient sources, especially in such apocrypha as the*
> *Acts of St Andrew, the Acts of St Thecla, the Apocalypse*
> *of Esdras, and so on. These include formulas such as:*
> *'Have mercy, O Christ, I beseech you'; 'Have mercy on*
> *us'; 'Have mercy, O sovereign Lord, and help me'. In the*
> *Acts of Philip there is an* eleison hemas *addressed to*
> *Philip.*
>
> *Eusebius, Cyril of Jerusalem, St Athanasius, St Basil,*
> *the two Gregorys—none of them have the* Kyrie eleison.

*The first time the formula occurs is in the liturgy
described in the eighth book of the* Apostolic Constitutions. *This dates from the second half of the fourth
century, from someplace near Antioch. Considering the
date and place, it is not surprising that St John Chrysostom is another witness to the* Kyrie eleison. *According to
the* Apostolic Constitutions *a deacon took his stand on an
elevated platform and lead the people in a litany: 'The
deacon says, "Pray for the catechumens." And all the
people pray devoutly for them saying,* Kyrie eleison. *The
people answered all the invocations of the deacon in this
way.*[6]

By coincidence or by more than coincidence, it is the
second half of the fourth century that also marks the rise of
monasticism. John Chrysostom had six years of experience as
a monk and held the life in greatest esteem. The
catechumens for whom the faithful prayed *Kyrie eleison* were
unbaptized and presumably sinners. The Church grew rapidly
after Constantine, and some of the baptized who had to do
penance for sins found themselves degraded to the rank of
auditors (*akroomenoi*), required to stand among the catechumens in the narthex and permitted to stay only for the
readings and instruction, not for the eucharistic prayer.[7]
Other penitents were classified as 'prostrators' (*hypopip-
tontes*) and were admitted into the nave of the church but had
to leave when the catechumens did. It was for all these
people that the faithful said their *Kyrie eleison*. There was
also a class of penitents known as 'weepers' (*prosklaiontes*),
who are mentioned by St Basil.[8] These were repentant
sinners who were obliged to stand for three years at the
entrance of the church and beg those going in to offer, out of
charity, fervent prayers for them to the Lord. Basil described
the remaining steps of their penance:

*After that they become auditors for three years; then, if
they beg for it with tears and great humility and*

compunction of heart they are permitted to be prostrators
for three years. Finally, at the tenth year, if they have
been serious about their repentance, they are permitted to
join the faithful for the eucharistic prayer; but they must
wait another two years before receiving communion.[9]

If we turn now to the monasteries, we can see customs,
attitudes and ideas that bear a striking resemblance to the
public penitential discipline of the church. Some monks were
no doubt guilty of grave sins. But the question to ask is
whether public penitents were permitted to become monks?
And, more important, whether monastic spirituality actually
encouraged or even demanded the sentiments and attitudes
of a public penitent?

An adequate answer to the first question would have to
take into account different regions and times. During the
fourth century the desert was open to anyone who wanted to
come 'in order to be saved', including former robbers such as
Abba Moses, assasins such as Apollo, and other criminals.[10]
But we know nothing of the background of the vast majority
of the hermits. In the rare cases when one of them did allude
to his past and accuse himself of something or admit someone
else's accusation, it is not always clear whether this should be
taken literally. Self-accusation was accepted as a basic
principle of asceticism, and the 'metany' was a daily exercise.
In all probability, most of these hermits had been ordinary
Christians, perhaps country gentlemen like Antony or civil
servants like Arsenius.

We are better informed about the admission requirements
for cenobitic monasticism. Pachomius 'permitted sinners to
become his disciples if he could keep them under proper
surveillance'.[11] But this was not a frequent occurrence since
the examples given are reported as exceptional cases; one
was a former mime, Silvanus, and others were 'individuals of
a sensual nature' who eventually left the monastery.[12] St
Basil's *Longer Rule* explicitly raised the question 'whether all
who ask for it should be admitted as members of the

community, or only certain ones?' Basil based his reply on a
principle from the gospel:

> *God, the lover of men, and our saviour Jesus Christ have
> said, 'Come to me all you who labor and are heavy
> burdened and I will refresh you'. How then could we dare
> drive away anyone who wants to give himself through us
> to the Lord and submit to his gentle yoke and take up the
> burden of his commandments which bring us to heaven?*[13]

According to St Basil, everyone who asks can be and even
should be admitted to the monastery. The conditions which
he went on to lay down were concerned with the candidate's
present dispositions and future intentions rather than with his
past. A candidate's past was of interest only insofar as it
could help determine what spiritual exercises would be most
helpful in his case. There is only one reason for excluding
someone: instability. As for other faults, vices and bad
habits, Basil held the principle that everything can be
corrected with the proper care. Good will and 'the fear of God
ultimately triumph over all shortcomings'.

This is already a very decisive point of doctrine, but even
more important is what follows. Basil was speaking for the
whole of monasticism when he said: 'Watch to see whether
this sinner can humbly confess his hidden crimes and act as
his own accuser.' That is the unmistakable sign of a good
will. 'The beginning of salvation is condemnation of self'—no
other sentence is repeated oftener, in various ways, by all the
masters of monastic spirituality including Antony, Arsenius,
Ammoe, Poemen, Theodore of Pherme, John Colobos,
Mathois, and the other great names of the golden age.

Examples of this doctrine being put into actual practice
are available in abundance. It was the consensus of all
monasticism that weeping for one's sins is the true starting
point of the ascetical life as well as the sign of progress and
the attribute of perfection. This follows the logic of the maxim
that all things reach perfection through the causes that

brought them about. If it is by confession of sins that one enters the way of salvation, then progress depends on a growing awareness of sinfulness and a growing sentiment of contrition. As one of the *apophthegmata* puts it: 'The more a man draws near to God, the more he sees himself as a sinner; the prophet Isaiah at the very moment of his vision of God called himself a man wretched and unclean.'[14] It was only in Syria that a monk was called *abilā*, a mourner, referring to the second beatitude, but in Greek-speaking countries monks were no less devoted to *penthos*, and the translators of Syriac ascetical writings could coin the word *penthikos* without fear of being misunderstood. Abba Poemen was not among the first generation of monks but he was a faithful witness to the earliest tradition when he wrote: 'Mourning is a traditional practice taught to us by Scripture and the fathers; they have told us that we must weep, for there is no other way than that.'[15] In what sense does Scripture teach the practice of mourning? Consider this saying attributed to St Antony himself: 'Even the praises of the psalter are mourning.'[16] In such a climate the publican's prayer was bound to flourish and prosper. It took either the literal form, 'O God be merciful to me a sinner' (Lk 18.13), or else analogous forms that would readily spring to the minds of men who were so familiar with Scripture.

If we compare this monastic tradition with the litany for penitents led by the deacon during the eucharistic liturgy, a question arises. Did the liturgical practice influence the monks or did the monks influence the liturgy? The latter alternative is less likely but not impossible. The monastic formula *Deus in adiutorium* so highly praised by Cassian found its way from the monastic office into the roman breviary.[17] Another possibility is a reciprocal influence; the *Kyrie eleison* of the liturgy of the catechumens may have come first, but subsequent monastic influence may have led to the ninefold repetition of *eleison* which is in line with the psychology of 'meditation' (*melete*).

The next point to be considered is the variety of formulas

taken by the prayer for mercy in the course of the centuries. The Jesus Prayer did not exist from the beginning in its classic and definitive form. Even in relatively late times, as with Symeon the New Theologian in the eleventh century, there was still great liberty in the choice of prayer formula. No one had yet thought of prescribing once and for all an invariable wording. Some said the Jesus Prayer without the name of Jesus. Others used different words for 'have mercy'. The old invocations 'help us' (*boetheson*) and 'protect us' (*skepason*) continued to be used along with the new formula, *Kyrie eleison*.

A few examples may be considered, in chronological order. A prayer of St Macarius goes, 'O God, be propitious to me a sinner.'[18] The *Apophthegmata* tell us that Ammonas 'had the words of the publican perpetually in his heart.'[19] In the sixth century St Barsanuphius recommended both the Our Father and the prayer of St Macarius. He said that the phrase 'lead us not into temptation' was equivalent to the words of Abba Macarius.[20] Which prayer of Macarius was he referring to? It may have been the one just quoted. But it may also have been, and this is more likely, the formula we have seen in the *Apophthegmata*: 'Lord, *eleison*, as you will and as you know, have mercy (*eleison*). If temptation crowds me, Lord help! (*boethei*).'[21] Barsanuphius did not yet know the stereotyped form of the Jesus Prayer, but he knew and freely used all the other traditional prayers. Answering a question posed by a novice he recommended either 'Lord pardon us' or 'God help us' or 'God protect us', according to the particular need. In another letter he has the following advice for times of temptation: 'Call the holy name of God to your assistance, saying "O Jesus, Master (*despota*), protect me and help my weakness." '

Symeon the New Theologian has been credited with inventing the method used by the Palamite hesychasts but there is no written evidence that he ever knew the Jesus Prayer in its final form. In one place he wrote: 'Weep and throw yourself down on your knees as did the blind man in

the gospel and say, "Have mercy on me, son of God." '
Instead of leaving it at that, Symeon added to it, making a
very long prayer, thirty-eight lines altogether. Although this
is a beautiful prayer, it is not one that could be easily
repeated hundreds and even thousands of times a day.[22]
Ever since his youth Symeon seems to have had a personal
habit of using the prayer of the publican; this much can be
gleaned from a lengthy discourse addressed to his brothers
and fathers in which he spoke about himself in the third
person:[23] 'One day as he was standing in prayer and saying,
"O God, be merciful to me a sinner," ' he fell into ecstasy.
His biographer amplified and altered this slightly: '...he cried
out, repeating in a loud voice the *Kyrie eleison.*'[24] The
prayer of the blind man is presumed to be the same as the
publican's prayer.

In the Typicon of Empress Irene, dating from about 1118,
we find fifteen profound bows (the greater 'metany')
prescribed for nuns. Three of these are to be done slowly
enough to say 'O God be merciful to me a sinner' three times
while bending over, and to say 'I have sinned against you,
Lord, forgive me' three times while straightening up.[25] The
remaining twelve are done more quickly, saying the same
invocation once for each bow. Next comes a catechesis and
then some troparies to be said for the empress, including one
which begins: 'Have mercy on us, O Lord, have mercy on us.'
At the death of the Empress troparies are to be said for her
eternal repose, followed by the *Kyrie eleison* fifteen times.

These examples could be multiplied. Even in later ages,
down to our own day, it is possible to find a number of
saintly people using short prayers that are spontaneous or
composed or borrowed from the liturgy, both before and
after the period when the Jesus Prayer was at the peak of
popularity. To quote one more example, we read that St
Joannice 'recited only this one, deeply theological, formula:
"My hope is God, my refuge is Christ, my protection is the
Holy Spirit."'[26]

As we have pointed out, in the centuries before

monasticism prayers for mercy were rare and prayers for help were almost universal. The first monks, of course, continued to use the prayer formulas they had learned in their youth. When attacked by evil thoughts they would stand up and pray, 'Lord, son of God, help me.'[27] But further on in this book of the *Vitae Patrum* we also read about an elder, perhaps the same one, who gave this advice: 'When thoughts begin to clamor in your heart do not answer them; instead get up, pray, make a profound bow, and say, "Son of God, have mercy on me."'[28] The same context contains the following instruction on meditation (*melete*):

> *One of the brothers said: 'Abba, I meditate but there is no compunction in my heart because I do not understand the meaning of what I say.' The Abba replied, 'Go on meditating regardless. For I have heard from Abba Poemen and others this saying: "The snake charmer does not understand the meaning of the words that he uses but the serpent understands and he submits humbly to the will of the enchanter." In the same way, even though we do not know the meaning of the words we are saying, the demons know it very well and they flee in terror.'* (Ibid.)

From that point of view it does not matter at all whether one prays *eleison* or *boethison*. There is another version of the same anecdote, this time attributed to the great Arsenius, which shows more clearly the broad freedom that was exercised in the choice of a formula:

> *One of the brothers said: 'I have no compunction because I do not understand the meaning of holy Scripture.' Arsenius answered: 'Nevertheless, my son, you must continually meditate the words of the Lord...even though we are unable to grasp the meaning of the divine Scriptures.'*[29]

St Nilus was in the same tradition when he wrote: 'Every

time erotic thoughts assail you in your hermitage, get up, throw yourself down before God, and cry: "O son of God, help me!"' [30] St Barsanuphius wrote similarly: 'Do not wear yourself down examining these temptations but cry out the name of Jesus saying, "Jesus, help me", and he will surely hear you.'[31] It would be incorrect to think Barsanuphius was restricting 'the name of Jesus' to those exact letters and syllables. Other names could be used just as effectively: 'Since Jesus is standing near you, cry to him, "Master!" (*epistata*) and he will answer you.'[32]

To sum up thus far, the practice of meditation (*melete*) or 'secret occupation' seems to have been universal from the very beginning of monasticism, and each person enjoyed the freedom of ruminating or chewing over the text of his choice. The earliest texts or formulas were petitions for help. As monasticism developed, these were gradually supplanted by the *eleison* formula which eventually predominated and monopolized the scene after the thirteenth or fourteenth century.

It is not enough simply to recognize this as a fact. What was the underlying reason and intention behind it? In the last analysis the motive was not zeal for self-accusation but a craving for continual prayer. The monks considered *penthos* the best and most effective means to continual prayer and the one least open to illusion.

The monastic concept of prayer was that of a hand held out to God to receive his gifts. St Irenaeus said that the essence of man was to be a recipient of God's goodness. By praying before receiving and by giving thanks afterward, man acknowledges and accepts his lowly yet magnificent destiny. He stand as a creature, wanting and needy, in the presence of his Creator who is infinitely rich and wants for nothing (*aprosdees*, in the terminology of the apostolic fathers). The monks certainly offered prayers of thanks but the parable of the Pharisee and the publican had warned them to be even more discreet about this than about their prayers of petition. They tended to regard the present life as a stretching forward towards a goal in the future, according to a phrase from St

Paul frequently found in hagiography (Phil 3:14). Thanks-giving implies a glance back to the past, and especially to the great public events of salvation history, the incarnation, the redemption, the sending of the Spirit. It belongs in a special way to the Church as a whole to express thankfulness because she and she alone can be called holy, the immaculate spouse of Christ without stain or wrinkle. The individual members of the Church have still to work out their salvation. Some of these devote themselves exclusively to this task, and they are the monks, 'those wishing to be saved' (*hoi sozesthai boulomenoi*). Monks believe that it is their duty to pray in the strict sense of the word, that is, to petition God (*deesthai*, as in Lk 21:36, not *proseuchesthai* in the Evagrian sense). Their prayer expresses the humble awareness of their spiritual poverty in the sight of God. One of the desert fathers said that man's chief needs are: 'to fear God's judgment, to hate sin, to love virtue, and to beseech (*deesthai*) God continually.'[33] The chief object of this supplication is eternal salvation and everything leading to it. Prayers for other things, not related directly to salvation, are also acceptable to the Lord and are even answered, with miracles at times, but these prayers too ultimately contribute to an increase of union with God. Miraculous results are visible proof of the power and efficacy of prayer, though the great ascetics of the desert paid scant attention to their reputation as miracle workers. They were preoccupied with praying for greater things, especially that supreme good which is God himself, and his grace, his love, his favor, his salvation.

When these monks prayed their suppliant invocations they were merely giving transitory expression to a permanent inner attitude of being a beggar before the Lord of heaven and earth, or at least the permanent desire to have such an attitude. They tried to bring about what the biographer of St Francis so aptly described as 'becoming prayer'.[34] The Eastern ascetics who had experienced the exhilarating reality of this state called it repentance or compunction or mourning (*katanyxis* or *penthos*) because the awareness of being a sinner was its indispensable beginning. For them prayer, both ejaculatory and habitual, was first of all the feeling or the expression of a profound awareness of being a sinner. This should always be kept in mind when studying the spiritual experiences recounted in Eastern hagiography. However, it is going a bit too far to say with Runciman that '[Eastern] monasticism tended more and more to develop into quietism; it set an almost hysterical store on the value of repentance.'[35] But it would be even more dangerous to underemphasize this characteristic, thereby to risk completely misunderstanding Eastern monasticism. Those who are interested in hesychasm or any of its manifestations must be aware of these extremes. The Jesus Prayer is first of all a petition for mercy. It is the prayer of one who is conscious of being a sinner, a prayer of contrition.

It would not be irrelevant to elaborate somewhat on the subject of *penthos*. Without attempting a systematic treatment we wish to highlight the relationship between prayer and the theory and practice of compunction. The treatise of St Nilus put it well: 'Pray first of all for the gift of tears so that you may soften by compunction the innate hardness of your heart; and when you accuse yourself and confess your inquity to the Lord, you will obtain pardon from him.'[36] This is exactly what is done in the Jesus Prayer as well as in the many other ejaculatory prayers we have been studying. The longer prayers paraphrase and amplify the sentiments expressed in the shorter formulas. One example of the lengthier type from Evagrius deserves to be quoted:

O God, have mercy on me a sinner! O God, forgive my offenses! Purify me, O Lord, from my iniquity for it is great. O my Creator, take pity on my weakness. Spare me, O my God and Maker. Your hands have shaped and fashioned me, do not let me perish. As you formed me in the dark womb, O Lord, and made me emerge into your beneficent light, so make me come out of my hideous darkness into the light of your gnosis. Now that I have left

*the world grant that I may not become enmeshed again in
the world's affairs. Since I have renounced the world's
concupiscences do not let me be soiled by them again. I
have turned my face away from the world; may I never
look back at it again. I gave up my patrimony, I tore away
from the affection of my friends, I left everything. It is to
you that I wish to come. But my sins have risen up before
me to make me stumble and robbers have jumped on me
from ambush to capture me; desires pound against me
like the waves of the sea. O Lord, do not leave me alone;
send someone from on high to deliver me and snatch me
up and draw me out of the sea of my sins. I am more than
ten thousand talents in debt and I have paid nothing of it
till this day; be patient with me and I will pay you in full.
I will never deny your love because it was you who shaped
me from the earth and you who stretch your hand over me
and protect me.—This is what you must meditate
on during the time of prayer.* [37]

Evagrius did not mean that everyone should be able to
break spontaneously into a highly literary and well-structured
formula like this every time he began to pray, but that the
heart should always be full of these thoughts and sentiments.
Then at the time of prayer, under the inspiration of grace,
ejaculatory prayers will well up intermittently as from an
underground pool. Or the model which Evagrius gave could
be used as a source for short prayers which the monk could
freely pick from and use. After about the fourth century there
existed so many of these compilations of short prayers
expressing compunction and contrition that they were put
together into special prayer books called *proseuchetarion
katanyctikon* or simply *katanyxis*. They seldom give the
impression of being spontaneous; most were carefully
composed with the public in mind. An example would be the
prayer at the end of the third *Century* of Thalassius which is
neatly divided into ten numbered paragraphs, from ninety-one
to one hundred. [38] Another example is the series of lengthy

precationes attributed to St Ephrem and placed at the end of
Volume Three of his Greek works.[39] They are beautiful from
a literary point of view. The prayers to the Virgin are
especially ardent but here too the devotion seems deliberate
rather than spontaneous. Although the effort of striving for
literary effect spoils to some extent the sincerity of these
prayers, they can still serve as examples of the self-
depreciatory character of Eastern spirituality. To consider one
sample, there is a very lengthy *Prayer to the Mother of God*
divided into two parts.[40] The first consists of a string of some
two hundred fifty titles of the Virgin, longer than any modern
marian litany. The second part begins with words which
clearly stamp it as compunction-oriented: 'See my faith and
my God-given desires, O most compassionate and powerful
One, and since you are the mother of the one good and
merciful God, look favorably on my most miserable soul....'[41]
Most of the prayers are in this same style.

The greatest masters of byzantine and syriac theology
were quite skillful in this genre of writing. For instance, St
Maximus the Confessor, a disciple of pseudo-Denys, can
discourse about the most sublime heights of mysticism, but in
his treatise on *The Ascetic Life* he shows himself true to the
heritage of the monastic fathers when he abruptly interrupts
his line of argument and goes off on a long prayer of petition:
'Do not cast us off forever, O Lord. Do not forget your
covenant. Do not withdraw from us your compassion and your
merciful love, O our Father who art in heaven....' He
continues in that vein for a column and a half. The latter part
is a tissue of scripture texts. 'The prophet Isaiah has written,
"You were angry and we sinned" (Is 64:5), but it is we who
have sinned and then you became angry.' After a short
reflection the prayer continues:

> *Look down from the heights of heaven and see! Save us*
> *out of love for your holy name. Help us discover the plots*
> *of our enemies and snatch us from their traps. Do not*
> *withdraw your assistance, for we are helpless to overcome*

*our difficulties but you are powerful enough to save us
from every adversity. In your goodness, O Lord, save us
from the temptations of the world so that we may cross
with pure conscience the sea of life and thus arrive
innocent and irreproachable before your terrible tribunal,
to be judged worthy of eternal life!*[42]

He goes on to tell us what fruit he expects from sentiments
like these:

*The brother who had listened to this instruction was over-
come by compunction and he said to his spiritual father,
'Father, as I see it there is no hope for my salvation.'
'Salvation,' replied the father, 'is impossible for men, but
nothing is impossible for God.'*[43]

Maximus concluded with a long series of quotations from the
Old and New Testaments which could be summed up in this
verse from Isaiah: 'If you convert and are moved to groaning
you will be saved' (Is 30:15, LXX). These groans springing
from compunction are ejaculatory prayers.

Symeon the New Theologian is another mystic, less
influenced by pseudo-Denys and more liturgical than
Maximus, and on the whole a more original thinker. But he
too was a disciple of the monastic fathers, through his own
spiritual master, St Simon Studite. From him he learned the
great importance of compunction and tears, and a method for
attaining them. Nicetas Stethatos, his biographer and
publisher, made it clear that Symeon practised heroic fidelity
toward his saintly master. Symeon's writings move back and
forth from the lyric pathos of a Jeremiah to the mystic
raptures of the Canticle, or rather they are an indissoluble
blend of the two. Everything he wrote would have to be
quoted, so it seems better not to give examples at all. Contact
with these ascetical-mystical writings will convince anyone
that the author was a true byzantine monk and poet who even
when he soared to the heights remained a worthy successor

of the fathers of the desert. In his ecstasies he would cry out repeatedly, 'Lord have mercy on me!' His biographer does not say that he used the name of Jesus. The fact that he could spontaneously repeat this plea for mercy at a time when ordinary volitional activity was in a state of suspension proves that Symeon had a deeply engrained habit of ejaculatory prayer, as did his famous monastic forefathers.

Compunction presupposes the memory of God (*mneme Theou*) and at the same time endows it with a special modality. Compunction makes the memory of God take on the attitude of a repentant sinner before his judge. The christian ascetics were not simply philosophers like the Therapeutae community described by Philo who were satisfied with praying twice a day. The christian goal was uninterrupted prayer. The best way to attain that goal proved to be a profound understanding of Christianity's fundamental doctrines about God, about man, and about the relationship of man to God. We know that God is love and infinite perfection, while man is sheer poverty made still more impure by the fall. When these truths are fully realized they force us down on our knees and make us beat our breasts or raise our hands or adopt some other attitude suited to a humble suppliant. Wisdom dictates that sinful man should completely lose himself in prayer to God as did St Antony, St Arsenius, St Francis of Assisi and their disciples. No one is capable of speaking incessantly to God, whether vocally or mentally, but we can manage to acquire and maintain an abiding awareness of our wretchedness and to stand thus before the holiness and kindness of God our saviour as the poor creatures we are and know ourselves to be. People who are truly poor, especially those who bear evident marks of their affliction for all to see, seem to speak very little or not at all; they know that they have only to show themselves in order to move the human heart to compassion. Abba Sisoe used to say, 'I go to sleep with the thought of my state of sinfulness and when I awake it is with the thought of my state of sinfulness.'[44]

The basic awareness of sinfulness can take on many different nuances. There is the terror of one who despairs of being forgiven and there is the false security of one who thinks he is confirmed in grace. Among the Messalians there was the state before receiving the 'great charism' of the Holy Spirit and the state after receiving it. Within orthodoxy there was the joyful Christianity of an Aphraates and the emphasis on weeping as with the austere St Ephrem; or compare St Antony at the end of his life with St Arsenius at the hour of death. Yet Aphraates took the sinful human situation as seriously as Ephrem, and Antony went through unbelievable tortures before attaining his radiant serenity. Symeon the New Theologian was one in whom these contrasts existed separately yet harmoniously, in a deeply monastic temperament. He was the author not only of the *Hymns of Divine Love* but also of numerous sermons redolent of compunction. Even in his *Hymns* the memory of sins is a recurring theme and one which was an essential part of his theology and psychology. Symeon knew that he was a forgiven sinner. He saw himself as one completely covered with sores, cuts, and bruises, and therefore he could cry out:

> *Have mercy, have compassion on this transgressor, O good physician who love souls. You are full of tender compassion and you did not hesitate to cure the sick and wounded. Dress my wounds and anoint them with your loving mercy. Heal my sores, remove my scars, set and bind my broken limbs, take all my hurt away....* [45]

Most of the saints—all of them in one sense—have been forgiven sinners. Remembrance of their former failings purifies and intensifies rather than lessens their joy because they see themselves fashioned 'for the praise of the glory of God's grace' (Eph 1:6). While waiting for the fullness of their redemption, the ones whom God has made his own for the praise of his glory (Eph 1:14) experience here below a thrill of sheer joy in knowing that they are the objects of mercy in

Jesus Christ for the glory of God the Father. There may have been certain cases of hysteria among the byzantine monks, but this does not prove that compunction is a basically unhealthy state of mind. The most respected representatives of byzantine spirituality as well as great ascetics like St Theodore Studite, and mystics like Symeon the New Theologian, all retained the attitude of a poor man and a sinner standing before God. Origen had already outlined the dynamics of this characteristic stance:

> *In confessing my own wretchedness, I find a source of happiness. If I humble myself and weep in sorrow for my sins, God will hear me and send me a liberator. Then I will say, 'Thanks be to God through Jesus Christ our Lord' (Rom 7:25). But when someone says, 'Wretched man that I am', it must come from the depths of his heart. It is not enough just to say these words; they must be accompanied by true compunction.*[46]

An answer is beginning to emerge to our question about how the fathers managed to transform their whole lives into prayer. As we have seen, they had a yearning for continual prayer and did not think it an impossible desire. Though they did not make it a matter of quantity alone, they realized that quantity or repetition did have something to do with it. All the great ascetics and saints had an insatiable thirst for saying prayers, and if their strength or the demands of charity had permitted they would have given all their time to prayer. Though this could not be done, they did not for that reason give up their ambition to 'pray always'. Instead they sought to attain a state of soul or of mind which would not be broken up into successive acts yet which could truly be called prayer.

At this point the differences in theory and in practice begin. Those who were more philosophically inclined described and preached a 'state of pure intellectuality' which would in itself be a lifting up of the mind to God. Others,

more numerous, aspired to the habitual 'memory of God'. For
them continual prayer was an enduring habit of the memory,
sustained by many intermittent acts. They almost always
combined the thought of God with an awareness of their own
misery and poverty, following the path of *penthos*.

All took for granted the existence of a secret, interior
operation or occupation (*krypte ergasia; endon* or *entos
ergasia; melete*). They maintained that all men had an inner
life in spite of all the distractions, diversions and evasions
that might encumber it. Every effort, as St Arsenius taught,
must be made to see that one's interior activity be 'according
to God'.[47] That was common doctrine. Evagrius, with his
philosophical preoccupations, stressed the noetic aspect of
this activity. Partisans of the *mneme theou* gave a big part to
the imaginative memory. The proponents of *penthos* concen-
trated on the underlying feeling of unworthiness as sinful
creatures. These were their theories. The question could well
be raised whether the pure Evagrian ideal was ever really
lived in practice. Evagrius himself, to judge by his letters and
monastic works, walked the path of compunction just as his
master, Macarius, and the other desert fathers had done.
Like them too, Evagrius made use of short and intense
prayers. These short prayers had a double function. They
contributed, along with reading, meditation, liturgy and the
whole ascetic life, to develop and maintain a desired psychic
state. And they gave to this state the value of prayer by
means of a frequently renewed attitude of supplication,
confidence and humility.

It was love of prayer that made the early monastic fathers
poor men, 'God's beggars'. They stood in the tradition of the
tax collector who beat his breast and who went away justified,
or of the prodigal son who said he was unworthy to be called
a son and whom the father clothed in the best robe, or in the
tradition of the ones who know they are poor and say so, and
who will inherit the kingdom of heaven. It is a tradition
formed by all men who believe that prayer is the essential act
of a creature and who for that reason wish to be praying—

thanking God or beseeching him—everywhere and at all times, for they have chosen to find their highest happiness in him.

NOTES

1. See Hausherr, *Direction spirituelle en Orient autrefois*, Vol. 144 of *Orientalia Christiana Analecta* (Rome, 1955) p. 152.

2. See Hausherr, *Penthos*, p. 11 and chaps. iv, viii and ix.

3. Clement of Rome, ed. by F.X. Funk, *Patres Apostolici*, p. 100.

4. C.M. Kaufmann, *Handbuch der altchristlichen Epigraphik* (Freiburg, 1917) p. 75.

5. A. Hamman, *Prières des premiers chrétiens* (Paris, 1951) pp. 308-325; English edition (Chicago, Regnery, 1961) p. 211ff.

6. *Dict. d'Arch. et de Liturgie*, Vol. VIII, p. 909.

7. Gregory Thaumaturgus, *Epistola canonica*, chap. ix; PG 10:1048AB.

8. St Basil, *Epist* Classis II, 217; PG 32:793-809.

9. Ibid., Note in passing the term 'converts' (those who have turned back—*hypostrephontes*) as found in Gregory Thaumaturgus, chap. viii, PG 10:1041D. Might this term have influenced the name given to the *conversi* in the middle ages? One reference work, the *Dict. d'Arch. et de Liturgie* Vol. III, 2, col. 2800, has an article on 'conversion' but says nothing about the *conversi* of the East.

10. See *Apophthegmata Patrum*, Alphabetical Series, 'Lot', no. 2; CS 59:103.

11. P. Ladeuze, *Etude sur le cénobitisme pakhomien* (Louvain, 1898) p. 278.

12. See F. Halkin, ed., *S Pachomii Vitae Graecae* (Bruxelles, 1932), *Vita Prima*, no. 38, p. 23; on Silvanus see pp. 124-128, *Paralipomena* 2.

13. St Basil, *Regula fusius tractata* X; PG 31:944C.

14. *Apophthegmata Patrum*, Alphabetical Series, 'Matoes' no. 2; CS 59:121.

15. Ibid., 'Poemen' no. 117; 155.

16. *Ipsa laudatio psalmorum planctus est. Vitae Patrum* VII, chap. 38; PL 73:1055C.

17. See S. Baumer, *Histoire de Bréviaire* (Paris, 1905) Vol. I, p. 146.

18. PG 34:445.

19. *Apophthegmata Patrum*, Alphabetical Series, 'Ammonas' no. 2. See also 'Apollo' no 2; CS 59: 22 and 31.

20. Barsanuphius, *Ep* 71; ed. by Nicodemou Hagioreitou (Venice, 1816) p. 38.

21. *Apophthegmata Patrum*, Alphabetical Series, 'Macarius' no. 19; CS 59:111, see above, p. 208.

22. See Hausherr, *La méthode d'oraison hésychaste*, Vol. 36 of *Orientalia Christiana Analecta* (Rome, 1927) p. 202, (106).

23. *Nicetas Stéthatos, Vie de Syméon le Nouveau Théologien* (Rome, 1928) Introduction, p. lix. The Greek text of this discourse can also be found in PG 12:693-702.

24. Stethatos, *Vie*, no. 5, p. 8, line 11.

25. *Typicum Irenes Augustae* cap. 32; *Analecta Graeca* (Paris, 1688) p. 209.

26. *Vie de S Joannice* no. 10; *Acta Sanctorum* Nov. II, p. 341B.

27. *Vitae Patrum* V, Lib V, 16; PL 73:877B.

28. Ibid., no. 32; PL 73:882B.

29. Ibid., III, *Verba Seniorum* no. 40; PL 73:764B.

30. Nilus, *De Octo Vitiis*; ed. by Cotelier, *Eccl. Graecae Monumenta* III (Paris, 1686) p. 209.

31. Barsanuphius, *Ep* 39; ed. Nicodemou Hagioreitou, p. 20.

32. Letter *Phia*; Nicodemou, p. 251. Compare the Ethiopian *'Eqabani* which is the reponse repeated forty times in the litanies to Christ: 'O my Lord Jesus Christ, protect me.' Each petition recalls an event from the life and passion of our Lord and his blessed mother. This belongs to the current of devotion we are considering at this point, and recalls the prayer of the 'spiritual sheik', John of Dalyatha, quoted above, p. 103. The word *'Eqabani* is equivalent to the Greek *skepason* or *philatte*.

33. Evergetinos, *Synagogé* (Constantinople, 1861), IV, chap. vii; p. 45, col. 2.

34. *Totus non tam orans quam oratio factus.* Thomas à Celano, *Legenda* II, chap. 61; ed. by Rinaldi (Rome, 1806).

35. S. Runciman, *Byzantine Civilisation*, p. 129.

36. Nilus, *De Octo Vitiis*, no. 5.

37. Evagrius, *Protrepticus*; W. Frankenberg, *Abhandlungen*, p. 588.

38. Thalassius; PG 91:1457AB.

39. *S Ephrem Syri Opera Omnia* (Rome, 1746), Vol III, pp. 482-552.

40. Ibid., pp. 527-532.

41. Ibid., p. 531B.

42. Maximus the Confessor, *Liber Asceticus* nos. 37-38; PG 90:444D, 948C.

43. Ibid., no. 38.

44. *Apophthegmata Patrum*, Alphabetical Series, 'Sisoes' no. 36; CS 59:184.

45. Denys Zagoraios, ed., *Oeuvres de Syméon le Nouveau Théologien* II, *Logos* 10, (Venice, 1790) p. 25.

46. Origen, *In Isaiam Hom* IV, iii; ed. Bahrens, p. 260.

47. See Evergetinos, *Synagogé*, IV, chap. vii, p. 43, col. 1.

CHAPTER SIX

THE JESUS PRAYER GAINS ACCEPTANCE

L EAVING ASIDE all other considerations we shall concentrate now on this one formula, 'Lord Jesus Christ, son of God, have mercy on me a sinner'. We have seen the matrix in which it originated and began its development. The Jesus Prayer is a prayer of contrition, a weapon against the attacks of demons, and a method for maintaining the continual remembrance of God. Its origin was in a monastic milieu, among athletes of the spiritual combat who stressed *penthos* and were dedicated to the search for God through continual prayer. The essence of the prayer is a continually repeated cry to the Lord from the heart of a man conscious of being a sinner.

Is it possible to pinpoint the date when the Jesus Prayer emerged in its classical formulation? One authority, Hieromonk Archbishop Vassili Krivochéine, concluded his article 'Date du texte traditionnel de la Prière de Jesus' with this statement:

> *We have the right to conclude that the traditional text of the Prayer was already in use towards the middle of the fifth century. This is basically an hypothesis, since Diadochus did not quote it in its full form. But after the period from the sixth to the eighth century its existence seems certain beyond a doubt.* [1]

The author's conclusion is neither certain nor completely satisfying. He has concluded his research with an hypothesis, leaving a broad margin for the possibility of error—the three hundred years between 500 and 800. Is it possible to fix the date more precisely?

In attempting to do so the first step is to define the problem with precision. The wording of the Jesus Prayer as given in the *Philokalia* and in *The Way of a Pilgrim* is, 'Lord Jesus Christ, son of God, have mercy on me', with or without the addition of 'a sinner'. This final word can be left out because the idea is already implicit in the *eleison*. The thrust of the prayer would be radically altered if the sinner's plea for mercy were replaced by a general petition for help or protection (*boetheson*). The preceeding pages have shown the different origins of these two invocations, *eleison* and *boetheson*. The Jesus Prayer was born in hearts given to compunction, to mourning for the lost soul, and to weeping for sins.

It is important to retain the precise notion of the Jesus Prayer in its classical formulation. We would soon be lost in a maze if we adopted any other definition. And other definitions have been given. A Monk of the Eastern Church says the Jesus Prayer is 'a technical term of byzantine spirituality referring to the invocation of the name of Jesus either all by itself or inserted into a formula of variable length'.[2] Archbishop Krivochéine has defined it as 'a particular form of mental prayer consisting in the constant interior repetition of short invocations centered on the name of Jesus'.[3]

Various short prayers containing the name of Jesus were certainly in existence long before the crystallization of the Jesus Prayer. The process of natural selection always singles out one individual or species from among several. But the antiquity of the emerging formula is not determined by referring to its antecedents or by claiming that it pre-existed in another shape in the earlier formulas. The Jesus Prayer came to be preferred over the previous, or previously documented, formula *Deus in adiutorium meum intende*. It is also true that Cassian's Abba Isaac attributed to his 'formula of spiritual contemplation' the same marvellous effects that the nineteenth-century Russian pilgrim attributed to the Jesus Prayer. But to conclude that the two formulas are therefore essentially the same would be to gloss over some crucial differences. What makes the Jesus Prayer is not the name of Jesus alone nor any of the titles of the Lord nor any combination of these. Neither is it the bare request for mercy or help addressed to God the Father or simply to the Lord. The essence of the Jesus Prayer requires a request for mercy together with a name or title of the Saviour that implies an act of faith in him as Messiah, as Son of God, as God himself.

Such a combination cannot be found in Diadochus of Photice. His interests lay specifically in the reintegration of the powers of the soul by means of the continual memory of Jesus. Nor can it be found in any of the great fourth and fifth century representatives of this school of *remembrance.*

The first historical evidence of the coalescence of the two essential elements into a single explicit unit of prayer occurs in the *Life of St Dosithy*. Until new discoveries are made this document deserves careful study. What is special about this young saint, and what his biography deliberately underlines for the reader's edification and imitation, is the struggle he had to go through against his self-will. All the little anecdotes which we read describe one or another aspect of his obedience or detachment or humility, for it was by means of these that Dosithy conquered selfishness. He obediently learned to cut down his daily ration of bread from six pounds to eight ounces. This was an obedience unto death, because tuberculosis brought this novice to the grave within five years. He learned not to lose his temper against the sick people he was nursing as infirmarian, for anger is the explosion of frustrated self-will. He was outstanding in the practice of opening his soul to his spiritual father (*exagoreusis*). This is the sovereign exercise in denying one's own will. He learned also to avoid the vice of complacency in himself and his capabilities or in the little articles for his personal use. After describing all this the biographer summed up in these terms: 'So he grew perfect in obedience, never once doing his own will in any matter, nor acting out of special attachment to anyone.'[4] He went on to describe the saint's final sufferings, noting how scrupulous Dosithy was about not seeking the satisfaction of his own desires. 'Thus even in the midst of a terrible disease he struggled against his self will'.

At this point the biographer inserted his account of 'the prayer':

> *For he lived in continual remembrance of God.* [*Dorotheos of Gaza, his spiritual father*] *had handed down to him the rule that he should always repeat these words: 'Lord Jesus Christ our God, have mercy on me! Son of God, save me!' He therefore said this prayer continually. When he fell ill, he* [*Dorotheos*] *said to him: 'Dosithy, do not neglect your prayer. Make sure that you never let go of it.' The sick man answered, 'I will do as you say, Father, only pray for me.' Later when he was almost completely worn out* [*by the disease*], *he* [*Dorotheos*] *said to him: 'How are you now, Dosithy? How is the prayer going? Do you say it all the time?' And he answered him, 'Yes, Father, thanks to your prayers'.*[5]

The first thing to comment on is the compunction *gar* which connects this paragraph with the preceeding one: 'Even in the midst of a terrible disease he struggled against his self-will, *for* he lived in continual remembrance of God.' This particle has a causal or explanatory force. Here it is used to call to mind the traditional ascetic doctrine of *mneme theou*. We have seen this doctrine in Diadochus: 'To purify the heart one must set it afire with the continual memory of the Lord Jesus, making this his whole meditation (*melete*) and his constant practice.'[6] Renunciation of one's own will is the surest sign of perfection, and those who have the remembrance of the Lord Jesus constantly in their hearts are on the sure path to perfection.[7]

'He [Dorotheos] had handed down to him what he should constantly say.' Dorotheos, spiritual father of Dosithy, was a celebrated disciple of Saints Barsanuphius and John the Prophet. In this context the verb *paradous* is clearly used in its technical sense of passing on to another what one has received from someone else. Barsanuphius and John are known from their letters to have recommended short prayers, including the very ones which Dorotheos in his turn transmitted to his novices. Dorotheos must have selected from all the formulas he had learned from his masters the one most appropriate for use by a young man as inexperienced as Dosithy. In doing so he still left the novice a certain freedom, much more than there would be later on when the Jesus Prayer had crystallized definitely in the *eleison* form to the exclusion of any petition for help (*boetheson*). Variants in the manuscript tradition indicate that some eleventh and twelfth century copyists were a little surprised by the double petition of Dosithy's prayer. Was this really a prayer of one word (*monologistos proseuche*)? The copyists did not surpress the second prayer but they indicated their preference for the first one by inserting an adverb: '...to say always "Lord Jesus Christ have mercy on me", and *sometimes* (*metaxu*) "Son of God, help me." '[8] This seems to imply that the habitual prayer should be *eleison*, but occasionally, at certain times (*metaxu*) one could interrupt this prayer with a *boetheson*. Step by step we draw closer to a monopoly of the *eleison* formula.

A few other details in this episode will be noticed by those who are familiar with byzantine ascetical literature. Dosithy has learned to follow the traditional teaching down to the fine points. When he was given a command or a suggestion he recommended himself to the prayers of his spiritual father; when the order was accomplished he gave all the credit to the father's prayers. It is probable that if it had not been for

Dosithy's illness no mention would have been made at all of
the famous prayer. The prayer remained simply a means. The
immediate goal or result which it had was the continual
memory of God. A further goal was the abnegation of all
self-will. The ultimate goal, which the biography did not
mention because it could be taken for granted, was spiritual
charity or perfect conformity with the will of God.[9] Notice
also that there came a moment in the terminal stage of the
disease when Dosithy was unable to say his prayer any
longer. Then, but only then, did Dorotheos tell him not to try
any more but simply to think of God and imagine himself in
God's presence. Perhaps we should ask why Dorotheos did
not tell him simply to say the name of Jesus as a prayer.

After Saints Dosithy and Dorotheos in the first half of the
sixth century there are several documents of uncertain date.
One of the most important of these, and one which may be
erlier than the *Life of St Dosithy*, is the account of a certain
Abba Philemon about whom very little is known. It was
published by Nicodemus the Hagiorite in the *Philokalia* under
the title 'The Most Profitable Narrative of Abba Philemon'.[10]

We are interested particularly in the date of this narrative
or composition and in what it says about the Jesus Prayer.
But worth looking at first is the introductory paragraph
written by Nicodemus, because it gives his evaluation of this
great proponent of hesychast spirituality. He called Philemon
'the most recollected, the most contrite of the god-bearing
fathers'. He added that his story contains no clue as to the
time when he flourished; for Nicodemus to make such an
admission the chronological problem must truly be desperate.
In the following lines he sang the praises of Philemon in
terms that reflect the hesychast tradition at its purest and
richest level. Each one of his remarks could be footnoted with
a reference to the writings of the great masters, beginning
with the treatise of St Nilus [Evagrius] *On Prayer*. The reader
was expected to be able to recognize allusions to this treatise
as readily as allusions to the Bible.

The beginning of Philemon's history is reminiscent of the

Apophthegmata: 'It is said of Abba Philemon....' This suggests that he might be found somewhere in the lives or sayings of the desert fathers, but there is no mention of a Philemon in Rosweyde's or Bousset's index. If there was an abba by this name none of his sayings found its way into the early anthologies. However, a Coptic calendar for the eighteenth of Kihak has this notice: 'Today we recall the memory of Heraclos, the martyr, and of Philemon, priest and hermit; may their prayers be with us, Amen.'[11] Nothing more than this bare mention of a name. But there is a good possibility that this is actually our Philemon because according to the *Philokalia* he was both a recluse and a priest. We are told that although he had been ordained he almost always refrained, out of reverence, from celebrating the sacred mysteries, and even from receiving Holy Communion on days when he had conversed with anyone.

When did this hermit live, and when was his story written down? It is not much help to know that he must have lived after Arsenius because he is said to have imitated Arsenius. What is important is to know his latest possible date. There is a shred of evidence in a paragraph which says that one of Philemon's disciples went down by boat to Alexandria and from there to 'the Queen of cities' on a lengthy journey concerned with some ecclesiastical matter. As Archbishop Krivochéine has observed, this must have taken place before the Arab conquest, and therefore before the early seventh century. It might be possible to set the date more exactly if we knew which heresy prompted Philemon to leave Alexandria and take up residence in the *laura* near the town of Nicanor, but there were many heresies in lower Egypt in the fifth and sixth centuries.

Philemon did not stay permanently at Nicanor. In the narrative this merely gives occasion for recounting a sermon which he gave and which is a compilation of quotations from various sources. After that Philemon and his disciple moved to the *laura* (never the word 'monastery'!) of St John Colobos. His rule of life, especially in the matter of liturgical prayer, is described in detail. Specialists in liturgy say that such practices were not uncommon around the year 600.

The writers mentioned by name are all fourth century or fifth century, St Basil the Great and Diadochus. Gregory Nazianzen is referred to as 'that most enlightened and theological mind' and an Origenist saying of his is quoted: '*Praxis* is the means of ascent to *theoria*.' [12] Evagrius was another source, never identified by name but sometimes quoted almost word for word: 'Virtues and vices both blind the intellect, the latter blinding it to virtue and the former blinding it to vices.' [13] Philemon's discourse at Nicanor quoted another Evagrian text: 'The mind is perfect when it has acquired essential knowledge and has been united to God.' [14] And a letter of Evagrius, wrongly attributed to St Basil, was cited in the same discourse: 'As the eye is directed toward material objects and takes pleasure in viewing them, so the pure mind is attracted to intelligible realities.' [15] The facility with which the author recalled and combined these Evagrian themes shows how deeply imbued with them he must have been. There is also a phrase (from Evagrius?) about being 'alone with the alone' (*monos pros mono*). [16]

Without attempting to study all of the author's work, let us look at one last saying attributed to the holy father, 'Moses':

> *Stillness* [hesychia] *gives birth to ascesis, ascesis gives birth to tears, tears to fear, fear to humility, humility to the gift of wisdom, and wisdom to charity. Charity makes the soul healthy and free of passion, and then a man may realize that he is not far from God.* [17]

This Abba Moses was actually Ammonas, a contemporary and acquaintance of Evagrius. These two very different men, Ammonas and Philemon, had in common a tendency to speak with great enthusiasm about solitude and silence. [18] The solitary life, said Philemon, is the only effective means of vanquishing demons which are more frightening than the monster so vividly described in Job (Jb 41:14-34). God's constant protection is absolutely necessary, and therefore we must pray for it constantly; and this can be done only in perfect solitude 'since even a single idle word can destroy our memory of God when the demons are pressing and the senses are on their side'.[19]

Philemon's insistence on prayer could give the impression that he had Messalian tendencies. His remarks on manual labor and on the possibility of falling into sin even after having received the charism of the Spirit are enough to dispel these suspicions.[20] Furthermore his idea of *apatheia* was not simply the total suppression of passion but the passions made ineffectual (*aprakta*). To attain this state of *apatheia* or, in other words, to maintain purity of mind, great labor and effort is required both spiritually and physically in practising the renunciation of self-will, compunction, strict poverty, and all the other traditional virtues and works of asceticism. Only at this high cost will a man 'preserve the image of God and enrich the likeness'.[21] This short phrase, with its two technical terms 'preserve' (*phylattei*) and 'enrich' (*ploutei*), reveals a mind perfectly at home with orthodox theology.

To get back to the question of chronology: there seems to be no reason why the history of Abba Philemon cannot come from the sixth century, even from the early sixth century. Philemon could have lived a little later than St Euthymius who around the year 430 had also taken Arsenius, former tutor of the emperor, as his model in the pursuit of *hesychia*. Euthemius, however, knew of the life of Arsenius only through the Egyptian pilgrims whom he questioned. Philemon, coming later, was familiar with the *Apophthegmata*.[22]

This date may not hold true for the entire Philemon narrative. Interpolations, paraphrases, and glosses are contained in so many other ancient documents, from the *Letters* of St Ignatius or the *Lausiac History* down to many biographies 'modernized' by later translators. It is possible also that subsequent critical examination of the Philemon text may reveal quotations from authors later than the fifth-century master, Diadochus. For instance, John Climacus. Why did Philemon, supposedly speaking to a single interrogator, forget himself and say, 'Brothers', as if he were addressing a community of monks?[23]

The next point to be considered is Philemon's teaching about the Jesus Prayer. First of all, he did not call it by that name. Also, the latter part of the formula, 'have mercy on me', is always the same, but the first half is not yet invariably fixed. Once it is 'Lord Jesus Christ', and the next time it is 'Lord Jesus Christ, son of God'. Philemon taught that the interior meditation of the psalms is a secret occupation just as useful as short prayers; the soul should alternate between the two.[24] In any case the important thing is always to be praying in the heart:

> *Whether you are eating or drinking, whether talking to someone in your cell or whether on a journey away from your cell never stop saying this prayer with recollected mind and undistracted intellect, and never stop singing psalms and meditating prayers and psalms. Even when taking care of urgent needs never let your soul cease to meditate in secret and to pray.*[25]

In this way it is possible to obey the Apostle's injunction: 'Pray without ceasing.' In recommending the Jesus Prayer, Philemon invoked the authority of the 'blessed Diadochus' and added that this was the prayer he prescribed for beginners. Philemon himself, to take his own word for it, had arrived at the *state of intellectuality*. In Evagrian terminology this is the state of perfection. It is the state of spiritual contemplation, of essential knowledge, of the perfection of the mind, and of overflowing joy. It had a special rule or liturgy proper to it:

> *The liturgy of the holy elder was as follows. At night he recited the entire psalter and the canticles without hurry*

or effort. This was followed by a pericope from the gospel. After that he sat down and repeated to himself, Kyrie eleison, *with as much attention and for as long a time as he could, until he could no longer utter a sound. Then he went to sleep. At dawn he recited psalms for the hour of prime. Afterwards he sat on his stool looking toward the East and recited psalms alternately [with another person?] Again he said by heart certain passages of the gospel and of the Apostle. In this way he passed the day, reciting psalms and praying continually, nourishing himself with the contemplation of heavenly things.* [26]

According to the teaching of Philemon, the prayer which would later be called the Jesus Prayer was an instrument for beginners to help them keep the memory of God, combat distractions and temptations, purify the intellect from all thoughts except the thought of God, and make progress toward uninterrupted prayer. Strict solitude was a prerequisite. Abba Philemon belonged to the school of Ammonas, Arsenius and Evagrius and spoke in their categories.

Recall also that Philemon was a priest although, out of reverence, 'throughout the many years of his ascetical combat he very seldom consented to officiate at the holy altar'. [27] Before Philemon the same custom had been followed by Abba Mathoes and his brother. Mathoes gave this reason:

I have confidence in God. He will not hold my ordination against me because now I do not offer mass. A man should be absolutely irreproachable before ever being ordained. [28]

This illustrates very well the mentality of these early hesychasts. They believed in the necessity of the most rigorous asceticism, with or without the use of the Jesus Prayer.

It has been necessary to dwell at some length on Abba

Philemon because he is not well known and he has something to teach us. Like Cassian's Abba Isaac he had his own 'formula for spiritual contemplation'. He praised the effectiveness of his formula, though not to the degree that Cassian did. Philemon saw in the Jesus Prayer a remedy against a wandering imagination, a means of keeping the memory of God, a method of concentration. For Cassian what was important was the efficacy of his prayer against every difficulty in life. For Philemon it was the pushing aside of all concepts and thoughts except one. Secret meditation had for its purpose 'the purification of the intellect'.[29] In the presence of so many Evagrian terms it is surprising not to find the notion of 'exclusion of thoughts' (*apothesis noematon*), but 'purification of the intellect' is equivalent in meaning. The ideal, certainly an exalted one, is not to have any passionate thoughts (*logismoi*) even in sleep.[30] To achieve this, the Jesus Prayer alone is not enough:

> *When you are struggling against the passions do not let them ever get the better of you, and do no lose courage if the battle is a lengthy one. Get up and throw yourself down before God, saying with all your heart the prophet's prayer, 'Fight, O Lord, against those who fight me, (Ps 35:1) for by myself I can do nothing against them.'*[31]

These redoubtable foes are the *logismoi*, or passionate thoughts, so subtly analyzed by Evagrius. Philemon wrote:

> *You must pray uninterruptedly for fear that another thought may catch you unaware, separating you from God and putting in your intellect some foreign object. The heart that is pure becomes the dwelling place of the Holy Spirit and can see in all clarity, as in a mirror, the full reality of God.*[32]

In conclusion, it is clear that for Philemon the practice of secret meditation held the same place it held among the fathers of the desert. It did not take the place of ascetical works or liturgical prayers or anything else. Its purpose was to fill empty moments and to help concentrate the attention and counteract distracting thoughts. It did not crowd out everything else; it remained always a part of *praxis*, not the whole of it. This is the sense in which Philemon understood the axiom which he quoted from Gregory the Theologian: '*Praxis* is the means of ascent to *theoria*.'[33] What is new with Philemon and marks a stage in the evolution of the Jesus Prayer is the exclusive use of one formula: 'Lord Jesus Christ (son of God), have mercy on me.'

In the course of history, as we have seen, many other short prayers have been used for the same purpose Philemon used his formula. Following the track of this particular formula leads us from Philemon to the later hesychasts, and especially to those in the region of Mt Sinai. At this time, after the sixth century, spiritual writers were beginning to compose collections of extracts from the fathers which were like portable libraries, condensing in systematic arrangement a complete spiritual theology. Today we would somewhat incorrectly call these compilations *florilegia*, meaning collections of select passages that appeal to the copyist. What Antiochus in his *Pandecte*, Paul Evergetinos in his *Synagoge*, and Nikon of the Black Mountain in his *Syntagma* were actually trying to do was to provide complete treatises of spirituality for refugee monks who were fleeing before the Turks or the Persians, or simply for all needy monks. Nikon entitled his work '*Syntagma* [or synthesis—*perilepsis*] of the Divine Commandments with Explanations and Some Teachings of the Divine Fathers'.[34] The equally long titles of his sixty-three chapters indicate that he left out very little. The eleventh century *Synagoge* of Evergetinos is still more complete, with four volumes of fifty chapters each.

In the seventh century Antiochus attempted in thirty discourses (*logos*) a résumé of 'the whole body of revelation, both Old and New Testaments, in such a way that no teaching useful for the salvation of souls is left out, and yet it does not form a volume too hefty to carry about.'[35] To consider a sample of his style, the chapter on prayer begins with the thesis that 'to give oneself to continual prayer is both necessary and profitable'. He quoted, without naming them, Diadochus and Evagrius. The selection from Diadochus is Chapter 97:

> *Whoever wishes to purify his heart should continually cherish the memory of the Lord, making it his meditation and his constant occupation. For if one wishes to be free of all his filthiness, it is not enough to pray intermittently. He must give himself to prayer at all times and keep watch over his intellect whether he is in a place reserved for prayer or not. Just as one who wishes to purify gold will find the metal getting hard as soon as he lets the fire in the furnace die down, so the one who does not stir up the memory of God continually will find himself losing by negligence all he thought he had acquired by prayer.*[36]

Antiochus had no special prayer formula to recommend. Toward the end of the chapter he referred to the Our Father, which was the Lord's answer to the request, 'Teach us to pray'. Antiochus had a chance to speak of the Jesus Prayer but did not do so; in fact when quoting Diadochus he even omitted a word, the name 'Jesus'. The chapter after this one is on compunction. Earlier chapters had treated *hesychia*, keeping vigil, and recitation of psalms. When he came to the problem of distractions he did not, as Philemon had done, suggest using a special short prayer. Instead he said, 'When you remember God it is good to ask him insistently to help you remember him again when you forget'.[37] Antiochus did recommend continual psalmody, but not the use of any particular psalm exclusively. Every psalm is an invocation of God. 'Let the psalm be uninterrupted, for thus we call upon God and put the demons to flight.'[38]

In the *Synagoge* Paul Evergetinos makes no mention of the Jesus Prayer. Nikon of the Black Mountain has five chapters on prayer, but the text is unpublished and the chapter titles alone, although very lengthy, do not provide sufficient evidence for firm conclusions. Everything, however, suggests that the famous prayer does not occupy a very great place in the *Syntagma*, if it is mentioned at all. It does not turn up in the actual titles, which run from five to twenty-five lines each. Nikon's preoccupations seems to be those of a canonist. He had misgivings about the freedom with which monks were borrowing elements from the parochial liturgy; he stressed the dangers of relying excessively on prayer alone, especially the intercessory prayer of others, even saints. Here is the title of the most relevant chapter:

About prayer and the methods of prayer: how it is possible, through vigilance (nepsis), *to pray continually and uninterruptedly in all places and in every occupation. And also the fact that when a man prays, calling God his father, and still commits sin, it is really the infernal author of all sin who becomes his father and takes him for a son.* [39]

The Jesus Prayer had not spread very far by the middle of the eleventh century. Nothing foreshadowed the widespread popularity it was to enjoy in the fourteenth century. Until now we have said nothing about the monks of Sinai, but now it is time to consider them. The existence of a sinaitic spirituality has been recognized for thirty years. [40] But a more profound familiarity with the total body of early monastic and ascetic literature indicates that the monks of Sinai played the role of transmitting rather than originating. [41] Their spirituality came to them from Egypt and Palestine. It came in the first place through living tradition, but then also through books, especially the *Lives of the Fathers* and the works of Evagrius, Palladius, Isaiah and others. All these influences inspired the Sinaitic authors, John Climacus, Hesychius, Philotheus. Sinaitic spirituality is simply a subdivision of hesychast spirituality in general, and as such it has only a limited importance, like that of a young branch of an illustrious old family. Diadochus and Philemon did not come from Sinai, nor did St Arsenius or any of the monks of Scete.

The most famous of the Sinai monks was John Climacus who wrote towards the middle of the seventh century. One edition of his works, together with a translation, runs to two volumes of four hundred pages each.[42] From this whole output only a few short phrases were picked out to be quoted again and again by hesychasts of later ages. One of these sentences reads: 'Whip your enemies with the name of Jesus, for there is no weapon more powerful in heaven or on earth.'[43] This occurs in a chapter entitled 'On unmanly cowardice', 'unmanly' in the sense of 'puerile': 'the emotion of a child in the heart of a vain adult'.[44] It is like the shuddering experienced in deserted or haunted or infamous places. This must be overcome, and John Climacus explained how:

> *You should not shrink from going even in the middle of the night to places that you find frightening. If you haven't the courage to do that, you are likely to carry this silly and childish fear around with you all your life. You must take up the weapons of prayer and go there. When you arrive lift up your hands in prayer and whip your enemies with the name of Jesus, for there is no weapon more powerful in heaven or on earth. Once you have freed yourselves from this disease, sing a hymn of praise to your Redeemer. If you thank him he will protect you at all times from everything.* (Gradus XXI, p. 37)

The ordinary reader may, if he wishes, see in these lines an exhortation to encourage him in the continual invocation of the name of Jesus. But the critical historian is not free to read into the text more than is actually there. And this text has nothing to say about the continual memory of God, about *penthos*, about the Jesus Prayer.

Another phrase from John Climacus was also popular

among the hesychasts, and with much more justification. To quote the Monk of the Eastern Church: 'The chief text in *The Ladder* on the invocation of the Name is this: "When you unite the memory of Jesus with your breathing, then you will know the benefit of *hesychia*."' [45] Because this is the principal text it deserves to be studied and seen against the background of its larger literary and historical context.

In the first place, John Climacus did not claim to be the author of this statement. Here is the whole passage Climacus wrote to John of Raïthu:

> *There is a saintly old man by the name of George the Arsilaite, with whom Your Reverence is acquainted. He is accustomed to speak in the following terms when instructing a beginner in the elements of* hesychia: *'I have observed that in the morning the demons of pride and lust present themselves, while during the day come the demons of* acedia, *sadness, and anger. At evening it is the demon of gluttony, the lover of pleasure. A poor man living under obedience, a cenobite, is better than a hesychast who is carried away by distractions. When a man practises* hesychia *wisely, apparently, but does not experience daily fruit it is either because he has not truly been practising wisely or because he is the victim of self-deceit.* Hesychia *is continual adoration of the ever-present God. Let the memory of Jesus be united to your breath and then you will know the benefit of* hesychia. *The downfall of a cenobite is self-will; the downfall of a hesychast is interrupting prayer. If you delight in receiving visitors in your cell you can be sure that you are opening yourself up to* acedia *and not to God. Take for your model of prayer that widow in the gospel who prevailed over the unjust judge (Lk 18: 1-5). The father and prototype of all hesychasts is the great Arsenius, equal to the angels. Ponder in your solitude the life of that angelic hesychast. Remember how often he would send his visitors on their way so as not to lose what was vastly more valuable....'*

As we will see, the expression 'let the name of Jesus be united to your breath' has a history that is older than Climacus, older also than George the Arsilaite, and it continued long after them. The meaning seems plain enough, especially when seen in its full context. The great sin for a hesychast was to interrupt his prayer, his memory of God, his awareness of God's presence, his adoration. The 'name of Jesus' here has the same broad meaning as in Diadochus and similar writers. It would be a misunderstanding to think that it means repeating the two or three syllables (depending on the language) of the word 'Jesus'. A good paraphrase would be: 'With every breath remember Jesus' or 'Renew the memory of Jesus as often as you breathe'.[46] Climacus was referring to what is commonly called in ascetical literature 'the memory of God' (*mneme theou*).

One way to prove that this is the correct interpretation would be to read the entire *Ladder of Paradise* with a mind that is familiar with hesychast thought patterns and modes of expression. Another way might be to compare a few select paragraphs. For instance, there is a section towards the end of Chapter Twenty-seven which describes some of the different forms of *krypte ergasia*:

> *Some of those who have chosen the path of* hesychia *continually fulfill within themselves what is written in the psalm, 'I set the Lord before my eyes at all times'* (Ps 16:8). *For the loaves of bread made from spiritual wheat are not all of the same variety. Thus there are some who fulfill the following verse: 'In patience you will possess your souls'* (Lk 21:19). *Others this one: 'Watch and pray'* (Mt 26:41). *Others this: 'Prepare your works with death in view'* (cf. Prov 24:27). *Others: 'I was brought down low and he saved me'* (Ps 116:6). *Others:'The sufferings of the present time are not worthy to be compared with the glory which is to come'* (Rom 8:18). *And still others ponder the psalmist's words, 'Take care lest he strike you and there be no one to rescue you'* (Ps 50:22). *All these run the race*

but only one of them receives the prize (1 Cor 9:24). *One who is far advanced in this practice can maintain it without effort not only while awake but even during sleep.*

The Jesus Prayer can likewise go on during sleep. In this passage John Climacus showed himself definitely on the side of freedom of choice as to formula. The precise formula for one's 'secret occupation' depends on the particular needs of the individual. The bread of interior meditation is not necessarily the same for all.

This discussion leads to another problem, the meaning of the phrase 'a prayer of one word' (*proseuche monologistos*). It has been understood in different ways by modern scholars and by spiritual writers through the centuries. The Abbé Saudreau, who did not claim to be familiar with Eastern writings on the Jesus Prayer, defined one-word prayer as 'that simplified form of prayer which later came to be called the prayer of simple attention to the presence of God'.[47] Father M. Viller, who quotes Saudreau only to disagree with him, defined it as 'the invocation of the name of Jesus continually repeated',[48] and cited Hesychius and John Climacus as references.

Viller's reference to Climacus deserves close examination. In *Gradus* XV we read:

Let the thought of death keep you company when you go to sleep and when you wake up, and with it the one-word prayer of Jesus (monologistos Jesou euche). *For nothing can come to you in sleep which is able to prevail over such protection.*[49]

The chapter in which this occurs has the general title: 'On that incorruptible purity and temperance which is acquired by corruptible beings through many hardships and much sweat.' The title is a fairly accurate résumé of the chapter, full of wisdom, practical experience, and humble confidence. The author managed to bring together a lofty moral ambition and a very realistic appraisal of the difficulties. 'That man is pure,' he wrote, 'who experiences no [erotic] physical stimulation even in sleep; that man is pure who has acquired perfect insensibility to the difference between man and woman.'[50] Such a state can only be reached by struggling for it; it requires hardships and sweat. Climacus filled a dozen columns—in the Migne edition—speaking about these struggles with remarkable psychological balance and insight. His remark about the prayer of one word takes up only a single line. Is this an indication of the small importance he attached to the matter? That remains to be seen. We know that a single word can have incalculable implications, especially in the inspired books of the Bible. But his is not sacred Scripture.

The passage in which this sentence occurs is analagous to the chapter 'On unmanly cowardice', where a formula was given for putting courage into timid hearts venturing into lonely places at midnight, the hour of crimes and demons. In the present case the hour is one which presents particular dangers to purity:

> *When you lie down to sleep, be careful! For that is the time when the mind has to wrestle with demons without help from the body. If the mind is inclined toward pleasure it will soon succumb. Therefore you should see to it that you go to sleep and wake up with the thought of death, and also the* monologistos *prayer of Jesus. For nothing can come to you in sleep which is able to prevail over such protection.* [51]

The author has made a choice between two possible tactics for dealing with Satan: prayer and counter argument (*antirrhesis, contradictio*). A century earlier St Barsanuphius had cautioned that *antirrhesis* was only for the perfect. John Climacus, less outspoken, was content to observe that 'He who drives away that dog with a prayer is like a lion in battle; he who puts him to flight by *antirrhesis* is like one who pursues a retreating enemy.'[52] This entire chapter on chastity shows a delicate sensitivity to differences of circumstance, of temperament, and of ability. Climacus saw that it would be unrealistic to impose lengthy and elaborate spiritual exercises on someone trying to go to sleep. The best thing would be to fall asleep as quickly as possible. And an excellent way of doing so was to concentrate on a monotonous thought which could also be a prayer—*monologistos euche.*

Nevertheless, Climacus chose not to insist on a particular formula: 'When we rise from sleep in a state of peace and devotion we owe this to the invisible protection of the holy angels; they console us especially when we have gone to sleep with much prayer and recollection.'[53]

There is also an exterior, corporal form of prayer which Climacus described as follows:

> *Those who have not yet acquired true prayer of the heart will profit by wearing themselves out in corporal prayer, holding the arms outstretched, striking the breast, gazing up toward heaven, moaning aloud, genuflecting frequently. Often it is not possible to do these things because of the presence of other people.... [In that case] you should cry out to him who is able to save you, not however with words of human eloquence but with expressions of humility, saying 'Have mercy on me, for I am weak' (Ps 6:2). Then you will experience the power of the Most-High and by his interior help you will spiritually drive off the invisible enemy.* [54]

The verse from Psalm 6 provides a formula equivalent to the Jesus Prayer and equal to it in efficacy. Or else, and this is more probable, this formula is the Jesus Prayer, in essence, for John Climacus. We know that the form of the Jesus Prayer was variable; the name 'Jesus' was not necessarily included. What is essential is a heartfelt cry for mercy, an *eleison* directed toward Christ our Saviour, whatever the name we call him.

In a later chapter dealing explicitly with prayer, Climacus wrote:

When you pray do not try to express yourself in fancy words, for often it is the simple, repetitious phrases of a little child that our Father in heaven finds most irresistible. Do not strive for verbosity lest your mind be distracted from devotion by a search for words. One phrase on the lips of the tax collector was enough to win God's mercy; one humble request made with faith was enough to save the good thief. Wordiness in prayer often subjects the mind to fantasy and dissipation; single words of their very nature tend to concentrate the mind. When you find satisfaction or compunction in a certain word of your prayer, stop at that point. Then your guardian angel will be there praying with you. Never pray in overly familiar terms even if you have acquired purity. Instead always go to God with great humility, and in doing so you will grow in greater intimacy with him. Even when you have climbed all the rungs in the ladder of virtue do not give up begging for forgiveness of sins. Remember the words of St Paul about sinners: 'Of their number I am the first' (1 Tm 1:15). [55]

A prayer of one word (*monologistos euche*) is for John Climacus any short prayer frequently repeated. It is identical with the secret occupation (*krypte ergasia*) of the early monks. Able to be adapted to changing circumstances, its constant factor is the note of compunction, the plea for forgiveness (*eleison, miserere*), exactly as in the Jesus Prayer. By no means does *monologistos euche* imply repeating the name 'Jesus' over and over.

Hesychius, a monk of Sinai, must have lived some time after John Climacus whom he quoted, referring to him as 'a certain wise man' (*sophos tis*).[56] Hesychius borrowed only two phrases from this wise man, and we have studied them already: 'Whip your enemies with the name of Jesus....Let the name of Jesus be yoked to your breath as long as you live and then you will discover the usefulness of *hesychia*.' The slight alterations in wording indicate a tendency in Hesychius to improve on his sources. In the second phrase he has replaced and strengthened the verb, adding a few words of his own as well. Rereading now what I wrote thirty years ago in *La méthode d'oraison hésychaste* (Rome, 1927) after my first contact with Hesychius, I have noticed several statements which I would still maintain and several which should be modified. I would still say this about Hesychius:

> *He is an author who seems to be almost obsessed with the idea of custody of the intellect. His two hundred chapters say the same thing over and over. Apparently he was one of those souls with an unlimited capacity for deep concentration who are drawn by nature to give themselves unreservedly to the interior life.*

But such judgments need to be illustrated and attached to concrete data if they are to be meaningful.

An examination of the data concerning Hesychius's use of the name of Christ reveals a very interesting fact. Like all the faithful in the early Church Hesychius loved to repeat the various titles of the Master whom he adored. But even more than they he loved, and dared, to call him by the name 'Jesus'.[57] This is something quite new, and what makes it even more significant is that Hesychius seems to have done this unconsciously and without intending to introduce novelties. He is far, far beyond someone like pseudo-Denys, or rather, far above him. With Hesychius we find spontaneity not contrivance. The compiler of the 'Office of the Most Sweet Jesus' was probably familiar with the writings of Hesychius, but he succeeded in making only a pastiche or even a caricature of them, just as others read Origin and copied his use of 'my Jesus' in an exaggerated fashion. This is not to say that Hesychius is the wrong place to search for the elements of a successful litany of the name of Jesus.[58]

The Jesus Prayer must be seen within the total thought of
Hesychius so as to avoid treating it like some rare tropical
flower artificially preserved in an environment foreign to it.
For Hesychius, as for John Climacus, the Jesus Prayer
functioned as a defense weapon, but it also took on the added
function of a means of acquiring something. It was seen as an
aid in repelling demonic temptations and in fostering
profitable thoughts. Perhaps the latter function was even
more important than the former. Like Diadochus, he used the
prayer to sustain the memory of God and eliminate contrary
memories, but Hesychius was not preoccupied with regaining
the original simplicity or unity of the intellect; he was more
interested in the possibilities of enriching the intellect with
the splendor and consolation of different spiritual intuitions.
He often used terms like 'concepts', 'perceptions', 'good
images', and 'insights' which are to fill up the space left open
by the removal of passionate thoughts (*logismoi*). When he
wrote these words Hesychius spontaneously added a number
of different adjectives which his own experience must have
taught him.[59] The impression given is that the writer is
completely enchanted with his inner contemplation:

> *A heart that is utterly purged of fantasies will give birth*
> *to mysterious, divine ideas which will spring up in him*
> *like fish frolicking or dolphins dancing in a tranquil sea.*
> *As the water ripples with a light breeze, so does the Holy*
> *Spirit move in the depths of the heart, making us cry out*
> *'Abba, Father'.*[60]

The last phrase is reminiscent of John Climacus,[61] but
Hesychius handled the thought far more poetically.

Traditional asceticism retained its place in the doctrine of
Hesychius but the word itself with its cognate vocabulary is
notably rare. The concept of recollection or vigilance (*nepsis*)
has replaced all that. The combat has become largely interior
and mental. And *nepsis* is completely centered around the
Jesus Prayer.

What precise formula did Hesychius use for the Jesus Prayer? He called it *Jesou euche*, with 'Jesus' as an objective genitive (a prayer addressed to Jesus, not a prayer said by Jesus), just as *pistis Jesou Christou* in St Paul means faith *in* Jesus Christ (Rom 3:22). This might suggest that for Hesychius the Jesus Prayer did not permit any other name or title than simply 'Jesus'. But the presence of so many different titles of Christ in the writings of Hesychius gives a contrary impression. He used 'Jesus' alone scarcely more than a third of the time, and then usually in the stereotyped phrase 'invocation of Jesus' or 'prayer of Jesus'. There is not sufficient evidence to say that the formula preferred by Hesychius was one using simply the name 'Jesus'. We find in the *Centuries* only two instances of direct address to Christ. The first occurence, 'O Christ God', is in an exclamation on the greatness of the virtue of vigilance (*nepsis*).[62] The second time is in an exhortation:

> *Like David in the psalms, be diligent in crying out the 'O Jesus Christ'. Do not worry about your voice getting hoarse and do not let the eyes of your intellect give up looking for the Lord our God* (Ps 69:3). *Remember the parable of the unjust judge....*[63]

The definite article before the vocative points to a well-known formula, while the words 'Jesus Christ' and 'Lord our God' allude to the actual content of the formula. This is as far as the evidence permits us to go.

By quoting the phrase from John Climacus about uniting the memory of Jesus to the breath, Hesychius did a great deal to assure the popularity and the long life of this phrase. The original import of the statement was explained above, but that exegesis may not be equally valid for Hesychius's use of it. He replaced 'unite' with 'cling', in accordance with his general preference for strong metaphors. Elsewhere he wrote: 'Attention and incessant *hesychia* of the heart,...continual, uninterrupted breathing and calling on Christ Jesus,

Son of God and God himself.'[64] He spoke of the Jesus Prayer
clinging to the breath, and of the soul clinging to the Jesus
Prayer, breathing the power and wisdom of God the Father
who is Jesus Christ.[65] Then he put it even more strongly:

> *To the breath of your nostrils unite attention* (nepsis)
> *and the name of Jesus, as well as meditation on death and*
> *complete humility. All these things will be of great*
> *profit.* [66]
>
> *Truly happy is the man in whom the Jesus Prayer clings*
> *to the power of thought and who calls on him continually*
> *in his heart, in the way that our body is united to the*
> *atmosphere or a flame to the candle wick.* [67]

At a later date these expressions would be taken very
literally and used to propagate a psycho-physical breathing
technique, but in Hesychius they remained simply metaphors.
He enjoyed preaching in a picturesque style about continual
prayer. Elsewhere he used the more traditional terms for
perseverance (*aennaos, epimonos, synechos, stenos*, etc.) and
spoke of laboring hard (*ponetikos*) and not losing courage (*me
ekkakein*) in the face of weariness or boredom.

Hesychius marks an important stage in the process of
restricting freedom of choice regarding the formula of
meditation (*melete*) to be used in tending towards continual
prayer through a secret occupation (*krypte ergasia*). John
Climacus was one of the last to speak of several different
short prayers for use according to circumstance or temperament. His disciple, Hesychius, no longer mentioned such
options. Nor did he speak of ascetical exercises. *Nepsis* has
supplanted *praxis*. In fact, in the very first paragraph of
Century I, the Evagrian definition of *praxis* as 'a spiritual
method for purifying the passionate part of the soul' has been
applied to *nepsis*, because Hesychius saw everything in terms
of the intellectual and the moral order.[68] The tendency to
synthesize and to simplify—a trait common among men who
have attained great spiritual depth—is clearly evident in

Hesychius's doctrine of secret meditation. The early monks gave everyone free choice of his own rule of life (*politeia*), insisting only on the necessity of having one. With Hesychius the choice is already made. He has decided in favor of the invocation of the name of Jesus, just as Cassian long before had decided in favor of the *Deus in adiutorium meum intende*.

In a previous chapter we studied the dynamics of this evolution towards uniformity by comparing St John Chrysostom, the partisan of freedom, with pseudo-Chrysostom, the plagiarist who favored uniformity. It would be tremendously helpful if we could date pseudo-Chrysostom precisely. Unfortunately we can only make conjectures, as is the case also with Hesychius, Philemon, and several other later writers of great importance to our subject. Apocryphal works, like that of pseudo-Chrysostom, are usually difficult to situate precisely in place and time. It took many centuries and many scholars to clear up the mystery of pseudo-Denys.

Basically however the uncertainty about chronology does not affect the general picture of hesychast spirituality. A little sooner or a little later the evolution towards a fixed formula was finally accomplished. At that terminal point, when we discover it, we will be able to write the name of Hesychius. Four or five hundred years elapsed between the early period of complete freedom and that later period which saw the discovery of a systematic method of prayer. During those centuries apprentice contemplatives nourished their secret meditation on a variety of short prayers, including the Jesus Prayer. But there is nothing to indicate that the Jesus Prayer was the most popular prayer-formula in the byzantine monastic world. It was not yet known at Mount Athos; even at the beginning of the fourteenth century it was not being used there. Only sporadic examples can be found for the transition period, all later than the year 1000.

In the eleventh century, and probably in the second half of that century, Nicetas Stethatos recommended 'the invocation of Jesus-God'. He appears to have read Hesychius but he

understood the 'invocation' more in the sense used by John
Climacus:

> *Before risking defeat in an open attack the demons often*
> *try to disturb the soul's imagination and deprive the eyes*
> *of sleep. But the soul that is filled by the Holy Spirit with*
> *bravery and courage does not worry about their attacks*
> *and their foolish hatred. He dissolves their phantoms and*
> *puts them to flight simply by making the life-giving sign*
> *[of the cross] and calling on Jesus-God.* [69]

The sign of the cross actually represents what may be the
most ancient form of invocation of Christ against the demons.
It has not been given a special consideration in this book
because there are good articles on it in all the theological
encyclopedias. [70] In the earliest monastic tradition we find St
Pachomius advising his monks: 'Always guard yourselves
against the demons by signing yourselves with the name of
Christ.' [71]

Nicetas Stethatos was the biographer of Symeon the New
Theologian. In the course of the biography he related an
interesting story about a bishop who became a monk at St
Mamas of Constantinople with the name 'Hierotheus'. This
saintly man was very emotional and demonstrative in his
devotions:

> *Hierotheus had reached such a great love of God that*
> *when he began to read he would stop every time he came*
> *to the name 'Christ' or 'Jesus' or 'God'. Then he would*
> *gaze at the name first with one eye then with the other*
> *and shed so many tears that he would drench the pages of*
> *the book and his own robe.* [72]

The three names were all equal in their power to arouse his
devotion.

Another monastic author was Elias Ekdikos. His country
and his dates are not known for sure, but he must have lived

later than the tenth century.[73] He mentioned the prayer of one word but without any further explanation.[74] There is nothing to indicate that he meant the Jesus Prayer. He wrote: 'The man who wishes to do battle must reduce his body to a single-dish diet and reduce his mind to a one-word prayer. Then he will become immune to passion and immune also to [false] ecstasies in his prayer.' *Monologistos* prayer is a means of recollection; what is essential is the repetition of a single petition such as the four or five hundred *eleisons* in one of the hours of the byzantine office. Elsewhere Elias Ekdikos said: 'A check on anger is silence at the right moment; a check on blind lust is a moderate diet; a check on wandering thoughts is the prayer of one word.' Elias did not prescribe a special formula for meditation any more than he prescribed a specific diet; he merely insisted that the prayer be simple, the diet frugal, and both invariable.

Not too surprisingly, the Jesus Prayer can be found at the beginning of the twelfth century in Russia. In the life of a certain Prince Nicolas who became a monk under the name 'Svjatocha', we read:

> *No one ever saw him idle. He always had his hands busy at manual labor (even making his own clothes) and all the time the Jesus Prayer was on his lips—Lord Jesus Christ, son of God, have mercy on me.*[75]

The old Slavic edition of 1759 omitted the words in parentheses and, interestingly, inserted a demonstrative pronoun before quoting the prayer, as if readers of that time would need a special reminder that this was the wording of the prayer.

With the next example we will no longer be groping in chronological incertitude. His name is Abba Isaiah and he is a rather important figure because he is fairly well documented and because he lived in the period of dusk between the end of the eleventh century when Nicetas Stethatos died and the fourteenth century when neo-hesychasm appeared.

Abba Isaiah was the spiritual director of Theodora, a nun and the daughter of Emperor Isaac II Angelus, who reigned twice between 1185 and 1204. Never did a spiritual daughter have a father in God who was so solicitous for her welfare. For Isaiah set himself to compose something that 'had never been attempted before in all history'—an anthology of feminine devotion.[76] He claimed to have labored arduously at the task and this is likely enough; he copied the *apophthegmata* of Saints Antony, Arsenius, John Colobos, Poemen, Hyperechios and others, and then attributed them to such women saints as Saints Theodora, Sarah, Syncletice, Pelagia, Melania, and others. And in doing so, 'he deliberately emphasized hesychast spirituality'. What did he say about the Jesus Prayer? He spoke of secret meditation (*krypte melete*) and then went on to spell out his meaning, as if the pious Theodora might not know: 'By this I mean praying continually in the mind, "O Lord Jesus Christ, have mercy on me! Son of God, hear my prayer!" '[77]

Is it likely that Theodora knew nothing of this prayer? Perhaps so, because she seems to have been completely ignorant of the writings of the fathers which were the daily reading and nourishment of all the Eastern monks. And if this was the case with the emperor's daughter, how much more true would it be with the common faithful. Fifty years earlier Anna Comnena had taken great pride in her knowledge of theology and had even read St Maximus the Confessor as had her mother before her.[78] Although Anna imagined she knew a great deal about theology, and made no efforts to conceal the fact, she wrote nothing that hints of any knowledge of secret meditation. The reason must be that this practice was reserved for monks and nuns until the age when hesychasm lost its original meaning and attempted to identify itself with all of Eastern Orthodoxy.

The next example is St Meletius of Galesios, the Confessor. His biographer was Macarius of Philadelphia, called the Golden-headed.[79] Meletius had been named Michael, but changed his name when he became a monk: 'At the same time he changed his style of life and kept only one spiritual *melete*, so that his life and actions might be in harmony with his name.'[80] With this spiritual *melete* St Meletius combined a frighteningly severe asceticism which soon drew the attention and admiration of the local population. For that reason he moved frequently—from Sinai to Jerusalem, from Jerusalem to Alexandria and parts of Egypt, then to Syria, living first in Damascus then for a long time at Mt Latros and then at Mt Galesios (hence his surname). Finally he went to Constantinople and ended his days at Mount Saint Auxentius. He was a wandering hesychast, one of many who have appeared in history down to the hero of *The Way of a Pilgrim*. But history does not tell us that St Meletius diligently practised the Jesus Prayer on his travels, as did the Russian pilgrim. The Jesus Prayer is mentioned only at the beginning of the saint's monastic career, and this occurs in a passage in which it is difficult to separate history from rhetoric:

> *O Meletius, who could describe your great humility even at that early age? Who could do justice to your fidelity to the divine office? ...you were a man of few words but many good works. You scrupulously obeyed whatever your spiritual father commanded. You were dutiful in rendering service. ...you passed whole nights in prayer without sleep, and whole days in tears. And there was scarcely a minute of the day when you were not meditating the name of Jesus Christ on your lips and in your heart, saying the prayer, 'Lord Jesus Christ, son of God, have mercy on me.'*[81]

The narrative continues with the recital of the saint's many virtues and good works, particularly his patience as a confessor in the face of persecution from 'Latinism'. In a biography that runs to seventeen columns of fifty lines each there are only the four lines quoted above about the Jesus Prayer. There is nothing to suggest that this holy monk who began as a novice at Mt Sinai ever did anything to publicize the wonders of this prayer, as the Sinaite, Gregory, did a century later.

After these two examples, both relatively certain as to date and place, we re-enter the realm of uncertainty and hypothesis. The 'Rule of the Blessed and Holy Fathers Sabas the Great and Theodosius the Cenobiarch' for cenobites and hermits is earlier than the fourteenth century but probably not much ealier.[82] It belongs to a literary genre which we have already encountered and which could be called cento or interpolated compilation, or even plagiarism. It is all these things at once. The author referred explicitly to St Basil and especially to St Athanasius, or the pseudo-Athanasius.[83] The work is very much like a typicon; it is based on earlier documents but modifies them to some extent. The following selection speaks of the Jesus Prayer:

Concerning prostrations [the great metany], the rule prescribes one hundred every day and one hundred every night. They are to be done in groups of fifteen, an hour for each group. These prostrations should be made in the following manner: Before the first three you say slowly, three times, with hands outstretched and in a low voice, 'O God, have mercy on me who am a sinner'. Then you prostrate on the ground and while in that position say to yourself three times, 'I have sinned against you, O Lord, forgive me'. The first three prostrations should be done with compunction and careful attention. The remaining twelve are done more rapidly. While standing you say once with hands outstretched, 'O God, have mercy on me who am a sinner'. When prostrate say once, 'I have sinned against you, O Lord, forgive me'. At the end, add the prescribed invocations.

It is to be noted that the Kyrie eleison *invocations are always to be said with hands slightly extended. This was the posture that our fathers habitually used for their devotions, according to the words of Scripture, 'May my prayer come before you like incense and the raising of my hands like an evening oblation'* (Ps 141:2), *and in another place, 'I lift my hands to you'* (Ps 88:9), *and the Apostle Paul says, 'Lift up pure hands without anger or dissension'* (1 Tm 2:8). *Woe to our generation and to the customs of our age, because all the best traditions have fallen into disuse!*[84]

This is another example of the Jesus Prayer being used without the name of Jesus. All the rest of the formula is there, including the final word, and the whole prayer is said with compunction and with a prostration. It is clearly a prayer oriented to contrition. It was to be repeated a specific number of times. Not simply 'often, very often' (*pykna, pykna*) as the fourteenth century hesychast zealot, Gregory the Sinaite, would prescribe it. Gregory's biography occurs immediately after that of Meletius of Galesios in the *Neon Eklogion*, but it must be admitted that something new came on the scene in the fourteenth century.

In the twelfth century a short treatise on the *Kyrie eleison* was written by Eustathius of Thessalonica.[85] I have been able to obtain a photocopy of this treatise but I am unable to decipher it. Still there is good reason to believe that this work is identical with that given in the *Philokalia* under the title, 'Explanation of the *Kyrie eleison* of great benefit to every Christian and therefore translated into the vernacular.'[86] Parts of this work are well worth quoting. Should it prove to be later than the thirteenth or even the fourteenth century it will at least show that certain of the earlier ideas persisted even alongside the psycho-physical technique.

The Prayer 'Lord Jesus Christ, have mercy on me' or briefly the 'Lord have mercy' was given to Christians in the age of the apostles. It has been decreed that Christians should say this prayer continually, as indeed they do. But rare are the men who know the true meaning of the Kyrie eleison *today; they say the words day after*

*day but never receive the mercy of the Lord because they
do not understand what they are praying for.*

This paragraph indicates that the *Kyrie eleison* is actually
a shortened form of the Jesus Prayer. The text goes on to
explain why we pray for God's mercy. It is because we are
sinners and the slaves of sin. What we are begging for is our
emancipation from slavery. We should go to God as a pauper
goes to a wealthy person, saying to him 'Have mercy on me',
or as a debtor goes to his creditor to implore him to cancel
his debt, or as an offender goes to the one offended to ask
pardon. But most people say the *Kyrie eleison* simply out of
routine.[87] The author writes:

*God's mercy is nothing but the grace of the Holy Spirit;
we ask God for mercy because we are sinners. We have to
cry out continually, Kyrie eleison. That is to say, 'Have
mercy, Lord, on me, a sinner, in the wretched state in
which I find myself, and receive me again into your grace;
give me courage to resist the devil's temptations and the
bad habits of sin.' [These are the sentiments to keep in
mind] so that you do not simply cry Kyrie eleison out of
sheer habit and with no intent or purpose.[88]*

All the evidence seems to agree. The Jesus Prayer,
despite its name, can call on the Lord under any title
whatsoever, without using the name 'Jesus', provided it be a
plea for mercy and pity. The anonymous saintly author of this
treatise, who was so exasperated by the state of piety in his
time, said exactly what had been said centuries before by St
Barsanuphius in a jubilant letter to a hesychast: 'With all
your strength say the *Kyrie eleison* and be full of
gratitude.'[89] During the period between these two writers
came Symeon the New Theologian who, in his ecstasies,
'used to cry out continually in a loud voice, "O Lord have
mercy on me" '.[90] Greater than all these men and long
before them was St John Chrysostom who drew a parallel

between the *Kyrie eleison* of continual prayer and the presistent supplication of the Canaanite woman of the Gospel.[91]

Widespread and persistent use of the *miserere* formula eventually provoked a certain opposition and resistance which would make an interesting study in itself. It seems that the opposition appeared only after the fourteenth century, as a reaction to the exaggerations of that time, and was soon drowned out in the general tumult of controversy over other sensitive points of doctrine and practice. On the whole it can be said that the *Kyrie eleison* has enjoyed a respectable history, due probably to the fact that this formula resonates with what is deepest in byzantine religious sensibility, indelibly marked by monasticism.

To conclude this chapter we might consider two of the critical reactions aroused by the Jesus Prayer. The first example is that of a monk named Denys, whom Dom Julien Leroy is inclined to identify with Thekaras, a fourteenth century composer of hymns.[92] Denys was the author of *Fifty Gnostic Chapters*. Dom Julien comments:

> *Despite the title this work might be disappointing to readers who are familiar with the* Centuries *of Evagrius or of Hesychius. The adjective 'gnostic' was put in the title to attract readers. Basically this work is a piece of propaganda dedicated to spreading devotion to the 'Divine Hymns' of Thekaras. The author repeats his thesis to the point of being wearisome—that a Christian's primary duty is to praise, glorify and sing to God using the hymns of Thekaras. A pattern of four words comes back again and again like a slogan throughout these short chapters: praise, glorify, bless, thank.*

The whole of Dom Julien's article should be read. He considers the *Fifty Gnostic Chapters* a counterattack against the progressive invasion of the Jesus Prayer and the concomitant hesychast doctrine. To quote Dom Julien's conclusion:

> *True prayer for Denys was neither the high, gnostic states*
> *described by Evagrius nor the humble, penitential prayers*
> *meant to foster compunction [the most popular of which*
> *was the Jesus Prayer], but rather the prayer of praise.*
> *This he saw as the essential work of the monk. Practising*
> *vigilance by means of short prayers was of value only as a*
> *means of safeguarding the fruits of the prayer of praise.*

It may be that Denys detected the danger of a certain impoverishment or narrowness in the exaggerated propaganda employed by some of his contemporaries in favor of their particular formula of short prayer.

The second example comes from the ranks of the hesychasts themselves. Some of them apparently found the Jesus Prayer too long to say in certain circumstances, which is not to say that they believed, with a contemporary author, that 'the power of this prayer lies not in its content, which is simple and plain like the prayer of the tax collector, but in the most sweet name of Jesus.'[93] If that had been their position, and especially if they believed that that was the traditional doctrine, they would certainly have said so. As we shall see, any ambiguity in their language on this point is only imaginary; clearly they were only saying that something was impossible, not recommending something new. They had no intention of propounding a theory, whether speculative or practical; they were simply recording a fact of their experience. But their experience was limited and their observations are formally contradicted by the recorded experience of the greatest byzantine mystic, Isaac the Syrian.

The spokesman for the opposition was Patriarch Callixtus, though he never claimed to be speaking for anyone but himself. The passage in question occurs in a work entitled *The Garden of Graces.*[94] It is worth quoting in full:

On the phenomena that may result from practising prayer of
the mind and heart, by Callixtus, the most holy Patriarch.

The first thing that the serious athlete of prayer will notice is a certain quivering in his body like a tremor beneath the skin, which he might attribute to an illusion of the devil. He will begin also to feel a warm sensation around is waist as if he were wearing a belt; and this too he might attribute to diabolical illusion. These things come however not from an illusion but from nature, as a natural reaction to the struggle of prayer. If someone were to take them as effects of grace rather than of nature, that would truly be an illusion. Phenomena of this kind, whatever their source, should not be desired and loved but instead resisted.

Then there is a sensation of warmth which comes from the region of the heart. This is to be considered an illusion of the devil if the mind has been indulging in lustful thoughts. But it is due to divine grace and is not an illusion if the mind has been kept pure and impassible, adhering to the deepest, inmost part of the heart.

Sometimes it happens that someone in this state will find himself covered with perspiration because of the great heat generated in his body. At this point a certain divine energy may begin to stir the heart, rising so to speak from the furnace of the heart and impelling the mind, which is united to this source of energy, to cry out frequently from its very depths 'My Jesus! My Jesus!' At the moment when the heart thus bursts open the mind can cry only these words and cannot complete the whole formula, 'Lord Jesus Christ, son of God, have mercy on me'. Because of the rapid succession of outbursts from the heart, all that can be said is 'My Jesus!' Anyone who claims that he can say the whole prayer while in this state has been deceived. As long as the mind adheres to the divine energy in the inmost depths of the heart it is unable to cry out anything more than 'My Jesus!'

This holy prayer ravishes the heart and the divine energy fills it with unspeakable consolation. Then tears of great sweetness begin to well up and spring from the heart and flood the eyes uncontrollably. This occurence is known as 'joyful sorrow' (karmolype).[95] *Next the heart is set on fire by contact with this tremendous divine energy until the whole body is aflame, and the mind in ecstasy cries out* Kyrie eleison.

For our purposes that will suffice. It is plain that here the Jesus Prayer has been reduced to the bare name of Jesus not by a process of simplification, not in the natural course of events, but because of an ecstatic state in which the subject is temporarily incapable of saying anything very lengthy. It is not a state which can be expected to last a long time. Nor is it the highest attainable state of prayer, for there is a further stage in which the soul is content simply to pray *Kyrie eleison*, as the final paragraph indicated. We have seen how Symeon the New Theologian was said to have repeated the *Kyrie eleison* even in his sublimest visions.

NOTES

1. Vassili Krivochéine, in *Messager de l'Exarchat du Patriarche russe en Europe occidentale*, No. 7-8 (Paris, 1951) pp. 55-59.

2. Un moine de l'Eglise d'Orient, 'La Prière de Jésus', *Irénikon* (Chevetogne, 1951) p. 7.

3. Krivochéine, *Messager*, p. 66.

4. Pierre-Marie Brun, *La Vie de saint Dosithée, Orientalia Christiana* 26 (1932) p. 114. See the Introduction to *Dorotheos of Gaza: Discourses and Sayings*, CS 33 (1977).

5. *La Vie*, p. 100.

6. Diadochus of Photice, *A Hundred Gnostic Chapters*, chap. 97; Sources Chrétiennes 5, p. 159.

7. Ibid., chap. 88, p. 148.

8. See Brun, *La Vie*, p. 116 critical apparatus to line 17.

9. See Diadochus, chaps. 89, 90, 100.

10. *Philokalia* (Venice, 1782) pp. 485-495.

11. See F. Wustenfeld, *Synaxarium, das ist Heiligen-Kalender der Coptischen Christen*, (Gotha, 1879) p. 186. Also J. Forget, *Synaxarium Alexandrinum*, Pars prior p. 248. (p. 164 of the arabic text).

12. *Philokalia* (Venice, 1782) p. 353.

13. Ibid., p. 354. Cf. Evagrius, *Praktikos* 62; PG 40:1249A.

14. Ibid., p. 348. Cf. Evagrius, *Cent III*, 48 and *Letter* 58; Frankenberg, p. 607.

15. Ibid., p. 348; cf. PG 32:265D.

16. Ibid., p. 348B.

17. Ibid., p. 347B.

18. See Hausherr, *L'Hésychasme, Orientalia Christiana Periodica* 22 (1956)

p. 33. On Evagrius and Ammonas see also F. Nau, 'Ammonas,' *Patrologia Orientalis* XI (1956 p. 481.

19.   *Philokalia* (Venice, 1782), p. 348. Compare St Basil's eulogy of *hesychia* in *Letter* 2, Classis I; PG 32:225.

20.   Ibid., p. 351A and 352B.

21.   Ibid., p. 353; see also p. 359.

22.   See Ibid., p. 347.

23.   See Ibid., p. 350B and 354A.

24.   Ibid., p. 345.

25.   Ibid.

26.   Ibid., p. 349. He must also have said the canonical hours of terce, sext, none and vespers, since he advised a disciple not to neglect them (see p. 351).

27.   Ibid., p. 354.

28.   *Apophthegmata Patrum*, Alphabetical Series, 'Mathoes' no. 9; CS 59:122.

29.   *Philokalia* (1782) p. 349.

30.   Ibid., p. 350.

31.   Ibid., p. 351.

32.   Ibid., p. 353.

33.   Ibid., p. 353; see Gregory Nazianzen, *Contra Julianum* (Paris, 1609) p. 102 or PG 35.

34.   PG 127:513A; 516B. Cf PG 106:1359D; 1382D.

35.   Antiochus, *Pandecte*; PG 89:1421B.

36.   Ibid., PG 89:1757.

37.   Ibid., PG 89:1752.

38.   Ibid., PG 89:1753.

39. Nikon, *Syntagna*; PG 106:1369.

40. See Hausherr, *La méthode d'oraison hésychaste, Orientalia Christiana* 36 (Rome, 1927). Its existence was rediscovered by L. Gillet in 1951, thank God. See *Sobornost*, series 3, no. 12 (Winter, 1952). Cf. Un moine de l'Eglise d'Orient, 'La Prière de Jésus,' *Irénikon* (Chevetogne, 1951) p. 25, note 1.

41. See Hausherr, 'La traité de l'Oraison d'Evagre le Pontique,' *Revue d'ascétique et de mystique* 15 (1934) p. 169ff.

42. P. Trevison, ed., *Scala Paradisi, Corona Patrum Salesiana, Serie Greca* Vols. VIII and IX (Turin, 1941).

43. Ibid., *Gradus* XXI; Vol. II, p. 37

44. Ibid.

45. *La Prière de Jésus* (Chevetogne, 1951) p. 28; the reference is to PG 88:1112C.

46. See Trevisan, *Scala*, II, p. 256.

47. A. Saudreau, *St Maxime, Vie Spirituelle* Vol. I (1920) p. 261.

48. M. Viller, 'Aux sources de la spiritualité de St Maxime', *Revue d'ascétique et de mystique* 11 (1930) p. 251, note 161.

49. Climacus, *Scala Paradisi, Gradus* XV; PG 88:889D.

50. Ibid., PG 88:880D.

51. Ibid., PG 88:889D.

52. Ibid., PG 88:881B.

53. Ibid., PG 88:896B.

54. Ibid., PG 88:900CD.

55. Ibid., PG 88:1132B; *Gradus* XXVIII.

56. Hesychius, *Cent* I, 99; PG 93:1512A.

57. Thirty-five times he uses simply 'Jesus'. In *Cent* I: 7 (twice), 8, 16, 20, 24, 28, 29, 39, 52, 86, 88 (three times), 89, 90, 93, 96, 99. In *Cent* II: 1, 18, 20, 28, 35, 46 (twice), 48 (twice), 64, 73 (twice), 80, 82, 87, 95.

Other titles and names occur as follows:

a. Christ Jesus, son of God and God himself: I:5 and 89.
b. Christ: In *Cent* I: 1, 5, 7, 20, 22, 29, 40, 41, 43, 47, 65, 80, 82, 96, 98. In *Cent* II: 56, 68, 73, 84.
c. Jesus Christ: I: 10, 11, 21, 26, 42; II: 2, 4 (twice), 5 (vocative).
d. Our master and God incarnate: I:12; II:14, 40, 41, 50 (twice), 66, 67, 69, 81, 82, 86, 95.
e. Master (*Despotes*): I:12.
f. Our Lord Jesus Christ: I: 30, 32, 97, 100; II: 9, 15, 67.
g. Christ Jesus: I: 39, 46, 52; II: 45, 47, 64.
h. Lord: I: 39 and 75; II: 5, 24, 49, 51.
i. Mighty King Jesus Christ: I:40.
j. Jesus Christ our God and Creator: I:42.
k. O Christ God: I:50 (vocative).
l. Jesus Christ our Lord: I:52 and 96.
m. Lord Jesus: I:62; II:46 and 94.
n. Our Lord: I:96.
o. Christ our God and great King: I:100.
p. The Lord our God: II:5.
q. Christ, King of the armies of Israel: II:15.
r. Lord God of all things: II:16.
s. Jesus our great God: II:51.
t. Jesus, God and son of God: II:72.
u. The Power and the Wisdom of God, Jesus Christ: II:85.
v. Christ Jesus our Lord: II:99.

57. Consider the following epithets and descriptions:

a. 'Have continual recourse against your enemies to Jesus the peace-maker' (*Cent* I:8).
b. 'The holy and adorable name of Jesus' (I:20; cf. 41).
c. 'The delightful (*glykeia*) invocation of Jesus' (I:86).
d. 'To call upon Jesus with a love full of sweetness and joy' (I:89).
e. 'To see with interior eyes the figure of Jesus flashing with light (*photomarmarygounta*)' (II:28).
f. 'The beauty and sweetness of Jesus' (II:46).
g. 'The sweet Jesus' (II:48).
h. 'Jesus reflecting justice like the sun' (II:64).
i. 'The divine light of Jesus' (II:73).

59. Some of these are difficult to translate: *pheggoeide kai asteroeide* (*Cent* II:95); *helioedes* (II:94); *phototokos kai astrapetokos kai photobolos kai pyrphoros* (II:69).

60. *Cent* II:54.

61. Climacus, *Scala Paradisi, Gradus* XXVI: PG 88:1073D.

62. *Cent* I:50: '...*nepsis* under your inspiration, O Christ God.'

63. *Cent* II:5.

64. *Cent* I:80. This is a further indication of the purpose of the Jesus Prayer.

65. See *Cent* II:8D, 81 and 85.

66. *Cent* II:87.

67. *Cent* II:94.

68. Hesychius, *Cent* I:1; Evagrius, *Praktikos*, 50, PG 40:1233B.

69. Nicetas Stethatos, *Cent* I, 97; PG 120:897B.

70. See *Lexikon für Theologie und Kirche*, s.v. 'Kreuzzeichen'.

71. *S. Pachomii Vitae Graecae* I, no. 73; Halkin, ed., p. 49.

72. Nicétas Stéthatos, *Vie de Syméon le Nouveau Théologien* (Rome, 1928).

73. See M. Th. Disdier, 'Elie l'Ecdicos et les hetera kephalaia attribués à S Maxime,' *Echos d'Orient* 31 (1932) pp. 17-43.

74. Elias Ekdikos, *Anthologion*, chap. 94; *Gnosticae sententiae* 65, 75; PG 127:1145A, 1161A.

75. *Kievopečerskij Patérik*, translated into modern Russian by Maria Viktorovna (Kiev, 1870) p. 44.

76. See *Le Métérikon de l'abbé Isaie, Orientalia Christiana Periodica* 12 (1946), pp. 286-301.

77. Ibid., p. 298.

78. Anna Comnena, *Alexiade* V, ix, 3; B. Leib, ed., (Paris, 1937) II: p. 38.

79. Macarius of Philadelphia, *Neon Eclogion* edited first by a Christian who was a lover of Christ and afterwards by Archdeacon Avvakum and the Monk Anthimius the Hagiorite (Constantinople, 1863) pp. 280-289.

80. Ibid., p. 380B.

81.   Ibid., p. 282.

82.   French translation of this *Rule* by Pl. de Meester, *osb* :Lille, 1937).

83.   St Basil, ibid., p. 9; pseudo-Athanasius 2, 14, 17; PG 28:252-282.

84.   *Rule*, de Meester p. 25.

85.   Eustathius of Thessalonica, *Kyrie Eleison*, Codex Escorial 262, fol 56-60. Cf. K. Krumbacher, *Geschichte der byzantinischen Literatur*, 2nd ed (Munich, 1897) 157.

86.   *Philokalia* (1782), pp. 1170-1186.

87.   Ibid., p. 1176.

88.   Ibid., p. 1170.

89.   Barsanuphius, *Ep* 81; ed. by Nicodemou Hagioreitou (Venice, 1816) p. 95.

90.   Nicétas Stéthatos, *Vie de Syméon le Nouveau Théologien*, nos. 5, 11, 27.

91.   St John Chrysostom, *In dimissionem Chanaanaeae* no. 10; PG 52:457. See also St Dorotheos, *Doctrina* 2:8; PG 88:1649.

92.   See *Dictionnaire de Spiritualité* III: 452-454. Cf. H.G. Beck, *Kirche und theologische Literatur* (1959) p. 704.

93.   Serge Boulgakov, quoted by Un Moine de l'Eglise d'Orient, *La Prière de Jésus* (Chevetogne, 1959) p. 87.

94.   Patriarch Callixtus, *Kyros kariton*, translated into Italian by Giardino de Grazie (Venice, 1819) p. 221.

95.   This is a term coined by John Climacus, *Gradus* VII; PG 88:804B. See Hausherr, *Penthos*, p. 152ff on the beatific sadness of compunction.

CHAPTER SEVEN

THE JESUS PRAYER

THE TWO preceeding chapters have shown that the secret meditation of the earliest hesychasts was practised with great freedom in the choice of formula, and that the practice gradually came to stabilize at one set prayer-formula. The process was plainly visible when we compared St John Chrysostom with the later pseudo-Chrysostom. In the century of pseudo-Chrysostom, which is difficult to pin down exactly, the Jesus Prayer was gaining acceptance but had not yet reached total predominance. The time was soon to come when this famous prayer would supplant virtually all others and receive for itself all the praise formerly given to secret meditation in general and to the *Deus in adiutorium* in particular.

We are much better informed today than we were thirty years ago about that era of history, thanks to some writings of Gregory Palamas which have been brought to light by a distinguished Romanian professor, D. Staniloae. They tell of a thirteenth-century Italian who converted from the 'degenerate religion' (*kakodoxia*) of his fellow Italians to the 'orthodoxy which we [the Greeks] possess'. In the words of Dr Staniloae, 'He renounced both his fatherland and his family, preferring ours to his own because of the word of truth which we teach with complete accuracy.' The new convert chose the most demanding state of life, that of a monk on Mount Athos. Probably it was at this time that he took the name 'Nicephorus'. According to custom Nicephorus was first a cenobite and then later was permitted to become a hesychast. Dr Staniloae writes:

> *He soon became a spiritual guide to many who were doing battle with the spirits of evil in their life of prayer. For their benefit he compiled a book of instructions from the fathers which would train them for battle, explain different tactics, and at the same time provide a preview of the prize to be won and the crown which victory would bring. But Nicephorus soon saw that there were many beginners who were incapable of controlling even to a slight degree the wandering of their minds. So in another work he offered them a method by which they might effectively resist the innumerable suggestions of the imagination.* [1]

Subsequently Nicephorus was exiled by Emperor Michael VIII Paleologus. While in exile he came in contact with men who afterwards became 'the salt of the earth and the light of the world', such as Theoleptus of Philadelphia, Seliotes, Elias and others. To them he taught the knowledge of divine things. The first part of the treatise of Nicephorus *On Vigilance* [*nepsis*] *and Custody of the Heart* consists of fourteen selections from the writings of the fathers. They were chosen, he tells us, with a view to convincing the skeptical that there exists 'a science, or rather a method, which can lead one without exhaustion or sweat to the door of *apatheia*, a method which is immune to the illusions and terrors of the demons'. [2] Thus Nicephorus had a particular purpose in mind; he reminded his readers of it by concluding each patristic selection with a brief comment of his own drawing attention to the lesson being taught. These concluding reflections are worth examining here in detail.

The anthology begins with an anecdote from the *Life of St*

Antony.[3] It illustrates how the great patriarch of monks 'was endowed, because of his vigilance of heart, with a vision of God and the vision of things at a distance'. It is the story of how Antony saw from afar two monks who were in danger of dying from thirst. For Nicephorus this demonstrated the power of *nepsis*.

Theodosius the Cenobiarch he quoted from his paraphrased biography, as one might expect; selections from two different parts of the biography are put side by side.[4] The result is an effective statement showing how 'this great St Theodosius was wounded with love for the Saviour by means of his habit of collecting the senses and *focusing them inward*'.

One of the *apophthegmata* of St Arsenius is related next, either from memory or from another paraphrased version.[5] Arsenius is said to have been careful 'to keep his attention within himself and to recollect his thoughts'. This permitted Nicephorus to comment: 'This holy man, an angel on earth, *gathered his thoughts within* himself so as to be able in this way to raise himself easily to God.'

St Paul of Latros is someone for whom Nicephorus evidently had great respect. This tenth-century monk is said to have taught his disciples 'a method' (*babai*).[6] Nicephorus was sure that this method could have been none other than '*custody of the mind*, because only the mind is equal to the task of expelling passionate thoughts'.

A similar idea concludes the passage selected from the *Life of St Sabas*.[7] 'You can see how the venerable Sabas also demanded *custody of the mind* from his disciples, and how he would not permit them to live alone in a cell until they could master the practice. How do we compare, when we sit in our cells in idleness without even knowing that there is such a thing as custody of the mind?'

A saying of Abba Agathon is quoted comparing exterior works of bodily asceticism to the leaves of a tree and custody of the heart to the fruit. The Abba affirmed that the leaves are necessary but not enough, for 'every tree that does not

bear good fruit will be cut down and cast into the fire' (Mt
3:10).[8] Nicephorus pointed out that this is a judgment on
those who rely only on their good works without guarding
their minds. 'Your words, O Father, are truly frightening!'
Here it should be remembered that the original, Evagrian
definition of ascetical works (*praxis*) was 'a spiritual method
to purify the passionate part of the soul' and to lead it all the
way to 'the contemplation of created things'.[9] But this
definition was subsequently turned into a definition of *nepsis*
by Hesychius.[10] Nicephorus placed himself clearly in the
tradition of Hesychius.

From the writings of Mark the Hermit Nicephorus chose
and greatly abridged a section speaking of 'a marvellous
spiritual method' for resisting, without physical exertion, the
three strong giants of forgetfulness, laziness and ignorance,
and thus attaining true *gnosis*'.[11] At the end Nicephorus
commented: 'Do you see how all the fathers agree in their
spiritual doctrine? They are all talking about the same
thing—vigilance (*nepsis*).'

St John Climacus is represented by half a dozen
quotations from different parts of *The Ladder*.[12] First there
are two definitions of a hesychast. Then a well-known maxim:
'Close the door of the cell to keep your body within; close the
door of your tongue against an idle word; close the door of
your heart to the spirits of evil.' Nicephorus selected three
other sentences, building up to a climax with the mention of
'prayer of the heart':

> When you are sitting [*as a hesychast*] look up if you
> know how and observe when and where and how the
> thieves try to break in and plunder the vineyard. See how
> many they are and their different kinds. If you should
> grow weary, do as a good watchman does; get up, pray
> for a while, then sit down again and resume your task
> with renewed strength.
> Controlling passionate thoughts is something, but
> keeping the mind itself under control is far greater and far

more difficult; they are as far apart as East is from the West.

Just as thieves think twice about breaking into a place when they see signs that a strong warrior is inside, in the same way the invisible robbers are not likely to attack a man who has united his prayer to his heart.

Nicephorus would soon explain his own method for prayer of the heart. At this point he commented: 'Can you see how clearly these texts reveal the wonderful spiritual life of this illustrious father?'

Next Nicephorus turned to Abba Isaiah. His only comment here is an exclamation of wonder at the 'great compassion and indulgence' of this father. Abba Isaiah said something which runs counter to the teaching of Abba Agathon quoted above: 'If we have not practised perfect *custody of the heart as our predecessors did*, let us at least do our utmost to preserve our bodies free of sin and for the rest trust in God's mercy.'[13] Probably Nicephorus quoted this text because of what it says about the existence of an early monastic tradition of custody of the heart, and not for the purpose of consoling the weaker brethren. Later he would say something calculated to take away any illusory consolations.

Macarius the Great was bound to be included in this gallery of illustrious witnesses to prayer of the heart. Macarius said: 'The chief task of the athlete [that is, the monk] is *to enter into his heart.*'[14] He distinguished two kinds of chastity, that of the body and that of the heart, just as our Lord distinguished two kinds of adultery (Mt 5:28). The thing that counts is purity of the heart and entering into the heart. Nicephorus remarked:

This illustrious father seems to be in contradiction to the teaching of Abba Isaiah given above. But on closer examination, Abba Isaiah recommends that we keep God's command and preserve purity of body; but God also commands purity of the soul; consequently, because of the gospel's commandments, Abba Isaiah prescribes the same thing [as Macarius].

Diadochus of Photice is quoted next: 'The man who lives always *within his own heart* is completely immune to the temptations of life.'[15] The theme is familiar already. Nicephorus added:

This holy father spoke truly when he said that the devil's wiles are ineffectual when we remain in the depths of our hearts, and this is the more true the longer we remain there. But I am afraid that I shall never end if I try to include in this little book the sayings of all the fathers. Therefore I will mention only one or two more and then conclude.

He mentions three more. One was Isaac the Syrian who is quoted without further comment by Nicephorus:

Try to enter the treasure chamber [tamieion) that is within you and then you will discover the treasure chamber of heaven. For they are one and the same. If you succeed in entering one, you will see both. The ladder to this kingdom is hidden inside you, in your soul. If you wash your soul clean of sin you will see there the rungs of the ladder which you may climb.

Then comes a passage from John Carpathios which drew the attention of Nicephorus by its mention of the heart: 'It takes great effort and struggle in prayer to reach that state of mind which is free from all disturbance; it is a heaven *within the heart* [literally 'endocardial'], the place, as the Apostle assures us, where Christ dwells in us' (2 Cor 13:5).[16]
Finally there is a passage twenty lines long which Nicephorus says comes from Symeon the New Theologian. After a careful search I have been unable to locate this passage in Symeon's works.[17] Whatever its source it is

another affirmation of the familiar theme of 'the memory of God engraved in the heart'. Nicephorus summed up at the end:

> *You can see, my brothers, from all these texts, that there truly exists a spiritual art or rather a method which can rapidly lead whoever practises it to* apatheia *and to the vision of God* [theopteia]. *It has been clearly shown that all* praxis *is like the leaves on a fruitless tree in God's sight, and is of no benefit at all, if a man does not practise custody of the mind. We should therefore strive diligently to bear good fruit so that we will have nothing to be sorry for at the end of our lives.*

Custody of the heart is therefore *the* method *par excellence* according to the monastic fathers. Other names for the same thing are: 'custody of the mind', '*nepsis*', 'vigilance', 'recollection', 'spiritual sobriety'. Nicephorus liked to speak of 'leading the mind into the heart' or 'union of the mind, or spirit, and the heart'. One question might be considered at this point, before we take up the second part of the treatise of Nicephorus. Was this doctrine of *nepsis* completely unknown in the thirteenth century until Nicephorus rediscovered it? The list of witnesses quoted goes from Antony the Great to Symeon the New Theologian (949-1022). Yet Nicephorus, a foreigner, could announce this doctrine to his byzantine confreres with full trumpet fanfare in words like the following:

> *Come, all you who are yearning to experience the marvellous and sublime illumination* [photophaneia] *of our Lord Jesus Christ! Come, all you who wish to set your hearts aflame with supercelestial fire! Come, all you who are eager for the feeling of being perfectly at peace with God! Come, all you who for the sake of discovering and possessing the treasure buried in the field of your hearts have given up all worldly possessions! Come, you who have renounced the things of this present world so as to*

be found with the lamps of your spirit burning bright!
Come, and I will explain to you the science of eternal life,
the life of heaven; I will show you a method which can
lead one without exhaustion or sweat to the odor of
apatheia. [18]

Such extravagant language could have been insulting to the
monastic audience for which it was intended. These monks
made the reading of the fathers their daily spiritual nourishment; how could they be accused of losing contact with
monastic tradition? We must suppose that the Greek
confreres of Nicephorus were already familiar with the
monastic doctrine of attentiveness (*nepsis*). But apparently
they did not know how to practise it; they lacked a method.
Thus they say to Nicephorus:

We are firmly convinced of the truth of your words, and
all our doubts have vanished. Now we ask that you
instruct us further concerning the nature of nepsis *and*
how to attain it. For of that we have not the slightest
notion.

Nicephorus answered their request by launching into an
explanation of his own system or method. This, in the words
of Callixtus and Ignatius, is 'the *physical method* of the
blessed and brilliant Nicephorus concerning entry into the
heart by means of nasal respiration, with the intention of
concentrating the thoughts of the mind'. [19] Callixtus and
Ignatius thought it very important to give an explanation of
this method in the correct terms; they transcribed the text of
Nicephorus verbatim and placed it at the very beginning of
their own lengthy treatise on prayer. The Jesus Prayer was
an integral part of the psycho-physical technique expounded
by Nicephorus. The mind should constantly be repeating this
prayer, so that this is its principal occupation. 'This practice,'
Nicephorus asserted, 'will keep the mind free from
distractions and make it invulnerable to the enemy's

suggestions.'

An explicit treatment of the psycho-physical method lies outside the scope of the present work. I mention it to show the close bonds that exist between the new method and the old invocation. The merging of the two marks the apogee of the Jesus Prayer. From that time on it predominated over every other prayer formula. Even when Nicephorus' method began to be downgraded by certain people the Jesus Prayer maintained the place of supremacy which it had gradually won for itself in the course of a dozen centuries. It seems unlikely that it would have enjoyed such a triumphant career without the help of writers like pseudo-Symeon the New Theologian and Nicephorus the Solitary.

However, there are indications that Nicephorus did not have very much influence in his own lifetime. We are told by Gregory Palamas that while he was in exile he taught the science of divine things to men like Theoleptus of Philadelphia 'who have since become the salt of the earth and the light of the world'. But a generation later, when Gregory of Sinai went to Mount Athos to observe the life of the monks he found things pretty much as Nicephorus had found them. There were only three monks whom he could call contemplatives in the hesychast tradition; he recorded their names—Isaiah, Cornelius and Macarius.[20] Even these three were poorly instructed. The rest of the monks led truly virtuous and edifying lives but they did not know how to go beyond the stage of ascetical practices to the contemplative life. The zealous efforts of Gregory the Sinaite changed all that. He is the one directly responsible for the great popularity of hesychasm and its new method.

Why didn't Nicephorus himself have such success? His exile and perhaps an early death would have prevented it. Only one of his three disciples, as far as we know, had any following as a spiritual master. This was Theoleptus of Philadelphia. Describing him, a modern author has written that he had neither a phobia nor a mania for using the psycho-pysical method: 'Theoleptus seems to have considered

the formula of invocation [the Jesus Prayer] less important
than the spirit of continual prayer which the invocation is
meant to facilitate.'[21]

After the fourteenth century the various spiritual writers
tried to outdo each other in celebrating the merits of the
Jesus Prayer. We shall quote from one of them, an
anonymous author, who is included in the *Philokalia*. The
editor, Nicodemus the Hagiorite, described his work as 'a
completely admirable treatise on the words of the divine
prayer, "Lord Jesus Christ, son of God, have mercy on me".'
The author used drawings and diagrams to illustrate his
words, a feature which almost gives his work the appearance
of a treatise on geometry or trigonometry. There has been no
modern language translation of this work since Nicodemus
put it in neo-Greek for the *Philokalia*, but it deserves to be
better known:

> *It would be impossible and completely beyond our
> ability to explain and describe all the powers possessed by
> the prayer, 'Lord Jesus Christ, son of God, have mercy on
> me', and all the graces it can procure for those who
> practise it and the state of dignity to which it raises them.
> The only thing we will attempt to say about the Prayer of
> the Lord Jesus Christ concerns its beginnings—where it
> came from and who were the first ones to pronounce the
> words of this Prayer.*
>
> *In the first place the Prayer is completely scriptural in
> its origin, and it was the three greatest apostles Paul,
> John and Peter, who uttered the words of this Prayer.
> From them we have received it as an heritage handed
> down from father to son. Furthermore these words are a
> divine oracle, a revelation from the Holy Spirit, the words
> of God himself, as our faith teaches us. For we believe
> that what the sacred and Spirit-filled apostles have said
> and written are the words of Christ speaking through
> them. We read in the gospel how the Lord himself
> promised that the Father, the Son, and the Holy Spirit*

would come and make their abode in the apostles and not only in them but in every Christian who keeps the Lord's commands.

So as it happened it was St Paul, a man permitted to ascend up to the third heaven, who said the first words of this Prayer, 'Lord Jesus'. He wrote: 'No one can say "Lord Jesus" except in the Holy Spirit' (1 Cor 12:3). And the Apostle Paul shows also that this name is sacred above every name known among men, and this is why no one can pronounce it except by the Holy Spirit.

Then St John the theologian, proclaiming things and theological with a voice of thunder, began where Paul left off and said, 'No spirit who fails to confess that Jesus Christ is come in the flesh is from God' (1 Jn 4:2). By affirming that every spirit confessing the name 'Jesus Christ' comes from God, the holy Apostle clearly showed that the name and the invocation of Jesus Christ is an effect of divine spiritual grace and not merely a chance occurrence.

Then Peter, head of the apostles, took up the word 'Christ' from St John and began from there. When our Lord asked his disciples, 'And you, who do you say that I am?' Peter answered, 'You are the Christ, the Son of God' (Mt 16:16). That was something which was revealed to him from heaven by God the Father, as our Lord himself, said in the gospel.

Notice how these three holy apostles of Christ join each other in the words they say, so as to form a circle. One takes up the sacred word of another and advances it a little further, and thus the Prayer is completed. Paul said, 'Lord Jesus'. John said, 'Jesus Christ'. And Peter said, 'Christ, Son of God'. And it forms a wonderful circle because the final phrase, which is 'Son of God', rejoins the first word which is 'Lord'. For it is one and the same to say 'Lord' and to say 'Son of God', since both express the divinity of the only-begotten Son of God. Let us draw that circle so that everyone will understand:

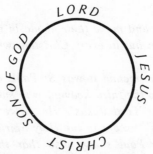

This is how the holy apostles handed down to us the custom of confessing and saying in the Holy Spirit, 'Lord Jesus Christ, son of God'. And since there are three witnesses they are worthy of belief. [22]

The text goes on to explain how the three degrees of the spiritual life are symbolized by the three apostles. Then the author examines the remainder of the Jesus Prayer, the words 'have mercy on us'. This need not be quoted because it repeats what we have already seen in our chapter on 'The Petition for Mercy'. Finally the anonymous author takes up an apologetic consideration, and with that we may bring our study to a conclusion.

The thesis is that the Jesus Prayer in its complete formulation constitutes a refutation of all heresies. There is another diagram and an explanation:

LORD	*CHRIST*
refutes Paul of Samosata	refutes the Nestorians

SON OF GOD	*JESUS*
refutes Eutyches, Dioscorus and the Monophysites	refutes the Armenians and the Theopaschites

The word 'Lord proclaims Christ's divine nature and thus denies the heresy of those who say that Christ is merely a man and not God. Opposite this, the word ''Jesus'' proclaims Christ's human nature and so refutes the heresy of those who say that he is simply God and not man and that he appears to be man only because of imagination. Next, "Christ" proclaims the unity of two natures, divine and human, in a single person and a single *hypostasis*. This is against the heresy of those who say that Christ has two *hypostases*, separate from one another. Finally the title "Son of God" proclaims that in Christ the divine nature remains integral even after having united itself with the human nature which likewise remains integral. This refutes the heresy of those who say that the human and divine natures in Christ have undergone a change and are somehow blended together.'

What makes the Jesus Prayer exceptionally important is its profession both of divine faith and of good human psychology. This is what makes it different from a practice like the repetition of the name 'Jesus' all by itself. The other practice, as our research has shown, never became popular among the faithful because it did not correspond well enough to their faith and their love. Because Christians believe in the Christ of revelation they delight in giving to Jesus, the son of man, all the titles which belong to him in virtue of his hypostatic union with the Logos, son of the Father. The custom of saying simply 'Jesus' runs the risk of reducing our relations with him to the level of a friendship that is more human than divine, more sentimental than respectful. It is only adoration that can transform our love for God into an all-powerful, all-consuming emotion before which all other loves turn pale.

Yet the anonymous treatise we have been quoting contains one passage a little out of harmony with this conclusion. The author wrote:

> *This is the doctrine that has been handed down to us by our inspired fathers who were perfect in all virtue and grace. They treasured and engraved on their hearts each of those sacred words left to us by the apostles*—Lord Jesus Christ, son of God. *Especially did they love the most sweet name of* Jesus; *they would use this name by*

itself in all their prayers. The whole effort of their lives
was to fill themselves with the sweetness of Jesus. *Their*
whole hunger and thirst was for Jesus. *This is what filled*
them with indescribable spiritual joy. They received
special charisms and were elevated above the cares of the
flesh and of the world. They became heavenly men or
angels on earth. It was calling on the name of Jesus *that*
led them to the heights of virtue. [23]

This paragraph seems contradictory to what the author
wrote earlier, and it is certainly in opposition to what we have
learned from historical research. The following paragraph
serves to some extent as a needed corrective:

Nevertheless, the fathers have prescribed that we who are
beginners and imperfect should say also the words 'have
mercy on us'. For us the full prayer should be: 'Lord
Jesus Christ, son of God, have mercy on us.' The reason
for this is that we might become aware of our true state
and condition and never forget how much we need the
great and abundant mercy of God most-holy. We are like
that blind man in the gospel who was moved by the desire
of regaining his sight to cry out these words when Our
Lord was passing by, 'Jesus, have mercy on me!' We who
are spiritually blind should continually beg God to show us
his mercy and open the eyes of our soul so that we may
see mentally. This is why the fathers have commanded us
to say the full prayer, with the 'have mercy on us'. [24]

If this is so, there were not likely to have been many
fathers who contented themselves with saying simply 'Jesus',
because the holiest (most god-bearing) among them were the
very ones who saw themselves as the least perfect. This
began (after the apostles) with St Arsenius and continued
with nearly all the desert fathers. 'The closer one draws to
God, the more one sees himself to be a sinner', said Abba
Mathoes, in perfect accord with his famous confrere,
Arsenius. [25]

NOTES

1. Professor Dr D. Staniloae, 'Două Tractate ale Sfântului Grigorie Palama', *Academia Teologică 'Andreiana'*, Annuarul IX, 1932-1933, (Sibiu, 1933) pp. 8-11. See also M. Jugie, 'Note sur le moine Nicéphore', *Echos d'Orient* 35 (1936) pp. 409-412.

2. Nicephorus the Monk, *Hyper tes nepsis kai tes kardias phylakes*; PG 147:945ff. See also E. Kadlouboŭsky-G. Palmer, translators, *Writings from the Philokalia on Prayer of the Heart* (London: Faber and Faber, 1962) p. 22ff.

3. *Vita Antonii*, no. 59; PG 26:928B.

4. Theodosius the Cenobiarch; PG 114:448AB and 509B.

5. See *Apophthegmata Patrum*, Alphabetical Series, 'Arsenius' no. 43; CS 59:16.

6. *Vita S. Pauli Junioris* no. 20; H Delehaye, ed., *Analecta Bollandiana* 11 (1892) 57ff.

7. See Cyril of Scythopolis, *Vita S Sabae*, no. 28; E Schwartz, ed., *Texte und Untersuchungen* 49, 2 (Leipzig, 1939) p. 113.

8. See *Apophthegmata Patrum*, Alphabetical Series, 'Agathon' no. 8; CS 59:18.

9. Evagrius, *Praktikos* 50; PG 40:1233B.

10. Hesychius, *Cent* I, 1; PG 93:1448D.

11. Mark the Hermit, *Ad Nicolaum*, nos. 12-13; PG 305:1048C.

12. John Climacus, *Scala Paradisi*, chaps. 26-27, passim; PG 88.

13. See Augoustinos, ed., *Isaie* (Jerusalem, 1911), *Logos* 21, no. 10, p. 132.

14. Macarius the Great, *Hom* 26, no. 12; PG 34:681D, 684A.

15. Diadochus of Photice, *A Hundred Gnostic Chapters*, chap. 57; E. des Places, ed., Sources Chrétiennes 5 (Paris, 1955) p. 117.

16. John Carpathios, *Capitula ad Monachos in India*; PG 85:1848.

17.　See pseudo-Symeon, *Méthode de la sainte oraison, Orientalia Christiana* IX (1927) p. 65.

18.　Nicephorus, *Nepsis*; PG 147:945ff.

19.　Callixtus and Ignatius Xanthopoulos, *Method and Canon*, chap. 18; PG 147:677.

20.　See J. Pomjalovsky, ed., *Vie de Grégoire le Sinaite* (S Petersburg, 1894), p. 10, note vii.

21.　S. Salaville, 'Formes de prière d'après un byzantin du XIV siècle,' *Echos d'Orient* 39 (1940-1942) pp. 25 and 19.

22.　*Philokalia*, Nicodemus the Hagiorite, ed., (1782) pp. 1163-1167. On page 966 there is another drawing illustrating the physical, theological, ethical and practical aspects of a certain 'chapter' in a work of Gregory Palamas. On three witnesses, see Deut. 19.15.

23.　Ibid., p. 1165.

24.　Ibid., p. 1166.

25.　*Apophthegmata Patrum*, Alphabetical Series, 'Matoes' no. 2; CS 59:121. See also Hausherr, *Penthos*, pp. 44-50.

CONCLUSION

T HE JESUS PRAYER is a superb formula of prayer. In it meet two elements of the highest importance: adoration and compunction. These signify everything that is divine and everything that is human, at the point where human and divine are most separate in the order of being and most united in the order of love.

For all that the Jesus Prayer, however admirable, remains simply a formula of words. A person deserves to be called 'formulistic' if he is 'overly attached to formulas, following them scrupulously'.[1] Things that come to a living organism from outside are useful only if they are assimilated, and they will be assimilated only if they fulfill some vital need in the organism. Such needs differ according to age, temperament, life history and particular circumstances.

The foregoing historical survey has shown that for centuries secret meditation (*krypte melete*) was practised with great freedom, each person choosing the text he wished to mull over. The only rule was enunciated by St Arsenius in these words: 'With all the strength at your command strive to make your interior prayer according to God.'[2] But there are many ways and means of praying, all pleasing to God. St Pachomius would exhort his monks to ruminate on a verse from Scripture (*de scripturis aliquid meditari*), presupposing

325

that every sentence of the sacred text has a saving power because it is the word of God and because of its intrinsic meaning. Some felt that this was true even if the meaning of the verse could not be understood. Cassian and his Abba Isaac had a clear preference for one particular verse, to which they freely attributed the most wonderful effects. Others would compose their own short prayer. What did the formula matter after all? As another saying of Arsenius goes, 'If we seek God, he will reveal himself to us, and if we hold him he will dwell with us'.[3]

The Holy Spirit cannot be tied to any formula of words. The Jesus Prayer is not even a sacrament, much less a magical charm—although history may record a case or two where the Jesus Prayer was used to introduce an incantation against rheumatism or headaches.[4] The human psyche, basically the same in all men, can take on an infinite number of variations depending on the heredity, environment and acquired habits of each individual. The 'multiform wisdom' of God (Eph 3:10) demands a corresponding sense of good judgment on man's part so that he may adapt himself to the Spirit's action.

'The Lord is a spirit, and where the spirit of the Lord is, there is freedom' (2 Cor 3:17). The Lord Jesus, although he urged his disciples to pray always, never took the initiative of teaching them a formula of prayer; John the Baptist, on the contrary, and the Pharisees, taught prayers freely (Lk 11:1 and 5:33). Perhaps Jesus felt that the best prayer which could be offered to the Father was the prayer each of his children made in his own words. If good thoughts spring from the heart (Lk 6:45), should it not be the same for good prayers? When the Master decided to teach his disciples the Our Father, he did not mean to suppress all other formulas of prayer, or even to insist that we all say the Our Father according to the version in Matthew. Luke's version, equally authentic, is slightly different. But the Lord's Prayer is normative in the sense that all liturgies and all personal prayers should in the last analysis be nothing more than an elaboration of the thoughts contained in the Lord's Prayer. This holds for *krypte melete* as well. Our prayer need not ask for many things, but for the same things many times.[5] Whatever the words used they should refer, in the intention of the one who prays, to something lofty and eternal, not someting picayune and transitory. This is the constant teaching of the fathers: seek first the kingdom of God and everything else will be given besides. This is what marks the deepest dimension of christian prayer. This is ultimately what it means to call on the name of the Lord. Every truly christian prayer has this dimension because the Christian has the mind and heart of the Spirit of God praying within him with ineffable groanings and making him a son of the Father. And he who searches the hearts of men knows what the Spirit means, because all that the Spirit asks for is 'according to God' and for our sanctification (Rom 8:26-27).

In christian spirituality everything is a calling on the name of the Lord even though the name 'Jesus' may be absent. Abba Isaac and his school, claiming to be faithful to the tradition of the earliest fathers, called on the name of the Lord by reciting the *Deus in adiutorium meum intende*. The name 'Christian' includes the name of the Lord without any need for additions like 'Jesuit Christian'. The sign of the cross is a preeminent trademark of the Christian but it does not contain the name 'Jesus'. The Church has always used the sign of the cross to exorcise demons, without fear of irreverence or of failure because the name of Jesus is missing. In the byzantine liturgy the *Kyrie eleison* lacks the name of Jesus but still it constitutes a perfect invocation of the name; and so the faithful repeat this cry almost innumerable times.[6] Similar examples could be multiplied.

A Russian Orthodox theologian has recently written:

The singing of the Kyrie eleison *in the liturgy goes back to the practice of the early Christians who, in order to obey St Paul's injunction to 'pray always', were accustomed to repeat the short prayer,* Kyrie eleison, *continually whatever they were doing. In the course of time this favorite christian invocation was lengthened to its present form: Lord Jesus Christ, son of God, have mercy on us. Certain fervent monks and laymen still say this prayer without interruption. But the liturgical litanies have retained the original short formula of this perennial christian prayer.*[7]

This explanation may not fit the historial picture presented by some of the writers in the *Philokalia* or by A Monk of the Eastern Church, but that is not important at the moment. The point to be noted is that all these sources witness to a desire and intention to call on the name of the Lord, whether by using the name 'Jesus' alone or the *Kyrie eleison*, or the full formula, 'Lord Jesus Christ, son of God, have mercy on me'. The fact that they all agree on their fundamental purpose is more significant than their disagreement on the choice of formula and their historical explanations. As St Paul says, 'What of it? All that matters is that in any and every way Christ is being proclaimed (*katangelletai*). Because of this I rejoice and shall always rejoice' (Phil 1:18). He would say anathema only to those who, although they knew the Lord, did not love him or adore him, that is, invoke him (Rom 1:20-22).

This corresponds exactly to the historical evidence we have concerning the reasons and intentions leading to the formulation of the Jesus Prayer. The russian author just quoted was perfectly correct when he said that the original purpose was the attainment of continual prayer. This was to be brought about by focusing the mind on a single point through the habitual memory of God. This was the explicit teaching of Diadochus of Photice who is the great authority in this matter. In fact all christian spirituality (not to mention other religions) aspires to a genuine 'life in God'. Prayer is the soul's very life breath, says a maxim whose author is unknown. Every religious person experiences the truth of this maxim in his own life. If there were some other bodily function more continually necessary to life than breathing, then prayer would be compared to that. John Climacus wrote the classic apophthegm on prayer and breathing, but the same point had been made by earlier and greater authors such as St Gregory the Theologian: 'Remembering God is of as much importance as breathing.'[8] And St Basil devoted a long question entirely to this subject.[9] Quoting the gospels and St Paul, Basil taught that a man had to abandon everything and be willing to undergo anything to reach this goal, 'that he carry about with him everywhere the holy thought of God, stamped in his soul like an indelible mark through continual and undistracted remembrance'. In St Gregory's case, although the maxim is characteristic of his spirit and his style of writing, he did not claim to have originated the idea. He mentioned it to say that he agreed with it, but he pushed the thought a step further by saying that there is no need to do anything but remember God.[10]

None of these great church fathers had a special formula to recommend for sustaining the continual memory of God. Their method consisted principally in the practice of detachment, which St Basil called 'the retreating (*anachoresis*) of self-will' or 'the total forgetfulness of the past'.[11] St Gregory once asserted that nothing was easier than the remembrance of God, but this statement occurs in a discourse to the citizens of Nazianzus during a time of great stress when they were being terrified by the threats of an angry governor.[12]

It was the monks who invented, or at least systematically practised and recommended, the method of secret meditation (*krypte melete*) as a means of maintaining the continual mindfulness of God. For this purpose each monk had his own special custom or rule of life (*politeia*). The desert reporters who collected the *Apophthegmata* were driven by a lively curiosity to unearth as many of these customs as they could, so that others might have a large selection from which to choose something that was well-suited to their particular tastes and talents. No one was under any illusion about discovering a quick and easy method that would bring instant results. Arsenius said it was necessary for a man to use all the strength he could muster.[13] And Diadochus was very careful to explain that if the soul be disturbed by anger or dulled by gluttony or weighed down by discouragement, 'the mind cannot, no matter how hard it tries, keep alive the memory of the Lord Jesus'.[14] In other words, no formula of prayer, whether it be the *Deus in adiutorium* or the Jesus Prayer, can accomplish anything by itself. There's no getting around the practice of mortification and the other exercises of the ascetical life.

If, however, the habit of secret meditation is found in the context of a sincere and virtuous life, it is likely to lead to the desired end of union with God through continual prayer whatever the prayer formula chosen for meditation and rumination. Every person who aspires to this sublime state will sooner or later discover his own way of frequently articulating that aspiration. It will be just so much the better if he is able to repeat or meditate (*meletan*) that aspiration almost continually except for interruptions caused by necessary duties. Even such interruptions may become another means or form of maintaining the memory of God. This may actually be the better way for some people. We have a record of the advice given by St Barsanuphius to an infirmarian monk who complained of the distractions inherent in his duties. Barsanuphius wrote: 'Having a job to do and doing it is at the same time obedience and *memory of God*; you have been immersed in the memory of God all day long without even knowing it!'[15] In teaching that holy thoughts have to be authenticated by good works, Barsanuphius, who was completely an Easterner and the descendant of an ancient Egyptian family, showed himself to be as realistic as any occidental writer. But the same point had been made long before by Abba Sisoes:

A brother said to Abba Sisoes, 'I can say, after examining myself, that the memory of God never leaves me.' Sisoes answered: 'It is no great thing that your thoughts are with God. What is really important is to see that you are lower than any other creature. This conviction, together with bodily toil, *will lead you to the virtue of humility.'*[16]

It is quite true that the thought of a virtue is not enough to bring about possession of that virtue or of virtue in general. Yet the fathers were well aware that the thought leads to the act, and leads the more surely as the thought is more intense. We read that St Dorotheos was asked the following question by a monk who was cellarer: 'Why is it that I can take delight with my mind in beautiful thoughts and can even desire to put them into practice but when the time comes for doing it I fail?' Dorotheos replied, 'It is because you do not *meditate* these thoughts always and everywhere.'[17] History shows that men of every land who strive for holiness have been in the habit of continually meditating or repeating short formulas, even if they did not think of promoting and advertising their particular form of meditation. And history shows too that some lacked discretion in their practice and overestimated their strength to the eventual ruin of their physical and even mental health.

In this concluding chapter it may be helpful to round out our study by considering a few examples of saints and spiritual writers of the West who practised and taught secret meditation just as did the famous fathers of the East. The examples will be those that come to my mind most readily. Others could add to this list and I would hope that they will. The complete list might be surprisingly long.

We may begin with the Carthusians, hesychasts of the West:

Among the Carthusians Hugh of Balma, writing towards the end of the thirteenth century, probably before 1290 [this would make him a contemporary of Nicephorus the Solitary], has left us a treatise De triplici via ad sapientiam. *This was eventually attributed to St Bona-*

venture and re-titled Theologia Mystica. *It had an extensive influence...serving as the point of departure for a
whole spirituality of aspirations which won favor among
authors of different schools such as Henry of Heep,
Alvarez de Paz, Cardinal Bona....*[18]

What should be emphasized is the phrase 'point of
departure'. The monk Nicephorus must also be called a point
of departure but he is clearly in continuity with the tradition
of the ancient fathers begun with St Antony. Cardinal Bona
was also conscious of being in a tradition. He quoted St
Antony, St Augustine, Cassian and St John Chrysostom
before quoting Tertullian, William of St Thierry, and St
Lawrence Justinian—all in favor of aspirations.[19] From St
Augustine he cited the well-known passage in the letter to
Proba: 'It is reported that the monks of Egypt say frequent,
very short, quick prayers, like arrows, so that their attentiveness (which is so necessary in prayer) may not slacken or
grow dull.'[20] In passing, it should be noted that this proves
St Augustine was aware of the practice of *krypte melete*
among the egyptian hermits and gave thse short prayers the
name 'ejaculations' (*orationes iaculatas*) by comparing them
with the flight of an arrow.

Cardinal Bona drew quotations from many other authorities, beginning with Christ our Saviour himself who used
short prayers during the agony in the garden and on the
cross. In the long list that follows there is no discernible
order: Nehemiah, Judith, the holy ones in heaven who cry
'Holy, holy, holy' continually, day and night. Then St Basil
who advised the sinner to cry out with the Canaanite woman,
'Have mercy on me, Son of David'.[21] And St Marcella who,
as St Jerome tells us, was constantly singing this verse from
the psalms: 'I have hidden yours words in my heart lest I sin
against you' (Ps 119:10). Also St Malachy, quoted from St
Bernard's biography, and Thais, the converted prostitute who
was taught by St Paphnutius to repeat, 'You have created
me, now have mercy on me'. Cassian is there, of course, with

his *Deus in adiutorium meum intende.* Then there is a general reference to the 'many examples in the *Lives of the Fathers*', especially Abba Isaiah, Abba Macarius, Moses the Ethiopian, Paul the Monk who regularly recited three hundred prayers, a virgin who recited seven hundred, Simon Stylites, and so on.

It is clear that the Latins who, like Cardinal Bona, were promoting the method of praying by aspirations could trace this method as far back in history as the Orientals could the Jesus Prayer. In fact, they traced it to the very same scriptural and monastic sources. Cardinal Bona stated his conclusion in these words:

> *I maintain, therefore, that the shortest way to God, to intimate union with the* Verbum, *and to the heights of mystical theology is the way of anagogic movements or the practice of aspirations. In support of this thesis I can quote the highest authorities. For instance, the Carmelite, John of Jesus Mary, writes as follows: 'It is the unanimous opinion of everyone I have read that the soul is elevated to the highest knowledge or experience of God by the use of aspirations, so that if the soul prefers this angelic exercise to all others and practises it diligently it will profit immensely.'* [22]

On the following page Bona quoted another Carmelite who was even more categorical. It was Thomas of Jesus:

> *According to the holy fathers and other mystics who have experienced it there is no shorter or easier or nobler way to ascend to God than that which is called in the language of the mystics 'unitive wisdom' or 'unitive love'. This consists of anagogic movements or aspirations by which the soul strives to raise itself to God and adhere to him by ardent longing.* [23]

The Cardinal assures us that he could fill pages and pages

with quotations in the same vein from the works of Bonaventure, Henry of Heep, John Gerson, Denys the Carthusian, Constantine of Barbanson, and others.

That should be evidence enough to show the existence of a spirituality of aspirations at least on the speculative, theoretical level. The West was definitely familiar with the traditional doctrine of the usefulness of short and frequent prayers as transmitted through Cassian and many others. And this form of spirituality was certainly practised by many in the West as well. Only a few indications of the fact will be given here but anyone who cared to make a thoroughgoing study of the subject would be doing a great service to the cause of truth and the history of spirituality.

We will begin with an early Jesuit text which is equal to anything in the *Philokalia*. It quotes from a homily of St Basil.[24]

This is what our Holy Father desired of the members of our Society,....that wherever they found themselves and whatever business they might be engaged in they should fly mentally to God by means of frequent aspirations and thus find God present everywhere. They should consider this to be the very best method of prayer since by it they refer themselves and all their actions to the greater glory and honor of God....If we truly appreciated this practice of directing the mind to God above by a prayer in which the soul consecrates itself to its Lord, we would see that this alone deserves the name of true prayer. For St Basil teaches that we ought to use every single moment for prayer by thanking God constantly and by directing the eye of the mind towards his supreme majesty. But you will manage to pray truly and perfectly without ceasing only when every occupation and activity of your life draws you into closer union with the divine will, so that your life itself may be and may deserve to be called a kind of continual and undivided prayer.

The author of this is Claudius Acquaviva, the fifth general of the Jesuits. This passage was taken from a letter he addressed to the fathers and brothers of the Society of Jesus, August 14th, 1599. The letter attempted to explain 'what is the custom in the Society concerning prayer and penance in accordance with our Rule'. In such a context it is not surprising to see the high respect paid to the practice of frequent, short prayers.

From the seventeenth century there is a six hundred forty-eight page book published at Lille by Antoine de Balinghem, a Jesuit from Saint-Omer, entitled *De Orationibus Jaculatoriis*. It was reprinted the following year at Antwerp. And there is a *Thesaurus Orationum Jaculatoriarum* dated 1626, with one hundred sixty-four pages, published at Cologne. In 1684 Michel Boutauld of Paris published a book of one hundred forty-one pages called *Méthode pour converser avec Dieu*. This work went through numerous editions and alterations and was translated into German, English,[25] Flemish and Italian (one Italian version was done by St Alphonsus Liguori).

Early in the eighteenth century an Italian Jesuit, Pietro Francesco Orta, a native of Dolina in Istria, published a book on ejaculatory prayer which is worth examining in some detail.[26] There is a list of one thousand ejaculations, each given in Latin followed by an Italian translation and a reference to the source and the names of holy persons who may have used that particular prayer. The names come from everywhere in Christendom, West and East; and include men and women, laymen and religious, ancients and contemporaries, the learned and the unlettered, Franciscans and Dominicans, hermits and missionaries. The author informs us that short prayers were in frequent use already in the Old Testament and that the saints of the New Testament all made use of them, to a greater or lesser degree.[27] At times the author's references are vague, at least by our standards, but at other times they are quite precise. For instance, he writes: 'It is recorded in the *Short Chronicle of Mark of Lisbon*,

Volume I, Book I, Chapter 99, Number 302, how the seraphic St Francis used to repeat frequently that familiar saying of his, "Blessed be the name of our Lord Jesus Christ."'[28] All such aspirations have the same purpose as the Jesus Prayer—fulfillment of the gospel precept, 'Pray always and never lose heart' (Lk 18:1) and 'Stay awake and pray always' (Lk 22:46). But fidelity to ejaculatory prayer leads also to numerous other benefits which Pietro Orta has enumerated in a lengthy list. This series of enthusiastic promises is in the same tradition as Cassian speaking of the *Deus in adiutorium* or the Russian Pilgrim eulogizing the Jesus Prayer. Orta wrote:

> *The holy fathers and the masters of the spiritual life had the greatest esteem for the practice of ejaculatory prayers. They tell us that such prayers promote strong and solid virtues which are prerequisite to the state of perfection. Further, they help root out faults, especially those that are the most habitual and engrained. They cool the heat of the strongest passions of the heart, hatred and lust, so that these passions are virtually extinguished. They provide consolation in time of trial, counsel in time of doubt and protection in time of danger. They sound the alarm in occasions of sin and help in recovering after a fall. They make the tongue more prudent in speech and the heart more careful in conversation. They inspire total confidence in God's provident love. They revive a flagging faith, confirm a wavering hope, enkindle a cooling charity.* [29]

Although there are a thousand different aspirations listed in the book, the Jesus Prayer is not among them. The one closest to it is this: 'Jesus the Nazarene, King of the Jews, have mercy on me' (no. 37). Something that is found much more frequently than in Eastern writings is the use of the name 'Jesus' without any title or with simply a modifier like 'most sweet Jesus' or 'good Jesus'.[30] There are also a number of aspirations directed to the Blessed Virgin Mary.[31]

Coming closer to our own time we can give a few examples of roman rite Christians who have practised secret meditation (*krypte melete*) with an intensity and freedom of spirit that easily rivals that of the Russian Pilgrim of interior prayer. This is not to suggest, of course, that there could ever be rivalry among men of God whose greatest wish is to share their riches with others.

Between the two world wars there appeared the biography of Father William Doyle, SJ. [32] His personal diary records his efforts to increase the number of aspirations per day from 10,000 to over 100,000. But Father Doyle was surpassed by Brother Mutien-Marie of the Brothers of Christian Schools, who is said to have made as many as 370,000 aspirations a day. Monsignor Picard, the biographer of Brother Mutien-Marie, compared the two men by saying:

Father Doyle exerted all his strength to say as many aspirations as he could. In 1911 he wrote: 'I felt urged today to make an effort to reach 10,000 aspirations each day....This would mean three and a half million acts in the year.' On July 26th, 1913, he resolved to do 20,000. On January 1st, 1915, he raised the number to 25,000 daily. He saw more and more clearly that to achieve this quota he would generously and resolutely have to banish every idle thought [recall here the doctrine of Diadochus of Photice on the memory of God]. And he spoke of making his life 'a martyrdom of prayer', of that continual prayer which had become his interior life. He resolved to make 50,000 aspirations daily beginning May 1st, 1916. After this the pace accelerated. On December 13th he wrote of reaching and trying to maintain 100,000 daily. Two months later, February 13th, 1917, he made a bargain with the Lord to give him a soul 'for every thousand aspirations made over the daily 100,000'. The final number which we read in Father Doyle's notes, dated just a few days before his death, is 120,000. Ten years before, in 1907, his beginning efforts could scarcely accomplish one thousand aspirations in a day.

Nevertheless Father Doyle fell far short of the record established by Brother Mutien-Marie [Gabriel Wiaux, 1895-1940]. Already in 1920 or 1921 Brother was completing a daily quote of from thirty to forty thousand aspirations. During his second novitiate the number climbed to 100,000 and beyond. His diary claims 120,000 on certain days, which was the maximum reached by Father Doyle. A few days of retreat in 1920 permitted Brother Mutien-Marie to reach 200,000. In 1925 he attained 300,000. The highest number he tells of saying is 370,000; this happened on January 30th, 1935. During the last years of his life he maintained and even accelerated this rhythm.

On the third of March, 1936, Brother Mutien-Marie wrote the following testimony:

> *A long time ago I needed to use many words to pray, but now for many years the loving thought of God has been enough for me. However, I still need to carry a chaplet in my hand at all times. I have a special chaplet, without cross or medal and with only one large bead on it. It never leaves me; I use it as an external aid to keep my mind and heart fixed on God. By holding it in my hand I can finger it constantly without being noticed. This is extremely helpful, I assure you. In the midst of trials or pain or headache or fever I am always touching it and always loving the good Lord, our good Jesus, and our good Mother in heaven. Vocal prayer quickly wears me out and distracts me. My habitual state for many years has been simple, loving union. I do nothing but love. My particular, personal vocation is to love. I love on behalf of those who labor.*[33]

The last example will be a Bavarian Jesuit who was a missionary in Brazil, Father Jean-Baptiste Reus (1886-1947).

His biography is being written by F. Baumann. Father Baumann also had an article in the periodical *Ewige Anbetung* (July, 1958, pp. 97-106) in which he said:

> *Father Reus firmly believed that perfect love was impossible without the continual practice of the memory of God. To achieve this he chose as an ejaculatory prayer the names 'Jesus, Mary, Joseph'. He repeated these names with many thoughts of faith and love and zeal all directed toward the goal of perfect love.*

Father Reus repeated these names with increasing frequency. He used a special chaplet which he held in his left hand; some thought that he was constantly praying the rosary. He did indeed have a special devotion to the rosary, for he wrote: 'I would not dare to offer the holy Mother of God a rosary which I did not say with as much recollection as possible; so I say my daily rosary, fifteen decades, in the presence of the Blessed Sacrament.' But on the chaplet in his left hand he was saying his short prayer: 2500 a day in November, 1917; 12,000 in 1935; and more than 20,000 a day in 1943, to make a yearly average of eight million. Numerically this is a figure far below the average attained by the Russian Pilgrim or by Brother Mutien-Marie. Father Reus said his prayers quite slowly, taking around six hours to say 12,000 invocations. In addition, he had his daily mass, breviary, meditation and rosary.

The objection might be raised that aspirations like these are indeed ejaculatory prayers but the Jesus Prayer is not an ejaculatory prayer. Personally I cannot see such distinctions. It is my conviction that except for the difference in words we have the same exercise of *krypte ergasia* with St Arsenius as with Father Doyle. The words have an entirely secondary importance—as all the authors maintained up to the time of pseudo-Chrysostom and Philemon. The formula used differs widely in the West, as it did among the earlier Eastern authors. There is no difference between East and West in the seriousness of their search for continual prayer or in the high esteem they have for effective means. The only difference is that in the byzantine empire *krypte melete* was taught primarily by monks, by hesychasts, so that the practice even came to be known as 'hesychasm', whereas in the West, especially in recent times, it seems to have been recommended and practised more by those in the active life who have made it the 'soul of their apostolate' and their own special means of sanctification. This difference may also explain something else. The hesychast tradition evolved naturally to the point where one single formula predominated because the life style of the hesychast was pretty much the same everywhere and in every century. But the life style of the apostolic laborer demands continual change and adaptation, and there is a corresponding multiplication and variation of prayer formulas. Someone in the active ministry has continually to confront new sources of distraction that present themselves as he goes about the daily duties of his apostolate. The hesychast need confront little more than the invisible enemy within himself; for that purpose Evagrius had collected a large number of scriptural formulas in his *Antirrheticos*, but subsequent tradition (St Barsanuphius) eliminated them as too cumbersome a system to operate.

The same impractical, idealistic mentality that inspired the *Antirrheticos* seems to lie also behind the efforts of some who have published books of collected aspirations. Cardinal Bona is a good example. He composed a 'little forest of aspirations' running to forty columns of small print which is, to say the least, too much to choose from.[34] His preface to Chapter Nine is very optimistic but it is not exactly a contagious optimism. Although admitting that it should not be hard for anyone to find in his own heart the makings of a suitable short prayer, he said:

> *Nevertheless, so that no ascetic may be left in dryness for lack of words, and so that the mystic fire may never die on the altar of the heart for lack of fuel, I have collected*

*from Scripture and the fathers a little forest of aspirations
for beginners, for the advanced and for the perfect.... You
will find them all here, arranged in groups of ten for easy
memorization. Spend a few days learning them by heart.
For what good is it to have a multitude of aspirations
written in a book if they are not also written and engraved
in the memory so as to be ready for use at any hour and
any moment?*

Cardinal Bona must have had, or thought that his readers
had, remarkable powers of memory. Today it would take
some people several days to learn just one or two of these
aspirations. Often they are five or six lines long.

The Cardinal's 'little forest' is about as far removed from
nature as an asphalt highway, but life and growth can
triumph over many an obstacle. Father Doyle, Brother
Mutien-Marie, Father Reus, and all who truly wish to live in
God will not be bothered for long with artificialities however
well-constructed. Each one will discover his own favorite
aspiration and will stick to it or vary it according to the
rhythm of his own spiritual development. It is also
interesting, though not surprising, that these saintly men and
women who may never have read John Climacus or any
Eastern author tend spontaneously to compare their practice
of saying aspirations with the process of respiration.[35] For
example, Mother Margaret Mary Hallahan, who never read
any of the hesychast writers, could say, 'Aspirative prayer is
to me almost as natural as breathing....'[36]

The Jesus Prayer can even evolve into what may be called
the Mary Prayer, and still produce the same effects. This has
been shown in a deep and delightful little book by a
Carmelite of Provence, Father John of Jesus-Mary, entitled
Notre-Dame de la Montée du Carmel. The demonstration is
all the more convincing because the author never says a word
about the Jesus Prayer and may not even be familiar with it.
He knows Cassian, however, and reprints part of the Latin
text of *Conference* X in an appendix. It is a pleasure to read

in Chapter five 'Trois sécrets de perfection' (pp. 68-82) how the Carmelite summarizes and comments on 'the narrative of Abba Isaac'. He sounds at times like St Barsanuphius criticizing the complicated Evagrian *Antirrhesis*. Father John writes:

> *It is a waste of time and energy to search in the arsenal of spiritual defences for a weapon that will be particularly effective against this or that enemy. It is useless even to know which enemy is attacking us. Besides it is often no more than guesswork on our part when we try to analyze the various movements and impulses that arise in our souls.* [37]

St Barsanuphius favored a simple invocation of the name 'Jesus'. Father John of Jesus-Mary, drawing on the tradition of St John of the Cross and St Louis-Marie Grignion de Montfort, maintained that 'the invocation of the name of Mary has the same theological meaning as the verse *Deus in adiutorium.*'[38] To prove his point he stressed the fact that all graces come to us through Mary. Consequently it should not be impossible that formulas such as the ancient marian petition, 'We fly to thy patronage, most holy Mother of God', should lead one to the goal of all secret meditation, which is continual interior prayer. This seems also to have been the opinion of St Seraphim of Sarov, who gave the following advice: 'In the afternoon, after resting, instead of saying the *molitva Iisusova*, say "Most holy Mother of God, save me, a sinner' ''.[39]

In a recent article Dom Bede Winslow, OSB expressed this wish: 'I would like to see the time when Orthodox monks might find Eastern Catholics imbued with the spirit of hesychasm and practising the Jesus Prayer.'[40] I think it can be said that his wish is already fulfilled, if not to the letter at least as to what constitutes the spirit of the Jesus Prayer. As for the letter, it has been said often enough that the letter kills. The letter leads to rigidity, narrowness, exclusivity. The 'multiform wisdom' of God (Eph 3:10) uses a variety of ways to lead all men to the same ultimate goal; the liberty of sons of the Father is a sign of the presence of the Spirit. There are indications even with the emergence of the Jesus Prayer that this liberty never completely disappeared from Eastern spirituality.[41] Freedom has certainly diminished, however, in the course of centuries according to ordinary psychological laws governing fashion and popularity which are valid even for religious devotions.

Bishop Palladius asked the question, 'How can the human mind be united to God without interruption?' The anchorite Diocles answered him, 'If the soul is concerned with a thought or action that is holy or devout, then it is with God.'[42] What is needed today is a similar attitude of respect toward the freedom of interior prayer. There is no need to impose laws on the prayer life of other people or to make propaganda for particular methods of interior prayer however marvellous they may seem to be. It is good, certainly, to make such methods known, but within the limits of humility and prudence, and without flaunting their superiority over other equally valid approaches.

St Francis Xavier, we may be sure, knew nothing about hesychasm. And surely his father in God, St Ignatius, never commanded him to practise the Jesus Prayer. But Francis did so. Here is the account left to us by the Chinese youth who watched Francis die at the age of forty-six and apparently as completely alone as Christ had been on the cross:

With his eyes raised to heaven and with an expression and a look full of joy he spoke at length in a loud voice with our Lord, using the various language he knew. I heard him repeat again and again, 'Jesus, son of David, have mercy on me; have mercy on my sins'. He continued in this state until Monday, November 28th, which was the eighth day of his illness. Then he stopped speaking and for three days, until noon on Thursday, he was not aware of anything and did not eat anything. Thursday at noon he

*regained his senses and his speech. I heard him call par-
ticularly on the Holy Trinity, Father, Son and Holy Spirit,
which was always one of his greatest devotions. And also
he was saying these words under his breath: 'Jesus, son
of David, have mercy one me! O virgin Mother of God,
remember me!' With these and similar words on his lips
he continued until Friday evening. A little before dawn on
Saturday morning, seeing that he was dying. I placed a
candle in his hands. Then with the name of Jesus on his
lips he rendered his soul into the hands of his Lord and
Maker, in great peace and tranquillity.* [43]

Some might still maintain that St Francis Xavier was not
reciting the Jesus Prayer. He was not, perhaps, using the
traditional formula. But surely, considering the spirit of his
prayer, it would be true to say that not since the death of the
good thief on the cross of the death of Stephen the
protomartyr has the invocation of the Lord Jesus and his
Blessed Mother known a more touching triumph.

NOTES

1.   E. Littré, *Dictionnaire de la Langue Français* (Paris, 1881) Vol. II; 1735.

2.   *Apophthegmata Patrum*, Alphabetical Series, 'Arsenius' no. 9; CS 59:9.

3.   Ibid., no. 10.

4.   See A. Vassiliev, *Anecdota Graeca* I (Moscow, 1893) p. 331ff.

5.   Not *polla legon* but *ta auta pollakis*. See John Climacus, *Ladder of Paradise*, Gradus 28, Schol. 2; PG 88:1140D.

6.   It is repeated five hundred times in succession on the feast of the Exaltation of the Holy Cross. See *Typicon of the Great Church of Christ*, M. Saliverou, ed., (Athens) p. 75.

7.   From an anonymous Russian manual (in Russian) in five volumes: *A Treatise on the Orthodox Faith*, (1956) Vol. II: p. 164, note.

8.   Gregory Nazianzen, *Oratio* 27, *Theologica* I, 4; PG 36:16.

9.   St Basil, *Regula fusius tractata*, question 5; PG 31:920B, 924D.

10.   The *Sacra Parallela* of St John Damascene attributes the maxim to St Gregory the Wonder Worker (PG 96:228). But see the objections of A.K. Holl in *Fragmente aus den Sacra Parallela, Texte und Untersuchungen* 20, p. 160, no. 407.

11.   St Basil, *Regula fusius tractata*, question 6; PG 31:995C.

12.   Gregory Nazianzen, *Oratio* 17, no. 2; PG 35:968.

13.   *Apophthegmata Patrum*, Alphabetical Series, 'Arsenius' no. 9; CS 59:9.

14.   Diadochus of Photice, *One Hundred Gnostic Chapters*, chap. 61.

15.   Barsanuphius, Letter 225; Nicodemou Hagioreitou, ed., (Venice, 1816) p. 168.

16.   *Apophthegmata Patrum*, Alphabetical Series, 'Sisoes' no. 13; CS 59:180.

17.   St Dorotheos, *Doctrina* XVIII; PG 88:1805B. [*Discourses and Sayings* XIX; CS 33:241].

18. J. de Guibert, *Leçons de théologie mystique*, Tome I (Toulouse, 1955) p. 62.

19. Cardinal Bona, *Via Compendii ad Deum*, chap. iv; *Opera Omnia* (Venice, 1764) p. 59.

20. St Augustine, *Ep ad Probam* x; PL 33:501.

21. St Basil, *Hort. ad baptismum*. This is Cardinal Bona's note.

22. Cardinal Bona, *Via*, chap. v, p. 58. John of Jesus Mary is quoted from his *Mystica Theologia*, chap. 9.

23. Thomas à Jesu, *De div orat* 4, 20 (Cardinal Bona's note).

24. St Basil, *Hom in Mont Iulit*. Later on Gregory the Great—Gregorios Dialogos as the Orientals call him—is quoted.

25. *A Method of Conversing with God*, tr. I.W. of The Society of Jesus (Sir John Warner). 2nd ed. London, 1789, and *How to Converse with God....* Brighton, 1883.

26. Pietro Francesco Orta, *Orazioni giacolatorie de molti santi e servi di Dio, con diversi racconti esemplari. Aggiuntevi alcune avvertenze, e maniere di practicare dette Orazioni, coll'Indice delle Materie, e catalogo de' Soggetti nominati nell'Opera, e nei racconti*. Gaetano Zenobj, Stampatore, e Intagliatore della Santità de Nostro Signore Clemente XI. Avanti il Seminario Romano. Con licenza dei Superiori. Rome, 1706.

27. Ibid., *Avvertenze* II and III.

28. Ibid., *Avvertenze* IV.

29. Ibid., *Avvertenze* XIII. This is followed by a list of aspirations recommended for people in particular states of life.

30. For example: 'O most sweet Jesus, pierce the heart and marrow of my soul with the gentle wound of your love' (ibid., no. 10). 'Most sweet Jesus, my Love!' (no. 17). 'Be not my judge, most sweet Jesus, but my Saviour' (no. 42). 'O Jesus most lovable!' (no. 56). 'O my Jesus, my love and my life!' (no. 90). 'O Jesus, true delight of the heart!' (no. 92). 'Come, come, O Jesus, come quickly!' (no. 131).

31. For example: 'Behold, O Mary, I give you my heart' (no. 196). 'If I possessed a thousand times ten thousand hearts I would love Mary with a thousand times ten thousand hearts' (no. 82). 'Behold, O Mother, now I come'

(no. 390). 'Show yourself my mother' (no. 473). 'May there be in me no heart other than the heart of Mary' (no. 801, attributed to St John Damascene).

32.   A. O'Rahilly, *Father William Doyle, SJ* (London, 1936). See also, *Merry in God*, anonymous (London, 1939).

33.   Mgr. L. Picard, *Fr Mutien-Marie de Ciney, Gabriel Wiaux, 1895-1940* (Namur-Brussels, 1943), p. 147ff.

34.   Cardinal Bona, *Via Compendii ad Deum*, chaps. xi-xix.

35.   See V. Poucel, *Pour que notre âme respire* (Paris: Art catholique, 1936), and also *Mystique de la terre* I, pp. 211-219.

36.   Quoted in O'Rahilly, *Father William Doyle, SJ*, p. 209, note 13.

37.   John of Jesus-Mary, *Notre-Dame de la Monteé du Carmel* (Tarascon, 1951), p. 71.

38.   Ibid., p. 79.

39.   See Posseljanin, *Russian Ascetics of the Nineteenth Century* (in Russian), St Petersburg, 1910, p. 275.

40.   Dom Bede Winslow *OSB*, 'Het christelijk Oosten en Hereeniging,' *Benedictijns Hereenigingswerk* (1952) p. 206.

41.   For instance, in the Orthodox work *Handbuch für rechtgläubige Christen* (Hersbruck, 1948), in which 160 pages out of 217 are devoted to prayer, the Jesus Prayer occurs only once, in the morning prayer, and then without title or commentary.

42.   Palladius, *Lausiac History* chap. 98; PL 93:1190B.

43.   *Monumenta Xaveriana* II p. 896. See also *Chronicon Soc. Jesu*, year 1552, no. 763. According to Francoise Darcy, *Quand la porte s'entr'ouvre* (Rome, 1955) p. 130, the Blessed Marie of Providence (Eugenia Smet) lived a life of continual prayer and universal charity and died after a long illness during which 'she repeated constantly her favorite invocation, "Jesus, eternal joy of the saints!" '

BIBLIOGRAPHY

Allo, E.B. *Saint Paul: Premiere epître aux Corinthiens*. Paris. 1934.

Apophthegmata Patrum. Migne, *Patrologia Graeca* 65:71-440. English translation by Benedicta Ward SLG, *The Sayings of the Desert Fathers*, Cistercian Studies Series, No. 59. Kalamazoo-London: Cistercian Publications-Mowbrays, 1975.

Ammonas. F. Nau (ed.). *Patrologia Orientalis* de Graffin, XI.

Anna Comnena. *Alexiade*. B. Leib (ed.). Paris, 1937.

Ante-Nicene Fathers Series. Rpt. Grand Rapids, Michigan: Eerdmans.

Aphraates. Dom Parisot (ed.). *Patrologia Syriaca* de M. Graffin. I, 1-2. Paris, 1894-7.

Aristophanes. *Scholia Graeca*. F. Dübner (ed.). *Lysistrata*. pp. 248-72. Paris, 1877.

Aristotle. *Opera omnia*. Paris, 1850.

        . *Ethica Nicomachae, Opera omnia* II: 1-130.

Asin Palacios, M. *Logia et Agrapha Domini Jesu apud moslemicos scriptores*. *Patrologia Orientalis* XIII: 335-431.

Athanasius. *Vita Antonii*. PG 26:835-976. See also *Patrologia Latina* 73: 125-170. English translation by Robert T. Meyer, *The Life of Saint Antony*. Ancient Christian Writers series, 10. Westminster, Maryland, 1950.

Augoustinos. See Isaiah.

Bacht, H. 'Das "Jesus-Gebet" seine Geschichte und Problematik'. *Geist und Leben* 14 (1951) 326-38.

        . '"Meditari" in den ältesten Mönchsquellen'. *Geist und Leben* 28 (1955) 360-73.

Baehrens. See Origen.

Balinghen, A. de. *De orationibus Iaculatoriis*. Lille, 1617. Antwerp, 1618.

        . *Thesaurus Orationum Iaculatoriarum*. Cologne, 1626.

Balthasar, Hans Urs von. 'Die Hiera des Evagrium'. *Zeitschrift für katholische Theologie* 63 (1939) 86-106; 181-206.

Barnabas.*Epistle*. See Funk (ed.), *Patres Apostolici*. Tübingen, 1901, pp. 38-97. *An English Translation of the Epistle of Barnabas*. London: SPCK, 1923.

Barsanuphius. Nicodemou Hagioreitou (ed.). Venice, 1816.

Basil. PG 29:32. J. Garnier and P. Maran (edd.) 3 vols. Paris, 1721-30. Translations in The Fathers of the Church series, vols. 9, 13, 28, 46 (New York, Washington, DC) and in A Select Library of Nicene and post-Nicene Fathers of the Christian Church, second series, vol. 8. Rpt. Grand Rapids: Eerdmans.

Bäumer, S. *Geschichte des Breviers*. Freiburg im Breisgau, 1895. French translation by R. Biron, *Histoire du Bréviaire*. 2 vols. paris, 1905.

Baumstark, A. *Geschichte der syrischen Literatur*. Bonn, 1922.

Beck, E. See Ephrem.

Bedjan. See Isaac of Nineveh and James of Sarough.

Behr-Sigel, E. 'La Prière à Jesus, ou le Mystère de la spiritualité monastique orthodoxe'. *Dieu Vivant* 8 (1947) 69-94.

Bekes, G. 'De continua Oratione Clementis Alexandrini Doctrina'. *Studia Anselmiana*, 14. Rome, 1942.

Benedict. *Regula Monachorum*. A.J. Schuster (ed.) Turin, 1942. Also Westmalle, Belgium, 1962. English translation by Leonard J. Doyle, *St. Benedict's Rule for Monasteries*. Collegeville, Minnesota, 1948.

Berguer, G. 'La puissance de nom'. Communication to the Sixth International Congress on the History of Religions, Brussels, 1935. *Archives de psychologie de la Suisse romande*, XXV, 1936.

Bertrand, F. *Mystique de Jésus chez Origène*. Paris, 1951.

Bidawid, F.J. 'Les Lettres du Patriarche nestorien Timothée I'. *Studi e testi*, 187 [Chaldean text and Latin translation]. Rome, 1956.

Bidez-Parmentier. See Evagrius.

Bietenhard, H. Article '*onoma*' in G. Kittel (ed.), *Theologisches Wörterbuch zum neuen Testament*, 5:242-83. See Kittel.

Bloom, A. 'Contemplation et ascèse: contribution orthodoxe'. *Etudes Carm.* 28 (1949) 49-67.

Bona, J. *Opera Omnia*.Venice, 1764.

Bonnet, M. *Acta Apostolorum apocrypha*. 2 vols. Leipzig, 1891-98.

——. *Acta Thomae*. Leipzig, 1903.

Boon, A. See Pachomius.

Boulgakov, S.N. *The Orthodox Church*. London, 1935. (Chap. xi: 'Orthodox Mysticism', p. 168ff.)

——. *Orthodoxie*. Sibiu-Hermannstadt, 1933.

——. *Philosophie du nom*. Paris, 1953. [Russian text]

Bousset, W. *Apophthegmata, Studien zur Geschichte des ältesten Mönchtums*. Tübingen, 1923.

——. *Kyrios Christos, Geschichte des Christusglaubens von den Anfängen des Christentums bis Irenaeus*. Göttingen, 1913. English translation by John E. Steely, *Kyrios Christos: A History of the Belief in Christ from the Beginning of Christianity to Irenaeus*. Nashville: Abington, 1970.

Brjančaninov, I. *On the prayer of Jesus*. Translated by F. Lazarus. London, 1952. Russian edition, St Petersburg, 1867.

Bremond, H. *Histoire de sentiment religieux en France*, vol. VII: *La métaphysique des Saints*. Parish, 1929.

Brun, P.M. 'La Vie de saint Dosithée'. *Orientalia Christiana*, 26 (1932) 102-23.

Buzy, D. *Vie de Soeur Marie de Jésus Crucifié*. Paris, 1926.

Cabrol, F. 'Kyrie eleison'. *Dictionnaire d'Archéologie chrétienne et Liturgie*, 8/1: cols. 908-16.

Cassian, John. *Collationes*. Edited and translated into French by E. Pichery, *Conférences avec Les Pères du Désert*, Sources chrétiennes, 42, 54. Paris, 1955, 1958. English translation in Nicene and Post-Nicene Fathers series, vol. XI. New translation projected for Cistercian Studies Series, 20, 31 (1979, 1980).

Cicero, M.T. *Ciceronis opera.* J.A. Ernesti (ed.) London, 1830. *De officiis:* Vol. XVI, pp. 1065-1277. *De finibus bonorum et malorum:* Vol. XIV, pp. 161-461.

Clement of Alexandria. O. Stahlin (ed.) Leipzig, 1905-1936. English translations are found in the Ante-Nicene Christian Library, vols. 4, 12, 22, 24.

Clement of Rome. See Funk (ed.), *Patres Apostolici.* Tübingen, 1911.

'Contemplation', *Dictionnaire de Spiritualité* 2: 1643ff.

Corpus Inscrptionum Graecarum published by the Academy of Berlin. 5 vols. A. Boeckh (ed.). 1882-1887.

Cotelier, J.B. *Ecclesiae Graecae Monumenta.* 3 vols. Paris, 1677-1686.

Crainic, N. 'Das Jesusgebet'. Translated by W. Biemel, *Zeitschrift für Kirchengeschichte* 60 (1941) 341-53.

Cyril of Scythopolis. *Vita Euthymii et Vita Sabae.* E. Schwartz (ed.), *Texte und Untersuchungen* 49, 2. Leipzig, 1939. See also the lengthier edition of K. Koiklylides. Jerusalem, 1905.

Daele, A. van den. *Indices pseudo-dionysiani.* Louvain, 1941.

Das Herzengebet: Mystik und Yoga der Ostkirche; Die Centurie der Mönche Kallistus und Ignatius. Munich, 1955.

De cultu ss. Nominis Jesus, a S. Bernardino Senensi propagato, et a S. Joanne Capistrano a calumniis vindicato. Acta Sanctorum tome X: 318-23. Paris, 1869.

Deissmann, A. 'The Name Jesus'. *Mysterium Christi: Christological Studies by British and German Theologians.* London: Bell and Deissmann, 1930.

De Lubac, Henri. *Histoire et Esprit. L'intelligence de l'Ecriture d'après Origène.* Paris, 1950.

De Santos Otero. *Los evcangelios apócrifos.* Madrid, 1956.

Diadochus of Photice. *Cent chapitres sur la perfection spirituelle.* Introduction and French translation by E. des Places, Sources chrétiennes series 5 bis. Paris, 1943.

Didache. See F.X. Funk (ed.), *Patres Apostolici.* Tübingen, 1901, pp. 1-37. English translation in the Ancient Christian Writers series, vol. 6 (1948) and by R.A. Kraft in *The Apostolic Fathers,* vol. 3. New York: Nelson, 1964-8.

Diekamp, F. *Doctrina Patrum de Incarnatione Verbi.* Münster, 1907.

Discussions about the Jesus Prayer [Besedy o molitve Iisusovoi]. Edited at the russian monastery of Valama in Finland. Serdobol, 1938.

Disdier, M.Th. 'Elie l'Ecdicos et les *etera kephalaia* attribués à S. Maxime'. *Echos d'Orient* 31 (1932) 17-43.

Dolger, F.J. *Ichthus I: Das Fischsymbol in frühchristlicher Zeit.* Münster, 1910.

——. *Ichthus II: Der helige Fisch in den antiken Religionen und im Christentum.* Münster, 1922.

Ephrem. *S. Ephrem Syri opera omnia.* Rome, 1732-46.

——. *Commentaire sur la Genèse.* R.M. Ronneau (ed.). Louvain, 1955.

——. *Hymni de fide.* Beck (ed.). C.S.C.O., 1955, pp. 154-55.

. *Hymni et sermones*. Th. J. Lamy (ed.). 4 vols. Malines, 1882-1902.

. *Prose Refutation of Mani, Marcion and Bardaisan*. C. Mitchell (ed.). 2 vols. London, 1912, 1921.

Estienne, H. *Thesaurus Graecae Linguae*. Paris, 1842-47.

Eusebius. *Historia Ecclesiastica*. E. Schwartz (ed.). 3 vols. *Die griechische-christliche Schriftsteller der ersten drei Gahrhunderte,* 9. Leipzig (1903)1909). English translation in the Fathers of the Church series, 19, 29 (1953, 1956), and in *A History of the Church*. Penguin Books, 1965.

Evagrius Ponticus. W. Frankenberg (ed.), *Abhandlungen der Gesellschaft der Wissenschaften zu Göttingen*, 1912. English translation by John Eudes Bamberger, *Evagrius Ponticus: Praktikos and Chapters on Prayer*, Cistercian Studies Series, 4. Spencer, Massachusetts-Dublin, 1970.

Evergetinos, Paul. *Synagogé*. Constantinople, 1861.

Fénelon. *Le gnostique de saint Clément d'Alexandrie*. P. Dudon (ed.). Paris, 1930.

Foerster, W. 'Kyrios', in G. Kittel, *Theologisches Wörterbuch*, III: 1038-56. See Kittel.

Folliet, G. 'Des moines euchites à Carthage en 400-401'. *Studia Patristica* II: 386-99. Berlin, 1957.

Forget, J. *Synaxarium Alexandrinum:textus et verso*. C.S.C.O. vols. 18-19. Paris, 1905-26.

Frankenberg. See Evagrius Ponticus.

Funk, F.X. See Barnabas, Clement of Rome, Didache, Hermas, Ignatius of Antioch.

Gardet, L. 'Un problème de mystique comparée'. *Revue Thomiste* (1952) 642-79.

Gorodetzky, N. 'The prayer of Jesus'. *Blackfriars* (February 1942) p. 74ff.

Gouillard, J. 'Un auteur spiritel du douzième siècle, Pierre Damascène'. *Echos d'Orient* 38 (1935) 257-78.

Grébaut, E. 'La prière "Eqabani" ou les litanies de Christ'. *Orientalia* IV (1935) 426-440.

Grégoire, H. *Recueil des Inscriptions Grecques Chrétiennes d'Asie Mineure*. Fasc. I. Paris, 1932.

Gregory Nazianzen. *Contra Julianum*. PG 35.

. *Les discours théologiques.*Translated by P. Gallay into French. Paris, 1942. English translation of 'select orations and letters...' in the Nicene and Post-Nicene Fathers, second series, vol. 7.

Gregory the Sinaite. J. Pomjalovsky (ed.) *The Life of Gregory the Sinaite* [in Russian]. St Petersburg, 1894.

Grumel, V. 'Acemètes', *Dictionnaire de Spiritualité* I: 169-75.

H. de B. 'La prière du Coeur'. *Messager de l'Exarchat Russe en Europe Occidentale*, 4. Paris (1953) 13-40.

Halkin. See Pachomius.

Hamman, A. *Prières des premiers chrétiens*. Paris, 1951. English translation by W. Mitchess, *Early Christian Prayers*, Chicago: Regnery, 1961.

Handbuch für rechtgläubige [Orthodox] *Christen*. Hersbruck, 1948.

Harvey. See Irenaeus.

Hausherr, I. *Direction spirituelle en Orient autrefois*. Orientalia Christiana *Analecta* 144. Rome, 1955.

. 'Le méthode d'oraison hésychaste'. *Orientalia Christiana* IX, 2 (1927) 'Les exercises Spirituels de Saint Ignace et la méthode d'oraison hésychaste'. *Orientalia Christiana Periodica* 20 (1954) 7-26.

. 'Le Traité de l'oraison d'Evagre le Pontique (pseudo-Nil)'. *Revue d'ascétique et de mystique*, (1934) 34-170.

. 'L'Hésychasme. Etude de Spiritualité'. *Orientalia Christiana Periodica*, 22 (1956) 5-40, 247-285.

. 'L'imitation de Jésus-Christ dans la spiritualité byzantine'. *Mélanges F. Cavallera* (Toulouse, 1948) 231-259.

. 'Note sur l'invention de la méthode hésychaste'. *Orientalia Christiana*, 20 (1930) 179-182.

. *Penthos: La doctrine de componction dans l'Orient Chrétien*. *Orientalia Christiana Analecta*, 132. Rome, 1944.

. *Philautie: De la tendresse pour soi à la charité selon Saint Maxime le Confesseur*. *Orientalia Christiana Analecta*, 137. Rome, 1952.

. 'Variations récentes dans les jugements sur la Méthode d'oraison des hésychastes'. *Orientalia Christiana Periodica*, 19 (1953) 424-428.

Heiler, F. *Das Gebet*. 5th edition, Munich, 1923.

Hermas. *The Shepherd of Hermas*. F.X. Funk (ed.). *Die apostolischen Väter*. Tübingen, 1906, pp. 144-238. English translation in *The Apostolic Fathers*, vol. 6. New York, 1964-8.

Holl, K. *Fragmente vornicänischer Kirchenväter aus den Sacra Parallela*. *Texte und Untersuchungenen* 20. Leipzig, 1899.

Holzner, J. *Paul of Tarsus*. Translated by F.C. Eckhoff. St Louis: Herder, 1944.

Humbertclaude, P. *La doctrine ascétique de saint Basile de Césarée*. Paris, 1932.

Hussey. See Socrates.

Ignatius of Antioch. F.X. Funk (ed.), *Patres Apostolici*. Tübingen, 1901, pp. 212-95. English translation by R.M. Grant, *The Apostolic Fathers*, vol. 5.

Irenaeus of Lyons. *Adversus haereses*. W. Harvey (ed.). Cambridge, 1857.

. *Contra haereticos, liber III. F. Sagnard [ed.], Sources chrétiennes, 34. Paris, 1952. English translation by John Keble, Library of the Fathers*, 42. Oxford, 1872.

Isaac of Ninevah. Syriac edition by P. Bedjan. Paris-Leipzig, 1909. Greek edition by Nicephorus Theotokis, Leipzig, 1770. English translation by A.J. Wensinck, *Mystic Treatises by Isaac of Nineveh*. Amsterdam, 1923. Rpt. Wiesbaden, 1969.

Isaiah Augoustinos (ed.). Jerusalem, 1911. Latin version by Pierre François Zinus of Verona. Venice, n.d. See A. Guillaumont, *L'ascéticon copte de d'abbé Isaie*. Cairo, 1956.

Isaiah, Abba. See 'Le Métérikon de l'abbé Isaïe'. *Orientalia Christiana Periodica*, 12 (1946) 286-301.

Ivànka, E. von. 'Byzantinische Yogis?' *Zeitschrift der deutschen morgen-ländischen Gesellschaft*, 102 (1952) 234-39.

James of Sarough. *Homiliae Selectae*. Bedjan (ed.). 5 vols. Paris-Leipzig, 1905-1910.

Jalabert, L. and R. Mouterde. *Inscriptions grecques et latines de la Syrie*. Paris, 1929-1955.

John Climacus. *Scala Paradisi*. Testo con introd. versione et note del Sac. Pietro Trevisan. *Corona Patrum Salesiana, Serie greca*, Vols. VIII-IX. Turin, 1941. Translation by Lazarus Moore, *The Ladder of Divine Ascent*. London: Faber and Faber, 1959, and by Rupert Martin, *The Illustration of the Heavenly Ladder*. Princeton, NJ, 1954.

John of Jesus Mary OCD. *Notre Dame de la Montée du Carmel*. Tarascon, 1951.

Joannes a Jesu Maria. *Theologia Mystica et Epistola Christi ad Hominem*. Freiburg im Br. 1912.

John Moschus. *Pré Spirituel*. Translated into French by R. de Journel. Sources chrétiennes, 12. Paris, 1946.

Jugie, M. 'Homélies Mariales Byzantines'. *Patrologia Orientalia de Graffin et Nau*. T. XIX.

——. 'Les origines de la méthode d'oraison des hésychastes', *Echos d'Orient* (1931) 179-185.

——. 'Note sur le moine Nicéphore', *Echos d'Orient* 35 (1936) 409-412.

Kaufmann, C.M. *Handbuch der altchristlichen Epigraphik*. Freiburg im Br. 1917.

Kievopečerskij Patérik. Translated into modern Russian by Maria Viktorovna. Kiev, 1870.

Kittel, G. (ed.). *Theologisches Wörterburch zum Neuen Testament*. English translation by G.W. Bromiley, *Theological Dictionary of the New Testament*, 9 vols. Grand Rapids: Eerdmans, 1964-74.

Klostermann. See Origen.

Knopf. R. *Ausgewählte Märtyrenakten*. 3 neubearb. Auflage von G. Krüger. Tübingen, 1929.

Loetchau. See Origen.

Kologrivof, I. *Essai sur la sainteté en Russie*. Bruges, 1953. German translation: *Das andere Russland*. Munich, 1958.

Krivochéine, R. 'Date du texte traditionnel de la "Prière de Jésus" '. *Messager de Exarchat du Patriarche russe en Europe Occidental*, 7-8 (1951) 55-59.

Krumbacher, K. *Geschichte der byzantinischen Litteratur*. 2nd ed. Munich, 1897.

Labourt, J. and Battifol, P. *Les Odes de Salomon*. Paris, 1911.

Laudeuze, P. *Etudes sur le cénobitisme pakhomien*. Louvain, 1898.

Lamy. See Ephrem.

Laurent, V. *Documents de sigillographie byzantine, La collection C. Orghidan*. Paris, 1952.

Leclercq, H. 'Conversion', *Dictionnaire de l'Archéologie et Liturgie* T. III, 2, col. 2797-2800.

Lefort. See Pachomius.

Lelong, A. *Les Pères Apostoliques*. Paris, 1910-1912.

Lemoine. See Philoxenus of Mabburgh.

Lipsius. R.A. and Bonnet, M. *Acta apostolorum apocrypha*. Leipzig, 1883-1903.

Livre des Degrés. M. Kmosko (ed.), *Patrologia Syriaca*, Vol. III, 1926.

Lorié, L.Th. A. *Spiritual Terminology in the Latin Translations of the Vita Antonii*. *Latinitas Christiana Primaeva*, fasciculus XI. Nimegen, 1955.

Macarius of Philadelphia. *Neon Eclogion*. Edited first by a Christian who was a lover of Christ and afterwards by Archdeacon Avvakum and the Monk Anthimius the Hagiorite. Constantinople, 1863.

Madoz, P.J. 'El amor a Jesuchriso en la Iglesia de los Mártires'. *Estudios Eclesiasticos* 12 (1933) 313-344.

Makarytchova, N. *Mitte des Herzens*. Zürich, 1957.

Maltzew, A. *Andachtsbuch der Orthodox-Katholischen Kirche des Morgenlandes*. Berlin, 1895.

Marsili, S. *Giovanni Cassiano ed Evagrio Pontico. Dottrina sulla carità e contemplazione*. *Studia Anselmiana*, 5. Rome, 1936.

Maximus the Confessor. *Centuries sur la charité*. Translated by J. Pegon, Sources Chrétiennes 9. Paris, 1943.

Melania. Cardinal Rampolla del Tindaro (ed.). *Vie de sainte Mélanie la Jeune*. Rome, 1905. Also D. Gorce (ed.) *Vie de sainte Mélanie*. Sources Chrétiennes, 90. Paris, 1962.

Mercenier, P.F. 'L'Antienne Mariale grecque la plus ancienne'. *Le Muséon* 52 (1939) 229-233.

Meyendorff, J. 'Le thème de 'retour en soi' dans la doctrine palamite du XIVe siècle,' *Revue hist. rel.* 145 (1954), 188-206.

Mitchell. See Ephrem.

Mollat, D. *L'Evangile de saint Jean*. Paris, 1953.

Moricca, U. 'Un nouvo testo dell'Evangelo di Bartolomeo'. *Revue Biblique* (1922) pp. 20-30.

Moulard, A. *Saint Jean Chrysostome*. Paris, 1941.

Nauck, A. *Jamblichi Chalcidensis De vita Pythagorica liber*. S Petersburg, 1884.

Nicétas Stéthatos. *Vie de Syméon le Nouveau Théologien*. Rome, 1928.

Nigg, W. *Des Pilgers Wiederkehr*. Zürich, 1954.

Nicene and Post-Nicene Fathers of the Church series. Rpt Grand Rapids, Michigan: Eerdman.

Nicodemus the Hagiorite. *'Egcheiridion symbouleutikon*. Athens, 1801; 1885.

Nicodemus. See Barsanuphius.

Nilus. *De octo vitiis*. Cotelier (ed.). *Ecclesiasticae Graecae Monumenta* III, 185-219. Paris, 1686.

——. *Opera omnia* (Greek and Latin). PG 79.

——. Texts on prayer in *Early Fathers from the Philokalia*. See Philokalia.

Nölle, W. 'Hesychasmus und Yoga'. *Byzantinische Zeitschrift* 47 (1954) 95-103.

Bibliography   355

O'Rahilly, A. *Father William Doyle S.J.* London, 1936.

Orbe, A. *La epinoia. Algunos preliminares historicos de la distincion kat' epinoian.* Rome, 1955.

Origen. *Contra Celsum.* P. Koetschau (ed.). *Die griechischen christlichen Schriftsteller der ersten drei Jahrhunderte,* 2. [G.C.S.] Leipzig, 1899. English translation by Henry Chadwick. Cambridge: University Press, 1953.

. *In Ezechielem homiliae.* Baehrens (ed.), G.C.S., 33. Leipzig, 1930.
. *In Exodum homiliae.* Baehrens (ed.), G.C.S., 29. Leipzig, 1920.
. *In Isaiam homiliae.* Baehrens (ed.), G.C.S., 33. Leipzig, 1925.
. *In Jeremiam homiliae.* E. Klostermann (ed.), G.C.S., 6. Leipzig, 1901.
. *In Josue Homiliae.* Baehrens (ed.), G.C.S., 29. Leipzig, 1920.
. *In lib I Regum homiliae.* Baehrens (ed.), G.C.S., 33. Leipzig, 1925.
. *In Lucam homiliae.* M. Rauer (ed.), G.C.S., 35. Leipzig, 1930.

Orlov, A.S.. *The Jesus Prayer in Russia in the 16th Century.* Russian book published in the Russian series *Monuments of Ancient Literature,* 185 (1914).

Orta, P.F. *Orazioni giacolatorie.* Roma, 1706.

Pachomius. F. Halkin (ed.), *S Pachomii Vitae Graecae.* Brussels, 1932.

A. Boon, *Pachomiana Latina.* Louvain, 1932.

L.Th. Lefort, *Les vies coptes de saint Pachome et de ses premiers successeurs.* Louvain, 1943.

Paul of Latros. H. Delehaye (ed.), 'Vita S. Pauli Junioris'. *Analecta Bolandiana* 11 (1892) 5-74.

Pegon, J. See Maximus the Confessor.

Peterson, E. *Eis Theos. Epigraphische, formgeschichtliche und religionsgeschichtliche Untersuchungen.* Göttingen, 1926.

. 'Jüdisches und christliches Morgengebet in Syrien'. *Zeitschrift für katholische Theologie,* 57 (1934) 110-113.

Philo, Jurdaeus. *De vita contemplativa.* F.C. Conybeare (ed.). Oxford, 1895. Has been reprinted several times; for instance: Athens, 1893, 1900, 1957-1958.

Russian version: Paisij Veličkovskij, *Dobrotoljubié.* Moscow, 1793. Reprinted in two parts, 1853 and 1855.

Russian version: Ignace Brjančaninov, *Dobrotoljubié.* St Petersburg, 1857.

Russian version: Theophane the Recluse (Govorov), published by the Russian monastery of Saiı Panteleimon on Mount Athos, 5 vols., 1877. Reprinted three times, 18. -1913.

Version in church slavonic published by the Synodol Press of Moscow, 1902.

French version: J. Gouillard, *Petite Philocalie de la prière du coeur.* Paris, 1953.

German version: Dietz-Smolitsch, *Kleine Philokalie.* Zurich-Köln, 1956.

English version: Kadloubovsky and Palmer, *Writings from the Philocalia on Prayer of the Heart.* London, 1951. *Early Fathers from the Philocalia,* London, 1954.

Philoxenus of Mabburgh. E. Lemoine, (ed.), *Homilies.* Sources chrétiennes, 44. Paris, 1956. Translation by E.A.W. Budge, *The Discourses of Philoxenus*, 2 vols. London, 1894.

Phokylides, J. *He Hiera Lavra tou hegiasmenou.* Alexandria, 1927.

Picard, L. *Fr. Mutien-Marie de Ciney, Gabriel Wiaux.* Namur-Brussels, 1943.

Plato. *Platonis opera,* J. Burnet (ed., tr.). 5 vols. Oxford, 1945-6.

———. *The Theaetetus and The Sophist,* tr. F.M. Cornford. New York, 1957.

Plutarch. *Opera.* Th. Doehner and F. Dubner (eds.). Paris, 1846-1882. Vol. IV, pp. 1295-1329: *De Communibus Notitiis.*

Pomjalovsky, J. See Gregory the Sinaite.

Popov, K. 'The teaching of Blessed Diadochús (5th century) on the Jesus Prayer'. (in Russian), *Travaux de l'Acad. eccl. de Kiev,* 3 (1902), 651-676.

Posseljanin, E. *Russian Ascetics of the Nineteenth Century.* (in Russian) S. Petersburg, 1910.

Poucel, V. *Pour que votre âme respire.* Paris: Art catholique, 1936.

Preuschen, E. *Palladius und Rufinus. Texte und Untersuchungen.* Giessen, 1897.

Probst, F. *Lehre und Gebet in den drei ersten christlichen Jahrhunderten.* Tübingen, 1871.

———. *Liturgie der ersten drei christlichen Jahrhunderten.* Tübingen, 1870.

Raabe, R. *Petrus der Iberer.* Leipzig, 1895.

Rabbow, P. *Seelenführung. Methodik der Exerzitien in der Antiki.* Munich, 1954.

Rauer, See Origen.

Recheis, A. 'Das Jesusgebet'. *Una Sancta* 9 (1954) 1-25.

Romanos the Melodist. N.V. Tomadakis (ed.). Athens, 1954. See also G. Cammelli, *Romano il Melode.* Florence, 1930. See also *Romanos le Melode: Hymnes.* F. Grosdidier de Matrons (ed.). Sources chrétiennes, 99, 110, 114. Paris, 1964, 1965.

Runciman, S. *Byzantine Civilisation.* London: Edward Arnold, 1933.

Sabas the Great. Pl. de Meester (trans.), *Règlement des Bienheureux et Saints Pères Sabas le Grand et Théodose le Cénobiarque pour la vie des cénobites et des kelliotes.* Lille, 1937.

Sabas the Younger. Biography by Philotheus Kokkinos, edited by A. Papadopoulos-Kerameus, *Anal. Hierosol. Stachyol.* Vol. 5.

Sabas. See also Cyril of Scythopolis.

Sagnard. See Irenaeus.

Salaville, S. 'Christus in Orientalium pietate'. *Ephemerides Liturgicae* 52 (1938) 221-236.

———. 'Formes ou méthodes de prière d'après un Byzantin du XIVe siècle, Theolepte de Philadelphie'. *Echos d'Orient* 30 (1940-1942) 1-25.

———. 'Office du Très Doux Jésus, anterieur au *Jubilus* de saint Bernard', *Revue d'ascétique et de mystique* 25 (1949) 247-259.

Saudreau, A. 'St. Maxime,' *Vie Spirituelle* (1920), 255-264.

Schlumberger, G. *Sigillographie de l'empire byzantin.* Paris, 1884.

Schmidt, K.L. 'epikaleo' in Kittel (ed.), *Theologisches Wörterbuch* III: 498-501.

Schultze, B. 'Der Streit um die Göttlichkeit des Namens Jesu in der russischen Theologie'. *Orientalia Christiana Periodica*, 17 (1951) 321-394.

. 'Untersuchungen über das Jesus-Gebet'. *Orientalia Christiana Periodica* 18 (1952) 319-343.

Schwartz. See Cyril of Scythopolis; Eusebius.

Severus, E. von. 'Meditari im Sprachgebrauch der hl. Schrift'. *Geist und Leben*, 26 (1953) 365-375.

Socrates. *Historia Ecclesiastica*. R. Hussey (ed.), Oxford, 1853. English translation: *A History of the Church*, in seven books...London, 1844, and in Nicene and post-Nicene Fathers, second series, vol. 2.

Stahlin. See Clement of Alexandria.

Staniloae, D. 'Douâ Tractáte ale Sfântului Grigorie Palama'. *Academia Teologicâ 'Andreiana'*, IX (1932-1933) Sibiu, 1933.

Stein, F.J. *Studien über die Hesychasten des vierzehnten Jahrhunderts*. Vienna, 1874.

Stengel, C. *Sacrosancti nominis Jesus cultus et miracula*. Augsburg, 1613.

Symeon the New Theologian. *Catèchése*, ed. B. Krivochéine, tr. F. Paramelle, 3 vols. Sources chrétiennes, 96, 104, 113. Paris, 1963-5. Denys Zagoraios (ed.). Venice, 1790. 2nd ed. 1886.

. *Traitès thèologiques et ethiques*. F. Darrouzès (ed.) Sources chrétiennes, 122. Paris, 1966.

Hymnes. F. Koder and F. Paramelle (edd.) Sources chrétiennes, 156. Paris, 1969.

Syncletice. *Vita et Gesta*. Cotelier (ed.). *Ecclesiasticae Graecae Monumenta* I. Paris, 1677, pp. 201-277.

'Technique et Contemplation'. *Etudes Carmlit*. Bruges, 1949.

Theotokis. See Isaac of Niniveh.

Thomas of Célano. *La légende de saint Francois*. Rinaldi (ed.), Rome, 1806.

Tischendorf, C. *Apocalpyses apocryphae*. Leipzig, 1866.

Tonneau. See Ephrem.

A Monk of the Eastern Church. 'La Prière de Jésus'. *Irénikon*. Chevetogne, 1959 .

. L'invocation de nom de Jèsus dans la tradition byzantine'. *La Vie Spirituelle* (1952), 38-45.

. *On the Invocation of the Name of Jesus.* Published by the Fellowship of SS. Alban and Sergius. London, 1950.

Un moine de l'Eglise orthodoxe Roumaine. 'L'avènement philocalique dans l'Orthodoxie roumaine'. *Istina* (1958) 295-328.

Vassiliev, A. *Anecdota Graeca*. Moscow, 1893.

Viller, M. 'Aux sources de la spiritualité de S. Maxime'. *Revue d'ascétique et de mystique* 11 (1930) 239-268.

Vitae Patrum. Rosweyde (ed.), Migne: *Patrologia Latina* 73:851-1024.

Wallis-Budge, E.A., *The Paradise of the Fathers*. London, 1907.

The Way of a Pilgrim. Sequel (Part II): *The Pilgrim Continues His Way*.

The original Russian edition was published at Kazan in 1884: *Otkrovennyje raskazy strannika duchovnomu svojemu otcu.* Part II was published in 1911 at the Laura of St Sergius of Moscow. A new edition was made by B. Vysešlavcev: Part I at Paris, 1930; Part II at Ladmirova (Czechoslovakia), 1933; Parts I and II at Paris, 1948.
Translations:

1925, Berlin. German translation by R. von Walter.

1928, French translation in *Irénikon-Collection*, nos 5-7.

1930, London: *The Story of a Russian Pilgrim*, translated by Th. Bailey.

1930, London: *The Way of a Pilgrim*, translated by R. French (Part I).

1943, London: *The Pilgrim Continues His Way*, translated by R. French (Part II).

1943, London: *The Way of a Pilgrim*, translated by R. French (Parts I and II).

Reprinted, New York: Seabury Press, 1972.

1944, Luzern. German translation by Meli Badgasarowa.

1945, Neuchâtel. French translation by J. Gauvain, *Cahiers du Rhône*, No. xii.

1951, Freiburg. German translation.

1955, Milan. Italian translation by L. Bortolon, *Raconti di un pellegrino russo.*

Wensinck. See Isaac of Nineveh.

Wilmart-Tisserant (eds.). 'Fragments grecs et latins de l'évangile de Barthélemy'. *Revue Biblique* (1913) 161-190.

Wunderle, G. *Zur Psychologie des hesychastischen Gebetes.* Würzburg, 1947.

Wüstgenfeld, F. *Synaxarium, das ist Heiligen-Kalender der Coptischen Christen,* Gotha, 1897.

Ziegler, J. *Dulcedo Dei. Ein Beitrag zur Theologie der grieschischen und lateinischen Bibel.* Münster, 1937.

CISTERCIAN PUBLICATIONS INC.

TITLES LISTING

THE CISTERCIAN FATHERS SERIES

THE CISTERCIAN STUDIES SERIES

* *Temporarily out of Print*   † *Forthcoming*

* *Temporarily out of print*   † *Forthcoming*